GOD AND THE MEANING

GOD AND THE MEANINGS OF LIFE

WHAT GOD COULD AND COULDN'T DO TO MAKE OUR LIVES MORE MEANINGFUL

T. J. Mawson

Bloomsbury Academic
An imprint of Bloomsbury Publishing Plc

B L O O M S B U R Y
LONDON · OXFORD · NEW YORK · NEW DELHI · SYDNEY

Bloomsbury Academic

An imprint of Bloomsbury Publishing Plc

50 Bedford Square	1385 Broadway
London	New York
WC1B 3DP	NY 10018
UK	USA

www.bloomsbury.com

BLOOMSBURY and the Diana logo are trademarks of Bloomsbury Publishing Plc

First published 2016

© T. J. Mawson, 2016

British Library Cataloguing-in-Publication Data
A catalogue record for this book is available from the British Library.

ISBN: HB: 9781474212557
PB: 9781474212540
ePDF: 9781474212564
ePub: 9781474212571

Library of Congress Cataloging-in-Publication Data
A catalog record for this book is available from the Library of Congress.

Typeset by Fakenham Prepress Solutions, Fakenham, Norfolk NR21 8NN
Printed and bound in India

To Joanna and all that her life will mean

CONTENTS

יְהוָה נָתַן וַיהוָה לָקָח[1]

(The Lord giveth and the Lord taketh away)

---

[1] *The Book of Job*, extract from Chapter 1, verse 21.

ACKNOWLEDGEMENTS

The authors of the works listed in the bibliography and in the suggestions for further reading have helped me in thinking more clearly about the topics covered in this book. I would like to record my gratitude to them, even those mention of whose thoughts was in the end squeezed out of my notes owing to considerations of space.

In addition, many people have helped me personally with the writing of the book: those attending Brian Leftow's work in progress group, who were kind enough to comment on a draft; those attending the Natural Theology Group that meets at the Athenaeum, who were kind enough to look over some material in even rougher form; and then especially Brian Leftow and Nick Waghorn, who read the penultimate draft.

Some of the ideas in this book appeared first in an article in *The European Journal for Philosophy of Religion* and I am grateful to the editor, Janusz Salamon, first for publishing it, and, second, for permission to reuse that material. Other ideas appeared first in a review article for *Philosophy Compass*; I am similarly grateful to Charles Taliaferro for first publishing that and for allowing me to reuse that material.

Finally, I record my thanks to those at Bloomsbury who have assisted in bringing this work to publication: Liza Thompson and Frankie Mace.

St Peter's College,
Oxford

INTRODUCTION

Some philosophers have thought that our individual lives can only be meaningful if there is no God of the traditional classical theistic sort – an eternal, omnipotent, omniscient, creator and ruler of the universe. By way of two examples, Jean-Paul Sartre and Thomas Nagel seem to have been of the opinion that if there were a God of this sort, then He would constrain our power of self-creation and autonomy in ways that would at least severely detract from the meaning of our lives, possibly even evacuate our lives of all meaning.

In a rightly famous passage to which we shall return and treat in more detail later, Sartre pictures our situation had there been a God. We would then be comparable with mere artefacts, things that exist solely to perform a function assigned to them by another. God's creating us would destroy the possibility of our creating ourselves and would thereby render our lives meaningless. Or at least meaningless *for us*.

I have it in mind here that the most plausible Sartrean view is that if Theism is in fact true, then our lives are still meaningful *for God*. On such a supposition, they would, after all, still have the meaning-giving purpose(s) that God had assigned them. Sartre's point is that they wouldn't then be meaningful *for us*. That is to say that I am taking it that the most plausible Sartrean view would have it that assigning another person's life a purpose gives that other person's life a meaning. It's not that someone other than oneself just cannot give one's life a meaning by assigning a purpose to it. Rather, Sartre's view is that the meaning a life gets by being assigned a purpose by another is valueless (or worse) to the individual to whom the meaning-giving purpose has been assigned. It's not the sort of meaning that he or she should be wanting – quite the opposite. As Rescher expresses it: 'What is central to the issue of the meaning of life is whether what we do can and does really matter – not ... to God or to the universe but to ourselves. It is clearly just this – namely, mattering for us – that counts *for us*, since that is who we are.'[1] If that is right, then Sartre's worry about God is best understood not as the worry that God can't make our lives meaningful. Rather, He can't make our lives meaningful *for us* because, by making them meaningful for Him, He'd made them meaningless for us.[2] And it is meaningfulness for us that is what we should value.

By contrast with the theistic worldview, according to Sartre, atheistic 'existentialism ... puts every man in possession of himself as he is, and places the entire responsibility for his existence squarely upon his own shoulders'.[3] Sartre's view then seems to be that we can have meaning in our lives, but only to the extent that we put it in ourselves. If there had been a God 'putting it in for us', that would have detracted from our ability to put it in for ourselves. The more meaning prescribed by God, the less meaning unconstrainedly chosen by us, and thus the less meaning for us. But, given that in fact there is no God (Sartre never seriously questioned his Atheism), we have unlimited space for self-creation[4] and thus meaningfulness.

Thomas Nagel seems to have thought along similar lines. In another oft-quoted passage, Nagel says this: 'I want atheism to be true and am made uneasy by the fact that some of the most intelligent and well-informed people I know are religious believers. It isn't just that I don't believe in God and, naturally, hope that I'm right in my belief. It's that I hope there is no God! I don't want there to be a God; I don't want the universe to be like that. My guess is that this cosmic authority problem is not a rare condition and that it is responsible for much of the scientism and reductionism of our time.'[5] Nagel's 'problem with authority' seems similar to Sartre's. But there are differences.

First, it is worth noting that Nagel is far more aware than Sartre of the irrationality of letting one's aversion to authority drive one to beliefs about what authorities are actually out there. Nagel's higher-order attitude towards the issue is clearly that if we are under divine authority, well, then that's that. We'll just have to get on with it (and probably Him). But his lower-order attitude is equally clear and, it seems to me, in essence at one with Sartre's. He – passionately – hopes that we're not under that sort of authority. We may safely presume then that Nagel doesn't regard his wanting not to be under authority as a perverse response to the true value of being under authority. He thinks that he's right not to want the world to be one where we're under the sort of authority that God would have over us. Why, according to Nagel, is that the right attitude? Well, he may have in mind other disvalues that he supposes would come in God's train, but it seems to me that high up his list would be that in any Godly world (i.e. one in which Theism is true) we are denied the scope for self-creation and autonomy and the resultant meaning-for-us-generating capacity, that he, like Sartre, values.

Another difference between Nagel and Sartre is that it is less clear whether Nagel supposes that we do in fact enjoy this sort of meaningfulness in any case, even given that Atheism is in fact true. This is because Nagel's position is complicated by the fact that it is not at all clear that he thinks that this sort of self-creation (even if undertaken in a spirit of ironic awareness of the ultimate absurdity of life) can add to meaningfulness in any case.[6] Notwithstanding that, I incline to think of the most plausible 'Nagelian' view as allowing that it can. The most plausible Nagelian view is then, I think, that, although there is – for all we know[7] – top-level absurdity (which entails, even if it is not identical to, meaninglessness), there is no necessity that this meaninglessness (if it exists at all) spread from the top, down. If we (in awareness of the potential absurdity of our lives as seen from 'the point of view of the universe', the top) wilfully create ourselves in manners that are appropriately responsive to value, then we thereby make our lives meaningful in spite of all that.[8] 'If *sub specie aeternitatis* there is no reason to believe that anything matters, then that does not matter either, and we can approach our absurd lives with irony instead of heroism or despair.'[9] And, once we so approach them, we may, by living them well, be living them meaningfully. Whether this is Nagel's view or not, it is certainly the view that was espoused by arguably the two most prominent British atheists of the twentieth century, Bertrand Russell[10] and Antony Flew.[11] And it is well summed up by E. D. Klemke, in the following passage:

It is true that life has no objective meaning. Let us face it once and for all. But from that it does not follow that life is not worthwhile, for it can still be subjectively meaningful. And, really, the latter is the only kind of meaning worth shouting about. An objective meaning – that is, one which is inherent within the universe or dependent on external agencies – would, frankly, leave me cold. It would not be mine. It would be an outer, neutral thing, rather than an inner, dynamic achievement. I, for one, am glad that the universe has no meaning, for thereby is man all the more glorious. I willingly accept the fact that external meaning is non-existent … for this leaves me free to forge my own meaning.[12]

There are other values that, while initially some distance away from meaningfulness, could be argued to be threatened by the existence of God and that might be tied to meaningfulness so as to generate a resultant worry here. In a recent paper, Guy Kahane, for example, says the following of a Godly world: 'It is a world where everything about us is known and fully understood by another, a world where even our innermost thoughts and feelings are not entirely private. It is a world in which we are never truly alone, away from the presence and attention of another.'[13] And that seems undeniably right – God is, by definition, omniscient and thus if there is a God, nothing is ultimately private. If we then suppose, as most do, that privacy is a value, we'll have to conclude that it's one that God, if He exists, cannot but help detracting from. Initially at least this detraction in the amount of privacy we enjoy does not entail a detraction in the amount of meaningfulness we enjoy. Privacy and meaningfulness are two different values, after all. (In order to exemplify their difference, one might consider the case of the British journalist, Martin Bell. He allowed his financial and personal life to be 'open books' for the electorate when he stood – successfully, as it turned out – against an incumbent MP who had been caught accepting money for asking questions in the House of Commons. Bell's life was, intuition suggests, made more meaningful but less private by all of this.) However, while distinct values, privacy and meaningfulness could be linked by a particular person in the manner that I'm about to outline (following Kahane), linked so that damage to the first leads inevitably to damage to the second.

The sort of background that renders most easily understandable the possibility of linking privacy to meaningfulness in the way I have in mind is, it seems to me, a certain sort of 'pluralism' about values and the good life. The word 'pluralism' means different things to different people and even a different thing as I am using it now from the thing it is going to mean when I use it later in this book.[14] All I have in mind with it here is the view that it is to some extent (though I would maintain only to some extent) up to us which of the smorgasbord of values we pick to shape our lives around, for some values at least are incommensurable.[15] Some people become singers; others, scientists; some, parents; others, not. All of these are generally permissible 'life choices', and in making them the way that one does, one commits oneself to values internal to (often peculiar to) the roles one thereby takes up. These choices having been made, these values then shape to at least an extent what gives one's life meaning thereafter. For example, it does not add much to the meaning of the life of someone who has dedicated themselves to singing if they find themselves in what is in its own terms a significant position in a centre for scientific research. It does not add much to the meaning of the life of a dedicated scientist if they find themselves performing a lead role at Covent Garden. The singer landing the lead role and the scientist the position in the centre would have added more meaning to each of their lives. If one admits this and that privacy is on the smorgasbord of values (as it is, after all, a value), then one will think that some people may permissibly choose to make it a more essential part of their lives than others. At one end of the spectrum, we will have the sort of person who we would naturally describe as a very private individual. At the other end, we will have the sort of person who posts the latest and most intimate details of their sex life online for all to see. For the private person at least, the meaningfulness of their life would then be reduced were there a God; the person who placed no value on privacy would obviously not be so threatened. I imagine most reading this will be somewhere in the middle. Thus most reading this will be somewhat threatened in this manner.[16]

The same sort of link can be made between other values that God seems to threaten and meaningfulness. So, most easily, consider someone who has committed their life to the promotion of the truth (as they see it) of Atheism. It seems clear that if we imagine that person in two worlds, $W1$ and $W2$, both of which are as similar as they can be in logical consistency given that in $W1$ there is a God and in $W2$ there isn't, then, as in $W2$ this person[17] has devoted their life to promoting a truth and arguably a not unimportant one, that has been them making their life meaningful relative to how it is on this score in $W1$. In $W1$, by contrast, this person has devoted their life to promoting a falsehood about an important issue. So, *ceteris paribus*, atheists are – to the extent that they live out their Atheism – going to be leading less meaningful lives if there is a God than if there is not (and less meaningful lives than otherwise similar theists are going to be leading if there is a God). Make Atheism a central enough part of your life then – as, incidentally, Jean Paul Sartre probably did – and, for this reason if no other, it'll be true for you that were there to be a God, your life would be at least somewhat less meaningful in virtue of that than it would be – *ceteris paribus* – if there were not a God.

So, as we have seen, some philosophers think that were there a God, He would detract from, possibly even remove all, meaningfulness from our lives. Other philosophers have sympathetically canvassed a more moderate 'pessimism' about what would follow from there being a God. They think that were there a God, He would detract from the meaningfulness of at least some people's lives. For example, those who had shaped a large part of their lives around the value of privacy would, in virtue of that, have proportionally less meaningful lives than those who had not. Those who had shaped their lives around the promotion of Atheism would similarly be relatively disadvantaged on that score. And so on.

It is worth interrupting the flow somewhat at this stage to stress a point even though it is merely a terminological one. The sort of pessimism (and, in a moment, optimism) spoken of here is merely pessimism (and optimism) about what God's existing detracts/adds or would detract/add to the meaningfulness of life.[18] Pessimism is the view that He detracts (or would detract); optimism is the view that He adds (or would add).

Pessimists in this sense need not to be pessimistic about how meaningful our lives actually are; indeed, they tend to be optimistic about *that*. That is, they tend to think that were Theism true, it would be bad news for meaningfulness, but Theism isn't true, so we may be optimistic about meaningfulness after all. That was Sartre's view, as we have seen. It may be Nagel's. It was certainly Russell's, Flew's, and Klemke's. Similarly, optimism about this issue – the belief that God does or would add to the meaningfulness of life – need not be allied with optimism about the actual meaningfulness of human lives, although often it is. Those attracted to the view we might call 'Nihilism' – they believe that life is totally meaningless – because they think that while God is necessary and would be sufficient for meaningfulness, He does not in fact exist, would count as optimists in the sense I am using the term.[19]

To return to the flow: we have seen that in this sense then, some philosophers are pessimists about the effect God has (would have, were He to exist) on the meaningfulness of our lives. Some are pessimists. But some are not.

Some philosophers are optimists. At the extreme, though very much in the minority, some have argued that life could only be meaningful *at all* if there is a God. The flavour is well captured by Wielenberg when he discusses (though doesn't endorse) it: 'Suppose that your life lacks supernatural meaning. This makes you a man (or woman) without a mission. There is nothing you are supposed to be doing with your life, no higher cause which you have been called to serve, no divine quest which you have been assigned. This means that there are no criteria by which to evaluate whether your life is a success or failure – and this in turn implies that there are no circumstances under which your life would be a successful one. Without some assigned goal, it doesn't much matter what you do; yours is a pointless existence … In a universe without God, without supernatural beings of any kind, there is no one suitably qualified to assign purposes to human lives.'[20]

If our world is a Godless one (not that those pushing this line typically believe that it is), then while of course some of us *think* that our lives have meaning, we are mistaken. Our thinking our lives have meaning doesn't make them have it. If anything, our being fooled into believing our lives have meaning makes our lives even worse, though not worse by reference to the value of meaning – everyone scores a flat zero there. Be that as it may, if we are in fact in a Godless universe, everyone's life – from that led by Gandhi to that led by that wastrel youth who lives at the other end of your street (you know the one; there's always [at least] one) – is entirely meaningless. Gandhi and the wastrel each score a flat zero. But that is a hard teaching. Who can believe it? As I say, not many theists actually believe that without God there is no meaning at all. Others then – the majority of theists – have held to the more modest optimistic claim that even though our lives might yet have a shallow or transient meaning if there isn't a God, they can only have a deep or permanent meaning if there is a God. On this view, it might well be true that Gandhi's life is more meaningful than that of the wastrel even if there is no God. But, if there is no God, then there's some deeper or more permanent sort of meaning that even Gandhi's life lacked because *all* our lives lack it. The most prominent contemporary defender of the more extreme view is John Cottingham.[21]

After having argued that a meaningful life 'must involve worthwhile activities or projects that enable us to flourish as human beings',[22] Cottingham considers arguments for and against adding God into this picture. In the end, he decides for. 'The religious perspective ... offers the possibility of meaningfulness by providing a powerful normative framework or focus for the life of virtue ... a framework within which that nature is revealed as more than just a set of characteristics that a certain species happens intermittently to possess, but instead as pointing to the condition that a Being of the utmost benevolence and care ... desires us to achieve ... To act in the light of such an attitude is to act in the faith that our struggles mean something beyond the local expression of a contingently evolving genetic lottery.'[23] Of course Cottingham believes that people who don't themselves adopt this religious perspective can still lead meaningful lives. They can, after all, still pursue the same sort of worthwhile activities and projects that enable us to flourish as human beings. But, without a God, the sort of absurdity that Nagel characterized would indeed engulf us from the top down, *pace* Russell, Flew and Klemke. In order to engage in worthwhile projects, we need to be in a world where something is worthwhile and, *pace* Nagel (and many others, of course), Cottingham thinks that God is needed to underwrite this. In addition, Cottingham argues that our lives – at least many of them – would have their meaningfulness vitiated by bad meaning-luck (my term, not Cottingham's) were there not a God: given that the value of many of the activities on which their meaningfulness hinges are 'success-orientated';[24] we thus need God again to underwrite what Cottingham calls 'the buoyancy of the good'. In short, we need to be in a world where there is objective good and also where that good will always ultimately triumph over evil. Only God can give the world both these features. If there is no God, then there is no objective value and it will be just dumb luck whether or not good ultimately triumphs over evil and thus extremely unlikely that it always does. So Gandhi and the wastrel really do score a flat zero. This, as I have said, is a hard teaching. That so few accept it just reveals the truth – so it would be claimed, *de facto* is claimed by Craig in various debates – of the thesis that there is objective value.

Other optimists have conceded to Sartre that our lives might well gain some meaning from the purposes that we might give them in a Godless world (*pace* Cottingham). Nonetheless they have argued against Sartre to the effect that God's giving them a purpose would *not* in fact inevitably subtract from their meaning for us. It could and would add. One might argue against Sartre in this fashion in either or both of two ways. First, one might accept, at least for the sake of argument, that meaning-for-us-giving through purpose-giving is a zero-sum game, but assert that it's not that if God's got in ahead of us and given our lives a purpose, we cannot put any purpose in ourselves – He may have left us space to do so. Second, one might deny the zero-sum game premise, asserting that we can gain meaning for ourselves from appropriating God's purposes to ourselves. If His purposes become our purposes, then they provide our lives with meaning for us, not just for Him.[25]

It is interesting to note that this optimistic view, whichever way it is argued for, shares a starting point with Sartre's pessimistic one. The starting point is the view that God would indeed be the sort of being who would have purposes for us, His creatures.

But, according to those taking this optimistic route from that starting point, Sartre did not fully consider two things: (a) the fact is that one of God's purposes for us may have been that we have, over some aspects of our lives, freedom to choose our own purposes – i.e. freedom of just the sort Sartre insists is needed for our lives to be meaningful for us; He didn't determinately 'fill in' every detail of a life plan for each of us; and (b) His more determinate/detailed purposes for us would be purposes that His perfect goodness would ensure were wholly desirable ones for us and ones that His omnipotence and omniscience would ensure were achieved. Thus, at least insofar as we willingly align ourselves with these purposes – make them our own – then they may add to, rather than subtract from, the meaningfulness of our lives for us. In that God is by definition the creator of everything other than Himself (including then us) and acts for good purposes, and in that the question 'What is the meaning of life?' and the question 'What is the purpose of life?' seem to some the same question[26] and to everyone they seem at least very similar questions, optimism on the grounds sketched under (b) is very natural.[27]

Stewart Goetz, for example, has recently written in this vein, endorsing the view that the meaning/purpose (tellingly, he uses the terms interchangeably) for each of our lives is that 'each experience perfect happiness'.[28] It had long-before been pointed out, e.g. by Nozick, that not just any old purpose imposed on us by our creator would suffice to give our lives meaning in the sense of meaning for us. A thought experiment effective in this context is to imagine us discovering that we had been created by Martians who sowed the Earth with appropriate genetic material many millennia ago, so as to ensure they had foodstuffs – us – when they returned from their round-the-galaxy trip. That humanity served the larger purpose of being the main course at a future meal for aliens would not add to the meaning of our lives for us.[29] If anything, it would detract from it. But concerns of this sort are obviously moot in the theistic context. The God of classical theism is such that He would not have allocated 'any old purpose' to us. He would have given us one that was compatible with His perfect goodness and thus one we could rely on being meaning-adding (rather than meaning-subtracting) for us (at least if we appropriate it, which of course we may).

Of course some – Baier, for example, and probably also Sartre – think that purpose-assigning by another per se degrades the person assigned a purpose. It degrades them in some way that makes it incompatible with its being meaning-giving for them however willingly they appropriate these purposes to themselves. We shall need to address this worry in more detail later. But we should perhaps say a few words about it now. It seems to me that some purpose-assigning actions can be degrading of the person assigned a purpose in such a way as to preclude them from being meaning-adding for the person assigned the purpose. But their being so relies on the person concerned being such that they cannot appropriate to themselves the degrading purposes. And thus the issue isn't so much one to do with degradation precluding meaningfulness for the person concerned. It's more to do with the psychology of the person concerned being such as to be incapable of appropriating the relevant purpose to himself or herself and *that* being what precludes it from being a meaning-adding purpose for him or her. The same issue could arise with an overly (for the person concerned) exalting (rather than degrading) purpose-giving action. The person concerned might not be able to appropriate to himself or herself the purpose and hence it too might fail to be meaning-adding for him or her. One case of too-degrading a purpose, we have already considered – that assigned to us by the Martians in the previous thought experiment. By way of another example, consider the following.

A certain person has pathologically low self-esteem and believes themselves to be unworthy of being treated as anything other than a slave by anyone, especially their spouse, who – as it happens – has a pathological condition of their own and enjoys nothing more than ceaselessly giving their slave needlessly degrading purposes. The slave – owing to their peculiar psychology – is fully able to appropriate those purposes to themselves. It seems to me that there is much wrong in this relationship, but that nevertheless these degrading purposes given to the slave by their master do make the slave's life meaningful – meaningful in that sense for him.[30] Now the spouse/master dies and the former slave is befriended by an egalitarian philanthropist. The egalitarian philanthropist gives the former slave a post on the board of one of their worthy charities – something respectable, indeed respected, and significant. This is a role that is in no way degrading, indeed the opposite: this new post entails for the former slave what I am calling exalting purposes. Sadly, the former slave's psychology remains as it was. They are completely unable to appropriate these exalting purposes to themselves. These purposes hence cannot make their lives more meaningful for them. Of course, whether or not a degrading purpose could be meaning-adding for particular people anyway is somewhat moot in this context: God just wouldn't give us degrading purposes. And, in the case of God, there is also the added complication that He can transfigure purposes that would have been degrading into exalting ones in any case – the servant King, and so forth.[31] What would be more *apropos* – but Baier fails to notice as he has fixated on the danger of degradation – is the worry that God might assign to us purposes that are too exalting. Indeed, I think that is a danger. We shall come to it later in discussing Jonah, someone who was – if the records are to be believed – given a purpose that was very exalting – saving Nineveh – and yet who was not able to appropriate that purpose to himself (at least initially). Thus it failed to be meaning-adding (at least initially) for him. But, in any case, it seems that we may allow ourselves for the moment to presume that purpose-assigning could in principle fail to degrade us in a way that meant it was meaning-subtracting. God would be able and – by definition – motivated to do the right sort of purpose-assigning. And He would have created us so that we are able to appropriate to ourselves the purposes He had assigned to us, at least in general and ultimately.

According to Goetz again, for example, our good just has to be happiness, which is why God has 'chosen' the achievement of this as the purpose for us and the same schematic answer can obviously be offered for other understandings of our good too. And the answer that works at the level of general providence can be made to work at the level of a more meticulous one. Perhaps God has a special purpose for me and this special purpose is that I do work in Philosophy. If so, my life is being made more meaningful by my writing this book than it would have been had I been sitting in the cocktail bar across the street from my rooms in College sipping on a succession of

Singapore gin slings, even if I'd have been in all other respects better off had I been doing that. As will have already become apparent, it seems to me – though this step need not be taken – that this purpose that God has for a person is probably best construed as contributing to the meaningfulness of a person's life even if that person doesn't know what the purpose is or even if they think that there's no purpose at all. But that is not uncontroversial. Cottingham, for one, would perhaps disagree, saying that 'for something to be meaningful to a [sic] agent, that agent must *interpret* it or *construe* it in a certain way'.[32] According to me, they need not interpret or construe it in any way, as they may be entirely ignorant of it and thus fail to interpret or construe it at all.[33] But be that as it may, I hope to have rendered it plausible that the purpose can contribute to the meaningfulness of a person's life *for* him or her if that person *does* realize what the purpose is and appropriates that purpose to himself or herself. If a worker finds himself in a particular job in the factory as a result of some prudent decision by the Managing Director, then his being there, rather than anywhere else, has a meaning-giving purpose and it has meaning for the Managing Director. But it will only have meaning *for* him – the particular worker – if he realizes this and willingly assents to it. Still, theists are unanimous that God has not left us entirely unable to fathom His purpose for us. We have natural reason and revelation. And – theological issues concerning God's prevenient grace not withstanding – we have at least some inclination to appropriate to ourselves God's purposes for us.

There is plausibility in the thought that our lives having a purpose – even when that purpose is a good one (or even the best); a good one for us; and one that we fully appropriate to ourselves – is not by itself sufficient for meaningfulness either. The purpose must be achieved. A thought experiment effective in this context concerns our imagining a man devoting his life to building a hospital in some needy part of the world. The day after it is completed, before it can open to patients, some natural disaster kills him and destroys the hospital utterly. It's hard not to see the frustration of his good purpose as depriving his life of at least some meaning. This is what I am calling bad meaning-luck.[34] Again though, such concerns are moot in this context, for the God of classical theism is omnipotent and omniscient. His good purposes cannot be ultimately frustrated and thus, insofar as we align ourselves with His purposes, our purposes cannot be ultimately frustrated either. Of course, this side of the grave we do not always see God's good purposes or ours being clearly fulfilled. But, according to Theism, this side of the grave is not all *or even most* of what there is.[35] After death, another – better – life awaits us.

There is as-yet-unexplored scope for additional lines of argument in favour of optimism. So, for example, there is a growing literature in the Philosophy of Religion on the Problem of 'horrendous' evils, these sometimes being defined in terms of their capacity to destroy the meaningfulness of a person's life. But connections have yet to be made between this and the growing meaning of life (as meaning in life) literature. Do we suffer from evils that *would be* horrendous were it not for God and the right sort of afterlife? A positive answer to this is often given in the Problem of Evil literature, which then suggests another line of argument for optimism. Of course, as always with the afterlife, we do need the 'right sort' of afterlife to ground optimism. The 'wrong sort' of afterlife – Hell as traditionally conceived – seems likely just to add to the problem. And thus there seems to me to be scope for further work arguing for pessimism at least with regards to the variant of Theism which holds to the traditional doctrine of Hell. There may even be scope for arguing for pessimism with regard to the variant of Theism that embraces Universalism. If we're all to get to Heaven when we die, does that make every-one's earthly suffering more meaningful or less? We shall come back to some of these issues in a later chapter.

We have seen, in our discussion of privacy and some other values, that pessimists may argue that God negatively affects these other values and that these other values can be linked to meaningfulness, so He negatively affects that too. Similarly, *mutatis mutandis*, optimists may argue that God positively affects values other than meaning-fulness and that these other values can be linked to meaningfulness, so that He positively affects that too. Some optimists, for example, have tied meaningfulness to morality and morality to God, reviving Kantian themes. Belief in a salient link between meaning-fulness and morality is widespread, even if not universal,[36] and it spans the optimist/ pessimist divide. The salient link is that meaningfulness requires moral engagement. In support of holding that there is such a link, one may consider the amoralist. The life of a totally amoral person, if there is such a person (a certain sort of psychopath perhaps?) is rendered meaningless (or at least significantly less meaningful than it might have been) in part, intuition suggests, because of his or her total inability to engage in actions that he or she can think of in moral terms. Now add to this the fact that it is hard – though by no means impossible – not to see permanently unresolved injustices as detracting from the meaning-generating capacity of moral engagement. Whatever one makes of Kant's original arguments here to the effect that only God and immortality can help, one may agree that retributive, re-distributive, reparative, and redemptive justice could all be optimally served by an omnipotent, omniscient and perfectly good God giving people the right sort of afterlife. One might concede that, *pace* Kant, something short of the theistic view of an everlasting afterlife might be sufficient for these purposes, but the theistic view *is* sufficient and thus grounds for optimism.[37] 'In an ultimately meaningful world, acting morally should be a necessary condition for the betterment of one's ultimate well-being, which is perfect happiness. However, what should be is not the case in a … world [where there is no God or afterlife as traditionally conceived] and, therefore, [such] a … world is ultimately absurd because it includes lives that are absurd in virtue of the failure of morality and well-being to meet and embrace.'[38]

In addition, one might argue that even if moral engagement in a world of perman-ently unresolved injustices is still as meaning-generating as it would be in a world without them, one's capacity for moral engagement is weakened by belief in permanently unresolved injustices. If that's right, then belief in Theism might help with meaning-fulness indirectly, through strengthening our commitment to moral engagement, which then in turn contributes directly. 'The thought of the ultimate victory of goodness over evil, of justice over injustice, gives us confidence to carry on the fight against injustice, cruelty, and hatred, when others calculate that the odds against righteousness are too great to fight against.'[39] Of course, as stated so far, this is not an argument for optimism as defined. It is rather an argument for optimism about what *belief in* Theism can add to the meaningfulness of our lives. But it could be transmuted into an argument for optimism as defined with a suitable premise concerning how, in a Godly world, belief in Theism is more likely than it is in an otherwise similar Godless one, because there's a God in the first world who is at least somewhat disposed to inculcate belief in Him by special revelation.

And then finally, the meaningfulness that's awaiting us on the other side of the grave seems to be able to add to the meaningfulness on this side. If my discussion of the meaning of life is destined not, as I fear, to remain entirely unloved, but rather all that is valuable in it will be preserved into eternity where it will be cherished by the person whose opinion I should most care about, then that makes my efforts all the more meaningful now. The fact that in this world it'll only be read by a handful of people (and get terrible reviews from some of those) won't have made my writing it pointless. God will ultimately eliminate the effects of bad meaning-luck. And knowing (or possibly even just believing) that may make me redouble my efforts and thus (insofar as they were meaning-generating efforts in the first place) add to the meaning of my *ante-mortem* life. William James says this at one point: 'Probably to almost every one of us here the most adverse life would seem well worth living, if we only could be *certain* that our bravery and patience with it were terminating and eventuating and bearing fruit somewhere in an unseen spiritual world.'[40] And one can lead an adverse life all the more fully if one – despite its adversity – finds it well worth living. Leading it all the more fully will dissipate at least some of the negative aspects of its adversity. If the sort of 'certainty' that has to be had for this to happen requires knowledge, then, as knowledge is factive, it requires this spiritual world to be out there.

It has long been appreciated that death – if understood as permanent annihilation – negates certain (relatively deep) senses of life's meaning, but not others. It appears that – regardless of what, if anything, happens for the individual after it – it will affect different people differently. For example, if I build my life around a lot of what Williams called I-desires (desires such as that *I see* my children get married (not simply that they get married; i.e. desires the satisfaction of which requires me to be alive[41]), then death before these desires are satisfied will detract from the meaning of my *ante-mortem* life more than if I had built it around non-I desires (e.g. that my children get married). A certain sort of selflessness then – as encouraged in fact by the world's major religions – robs death of at least some of its meaning-negating power even if death does mark permanent annihilation. Of course this argument is rather compressed and could do with unpacking. But as nothing with regard to my main line of argument turns on it, I leave it there and to the judgement of the reader. In this way and others various religions (and non-religious philosophies) have reacted to the 'problem of death', the most radical solution being its 'dissolution'. Death – in the sense of permanent annihilation – never happens at all: we all live on in an everlasting afterlife. It is this most radical solution that Theism provides for us and that later I shall argue is key in finally resolving the optimism/pessimism issue.

Of course those who are inclined to think that God would detract from the meaningfulness of our lives are inclined to turn these optimistic arguments on their heads. For example, consider the issue of immortality. So far, I have been rather uncritically accepting of the idea that it would help with meaningfulness if only because it would add to our total lifespan and thus add to the total meaningfulness quantitatively[42] and add potentially infinitely. Atheism predicts for us a lifespan of the sort actuarial tables detail, i.e. merely an *ante-mortem* life;[43] Theism predicts for us a lifespan constituted by *ante-mortem* life and *post-mortem* life, the second of which is potentially infinite. But it's not at all clear to everyone considering the issue that God's giving us immortality would add to, rather than subtract from, our lives' meaning.

Several decades ago now, Bernard Williams wrote an influential article alleging that immortality would either become tedious and hence – though this is implicit, rather than explicit in his writing – meaning-subtracting for us or it would not be us who were experiencing it (as the conditions of our personal identity would have been vitiated).[44] I shall return to the argument in a later chapter. But for now we may summarize. In essence, there's only so much any one person can experience and, having experienced it, one either repeats and ultimately gets bored with it, or one is altered so as to avoid boredom and yet ultimately such alterations will cause one to cease to exist. These and similar reflections continue to garner approving remarks.[45] The details differ, but the central claim is that even if some sort of afterlife might help with the meaningfulness of some or even all people's lives, the sort of everlasting afterlife predicted for us on Theism would of necessity be or become meaning-subtracting.

It is sometimes held that the problem arises for Theism from its committing us to immortality per se. That is, it is sometimes held that mortality (our lives having a real end) is necessary for meaningfulness. The (putative) fact that life is fleeting is what gives it the right sort of gravitas and importance. This though doesn't seem to me to be the best way of articulating the objection to grounding optimism on immortality. This is because it seems to me that the best explanation of why death, if it were permanent annihilation, would be bad is that it would permanently end our enjoyment of a good – life. That being so, it seems to me, on the one hand, that one had better not argue that immortality is necessary to make life good. Life would be good even if it did have an end, if we were mortal. But, by the same token, on the other hand, neither should one think that immortality couldn't be a good. After all, it would add (even if only quantitatively [though no doubt a good case could be made for its adding qualitatively too]), to that thing, life, which, as just argued, we do well to accept as a good. If that's all right, one cannot then consistently hold that mortality per se makes (or would make) life better. Why think it makes (or would make) it more meaningful? (Or at least more meaningful in some sense we should care about?[46]) Frankly, it seems to me obviously implausible to think that mortality per se adds to overall meaningfulness. I tell you of a society in which human life is twice as fleeting as it is in ours, i.e. life-expectancy is half what it is in ours. Do you incline to infer that *ceteris paribus* people in that society must be leading overall more meaningful lives than us? I doubt it. So, the person who wishes to argue that the sort of immortality predicted for us on Theism is actually grounds for

Pessimism (rather than Optimism) is, it seems to me, best advised to argue that it is not the immortality per se that detracts from or at least fails to contribute to our lives' meaningfulness, but something about that immortality, something of the sort perhaps that Williams was talking about.[47] Once more, how this all plays out turns on what sort of immortality one thinks Theism *does* actually predict for us. In making the case that immortality helps meaningfulness, as I have already indicated, one needs to use immortality of the right sort; Hell wouldn't do the job. But – to reveal my own hand early in the game – Heaven, it seems to me, would. Why would such a good as Heaven be meaning-subtracting? Worshipping God in the full glory of the beatific vision is precisely the sort of 'guaranteedly-absorbing' activity that Williams himself originally demanded if one were to defeat his argument. It is not boredom-worthy and we wouldn't be bored by it.

There is a view that is worth flagging up at this point as a sort-of hybrid between pessimism and optimism. I have in mind the view that concedes to the optimist that the overall package of *ante-mortem* plus *post-mortem* life that Theism predicts for us would be more meaningful than the overall package that Atheism predicts for us[48] (*viz. ante-mortem* life only), but asserts that, nevertheless, the *ante-mortem* section of the theistic package is less meaningful than the corresponding *ante-mortem* section (i.e. totality) of the atheistic package. God detracts (would detract) from the meaning of our *earthly* lives. When this earthly life is all that there is, there's more meaning in it than when this earthly life is but an infinitesimally small section of what there is. To reveal my own hand once more, that seems to me a much more plausible view.[49] But, even if true, it is of course compatible with the theistic package (*ante*- plus *post*- *mortem*) being more overall meaningful than the atheistic package (*ante-mortem* alone). So an optimist need not avoid this 'concession'. I also report though that it seems to me personally that much of how one rates opposing views here turns on temperament. If we are to have pie in the sky when we die, does that make the pies we have now less valuable or more? Do we have all the more reason to develop a taste for pie now, for it's what we'll be eating lots of later? Or does it follow that we should not eat pie now, for we'll have plenty later? I find it hard to come up with arguments for one set of answers that may not be turned on their head by those of differing temperaments. You'll see me finding it hard later on in the book. Sorry about that.

Another example of an argument that may be turned on its head by those of differing temperaments is the one that I sketched earlier which focused on whether belief in Theism adds to or subtracts from meaningfulness. Earlier, I put forward a case for thinking that belief in Theism will motivate moral engagement. Thus, on the widespread and plausible assumption that moral engagement is necessary for – or at least helps with – meaningfulness, it will indirectly add to (or probably add to) meaningfulness. But an alternative suggestion is often made. Theism makes it more likely one will disengage – 'I'll let God sort this out later'[50] – or perhaps engage but in the *wrong* morality – 'Kill them all! God will know His own!'[51] Clack and Clack, for example, say this of views that encourage reflection on the afterlife awaiting us:

Such views are potentially dangerous, undermining the kind of ethic that might stem from considering this world to be all that we have. To accept this world as all that is means that we need to work constructively at our relationships with the people with whom we share this fragile planet, as well as with the world itself. Cultivating such an attitude necessitates accepting the fleeting quality of our own lives, and resisting the idea that this is simply a temporary state before we enter into the 'real' world.[52]

Immediately after this passage, Clack and Clack juxtapose a quotation from one of my own works, in which I say something (as I would have thought it, something cheering) about the afterlife, with one from a note found in the baggage of one of the '911' terrorists. Their readers are then encouraged to draw parallels between my thinking and that of this particular mass-murderer. Needless to say, I am not delighted beyond qualification at finding myself placed in such company. I pass over that with a dignified silence (or at least as much dignified silence as is compatible with my huffily telling you that this is what I'm doing). In any case, the view is that, whether it's by discouraging engagement; encouraging engagement with the wrong sort of morality; or a bit of both, belief in Theism undermines, rather than undergirds, the sort of moral engagement that plausibly has meaning-generating capacity.

Metz has recently sought to explore the possibilities of arguing for why God would be especially suitable for grounding meaning by appealing to properties peculiar to Him, such as atemporality and immutability. Of course, it might be argued that things other than God could have these properties – angels or Platonic forms. Be that as it may, one of God's peculiar properties is necessity. One of the traditional sources of worry about the meaningfulness of our lives has been the apparent arbitrariness and contingency of what we do with them. I care about something, but I could easily have cared about something else; what seems important from a narrow perspective seems unimportant from a wider one. From the widest perspective, isn't it all arbitrary and isn't nothing I do important? God seems a good contender for being able to stop such problematic regresses/widenings-of-perspectives. In God one would reach a point of view that couldn't have been different from the way that it is; that it's impossible to get beyond; and that does regard some of what I do as important. As such, it seems God might be uniquely capable of removing the absurdity that Nagel characterized.

Finally, I mention one argument that may be used by both sides in the optimist/pessimist debate. Audi[53] argues that believing one's life to be meaningful can in and of itself enhance the meaningfulness of one's life, presuming other things are in order – he's not a subjectivist. So, theists who believe that optimistic views are right – as most do – might thereby actually be making their lives more meaningful than they would otherwise have been (as long as these other things are in fact in order). Of course one could deny this possibility, arguing that optimistic views are wrong and that one of the things that needs to be in order before one can 'super-add' meaningfulness to one's life simply by believing of it that it is meaningful is the line of reasoning that has led to the belief that one's life is meaningful. But *if* optimistic views *are* right and there is a God, then this super-addition of meaningfulness is surely the cherry on the cake for theistic optimists. In a similar manner to Audi on this topic, William James says this: 'Believe that life is worth living, and your belief will help create the fact. The 'scientific proof' that you are right may not be clear before the day of judgment … is reached. But the faithful fighters of this hour …may then turn to the faint-hearted, who here decline to go on, with words like those with which Henry IV. greeted the tardy Crillon after a great victory had been gained: "Hang yourself, brave Crillon! we fought at Arques, and you were not there."[54] Well, quite. Words *like* that. Personally, I expect that I myself will choose slightly different ones. And the same cherry – well *mutatis mutandis* the same cherry – can be popped on their cake by pessimists. Remember, the pessimists spoken of here are pessimistic by definition solely about what God would do to the meaningfulness of our lives were He to exist. They may well, if atheists, think that our actual lives are meaningful. If one supposes then that there is no God and considers an atheist who believes in pessimism, as most do, he or she might actually be making his or her life more meaningful than it would otherwise be by believing of it that it is meaningful. Of course, optimists could pull the same move here as was used against them by pessimists earlier: argue that pessimistic views are wrong and that one of the things that needs to be in order before one can super-add meaningfulness is the line of reasoning that has led to the belief that one's life is meaningful. But *if* pessimistic views *are* right and there is no God, then this super-addition is the cherry on the cake for atheistic pessimists.

So, to sum up: on the one hand, we have those who think that God would hinder, perhaps even entirely prevent, meaningfulness for us; these I have called pessimists. On the other hand, we have those who think that God would help, perhaps even is necessary for, meaningfulness for us; these I have called optimists. Even though I have been brief, I hope I have done enough to show that each side in this debate has weighty arguments, arguments that have been well developed and gone through many iterations as a result of their interactions with counterarguments. And thus I hope to have done enough to render of philosophical interest the following question: Which side is right?

One way of understanding what I am about in this book is by thinking of me as seeking to explore at each stage in my discussion of the question 'What is the meaning of life?' the truth in *both* these schools of thought. Think of me as answering the question then of what God could do and what God couldn't do to make life more meaningful (as well as what He would and wouldn't do) and what He could/Has to do to make it less meaningful (I don't in fact think He can make it entirely meaningless). For brevity, I shall sometimes call this the issue of what He brings to the party and what He takes away from it. My view is that He both brings *and* takes away; thus, there's rightness on both sides of this debate. How can He both bring and take away?

In this book, I argue for a version of the 'amalgam' thesis about the issue of life's meaning, which thesis I locate within a wider one that I call pluralism[55] or – more often – polyvalence. In essence, polyvalence at the level of connotation is the thesis that there are a number of different legitimate meanings of 'meaning' and 'life' in the question of life's meaning. When one asks the question 'What is the meaning of life?' one thus asks a number of different questions at once. And polyvalence at the level of denotation is the thesis that these different questions have different answers. In short, there are many meanings of life.[56] If one asks what God could or couldn't (or would or wouldn't [or has to]) do to help or hinder meaning in one of its senses for life in one of its senses, one gets a different answer from the answer one would have got if one had asked what God could or couldn't (or would or wouldn't [or has to]) do to help or hinder meaning in another of its senses or for life in another of its senses. It seems to me – and a large part of this book will be taken up arguing this point in various forms – that God, were He to exist, would help with making life in its various senses meaningful in some of its senses and hinder in some other senses. That's why there's truth in both schools of thought, why Sartre and Nagel, say, are (partially) right, but Cottingham, say, is (partially) right too. I'm also going to argue that the same applies to what God could and would do to resolve 'trade-off' issues between differing meanings of life and secure 'deeper' and 'overall' meaning, for I shall argue that some meanings of life can be ranked as determinately deeper than others and so it's not just a quantitative 'What's God bring (or take) net?' question that one needs to be asking (and answering).

The notion of the relative deepness of certain sorts of meaningfulness as it applies to human lives is used by people writing in the field more often than it is analysed. A life, a period or an aspect within a life, or even an individual action within a life is said to be more deeply meaningful than another and there is a notable consensus on such first-order judgements, a consensus that spans very different theories of what the meaning of life is. Given the Monism – the view that meaning in life is just one thing – that is almost universally the shared presumption of those philosophers reporting and making these judgements, one wonders what the dimension of deepness could be being supposed to be if not simply that of how much meaningfulness is had by whatever things are being compared. The consensus that there would be, for example, on the first-order judgement that Gandhi's life as a whole was more deeply meaningful than that of my paternal grandfather can surely, on Monism, only amount to the consensus that there would be on the fact that Gandhi's life had more meaning in it than did that of my paternal grandfather.[57]

Given my Pluralism, other possibilities for using the term 'deepness' and its cognates open themselves and I shall avail myself of one.[58] According to the usage adopted hereafter then, the deepness of a particular meaning of life is the same as its desirability in itself *qua* a meaning of life. In due course, I shall also introduce the notion of the overall meaningfulness that a life (a period, an aspect, or even an action) has, which I shall define as the overall desirability of the life (period, aspect, or action) with respect to meaningfulness. An analogy will help, I think, in making things clearer at this stage, though one needs to read on for them to become as fully clear as I can make them. The area of which value pluralism (or polyvalence, as I prefer) strikes most people as most plausible is Aesthetics. So I shall choose my putative analogical case from that field.

Suppose then my wife and I have been to see two plays in the recent past: one, a production of *Waiting for Godot*, with Sir Patrick Stewart and Sir Ian McKellen in the lead roles; the other, our daughter's nursery's nativity play, in which she – as did every child – had a walk-on part, whilst adults corralled them on the stage and a narrator did their best to explain to us why children dressed as toys and Disney Princesses were visiting the infant savior. My wife and I can easily be imagined to have effortlessly pushed past the warmth we felt towards the second of these performances as a result of sentiment and to have agreed that the first was overall the greater artistic success. It seems to me plausible that there are a number of discrete values that go up to make a performance of a play an artistic success. The raw material of the script itself, of course – does it have fundamentally coherent characters doing what people with their characters would do in the situations in which they find themselves? The set – does it fit the play without being too intrusive or didactic in its own terms? The actors, of course – can they hold the stage? More prosaically, are they audible? And a myriad of other values. On all fronts, the first won out over the second. Thus our judgement: the first was a greater overall artistic success than the second. But suppose we considered a less easy comparison. We are trying to judge between two significant West End plays we have seen. We might find that one did rather better on one front than the other, but that the other did rather better on another front than the first. Yet – nevertheless – we might find we were able to make an overall judgement, because we judged that one of these fronts was less important – less deep, we may put it – than the other. Thus it is, I shall suggest with various meanings of life. Some are more desirable, than others – they are deeper. And we may sometimes – but not always (the issue of incommensurablity stands in the way on occasion) – make judgements of overall meaningfulness in the light of that. Sometimes we may do so as we'll be comparing lives where one has a lot of several deep meanings of life and the other has just a small amount of an obviously-less-deep meaning of life or none at all (similarly then to the *Waiting for Godot* verses nursery nativity play case). But sometimes we'll be able to make a judgement of the following kind. Although life A was more meaningful than life B with respect to meaning of life *p*, nevertheless, overall, B was more meaningful than A, in virtue of being more meaningful in senses *q*, *r* and *s*, which senses – even though each *less* deep than *p* – when taken together outweigh the only slightly greater *p*-meaning that A had over B, thus leaving B ahead overall.

So, the view I'll be defending is that there's truth on both sides of the pessimist/optimist debate. 'The Lord giveth, and the Lord taketh away.'[59] But, one may legitimately press me at this point: 'Does the Lord giveth more than He taketh away? If so, then Blessed be the Name of the Lord. Or does He taketh away more than He giveth? In which case, I shall curse Him (even if not to His face [prudence is, after all, a virtue]).' In other words, one may ask is there *more* truth on one side of the optimist/pessimist debate than there is on the other? I think that there is. My conclusion will be, roughly, that while there could be meaning in our world even were it a Godless world, there could be more and deeper sorts of meaning in it were it a Godly one; and there could be more overall meaning too. There are a number of reasons to think this, but I shall argue that the major way in which God ends up bringing more to the party (or, if you will, afterparty) than He takes away is through giving us eternal life. This keeps the meanings of life we have *ante-mortem* going; going infinitely; and going infinitely *for us*. In that my view is that He *does* take away from the party, I'm not an unqualified optimist. But in that my view is that He brings more than He takes away, it seems least misleading to think of me as ending up on that side of the debate. That's the conclusion of the book in a nutshell. Now I need to argue for it.

CHAPTER 1

Those unexposed to Philosophy as an academic discipline often suppose from the outside that a central question – one occupying most, if not all, of its practitioners for most, if not all, of their time – must be, 'What is the meaning of life?' Those on the inside know better.

Until the past few decades, hardly anybody who would have called themselves a professional philosopher was willing to consider the question 'What is the meaning of life?' at all, or at least admit to considering it.[1] Even now, interest in it is confined to a sub-section of a sub-section of the discipline, a branch of the branch of Philosophy that is sometimes called Value Theory.[2] (Tellingly, it didn't really fit in anywhere under older taxonomies, ones that tended to speak of Moral Philosophy and Aesthetics.[3]) Even now, the number of philosophers addressing it is very small relative to those, say, addressing topics in Epistemology or the Philosophy of Mind. And even now the question attracts suspicion more often than it attracts genuine interest from those professional philosophers who are not themselves directly working on it.[4] As Susan Wolf says, 'when the question is brought up by a naïve student … or a prospective donor to the cause of a liberal arts education, it is apt to be greeted with uncomfortable embarrassment.'[5] When someone employed as a philosopher by a university tells an outsider that that's what they do and gets the response, 'On yes. So, what's the meaning of life?' as – if my experience is anything to go by – is not that unusual, they are likely to feel about as perplexed as did a colleague of mine who got the response, 'Oh yes. So, what are your sayings?' That a Philosopher would be asked this by a non-Philosopher reveals a deep gulf between the outsider's and the insiders' understanding of what Philosophy must be about.

Sometimes, in my experience, there's an air of challenge in the outsider's question – rather as there might be in 'So, you say you're a medical researcher. What's the cure for cancer then?' But even when asked in this spirit, the fact that it is asked reveals the outsider's supposition that that this is what philosophers should be thinking about. Even if they've shamefully failed to answer the question, they should at least be trying. If one answered 'Well, actually I'm an Epistemologist, so I don't look at that sort of thing at all. I look at ways of adapting the safety condition on knowledge to cope with knowledge of necessary truths', one might get as a reply (if one was speaking to someone who valued candour over etiquette) 'Well, you shouldn't; you should be thinking about the question of the meaning of life … But, then again, you wouldn't come to any satisfactory answer if you did. So really you should just give up on Philosophy and get a proper job.' A point of dis-analogy suggests itself then with people's attitudes to medical research. Nobody suggests that medical research should just stop because it hasn't yet found the cure for cancer. But at least some of those on the outside *do* think that Philosophy should just stop. The difference in attitude is justified by a widespread presumption – held by many of those outside and indeed many inside – that the question of the meaning of life just cannot have a satisfactory answer. For those on the outside, the argument goes as follows: 'Philosophy should be about answering this question satisfactorily. But the question can't be answered satisfactorily. So Philosophy should just stop.' For those on the inside, it goes slightly differently: 'This question can't be answered satisfactorily. And Philosophy shouldn't just stop (a selection effect explains the universality of the belief in this premise amongst those on the inside of the discipline). So Philosophy should be about answering other questions.' While I, an insider, think that there are many important questions other than this one that Philosophy should be about answering, I am sympathetic to the outsider's view in the following two ways.

I think that one question Philosophy should be about answering is the question of the meaning of life. It's not *the* central question, but it is *a* central question. I also think that the widespread presumption that the question cannot be answered satisfactorily – widespread, as I say, both within and without the discipline – has some truth in it. This book has as one of the main themes running through it an attempted diagnosis of why it is that the sorts of answers that the person on the outside wants – in essence, 'sayings' of the sort that my colleague was asked for – they rightly suppose won't be satisfactory even as they continue to demand them. No saying – even a long one – can be the answer. This theme is tied to the first, mentioned at the end of the previous chapter, in that one of the main reasons why no answer can be fully satisfactory is that not even an omnipotent, omniscient, perfectly good being could make it so. And that itself is unsatisfactory whether or not there's a God. If God exists, He takes – *has to* take – as well as giving and in taking He makes things less than fully satisfactory, even if He may be relied upon to make them as fully satisfactory as is possible. If God doesn't exist, then how satisfactory 'as fully satisfactory as possible' amounts to is different again, and – though the argument for this will not be given until a later chapter – worse. One problem is that one cannot clearly see at the outset (or even, I shall argue, at the end) quite how unsatisfactory 'as fully satisfactory as is possible' is under either a presumption of Theism or a presumption of Atheism. And that itself is of course … well, the word that suggests itself is 'unsatisfactory'.

It seems to me that to ask the question 'What is the meaning of life?' *seriously* and after thought is already to know that no answer capable of easy formulation will be immediately and entirely satisfying. Of course the question is often asked non-seriously – playfully or in any case without any willingness to engage in serious thought about it and any answer presented. But it is not always asked non-seriously. I'd even venture that everyone who has achieved the age of reason has at some stage asked the question in a spirit of seriousness. They've earnestly wanted to know the answer and been willing to engage with various putative answers sympathetically – indeed, more than sympathetically, willing them to be right. And, if that spirit of seriousness has maintained itself through engagement with a variety of putative answers, they'll have reached the stage

I'm talking about now – the stage of seriously asking it once more, but asking it with the confident expectation that any answer they receive will be unsatisfactory. Indeed, it is this expectation of dissatisfaction if one continues to take the question seriously and engage with putative answers that explains the relief gained by exposing oneself to comedic treatments of the question and jokey answers. And it explains why many who may at some stage have asked the question seriously now ask it with an air of challenge to those they encounter who have the hubris to call themselves 'professional philosophers' and thus, they presume, are still wasting their time with it. Why try to ponder imponderables? Why try to answer unanswerable questions? It also explains why many more simply fail to engage with it at all any more, either jokingly or by way of challenge. They have given up on it entirely. Philosophers then may be compared to Politicians in this respect: When they don't give the people satisfaction, the people find relief in laughing at them; being angry with them; or simply ignoring them. But – as you'd expect me, a philosopher writing a book on the meaning of life, to say – this is unfair. Davis says this: 'Philosophers do not get much credit for solving mankind's fundamental questions, but they have achieved a modest success in identifying those questions.'[6] And we may expand on Davis's thought thusly: if philosophers deserve the credit for having identified the fundamental questions, then, as the question 'Which are the most fundamental questions?' must itself be the most fundamental question (or at least among the most fundamental), so this act of identification is the answer to the most fundamental question (or at least one of the most fundamental). Thus, if Davis is right, philosophers deserve more credit than they are currently getting. And they deserve credit for *solving* mankind's most fundamental question (or at least one of them). The question 'What is the meaning of life?' is obviously a fundamental question; one doesn't in fact need a philosopher to tell one that. And I hope my attempts at identifying it and answering the question one may suppose even more fundamental than it (as it is a question about it – why is the question 'What is the meaning of life?' so difficult to answer satisfactorily?) will thus be worthy of credit.

So, what answers to the question 'What is the meaning of life?' are we already familiar with?

'The meaning of life is to give and receive love.' 'The meaning of life is to gain in wisdom and knowledge.' 'The meaning of life is to find union with God.' 'The meaning of life is to escape the suffering inherent in the cycle of rebirth.' 'Life has no meaning.' At the stage of seriously asking the question of the meaning of life after thought, one will have already heard and rejected these, these and a multitude of alternative answers. One will have rejected them at least as *definitive* of, as saying all that there is to be said about, life's meaning. There may be some truth in that, one may well have thought, but it can't be right that that's *it*; there must be more to it than that. If one picks through the scrap pile of answers one has thus generated, of most melancholic interest among them will be those answers that one found wanting in completeness while recognizing that there is nevertheless something of value in the modes of life that they license. Most puzzlingly melancholic will be any answer that one found wanting whilst believing that there is something of unsurpassable value in the mode of life that it licenses – for example, if one believes in God, the answer involving union with Him; if one believes in suffering inherent in a cycle of rebirth, the answer involving escape from this cycle.

Presumably, whatever one's worldview, one thinks that there is something of value in giving and receiving love and in gaining in wisdom and knowledge. If one believes in God, presumably one thinks that there is something of unsurpassable value in finding union with Him. If, instead, one believes in suffering inherent in a cycle of rebirth, presumably one thinks there is something of unsurpassable value in escaping this suffering by escaping this cycle. But, even as one believes oneself to recognize value – even unsurpassable value – in these things, on reflection such answers appear to connect at best only partially with one's concerns when asking the question of the meaning of life. 'That can't be all that there is to be said about it' is, I hazard, the thought that occurs again and again, in response to every answer to the question of the meaning of life, even the answer that there is no answer. And, with only slightly less insistence does one think 'That can't be all that there is to it'; does one think 'There must be more to it than that'. Again, I hazard that this thought occurs whatever the precise nature of the 'that' which is offered, even when the 'that' offered is as impressive a 'that' as union with God or as ultimate a 'that' as escape from existence altogether.

In the case of a religious answer, if one is oneself of that particular religious persuasion, perhaps one hesitates in having the thought 'There must be more to it than that' when one reaches the object of ultimate religious reverence. If one believes in God, for example, one feels perhaps rather impious in thinking this about finding union with Him. One inclines to worry that the thought 'There must be more to it than that' must finally be misplaced here, as there could be no 'that' more impressive – more ultimately satisfying of every valuable aspect of one's being – than union with God. But, I speculate that, even if one believes in God, one thinks the thought nonetheless, even here. One thinks it tentatively perhaps and with some embarrassment. One thinks it quietly to oneself in church and doesn't mention it to the vicar over tea afterwards. But one thinks it, nevertheless, and persistently. And I speculate that the same goes, *mutatis mutandis*, if one is of another religious persuasion. If one believes in the 'noble truth' that all existence is characterized by suffering and has committed oneself to the 'noble eightfold path', which one believes will lead one ultimately to escape from it, this too, I hazard, strikes one as, even if complete and sufficient as a guide to life, incomplete and insufficient as an answer to the question of the meaning of life.

Of course, if one eventually finds oneself face-to-face with God, one will not, at that time (if time may still be spoken of in such a context), be thinking 'There must be more to it than this'. And if one ultimately escapes existence altogether, one will not be able in such a non-state to think anything at all, so *a fortiori* one will not then be thinking 'There must be more to it than this'. But the fact that, in such states/non-states, such thoughts would be obliterated does not make any less well-grounded now the thought in question. For the thought one has now is not that such things cannot happen or that their happening wouldn't then remove any dissatisfaction one might feel about one's life and indeed everything else, but rather that ending up at such points cannot be all that there is to making meaningful the lives that led up to them. There must be more to the meaning of life than simply passing through it to what (if anything) lies beyond. And if there is an afterlife beyond, what then would be the meaning of that? Not, one presumes, to pass beyond it to something else, surely.

This dissatisfaction with what one takes to be one's religion's answer to the question of the meaning of life is likely to be puzzling to the reflective believer. Surely, if I recall a phrase from the catechism that I learnt when being prepared for confirmation to the effect that the purpose of humanity (and thus oneself as an individual) is to glorify God and enjoy Him forever and I still wholeheartedly believe in the religion in which I was duly confirmed, I should not now be inclined to ask of it 'Is that it?' voicing as I do so the thought 'There must be more to it than that' when I reflect on the thesis that this is the meaning of my life. I should be satisfied. But I am not. Do I not then really believe in my religion after all? The puzzlement may gain an extra layer from the fact that when it comes to my religious praxis, I find that I would say that my religion gives my life a great deal of meaning. It shapes my year; my week; even my day; it affects my attitudes towards others; my aesthetic choices and responses; and much more. So, perhaps I am a true believer, after all? But then again, religious praxis doesn't shield me and nor, it seems, *could* it shield me from all meaninglessness. If all of those whom I love were to die in a fluke accident (one might naturally say a 'meaningless' accident), my life would be rendered less meaningful thereby whatever my religious response. I might hope, even expect, that my religion would give me some solace in such a case, perhaps even provide me with a reassurance that one day I would see them again in Heaven. But that would still leave the meaning-negating aspect of their deaths untouched. My life – or *ante-mortem* life, in the short term anyway – would still have been largely ruined in respect of its meaningfulness by this disaster. It seems obvious that the death of a loved one attacks the meaning of the lives of those who loved him or her and that religion, whatever its comforts, offers no real defence against that loss or at least that loss as it occurs at that time. Even if God ultimately restores to one all who are lost by death and adds immeasurably to the meaningfulness of one's existence *post-mortem*, that *ante-mortem* loss in meaningfulness is still a loss in meaningfulness, and one that is as close to a total loss as to make no difference. Forgive me for the intrusion, but, if you doubt this, draw up a list of the people you love; reflect on them fondly; spend a few minutes doing this; and now imagine yourself in the instant after you discover that all the people on that list have been killed in a fluke accident. Whatever your hopes for future meaning might be, would it not be that your life had – at that moment at least – been rendered almost entirely meaningless? It is as Seneca almost[7] said, 'One may gain security against many things, but, when it comes to [the] death [of the ones that he loves], each man lives in a city without walls.'

If you are of a particular religious persuasion, you may need to step back for a moment from what you take your religion to be telling you to feel, so as to be able to recover the feeling you actually have towards what you take it your religion is telling you the meaning of life is. Remember, you're not in front of a vicar who is mild-manneredly expecting a cup of tea now. You're in front of a philosopher (yourself). You can, indeed must, be honest, brutally so if need be. Reflect on what you think your religion tells you the meaning of life is. Reflect on how you *really* feel about that. Dissatisfied, yes?

If you are not of any particular religious persuasion, I hazard that you will probably find it easier to know you feel the same dissatisfaction towards each answer to the question that you have considered, because you will probably not consider yourself under an authority who you take to be telling you not to feel this towards any in particular, or in general.

These speculations as to the feelings of dissatisfaction one is likely to have with putative answers to the question of life's meaning may be wide of the mark in any individual reader's case. But I maintain that, in general, they hold true and thus I trust that the majority of my readers will find their own thoughts echoed in what I have said so far in this chapter.

Be all of that as it may, I shall argue that the thought 'There must be more to it than that', if and when it does occur in response to particular answers to the question of life's meaning, is not impious or misplaced even when had of the object of one's greatest religious reverence. It is right and important. For every particular answer to the question – even every particular religious answer – there is always more to be said about the meaning of life than that and there is always more *to* the meaning of life than that. And that *must* be so, whichever religion, if any, is true. You are right to be dissatisfied. No part of my aim in this book is to remove that dissatisfaction. But it is a part of my aim to help you to understand it by understanding what more needs to be said and what difficulties lie in the way of saying it. What is more, it is part of my aim to help you to transcend this dissatisfaction, that is to say to become, as I shall put it, satisfied with your dissatisfaction.

After giving a brief history of the subject in recent years, which will serve – I hope – simultaneously both to introduce and to dismiss the first explanation of this dissatisfaction that will suggest itself to anyone trained in Analytic Philosophy, I shall state in outline what more needs to be said than is offered by any particular answer to the question of the meaning of life and thus indicate why there is always more to the meaning of life than whatever is said by any particular answer to it. This then will afford us with a characterization of what I diagnose in this book as the *primary* source for the dissatisfaction that I am speculating we feel with each answer to the question of the meaning of life, even if we rightly judge that no answer could be more satisfying or ultimate than the particular one under consideration. The nature of what I call the primary source of dissatisfaction with answers to the question of the meaning of life immediately suggests a methodology for investigating it, the methodology that informs the investigation into it as it is described (and even partially/inconclusively conducted) in the rest of the book. It also enables us to see what dissatisfaction we must reasonably expect will remain at the end of as full and conclusive an investigation as is possible conducted using this methodology. There are – sadly – sources of dissatisfaction other than the primary one. These other sources of dissatisfaction will be diagnosed as the book goes on. And some of them, I shall argue, are in-eliminable, even in principle, even – as I say – by an omnipotent, omniscient, perfectly good being (should one exist). Dissatisfaction that springs from sources that one can be brought to see are ineliminable – even if ineliminable in this, the strongest of senses, ineliminable even by God – is no less dissatisfaction for that. But it is the sort of dissatisfaction about which, if my experience is anything to go by, one can become satisfied. That is what I meant by 'transcend' a moment ago. Kant famously closes one of his works by saying of a certain philosophical issue that it is one that we cannot comprehend. Yet, he says, we can comprehend its incomprehensibility and this is the most we should expect from a Philosophy that finds itself at the limits of human reason. While I would not maintain that in this book I am working at the limits of human reason (just, I hope, not beyond them as they find themselves in my own person), I shall maintain in a similar fashion to Kant that while we cannot remove our dissatisfaction with answers to the question of the meaning of life, nevertheless, by coming to realize why it is that we cannot remove it (and especially in coming to see why it is that not even God could remove all of it), we should become satisfied with our dissatisfaction. And, as I say, if my experience is anything to go by, we can do that which we should do. This is the most we should expect when investigating the meaning of life. And this I aim to provide.[8] I find you dissatisfied; I aim to leave you dissatisfied, but satisfied with your dissatisfaction.

It will be instructive then for us to lead up to the diagnosis of what I shall call the primary source of our dissatisfaction with answers to the question of the meaning of life by briefly looking at the recent history of the question in Anglo-American Philosophy. Given what I have already said about how those on the outside of the discipline often suppose that the question has a much more central place within it than do those on the inside, this history (in that it is a history of almost total, if wilful, neglect) will be a surprising one to many reading it. Even those already on the inside, for whom it will obviously not be so surprising, will, I think, find it interesting and informative, for how we've got to where we are now in thinking about the question gives causal, if not rational, impetus to what views on it are going to be popular in the next stage of its history. And, more importantly, giving this history will also allow us, I hope, to get beyond what will first suggest itself to those trained in Analytic Philosophy as the most probable explanation of our dissatisfaction with answers to the question of life's meaning, an explanation as simple as it is wrong. This is the view I have in mind: the question just doesn't make sense, so no wonder no answer to it is satisfying. Independent of all of these reasons, there is an obvious methodological rationale for dealing with the view that the question that we are investigating – 'What is the meaning of life?' – doesn't even make sense prior to dealing with any other views on it.

In giving this brief history for these purposes, I shall pick out some characters from the unfolding drama, but these are by no means the only or even always the most significant thinkers of the period; nor are they always the first thinkers of the ideas that find expression in their works. Rather, they serve as indicative in their thoughts of certain broad themes in the developing story into which this book fits, even if it fits only as a footnote to the current chapter and even though the story is one that will no doubt continue to be told for as many years as the human race has left to it. Somewhat arbitrarily, I choose to pick up the story at the turn of the twentieth century.[9]

Although driven by a philosophical movement, Pragmatism, to which by no means all Anglo-American philosophers subscribed, even at the time at which he wrote, William

James expressed what was to become a common theme in the treatment of the question of life's meaning in his *fin de siècle* essay, 'Is Life Worth Living?' The theme in question is a tendency to 'pathologize' the person asking the question of the meaning of life, rather than philosophize directly concerning the question itself. It is perhaps significant in this connection that, rather than addressing himself directly to the question 'What is the meaning of life?', James addresses himself to the question that is the title of his essay – a question that perhaps more naturally lends itself to such a treatment. In any case, James thinks most *apropos* the suggestion that this and similar questions – such as ones overtly focused on life's meaningfulness – would not arise were we all ceaselessly happy. Of such an apparently idyllic situation, he says this:

'No philosopher would seek to prove articulately that life is worth living, for the fact that it absolutely is so would vouch for itself, and the problem disappear in the vanishing of the question rather than in the coming of anything like a reply.'[10]

It is difficult to be sure of James's meaning here. Even when one consults the text surrounding the passage quoted, the notion of happiness on which James draws remains opaque. Its being so makes it difficult to come firmly to grips with the view he is espousing and to assess thereby its strengths and weaknesses. Nevertheless, we may say that it would not be at all plausible were James to be suggesting, as those influenced by Pragmatism *do* tend to suggest, that in general problems of this sort appear or disappear with one's awareness of them. It would not, for example, be at all plausible to suggest that were I to put something in the water supply such that everyone became deliriously happy in the hedonist's sense of happiness, so happy in this sense indeed that they simply collapsed into heaps wherever they were (imbecilic, slobbering, yet smiling from ear to ear), I would have made their lives more worth living or more meaningful. Rather, one would have thought, the opposite. Or consider the following possibility. If everyone were in ceaseless and mind-blowing agony, questions of whether life was worth living or meaningful would again not arise in anyone's mind; everyone would be too busy screaming. Yet such questions may still be asked about the lives of such people. Questions may be asked of the lives of people unable to ask these questions of themselves. In other words, it would certainly be quite fallacious to reason, as in this passage James appears to be in danger of reasoning, from the premise that in a certain situation the sorts of problems that concern us disappear from the consciousnesses of people to the conclusion that in that situation the problems disappear per se. Some problems can be there even when nobody notices them. Their being unnoticed may indeed itself be a part of the problem. Such would be the case, I suggest, were I to treat the water supply as just imagined or inflict unremitting agony on every sentient being.

We, who are neither in a state of unalloyed idiotic bliss, nor in one of unremitting equally idiotic agony, are able to contemplate detachedly both possibilities. We thus are able to see that there is more reason to answer the question of whether their lives are worth living affirmatively on behalf of people in the state of persistent thought-denying bliss than there is on behalf of those in the state of persistent thought-denying agony. This is because, even if Hedonism is wrong, there's at least this much truth in it: *ceteris paribus* pleasure contributes to making life worth living. It is not so obviously the case that *ceteris paribus* pleasure contributes to making life meaningful, which gives us reason to suppose that the question James treats in this fashion may not be quite the same as our question, even if it overlaps it significantly. But – as I say – the notion of happiness as used by James is a somewhat vague one and it may well be that he would not call 'happy' people who were drugged into hedonic bliss. In that case the question he directly treats of and our question may more closely approach one another.[11] Be that as it may, in this essay James is harbinger of a theme in twentieth-century Anglophone Philosophy's treatment of the question of life's meaning: people asking such grandiloquent questions as whether or not life is worth living; whether or not it has any meaning; or whether or not anything, ultimately, matters, are more expressing (unhealthy) emotions than they are raising philosophical issues. As Flew summed it up, 'These [questions] are most charitably to be regarded not as questions requiring an answer but as symptomatic utterances.'[12] This thread was to be woven into emerging patterns in the fabric of the philosophy of language. It tied the doubts they successively engendered concerning whether such questions had any meaning at all together with an explanation as to why people might, despite the meaninglessness of such questions, still utter them. It gave the insiders a way of explaining the foolishness of the outsiders in keeping pestering them with this question (or, better, pseudo-question). It enabled philosophers to feel smug, and smugness is, of course, very comfortable. A discipline can luxuriate in it for a long time. It's not a fairytale to say that it can even curl up and fall asleep in it for a hundred years.

As the twentieth century progressed, a consensus developed among philosophers working in the English-speaking world on the reason why one should not ask the question of life's meaning and the reason why dissatisfaction with answers to it is well placed: the question doesn't make sense, so there's no point in asking it and there's no surprise that answers to it are unsatisfying. Logical Positivism had denied meaningfulness to any questions that did not yield themselves to scientific investigation.[13] 'What is the meaning of life?' obviously does not yield itself to scientific investigation. So, the question itself is – Logical Positivists held – meaningless. The correct 'answer' to it is simply to ignore it. Of course we may *feel* that there's more to ask about than the sorts of things science can tell us about, and this feeling no doubt sometimes finds an outlet in one's articulation of strings of words such as 'Is there any ultimate point to anything?' or 'What is the meaning of life?' But this feeling misleads us. We may express emotions with such words, but we *mean* nothing by them. Such a view gains expression in the Early Wittgenstein thus:

'We feel that even if all possible scientific questions be answered, the problems of life have still not been touched at all. Of course there is then no question left, and just this is the answer. The solution of the problem of life is seen in the vanishing of this problem.'[14]

In the Early Wittgenstein then, the 'solution' offered is in essence James's: the problem of the meaning of life would disappear if only people would stop asking about it, for the only real problem *is* that people wish to ask about it. They have and express a certain sort of emotion with what is, strictly speaking, a meaningless jumble of words. The thought of Wittgenstein here may be more subtle than I indicate: he had of course a distinction within the category of nonsense; some sorts were more important than others. Sweeping that concern aside, suppose we are convinced by Logical Positivism, we've then no need to imagine with James a world where we are all ludicrously happy and thus do not think to raise the question in order to motivate ourselves not to raise the question in the actual world. We can see that we are *already* in a world where the question does not fall within the set of questions we may meaningfully raise. We are already in a world where we should not raise it.

Logical Positivism was replaced for good reasons. Not least among these was that trying to state it is self-refuting and drawing conclusions about what we 'should' or 'should not' say having become convinced of it is, by its own lights, descending back into the meaningless talk from which it seeks to elevate us. But it was replaced by a philosophy of language that was not much more hospitable to the question of the meaning of life than Logical Positivism. Towards the latter half of the twentieth century, the consensus among Analytic Philosophers became that asking for the meaning of a thing makes sense only when the thing in question is a word or sentence; 'meaning' can only mean 'linguistic meaning'. As Quinn reminisces, 'When I was younger, more than once I heard the reason for suspicion put this way. The bearers of meaning are linguistic entities such as texts or utterances. But a human life is not a linguistic entity. Hence attributing meaning to a human life involves a category mistake. To ask what a human life means is therefore to ask a pseudoquestion.'[15] So now the question 'What is the meaning of life?', when allowed to have a meaning at all, was allowed only to mean, 'What is the meaning of the word "life"?', a question to be delegated in the final instance to the compilers of dictionaries. Thus, in his article 'What is a Philosophical Question?' Uygur says this: 'What is needed is, first of all, to stress an important fact: that the question-pattern of philosophy, "What is the meaning of … ?" is as a question concerned *with language*. For the empty space (…) in the question-matrix must be filled each time with a *word*.'[16]

This approach, while usually explicit in espousing the view that philosophers should defer to the facts of 'ordinary language' in addressing these sorts of questions, was somewhat reluctant to engage with the fact that those who ask the question 'What is the meaning of life?' ordinarily do *not* think that using a dictionary to look up the word 'life' is the way to answer it. The meaning of 'meaning' in the question 'What is the meaning of life?' is not characteristically taken by the people who actually ask the question to be simply 'linguistic meaning'. And the word 'life' in the question in not usually taken to refer to the word 'life', but rather to that word's referent. As a result of what engagement took place between Analytic Philosophy and these facts of ordinary usage, the flame of sympathy was rekindled for the people asking the question of the meaning of life, even if little warmth was yet generated for the question itself.

Just as Moore had replied to those who tried to raise with him the traditional 'Problem of the External World' with deliberately 'flat-footed' questions of his own such as 'Are you saying you do not know the way to the bus station?', so those who persisted in asking the question 'What is the meaning of life?' were now sometimes greeted by Analytic Philosophers with questions such as 'Are you saying that you find it difficult to get out of bed in the morning?' Perhaps – such Philosophers conjectured – the people asking this question are working too hard and need instead to lose themselves in play. Perhaps they just need to take the day off studying Philosophy and go to the races instead.[17] In any case, a paradigm of the person who would have been taken by philosophers of this period to have overcome the relevant psychological hurdle is given by Cottingham. 'Consider Alan, a golfer. He has retired, has a pension sufficient for his needs, is reasonably healthy, and enjoys above all his thrice-weekly game of golf. Let us assume that he is free from the self-deception and social manipulation that blight the lives of some of his fellow members of the local club: he is not there as a social climber, or to make business contacts, or to show off his expensive golfclubs; he just genuinely enjoys the game. His playing gives his life a structure; each week he looks forward to the coming games, and feels satisfied when they go well ... why not say ... that he has succeeded in finding a meaning, or some meaning, to his life; and that this, and countless similar stories for countless other individuals happily absorbed in their own favoured pursuits, amounts to all that can be said, or needs to be said, on the matter?'[18] So, the people asking the question 'What is the meaning of life?' may, as the Logical Positivists had held, be taken to be expressing a particular mood or perhaps an emotion of dissatisfaction directed towards a rather ill-defined or all-encompassing object, the world as a whole. And, in addition, perhaps they are raising some confused (as overly general) scepticism about the basis for rational action. The therapist thus has some obvious work to do with people asking the question of the meaning of life. So perhaps does the membership secretary of the local golf club. For his or her part, the Analytic Philosopher does best in dealing with such people by coolly deflecting their pseudo-question into other, genuine, questions.

One of these other questions may well be the purely definitional one. So the Analytic Philosopher may ask the questioner 'Are you asking what you would find were you to look up the word "life" in a dictionary?' But the person asking 'What is the meaning of life?' – not being apprised, we may be sure (for otherwise they would not ask it), of the latest findings in Analytic Philosophy – is, it may now be conceded, unlikely to respond positively to the suggestion that he or she was asking this. Such a question, we may now concede, is probably *not* one that they were in fact asking. And there are other questions, questions which, while they formed no part of what was being asked about originally (for nothing was strictly being asked about originally, except potentially the definitional question), are such that one's providing answers to them may remove from the questioner the emotional turmoil that expresses itself in such pseudo-questions as 'What is the meaning of life?' and keeps them from action. For example, were it to be established that the person asking 'What is the meaning of life?' was already committed to premises from which it followed that maximizing society's happiness was a good reason for action, so it could be shown to them by the right sort of Socratic interchange that they would be irrational (on various other easy-to-fill-in assumptions, assumptions that it could realisti-cally be hoped they would accept) were they to stay in bed asking about the meaning of life. At last: problem solved ... or at least almost solved. What should we say to someone who is unwilling to commit themselves to the necessary premises?

Hare provided an answer to this. His essay 'Nothing Matters'[19] was occasioned by a visit from a disaffected teenager, who lodged with Hare in Oxford during the time Hare was White's Professor of Moral Philosophy. It is touchingly obvious from his text that Hare felt a rather fatherly duty to lift this young man out of the *tedium vitae* that had engulfed him after reading the work of Camus. Cold baths and bracing walks across Christ Church Meadow would no doubt play their part in the process, as would perhaps a change of reading matter – W. E. Johns perhaps. But Hare also felt a professional duty as a philosopher not to leave idle the tools in the use of which his profession had trained him. Thus, in 'Nothing Matters', Hare argues against the possibility of anyone non-self-defeatingly making the claim that gives the essay its title.

Hare suggests that saying that something matters is expressing concern for that thing; that every action manifests concern for something, the object at which the action is directed; and thus that for every agent, there is something that matters. For everyone who does anything, there is something for which they express concern in their action, even if it is only the fact that there is nothing, other than this, over which they are concerned. Thus, a *reductio ad absurdum* is provided, at least for all agents, of the claim that nothing matters. Any teenager one actually finds in bed languorously spinning pretentious themes about the meaninglessness of life or nothing really mattering will in fact already be committed thereby to premises from which they can be shown to be insincere or confused. They can be shown to be already finding meaning, at least in the sense of purpose, in such actions, to be already thinking that such actions as articulating the fundamental meaninglessness of life matter. History does not record whether the teenager whose visit to Hare occasioned this train of reasoning on his host's part found it easier to get out of bed in the morning after having been exposed to it. Perhaps he just regretted having poked his head out from under his bed covers to get into a conversation with his host in the first place and retreated back under them in indolent adolescent silence.

This brief sketch of this period in the history of the treatment of the question of the meaning of life by Anglo-American Philosophy has, I trust, been sufficient to reveal common themes in its reception. These common themes are that the question 'What is the meaning of life?' has no legitimate meaning at all (beyond possibly being an inquiry into the linguistic meaning of the word 'life'). Rather, it is expressive of a certain sort of emotion or, perhaps better, mood – a desperate existential malaise. Philosophers do their part to lift this mood by refocusing the attention of the person asking the question on what are genuinely meaningful, and thus potentially tractable, questions. These are questions that perhaps – if one wishes to be generous-spirited – one might suggest the person asking the original question really intended to ask, maybe even was already asking in their own confused and overly general way. A desolate beggar starts shouting an inchoate request to you in the street. It is obvious that he has no clear idea what he is asking for, let alone what it would be in his best interests for you to give him. The best you can do is try to lift his mood and present some genuine questions back to him – 'Chin up. Tell you what: would you like me to buy you a sandwich? What's that you're shouting now? That you don't want anything? Surely, you must admit that your very action in shouting that you don't want anything commits you to the view that you want at least to shout that you don't want anything. Now, you may of course continue with that self-defeating shouting, but isn't that sandwich rather more tempting than it was a moment ago?' And so on. Thus it is with those who ask Philosophers to tell them the meaning of life. Or rather thus it *was*, for things have now moved on.

In the past thirty or so years Analytic Philosophers have started to show more patience with the question itself. In a lecture written just a few months before his death, Ayer, who had himself of course bodied forth in its most strident form the Logical Positivist stage of the tradition, revealed himself to have mellowed to the idea that in asking 'What is the meaning of life?' one may, after all, be asking something meaningful and not merely something meaningful about the linguistic meaning of the word 'life'. But, even at this stage, Ayer was still drawn towards the apparently irresistible 'psychologizing' (even if not 'pathologizing') tendency. The person asking the question of life's meaning is, Ayer now allowed, asking something with a cognitive content that has nothing to do with the meaning of the word 'life'. He or she is asking how he or she can avoid the delocalized feeling of dissatisfaction that earlier generations of philosophers (in whose number one would have to count the younger Ayer himself) had thought of the words 'What is the meaning of life?' as merely expressing. This is not much progress, one might think, but at least with this move from non-cognitivism to cognitivism, there is a now topic to investigate. One can, after all, inquire scientifically into which stimuli seem to facilitate and which stimuli seem to block the emotions-cum-mood behind a tendency to utter any series of words, including the series 'What is the meaning of life?' Ayer gives his answer to the question as so interpreted in these terms:

'There are many ways in which a person's life may come to have a meaning for him in itself. He may find fulfilment in his work, though this cannot be guaranteed to last until old age. The same is true of the satisfaction which some people find in their domestic lives … There are hobbies, like chess or stamp collecting, which may become a passion. I am not suggesting that these activities are of equal worth but only that they may be equally absorbing. Some people are absorbed in making money, presumably in most cases for the sake of the luxury, prestige, or power that the possession of it brings, but in some cases simply for its own sake.'[20]

As with James a hundred years before then, the 'answer' to the question of life's meaning is still being supposed by Ayer to be found simply in dissipating the desire to ask it. As with Schlick and Wisdom, the person asking 'What is the meaning of life?' is a person whose predicament is solved by introducing him or her to some sufficiently absorbing pastime, the criterion for sufficient absorption simply being, one would suppose from Ayer's essay, that, once so occupied, he or she is no longer inclined to ask the question. But the shouting beggar is now being allowed at least to have shouted a coherent request: 'How can I stop myself wanting to shout this?' And there is then, for the first time, something of substance to investigate and potentially something of substance to proffer in genuine answer to what may now be seen as a genuine question.

Similarly, in his 'Has the Question About the Meaning of Life any Meaning?', after making a few verificationist remarks which, while relatively mild, would not have seemed out of place in Ayer's earlier *Language, Truth and Logic*, Wohlgennant says the following:

'I can define 'meaning of life' as a *feeling* that human beings generally have when they achieve a sufficient number of objectives that they have set themselves, or when they can bring about the realization of values they recognize.'[21]

It is not immediately clear precisely what feeling it is that Wohlgennant is suggesting may be identified with the meaning of life here. Very different feelings may be generated in the two circumstances he envisages, the one where one has achieved a sufficient number of one's objectives and the other where one can bring about the realization of values that one recognizes. Even if one makes the assumption that Wohlgennant wishes to talk merely of the supposedly unitary feeling which one has in these two circumstances when in each case one realizes that one is in them (thus ruling out differences in feelings arising from differences in one's perception of one's situation), and even if one interprets bringing about the realization of values that one recognizes as being simply one and the same thing as achieving a sufficient number of one's objectives, the feelings are still very different. The feeling one has knowing one has accomplished something that one believes to be of value is very different from the feeling one has prior to accomplishing such a thing, even if one is confident in one's the belief that one will in due course accomplish such a thing.

However, we may be charitable to Wohlgennant and push these concerns aside as pedantic niggles. We may suggest that Wohlgennant is seeking to pick out a recognizable feeling of overall satisfaction with the way one's life has gone; is going; and will go. This is the feeling of existential repletion, as it were, that, if one is fortunately circumstanced, one sometimes obtains as one reflects on broad themes in one's life's ongoing and developing story. This feeling sometimes comes upon one at the end of a long but fruitful day's labour at some ongoing project, as one folds oneself into bed, tired but happy, and drifts into a sleep populated by dreamy reflections on what will flow from one's labours on the morrow. In another sphere of life, perhaps one is most vividly aware of the feeling at a joyful and significant family occasion, for example when at the wedding of one of one's children to someone of whom one wholly approves, reflecting on the happy life they seem destined to have together and one's own part in bringing them to this state. Perhaps one is most serenely aware of it when one has reached a point in life from which one is able to look back on what one supposes to be a relatively substantial portion of the time one has been allotted and say something along the lines of 'Regrets. I've had a few, but, then again, too few to mention.' One can even imagine having the feeling on one's deathbed whilst supposing that one has no future ahead of one at all. As he lay dying on his flagship, after he had heard enough to know that he had won a nation-saving victory at Trafalgar, amongst the last words Nelson spoke were 'Thank God, I have done my duty'. I hope that such gesturing on my part will be enough to identify the feeling that I am suggesting Wohlgennant is most charitably interpreted as defining as the meaning of life and I hope that all my readers will know the feeling first-hand from moments or periods in their own lives.

According to Ayer/Wohlgennant so-interpreted then, we may say that the person asking the question of the meaning of life is asking how it is that he or she can get himself or herself to have the feeling sketched in the previous paragraph. If a person has this feeling towards his or her life, then his or her life is thereby meaningful as judged by the criterion of his or her then not wishing to ask the question of life's meaning, for this feeling will dissipate the tendency to ask it. If he or she does not, then it is not as judged by the same criterion, for no other feeling will dissipate it.

Obviously various elements in the Ayer/Wohlgennant thesis as so far described may be teased apart and given different inflections and at least one of these elements, when teased apart from the others, is probably best discretely dropped entirely as it rather weighs down an otherwise plausible thesis. Presumably the more plausible Ayer/Wohlgennant line to take will not identity the feeling itself by its effect of dissipating the desire to ask the question. Rather it will identify the feeling in the manner of the previous paragraph (ostensibly) and then posit, as a contingent psychological matter, that the feeling so-identified always does (and perhaps – to push the boat out a bit – no other feeling ever does) remove the tendency to ask the question. And presumably, if going down the Ayer/Wohlgennant line, one does best to suggest that a meaningful life need not have this feeling present in the consciousness of the person living it at all moments, but just that a person leading a meaningful life needs to be in general disposed to have such a feeling whenever he or she reflects on his or her life as a whole in the right way. Once these amendments have been made, one may in fact entirely drop from the account what seems to me the least plausible feature of it – that the feeling must dissipate the tendency to ask the question (and one has even more reason to drop the claim that no other feeling ever does that) – and leave the rest of it intact and all the more plausible as a result. One may then say simply that having meaning in one's life is one's having this feeling at appropriate moments towards one's life and leave it at that. Or perhaps one may add merely as a generalization (a commitment to the universality of which is no part of the theory) that if one does have meaning in one's life so defined, then one will not be disposed to ask the question 'What is the meaning of life?' I do not in fact see any reason to add that generalization to the theory, though it seems quite harmless philosophically (empirically, it seems to me it could easily be shown to be false). The temptation to add it comes, I think, from the momentum that one may still detect in Ayer/Wohlgennant behind the tendency to pathologize/psychologize concerning the person asking the question. The prejudice is still to think that the fact someone asks the question is expressive of there being something wrong with them and the right answer to the question is thus in part shown to be right by correcting this thing, which correction having been made then will entail that they no longer ask the question. In any case, it seems to me that as a generalization this claim is too strong to be true.[22] Be that as it may, when I speak of the Ayer/Wohlegennant view in what follows I'll have in mind the view sketched in this paragraph absent this sort of psychological claim even as an inessential empirical 'bolt-on' extra. That seems to me to be the most plausible variant of the Ayer/Wohlgennant view. And indeed it seems to me not entirely implausible 'straight out of the gate', as it were, as the answer to the question of the meaning of life. The meaning of life is to do those things, whatever they may be, that afford one this feeling as one reflects upon one's life. Be that as it may, on this view or its variants, we have at last in 'What is the meaning of life?' a meaningful question, and one that yields itself to investigation by the procedures one may find in innumerable 'self-help' books. We have moved on from 'pathologizing-cum-psychologizing' the person asking the question to 'psychologizing' the question itself. A slight movement perhaps, but a significant one.

All reading this will probably have been asked on some occasion to conduct the thought experiment where one imagines oneself observing in some detached way a funeral, eavesdropping on people speaking – both informally before the service starts and then formally in the eulogy – about the deceased. Gradually one realizes that the person they are speaking about is oneself: it is one's own funeral! The person guiding one through this thought experiment then usually asks what is it that one finds oneself hoping that the people will be saying about one. To which one may incline to reply that one most hopes they will say something along the lines of, 'Wait a second. He's not dead! Quick, open the coffin; he's completely recovered; it's a miracle.' But such is not the reply the thought experiment is intended to elicit. Rather, the intention is that, with an idealized funeral eulogy for oneself in mind (an alternative version of the exercise actually has one writing out such a eulogy), one will be enabled to order one's life's projects in a manner that will be more satisfying to oneself in the sense that it will give one the disposition to feel the feeling that Ayer/Wohlgennant suggest is necessary and sufficient for one's life to be meaningful, 'existential repletion' as I have called it. No doubt such exercises are sometimes useful in achieving this goal. But it is a feature of exercises of this sort, often trumpeted as an attractive feature, that they have no direction other than that imparted to them by the affective responses of the persons engaged in them. Such a procedure cannot do anything to avoid what we may think is at least potentially a problem. To put it in terms of a computing dictum, 'Rubbish in, rubbish out.' If in fact, as one contemplates being an observer at one's own funeral, one finds oneself warming to the following eulogy, they have nothing to offer by way of explaining what's gone wrong with one.

I'm sure I speak for all of us gathered here today when I say that it would be a source of complete puzzlement how [**INSERT YOUR OWN NAME HERE**], the deceased, could have accomplished so little; been despised by so many; and yet have been – through it all – as supremely and imperturbably existentially replete as the deceased was. It would be a source of puzzlement were we not all to know that this absolute life/self-satisfaction was generated by the deceased's practice of constantly performing the thought experiment where one imagines oneself listening to the eulogy at one's own funeral and the deceased's constantly warming to the prospect of having just these words, which I speak now, read out.

Something, surely, is missing. The simple problem is that the Ayer/Wohlgennant view is too subjective. While it captures – well captures, it seems to me – what it is for a life to *feel* meaningful (at least in one sense) to the person living it, what we might call subjective meaning in their sense, it does not capture what it is for a life to be the worthy object of such a feeling, what we might call objective meaning in their sense.[23] John Kekes is one of many who gives a good account of the multitude of good arguments not to rest with subjectivism.[24] I shall not repeat these arguments here, just the 'bottom line': we don't just (or even most) want our lives to *feel* meaningful; we want them to *be* meaningful. And to this desire Ayer/Wohlgennant do not speak.

Towards the end of his essay, Ayer points the way to a more objective concern, one the investigation into which would, for the first time, raise the question of life's meaning out of the realm of Psychology and place it into that of Philosophy. He himself suggests – though ultimately fails wholeheartedly to endorse – a more 'objectivist' spin on what had hitherto been unabashedly a subjectivist idea. He puts to himself a question to which he says he does 'not know the answer', *viz.* whether there may be some ways of giving us the disposition towards this feeling of existential repletion, of removing the beggar's desire to shout as it were, which are more objectively justified than others. Are there some imagined eulogies that would more appropriately ground a feeling of life/self-satisfaction than others? In a most telling passage, Ayer closes his essay by saying this:

'Let us take the example of a nun, belonging to a strict order, leading a life of austerity, but serene in the performance of her devotions, confident that she is loved by her deity, and that she is destined for a blissful future in the world to come. ... The question is whether it matters that the deity in whose love she rejoices does not exist and that there is no world to come. I am inclined to say that it does matter ... I am yielding to what ... [Moore] called "a strong respect for truth". But what is our argument? It is not as if there were some end that the nun's life is failing to achieve. So far as one can survey the Universe *sub specie aeternitatis* one has to agree with Macbeth. It *is* "a tale, told by an idiot, full of sound and fury, signifying nothing". What is wrong with this quotation is its aura of disillusionment. It is not that we are sentenced to deprivation. It is open to us to make our lives as satisfying as our circumstances allow. But to return to the nun. It would indeed be terrible for her to discover that the point of her life was nonexistent. But *ex hypothesi* that is something she will never know.'[25]

From this, it is obvious that Ayer himself is drawn to the idea that, given that there is no God or afterlife of the sort the nun supposes, the nun's life is less meaningful than that, for example, which he himself, apprised of these truths, has managed to live; truth matters. And Ayer, we may guess, would maintain this relative ranking even were one to add the hypothesis that the nun feels *more* satisfied with her life – more absorbed in her day-to-day activities and existentially replete as we have put it – than Ayer does with his. This is, he would have said, by the by, for it is; he would have echoed Mill in saying, more meaningful to lead the life of a dissatisfied Socrates than that of a satisfied fool.

In fact it does not seem that Ayer himself was much troubled with a sense of dissatisfaction when he looked back on his life as a whole. I am told that, towards the end of his life, Ayer attended a party at which the famous boxer Mike Tyson was also present. Tyson was acting somewhat boorishly towards a young lady and Ayer interposed himself between the two. Tyson snarled, 'Do you know who I am? I'm Mike Tyson,

Heavyweight Champion of the World'. Ayer replied, 'And I am Sir Alfred Ayer, Professor of Philosophy at the University of London and Fellow of the British Academy. Each of us then has risen to pre-eminence in our chosen fields. I feel sure, therefore, that we shall be able to settle this matter like gentlemen.'[26] Such a riposte does not suggest that Ayer was a man who felt insecure or unsatisfied with the way that his own life had gone up until that point. Indeed it reveals him to have been pleasingly indifferent about the prospects of its being brought to an end with a punch. It is also almost impossible not to read the casual way in which Ayer suggests in this reply that he himself regards Pugilism and Philosophy as comparable fields of human endeavour as an entirely disingenuous deployment of *captatio benevolentiae*, one which must have afforded Ayer pleasure in knowing as he offered it that Tyson would not notice as such. (It seems unlikely that the concept of *captatio benevolentiae* is one for which Tyson finds much use.) In any case, Ayer, we may be confident, would have disdained to lead the life of an unthinking thug, even a pre-eminent and life/self-satisfied one, over that of a philosopher, even had this philosopher, unlike Ayer himself then, been condemned to be less eminent and less self-satisfied; truth matters.

From this realization, it is but a short step – albeit one that, at the last moment in his essay on the topic, Ayer himself stumbles over – to thinking of the person who raises the question 'What is the meaning of life?' not as a beggar simply shouting out his desire to have the desire to shout out removed by whatever means are as a matter of fact most efficacious, but rather as someone inquiring, potentially calmly, into what features, if any, of a life would objectively justify one in having this feeling of existential repletion when contemplating it. Not 'What sort of eulogy, as it happens, would give me a feeling of satisfaction as I imagine it being delivered at my funeral?' Rather, 'What sort of eulogy, if any, *should* give me this feeling if I imagine it being spoken truly at my funeral?' But this sort of inquiry is no psychological one, whatever the psychology that drives one to engage in it and however feverishly or calmly one conducts it. It is an inquiry into what sort of features, if any, rationally ground what sort of responses, and such an inquiry is properly the subject matter of Philosophy. This move then from Psychology to Philosophy is the next step in the journey taken by the question.

There are of course arguments, for example those of the Logical Positivists or those of certain Existentialists, that would challenge the assumption that there exist the sort of objective values that would need to exist were one to be able in principle to answer this question now in its own terms. Absent such values, the question of the meaning of life might – someone might suggest – be reduced back to one of Psychology.[27] But at least these arguments may now be seen to be needed. A gap has opened, at least in thought, between facts about whether or not one is feeling a certain way towards one's life and facts about whether or not one is living a meaningful life. And one's attention has now focused on the latter sort of facts. If some sorts of lives are or could be more properly the object for the feeling of existential repletion by the people living them, if 'respect for truth' matters in generating this feeling in the proper way, then the feeling at which – if Ayer and Wohlgennant are on the right track – one is aiming at instilling in oneself when trying to make one's life meaningful is one that one is aiming in addition at grounding in some feature or features of one's life other than and prior to one's affective response to it or them. These are features that themselves are *worthy* of this type of affective response whether or not it has yet been given. If the life of a dissatisfied Socrates really is being supposed to be more meaningful than that of a satisfied fool, then there is being supposed to be something to the meaning of life other than simply removing the desire to ask the question of life's meaning by generating the feeling of satisfaction with one's life in whatever way is most efficient. Indeed it becomes possible for the first time to think that it is not this feeling at which one is aiming *at all* when one is aiming to make one's life more meaningful. Rather one is aiming at the feature or features that would properly ground this feeling were one to perceive it or them. Nelson said, after all, 'Thank God, I have done my duty', not 'Thank God, I *feel* I have done my duty'. (Nor even, 'Thank God, I have done my duty, and, thank God, I feel I have done my duty' – admittedly that suggests a more plausible view and one to which we shall return in a moment when discussing Wolf.) So, for the first time in the history of the question within Anglophone Philosophy, we are enabled to resist the pull of the psychologizing tendency, to see that instilling a feeling and/or removing the desire to ask the question of life's meaning is potentially no part whatsoever of making one's life meaningful in this more objective sense. A philosopher such as Ayer could have removed his desire to ask all questions most efficiently by going a few rounds with Mike Tyson. But this is not, we imagine, the 'solution' the effecting of which he had in mind when he spoke to Tyson of his confident hope that the two of them would settle the issue of Tyson's behaviour at the party 'like gentlemen'.

So it is that Analytic Philosophy has in large part now come to an appreciation that the question 'What is the meaning of life?' is not simply, or even essentially, an inchoate cry of existential desperation. It is of course true that questions such as 'What is the meaning of life?' or 'Does anything ultimately matter?' do find themselves on the lips of teenagers who cannot easily be persuaded to get out of bed in the mornings and the suicidal. But they are not exclusively to be found there. Often, the people articulating such questions are not subject to any emotional disquietude of the sort caricatured in Hare's Camus-reading houseguest precisely because these people believe themselves to have a good argument for particular positive answers to these questions. In some cases we know this because they've got out of bed and written down these answers for us to read. Hare, for example, must be taken to have been addressing the same issues as his disaffected houseguest, yet without any of the disaffection felt by the latter, coolly writing a paper showing that to articulate the thesis that nothing matters is to prove it false, at least as it pertains to oneself. Similar claims could be made of Ayer and Wohlgennant and indeed of many other philosophers and religious thinkers, people who have written sober and careful accounts of how life is worth living, meaningful, and the like. Of course many have only written these accounts after 'dark nights of the soul'. But they have in the main written them once they have come to the belief that, for their souls at least, the day has dawned and their treatment of the issues is thus as lucid as any other work in the Analytic tradition.

Even if we look back to Camus's *Le Mythe de Sisyphe*[28] – a work by a continental thinker who suffuses his text with urgent emotion and embraces the view that life has no meaning – we cannot suppose that the most careless reader would be able finish reading this work without having noticed that there is, despite all this, an *argument* to be found within it.

As Camus tells the famous eponymous story, Sisyphus is sentenced by the gods to the everlasting punishment of pushing a boulder up a hill by day, only for it to roll down the hill again at night. But Sisyphus has an awareness of this as his situation and, in holding this awareness in the right spirit, Camus argues, Sisyphus gains a certain sort of 'victory' over his fate. By recognizing the meaninglessness of his continuing existence – that he is accomplishing nothing by his endless labours – but reacting with 'scorn' to his 'tragic' state, Sisyphus remains unbroken and this represents something worthy in his state. It is a type of worthiness that does not in any way detract from the meaninglessness of the life that he leads. Indeed the unmitigatedness of Sisyphus's life's meaninglessness is a necessary condition of the unsurpassability of the victory that he gains over it with his scorn. Camus finishes his text by seeking to transfer to our workaday world the principles that he has, he believes, shown to hold by reference to this imaginary one. He says this:

> The workman of today works everyday in his life at the same tasks, and his fate is no less absurd. But it is tragic only at the rare moments when it becomes conscious. Sisyphus, proletarian of the gods, powerless and rebellious, knows the whole extent of his wretched condition: it is what he thinks of during his descent. The lucidity that was to constitute his torture at the same time crowns his victory. There is no fate that cannot be surmounted by scorn.[29]

Indeed, in a rather hard-to-interpret sentence, Camus tells us that we must even think of Sisyphus as happy ('il faut imaginer Sisyphe heureux'). If we must indeed do so, then I tend to think of this needing to be a rather grim-faced, stoic, through-gritted-teeth version of happiness – one not likely to appeal to the hedonist, but perhaps no less edifying for that.

Of course, there is no way that this would be published in a journal of Analytic Philosophy. But there is, nevertheless, clearly an argument within Camus's telling of the story of Sisyphus. Recognizably the same argument is endorsed as valid, at least in its earlier stages, by certain religiously minded thinkers – valid, but unsound, for these thinkers deny the inescapability of meaninglessness in Camus's sense. They would rather say that *were* their religious hypothesis not true, then life would indeed be meaningless, more or less for the reasons and in the manner Camus suggests. It might indeed then be the case that the best we could do would be to react to the world with scorn. However, in fact, they would say, as their religious hypothesis *is* true, such a conclusion does not follow. It is no doubt the case that this argument could do with conceptual clarification and closer analysis. Is it valid? Is it not? But clarifying the concepts used in an argument and assessing the validity of its structure are properly topics for Analytic Philosophy.

If the concepts used in such an argument are hopelessly confused and if the structure is hopelessly invalid, believing that this is the case requires some relatively weighty argumentation behind it, given that thinkers with very diverse worldviews seem to understand one another when discussing it and seem to accept it as valid. All of this is now open for appreciation in a way it never was before.

In short, we have now reached a stage in Analytic Philosophy's treatment of the question of the meaning of life where, owing to the question's being relocated from the realm of Pathological Psychology into that of Philosophy, the people asking and answering it can be seen, as a class, not to be in any more or less emotional turmoil than those philosophers who address themselves to other questions. In a tradition that eschews emotionalism, this gives the question the hope of respectability. Furthermore, the matter into which they are inquiring can be seen to be one that it is sensible to argue cannot be represented as a purely psychological matter (at least without argument). One is not asking merely how as a matter of fact may one generate a certain type of feeling towards one's life as a whole. Rather, it can be seen to be a philosophical matter. Perhaps it is wholly an inquiry into what in principle could appropriately ground such a feeling and whether the conditions necessary for appropriate grounding are or are not met in practice. But perhaps it is more than that. Perhaps it is an inquiry into something else entirely. And, as observed, even if it is only that, then for this sort of philosophical question to be turned back into a psychological one, as some philosophers have of course held that it must be, requires philosophical, not psychological, argument. And if it is an inquiry into more than that or an inquiry into something else entirely, then turning it back into a psychological question or making it disappear from the proper subject matter of Philosophy in some other way will prove all the more difficult. And, finally, we can see that the people asking and answering the question of life's meaning appear to have a largely overlapping understanding of what it is they are asking about; the potential cogency of one another's answers; and even the validity of certain types of argument as they are advanced in favour of these answers, arguments that may be extracted from thinkers who fall outside the analytic canon. The subject matter of the question then seems now to be planted squarely in the land of Philosophy and to be well-nourished with a goodly quantity and variety of literature.

The majority of those contemporary Analytic Philosophers who have considered the question now concur then with the community of language users whose opinions they had always claimed to respect. It has, after all, a perfectly legitimate meaning and that is nothing to do with the linguistic meaning of the word 'life'. The question of the meaning of life has thus finally clearly emerged from languishing in the post-Logical Positivist doldrums. It now has a fair wind behind it, a wind that admittedly is blowing it in a variety of directions under a variety of captains. But some common ground has already been reached and, even where different positions have been staked out, there is often a common currency of argument across the borders.

Within the analytic tradition, an idea has gained widespread assent in the past few decades: whatever the vague and enigmatic nature of the phrase 'the meaning *of* life', we may sensibly speak of meaningfulness *in* a life as a particular, positive, normative feature that some individuals' lives may well have and this feature is to be distinguished from, though closely related to, other positive features – satisfaction, well-being, virtue, and so forth. Even if many – though by no means all – philosophers retain a knee-jerk scepticism towards the phrase 'the meaning of life' (for it seems to them to connote vague and/or impossible-to-fulfil cosmic expectations[30]), analytic philosophers nowadays are not generally so sceptical about talk of meaningfulness *in* a life. Thus they are not so sceptical about the phrase 'the meaning of life' if it is taken to be referring merely to this. And indeed, in recent years, this is how the majority of Analytic Philosophers who have looked at the question 'What is the meaning of life?' have taken it. They have eschewed the cosmic interpretations,[31] embraced the individualistic ones, and not been at all averse to proffering their own answers to the question as they have so interpreted it. In fact, in the past few years there has been a veritable *profusion* of philosophers offering their own theories about what this property is, summed up in their own formula – sometimes, pithy; oftentimes, not. They have started to engage with thinkers in the continental tradition who had never suffered (or benefited) in the same way from Logical Positivism. And they have laid down some clear paths for future thinking about the nature of this property that individuals lives may have. Where are these paths leading us?

As we have seen, Ayer (probably) could not in the end bring himself to admit that some features of a life might better ground the feeling of existential repletion than others. That view still has support. Contemporary philosopher Harry Frankfurt, for example, argues that meaningfulness in an individual's life is that individual's making a certain sort of commitment to care about or love something and then being swept up by that; for Frankfurt, it doesn't in itself matter what that thing is. It might be being a nun. It might be being a Philosopher. It might be improving one's golf handicap. Of course some of these things will be harder or easier for those of particular temperaments to care about than others. And perhaps – though Frankfurt himself doesn't dwell on this possibility – there may be some universalities in human temperament, ones that will make us generally less likely to tire of some activities than of others. As Singer puts it, 'some people find collecting stamps an entirely adequate way of giving purpose to their lives. There is nothing irrational about that; but others again grow out of stamp collecting as they become more aware of their situation in the world and more reflective about their purposes. To this … group the ethical point of view offers a meaning and purpose in life that one does not grow out of.'[32] And not tiring of the object of one's affections does seem to be a condition to be included in any plausible Frankfurtian position. Indeed there's truth in the claim that it's 'necessary that we are really *inspired* by the idea we adopt as the meaning of our lives'.[33] Be all that as it may, in a later work, Frankfurt sums up his view thus: 'Devoting oneself to what one loves suffices to make one's life meaningful, regardless of the inherent or objective character of the objects that are loved.'[34] But such a view only really sits easily within the context of a subjectivism about value, and on this topic too, Analytic Philosophy has moved on. Objectivism is now much more respectable than it was a generation or so ago. The two contemporary philosophers we shall look at next – Wolf and Metz – explicitly take the step of denying that the inherent or objective character of the objects loved or attended to is irrelevant. And in doing so, it seems to me, they drive the roots of the question of the meaning of life even more securely into the soil of Philosophy.

Wolf says that meaning in life is 'subjective attraction [meeting] objective attractiveness';[35] or again, 'meaningful lives are lives of active engagement in projects of worth'.[36] She calls her view the 'fitting fulfilment' view. It's not enough that what one does is fitting, nor that one be fulfilled by what one does, but bring the two together and one's life is meaningful. As Wolf contends that meaning in life comes from subjective attraction (characterized not dissimilarly to the way Frankfurt would characterise it) to that which is objectively worthy of it, there is still a psychological element in her theory. One must feel a certain way (though not necessarily towards one's life, *pace* Ayer/Wohlgennant) for one's life to be meaningful. Without that feeling of attraction, meaningfulness cannot be had. So, by way of illustration, it came as something of a shock for some of us to discover after Mother Teresa's death that she had not felt as many of us had assumed she must have done based on the fact that she had so completely – and thus we had supposed wholeheartedly – committed herself to relieving the suffering of others. To the extent that she did not have subjective attraction towards what she was doing, even though what she was doing met the standard of being objectively worthy (I take this for granted [apologies to Ayer: she was a nun, after all]), she had a less meaningful life on Wolf's account than if she had been able to feel more warmly towards it. Similarly Flannagan tells us that 'Life's meaning comes, if it does come, from having chances to express and carry through on projects that matter, that have value and worth, first and third personally'.[37] If the project has worth only third-personally, i.e. objectively, then that's not enough. It has to have it first-personally, i.e. subjectively, too.[38] Or consider these comments of Baird: 'On the one hand, if an individual's life is to be judged meaningful in the fullest sense, that person must feel that his or her life is worthwhile. Even if we judge a person's life to be meaningful, there is obviously something amiss if that person sincerely declares verbally or behaviorally (as, for example, in suicide) that life is not worth living. Meaning must involve the pursuit of "projects that afford satisfaction to the pursuer." Without subjective satisfaction, meaning is incomplete. On the other hand, one may feel that one's life is meaningful, one may be daily and enthusiastically involved in the pursuit of a goal, but one's name may be Hitler, and the end pursued may be the destruction of a race of people.'[39] With Metz, the next philosopher we shall look at, we finally sever this last strand of the cord that links us back to the psychologizing tendency.

Thaddeus Metz is the philosopher who has done the most significant and sustained work on the topic of the meaning of life (construed in the individualistic way, as what it is that constitutes meaningfulness within individuals' lives) in recent decades. In his recent book, *Meaning in Life*,[40] Metz draws together work spanning these several decades to conclude that 'A human person's life is more meaningful, the more that she, without violating certain moral constraints against degrading sacrifice, employs her reason and in ways that either positively orient rationality towards fundamental conditions of human existence, or negatively orient it towards what threatens them, such that the worse parts of her life cause better parts towards its end by a process that makes for a compelling and ideally original life-story; in addition, the meaning in a human person's life is reduced, the more it is negatively oriented towards fundamental conditions of human existence or exhibits narrative disvalue.'[41] Now that, whatever else it is, is quite a mouthful. It is not as pithy a formula as Wolf's, even if it is – significantly (we shall return to this later) – still a formula. For our purposes at the moment, we do not need to get into the detail of what is in Metz's formula. We are more interested in a significant absence. According to Metz, for a person's life to be meaningful, they don't need to *feel* any particular way about it or about anything else. The psychological element of meaningfulness (the sense of 'existential repletion' as I have been calling it, which was all that there was to it for Ayer or the attraction to something in it which was still a necessary part of it for Wolf et al.) has now dropped out of the picture entirely. As long as the person's rationality is orientated in the right direction and his or her life has the right narrative value, the job is done.[42]

This then is where we have got to in the debate at the time of my writing. Indeed Metz finishes his book by saying that his characterization of meaningfulness, which he calls 'the fundamentality theory' is now 'the one to beat'. His last words in fact are 'Is the fundamentality theory the holy grail of Western normative philosophy, *the* respect in which the good, the true and the beautiful genuinely constitute a unity, *the* principle that captures all and only the myriad factors that make up Meaning in Life? It would be presumptuous to say that the search for an adequate theory of what makes a life meaningful is over, given how few philosophers have undertaken the enquiry in earnest. However, the fundamentality theory is now the one to beat.'[43] One can only, well, I suppose the word is 'presume', that Metz thinks that that which it would be presumptuous to say it would not be presumptuous to use conversational implicature to suggest.

As one surveys the field of contemporary analytic philosophers contributing to the debate, one observes that a residual element of subjectivism remains in many.[44] One must feel a certain way about something – perhaps one's life, perhaps merely some aspect of it – for one's life to be meaningful – but by no means all – as long as one's life meets various objective criteria, it is meaningful, regardless of the way one feels about anything. The consensus is that meaningfulness is a particular objective (or at least partly objective) and positive normative property that our lives can (and often do) have. The presumption is that we can get on and investigate this property – the individualistic-meaning-of-life issue – without needing to investigate any more cosmic meaning-of-life issues. Theories of that property are being touted as beating other theories. One at least is being held up as a good contender for being The Holy Grail.

We have looked at various philosophers from the past hundred or so years. No doubt we could have looked at more. But at least one aspect of our current purpose does not require us to do so. That aspect, it will be recalled, is to start us on the road to giving a general explanation of a phenomenon that we will find when we look at the answers proffered by contemporary philosophers: *these answers are just as dissatisfying to us as those proffered by sages in the past.* At the start of the recent history of the treatment of the question, an explanation as to why we were dissatisfied with answers to the question of the meaning of life was readily available. Indeed it would have been irresistible to any analytic philosopher. But I hope we have already seen enough to know that it cannot now commend itself to us. That explanation was that the question 'What is the meaning of life?' just doesn't make sense. If a question doesn't make sense, it is no wonder that we're dissatisfied with treatments of it. While that diagnosis was never really credible to those outside the discipline of Analytic Philosophy, the developments of the past few decades have meant that it is no longer credible even to those inside. *This is to be counted as significant progress.*

If the source of our dissatisfaction with the answers proffered to the question is not then that the question of life's meaning makes no sense, the next answer that might suggest itself is perhaps this: it is simply that all of the answers that have been given to it hitherto are wrong. One could be forgiven for thinking that this is the view of everyone writing in the field today. This would be especially so if one were to judge by the proportion of their time spent pointing to the weaknesses of extant answers (rather than to their strengths) and asserting their own answers as characterizing what had remained, prior to their own contribution to the debate, the elusive property of meaningfulness. But, on a moment's reflection, the suggestion that everything said in answer to the question prior to whatever particular paper or book the author is at that time penning was wholly mistaken seems equally incredible and no contemporary philosopher is so foolish as to commit themselves to it explicitly. The question of the meaning of life is of course widely held to be exemplary of difficulty. But it is not, we must suppose if we reflect for a moment, so intractable that no thinker to date has illuminated it or its answer to any extent at all. Most contemporary philosophers thus find something at least to praise (lightly) in a selection of the writings of others on the topic. There is, after all, some gold here and there amongst the dross. (Significantly, if unsurprisingly, what one author offers up as gold, another discards as dross.)

My own position is more generous still. Rather than saying of all the answers offered to the question so far that they are wrong or even saying of most of the answers offered so far that they are wrong, my position is that it would be less misleading to say of all of them that they are *right*. But that seems to make the prospects of explaining our dissatisfaction even slimmer. How *then* can it be right to feel dissatisfied with each of them? If all – or almost all – of these answers offer us more gold than dross, we surely have an embarrassment of riches on our hands.

The answer comes with a central claim of the current work: the question of the meaning of life is best approached first and foremost by recognizing that it is several questions. The way different – and indeed, what is more, straightforwardly conflicting – answers can be all be right is that they are answering different questions. This is the fact that, on my diagnosis, forms what I call the primary source of our dissatisfaction with answers to the question of the meaning of life.

Whether or not one accepts this is, it seems to me, the next significant fork in the road of Analytic Philosophy's treatment of 'the' question. It's the decision we as a discipline now face. Naturally, I hope that in time many will follow me down the path that I take from accepting it – the path I shall outline in a bit more detail in the next chapter and then explore the implications of in the rest of this book. And the general Value Pluralism within which my thesis can be fairly presented as finding itself as a focused-instance[45] seems to me to be growing in popularity. But its time is not yet. At the time of writing, most are still taking the path of supposing that meaningfulness is a singular – even if complex – property that individuals' lives may or may not have to various degrees and almost all are bracketing-off as a different issue (from the meanings-in-individual-lives issue) the cosmic issues of the meaning of life. Different and (the methodological presumption behind bracketing-off is) irrelevant to meaningfulness-in-individual-life issues. My view is that in doing this they are all mistaken. On the issue then of meaningfulness-in-individuals' lives, their formulae for this property differ. Wolf's, as we have seen, is simple; Metz's, complex. But even when they show sympathy with a pluralistic claim along the lines of my own, this turns out to be an *en passant* sympathy, soon moved past as they argue for their own formula of what they suppose to be a unitary value, meaningfulness.[46] My view, by contrast, is a pluralist one in the sense that it asserts that there are many senses of meaning and many senses of life and thus there are many meanings of life. This is the point at which I start the argument that is peculiar to me. And it is worth spending a moment or two signposting this fork in the road a bit more clearly and signposting which of the later branches I shall take when travelling on from it. Knowing where I'm going will help in seeing the rationale behind how I'm proposing to get there. This is what I shall do in the next chapter.

CHAPTER 2

I finished the previous chapter by saying of myself that I was a pluralist about the meaning of life, understanding pluralism as the view that there are many different meanings of life. There are not many pluralists in this sense, though there are more in another sense. There are plural meanings of 'pluralism'. Some clarification is in order.[1]

In the book that I have already quoted from, under the subtitle, 'A pluralist analysis', Metz says, 'I advance a family resemblance approach'.[2] He then goes on to list some questions that it is plausible to suggest any theory of the meaning of life must enable one to answer (rather in the manner that I am about to do). Nevertheless, I do not count Metz as a fellow traveller down the pluralist path as I understand it in that, in the end, he has a monistic theory of what the answer to these questions is. We've seen his formula already. Metz's view is a 'family resemblance model ... of what talk of life's meaning connotes', but a monistic view of what it denotes – *viz.* that a 'single property grounds the best answer to all the variegated questions associated with enquiry into life's meaning'.[3] Life's meaning is of course being understood to be simply what it is in virtue of which individuals' lives are meaningful. He eschews cosmic interpretations of the question from the start.

In another piece, Metz helpfully says the following. 'Many analytic philosophers writing on life's meaning are monists who hold that a theory of meaning is possible – i.e. that what constitutes the meaning of a person's life can be at least largely expressed by a general and fundamental principle.'[4] As already stated, I count Metz as a monist in this sense. His formula is his attempt to articulate such a general and fundamental principle. I also see Wolf as a monist in this sense and for the same reason. She has a formula for what she takes to be the single value of meaningfulness. But Metz himself doesn't see Wolf as a monist. Why not? He goes on in the same passage thusly: 'However, there are some prominent pluralists in the literature – those who maintain that no theory of meaning in life is possible because what constitutes it varies too much to admit of unification in the form of necessary and sufficient conditions or anything close to an "essence." That said, most friends of pluralism do not merely list many constitutive conditions of meaning ... Instead, what many pluralists do ... is provide a very abstract characterization of meaning in life as being conferred when, in Wolf's pithy and influential phrase, "subjective attraction meets objective attractiveness"[5] – i.e. when an individual is fulfilled by, identifies with, or cares about a project that is intrinsically desirable, where the latter is left wide open.' But it seems to me that at least this last sort of 'pluralist' is unworthy of the name 'pluralist'. (Do we get a hint that Metz himself thinks so provided by his talking of them once as 'friends of pluralism' rather than pluralists *simpliciter*?) In any case, it seems to me that such an 'abstract characterization' of meaning is a monist one – it's their theory of what meaningfulness is. The fact that they think that the things that can appropriately anchor the subjective end of meaningfulness (the thing towards which one is attracted) are varied – 'left wide open' – doesn't make them pluralists about meaningfulness. They are just pluralists about what can ground meaningfulness. Ayer and Wohlgennant probably, and Frankfurt certainly, were – as we have seen – equally open-minded about what could ground the subjective feeling that was all that there was for meaningfulness in their sense. But that didn't make them pluralists either, at least in the sense that I am using the term, where to be a pluralist about life's meaning one must think that the things that go by the names 'meaning' and/or 'life' are plural, not simply that plural things undergird the monistic value of meaningfulness as it may be found in some individuals' lives.[6]

That Metz uses the term 'pluralist' more inclusively than I would incline to use it is confirmed by Metz's characterization of the views of those he then goes on to cite as pluralists in the same piece. Dworkin, we are told, endorses 'a "challenge" model of meaning, according to which one's life is meaningful insofar as it is a skilful performance that one endorses, and claims that what constitutes a skilful performance cannot be captured in principle'. And Kekes,[7] we are told, argues that 'meaning consists in identifying with, and carrying out, projects that make one's life better, where the latter does not admit of a monistic account.' Even if one believes in one of these theories of meaning and one believes that a skilful performance cannot be analysed and/or that there's no general account to be given of the projects that make one's life better, again, on my definition, that doesn't make one a pluralist about meaning. To be a pluralist about the meaning-in-individual-life issue in my sense of pluralist, one has to believe not only (or even[8]) that 'meaning' and/or 'life' is an ambiguous term. That amounts to the connotation element that Metz endorses (or appears to endorse) with his 'family resemblance' talk. But also (or in any case) one has to believe that it that it refers to different values.[9] That amounts to the denial of Metz's monist understanding of its denotation.[10]

That Metz is a monist (in my sense) is confirmed by other comments he makes. Metz says at one point that a family resemblance theory of what talk of life's meaning connotes might give one to think one has 'strong reason to doubt the existence of a conception of life's meaning that is monist, sought for in chapters 5 to 12 [i.e. the rest of his book bar the last, short concluding chapter]. Admittedly it does provide some ground for doubt.'[11] He then cites a person whose importance he rather overinflates by dubbing him 'a scholar' as someone who would give the evidence this reading. Metz, however, remains unconvinced by said 'scholar' and thus he goes on his search for the rest of the book and thinks he finds the answer by the end of it. And *that* is what makes him ultimately a monist.

To be a pluralist in my sense then requires one to believe that meaning is, as I shall put it, polyvalent. All pluralists in my sense are pluralists in Metz's. But not all pluralists in Metz's sense are pluralists in mine.[12] I shall therefore tend to prefer the term 'polyvalence' over 'pluralism' in what follows simply to avoid confusion. Few writing in the field today hold to polyvalence.[13] Those who do hold to it leave these different meanings of life entirely separate in their discussions. They do not relate them to one another except perhaps now and again causally: i.e. they do not advance a theory as to how any are related metaphysically or logically.[14] I shall advance such theories and in doing so my view has the property – for good or ill – of uniqueness even among the small group of people who endorse polyvalence.[15] I call views that do tie the various values of meaning together into larger wholes, of which mine then is the only extant example, 'amalgam' versions of polyvalence. It is worth spending just one more moment on the detail of what an amalgam thesis amounts to before we move on for two reasons. First, the fact that it is my view has escaped at least one, albeit that this is one who has been so forgivingly inattentive to my work as to allow him to label it that of a scholar. Second, a legitimate question one may raise of any amalgam thesis, and mine is no exception, is just how much does the endorsing of amalgamation conflict with the endorsing of polyvalence? And it's as well to address this question now.

At one stage, Metz says this: 'Although relatively few have addressed the question of whether there exists a single, primary sense of "life's meaning," the inability to find one so far might suggest that none exists. In that case, it could be that the field is united in virtue of addressing certain overlapping but not equivalent ideas that have family resem-blances ... Perhaps when we speak of "meaning in life," we have in mind one or more of these related ideas: certain conditions that are worthy of great pride or admiration, values that warrant devotion and love, qualities that make a life intelligible, or ends apart from base pleasure that are particularly choice-worthy. Another possibility is that talk of "meaning in life" fails to exhibit even this degree of unity, and is instead a grab-bag of heterogenous ideas ... Mawson.'[16]

So, to be clear: I agree with many of the views that Metz is discussing in this passage. In particular, I agree with those he has in mind in the first part, where he is discussing what might drive one to a polyvalence theory of the connotation of the question – the thesis that the question is really many questions. I also agree with the views he has in mind in the second part, where he is discussing what might drive one to a polyvalence theory of the denotation – the thesis that these many questions are answered by pointing to many values (and indeed, I would say, some things that are not values[17]). So far then, yes, it is my view that is under discussion. But I do not agree with what he talks of in the end as 'another possibility'. My view is not the 'grab bag' one he seems to suggest that it is, at least it is not if I am understanding correctly what a grab bag is. The way I under-stand the notion of a 'grab bag' is that the things within a grab bag are entirely separate from one another or, when the analogy is cashed out, if not entirely separate then at most linked now and again with causal chains. One might well pluck one thing out of the bag and – absent causation – leave the rest behind. And, if one was omnipotent, one might well pluck out any one thing and leave all the rest behind. Or, if one had wished to do so with one's omnipotence, one might well have linked any or all of the different sorts of things in the bag together causally, so that one could have made it that any combination, including all of them, came out at once if one plucked out any one. My polyvalence isn't a grab-bag polyvalence in that sense. It's an amalgam polyvalence.

I choose the word 'amalgam' with some reluctance as it too has been used in the literature already. Hepburn says at one stage, 'According to the interpretation being now worked out, questions about the meaning of life are, very often, conceptually obscure and confused. They are amalgams of logically diverse questions, some coherent and answerable, some neither.'[18] As will be clear as the book goes on, the amalgam thesis I endorse is a thesis about the answer to the question and it does not commit me to the pejorative attitude towards the question that is suggested by Hepburn's comments. While, for example, I think that there is certainly something conceptually obscure about the question 'What is the meaning of life?' and about at least some of the questions into which it may be broken down, this is only because it is typical of every question of philosophical significance worth talking about. If the issue inquired about wasn't conceptually obscure, it wouldn't be philosophically significant and worth talking about. I don't think the questions into which the question of the meaning of life may be broken down are very often confused, though some may be. And so on.[19]

With regard to meaningfulness as a value that individual human lives may have, as already alluded to in a few endnotes, my view here is similar to that which I would hold of some other values. So, one might ask 'What is human flourishing?' Some philosophers, one will have noticed, have certainly asked that. My view is that it would be a mistake to think that there is a single unitary value – human flourishing – the right characterization of which is the answer to this question. There are several. But that is not to say that asking about these things is confused or ill-conceived. Nor is it to say that these things are entirely unrelated (except perhaps causally). Nor again is it to say that one cannot say informative and universally true things about human flourishing, e.g. that it is incompatible with certain things – protracted and significant physical suffering, for example. Someone who had spent the whole of their life suffering from a genetic condition that meant they were paralysed and in constant pain might have lived bravely, estimably, and so forth, but they could not have flourished. Their life would not have been a good one, well lived. It would have been a poor hand, well played. Similarly, someone born into great material and social privilege and in excellent health, who, as soon as they reached the age of reason, used all their choices so as to squander their native possibilities and sink themselves into debauchery and selfishness would not have flourished from the moment they reached the age of reason onwards. So, conditions that are not of one's own making (e.g. one's health and position in society) as well things that are of one's own making (one's response to one's situation) are both important for human flourishing, both important of non-causal necessity. Given that, it seems to me then that there is no one value – physical health or moral rectitude, say – that is the nature of human flourishing. Rather, human flourishing is polyvalent. But it is not that the many values that go up to make human flourishing are a 'grab bag' – unconnected except perhaps causally. For example, certain of the virtues conceptually require one to be efficacious as well as well intentioned in one's actions. They thus require both that things beyond one's control go certain ways and that things within one's control go certain ways. Human flourishing then is an amalgam of values. There are multiple other questions that seem to me similarly best approached by realizing that they display the same sort of polyvalence and yield themselves most plausibly to their own type of amalgam answer. Other examples would be 'What is a healthy economy?' 'What is an aesthetic success?' and 'What is a good wine?'

Let us turn now to the second issue that I said one needs to address. Given my commitment to an amalgam version of polyvalence, one might legitimately press me on the issue of the extent to which my claim that meaning understood as meaningfulness in an individual's life is best thought of as an amalgam (the amalgam thesis) detracts from my claim that there are many sorts of meaning (the polyvalence thesis) or at least it does so if one continues to bracket off cosmic interpretations. If I'm suggesting that these 'many' are ultimately to be combined into 'one', isn't mine ultimately *not* a polyvalence thesis at all, at least at the level of individualistic meanings of life? My short answer to this is that a putative amalgam thesis ultimately fails to be a polyvalence thesis if it claims that *all* of the many are combined into one.[20] But in fact, as we shall see, that is not the sort of amalgam that we have here. Even continuing to confine ourselves to the individualistic meanings of life, not all the values of meaningfulness in an individual life *can be* combined into one (even by an omnipotent being) and there are reasons for doubting that there is only one amalgam (there are, I shall argue, several). It's worth pointing out that even had, say, all the different sorts of meaningfulness that an individual's life might have been shown to be elements of just one amalgam, an amalgam isn't a disjunction or even simply a conjunction of several sorts of metal. It's an alloy. So this sort of amalgam thesis would not be a 'conjunction' or 'disjunction' thesis about meaningfulness in human life even if one might with justification say that it's the alloy that is true meaningfulness and thus push the suggestion that such a view would be a monist one after all, at least about meaningfulness in individual human lives. Indeed it's because an amalgam is an alloy, not a conjunction or disjunction, that the charge of Monism would thus stick (at least of meaningfulness as a property that individuals' lives may have).[21] In short, an 'amalgam' thesis that amalgamated all the 'different' meanings of life would in the end not be a polyvalence thesis, but a monistic one, one that had it that the meaning of life could be described in a no-doubt-complex formula. This would be more complex than something like 'p and q and r' or 'p or q or r', but a formula for what was in the end a unitary thing after all. But, as it is, because my view is that not all meanings of life are elements in one amalgam, so my view remains a polyvalence one.[22]

One may certainly suggest that on at least one aspect of this debate the differences between my fellow polyvalence theorists (not that there are many of them for me to have differences with at the moment, sadly) and myself are merely terminological. Again, if one focuses down just on the individualistic interpretations of the question, I am saying that there is no one thing that is meaningfulness, but that some (though not all) different sorts of meaningfulness are formed together into an amalgam (or into several amalgams). Another is saying that there is one thing called meaningfulness, but that this one thing has a disjunctive character. We are, I concede, arguing only about words at that stage. By way of an analogy, suppose we discover that a certain proportion of the stuff that falls as rain; that makes up our oceans; that boils at 100 degrees centigrade at sea level; and that we all refer to as 'water' is made of H_2O and the rest of XYZ. Chemists are astounded and meet at an international conference to decide what to do with this discovery. One group favours their reporting the discovery to the wider world as the fact that there is no such thing as the essence of water. Rather, the term 'water' is ambiguous, not in connotation, admittedly, but in denotation. It denotes two distinct substances – the H_2O one and the XYZ one. Another group favours reporting the discovery as one that while there is such a thing as the essence of water, that essence is a disjunctive essence. The term 'water' is no more ambiguous in its denotation that it is in its connotation. It denotes one and the same substance the essence of which is to be either H_2O or XYZ.[23] It seems to me that there is merely a terminological difference between the two groups. Similarly, there are issues here that are merely terminological. But stressing that at this stage we're arguing merely over words seems to me more likely to obscure the issues than reveal them. For this is an internal dispute – if it need be a dispute – between polyvalence theorists, a dispute about how best to talk. It is not a dispute about whether or not polyvalence theory is correct or even about whether or not an amalgam or grab-bag version of it is correct.

Having stated the sort of view that I am aiming to support, it is time to argue for it. In that context, it makes sense to start at the connotation end of it – what is it that one means when one asks 'What is the meaning of life?' The claim to be considered at this stage then is that one means several things: there are several legitimate meanings of 'meaning', and indeed of 'life'. Thus when one asks 'What is the meaning of life?', one asks an ambiguous question. Perhaps better, one asks an assemblage of – largely overlapping, but significantly different – questions at once. If one wishes, one may use the notion of family resemblance here, or polyvalence – 'the' question has many meaning values. This then is the polyvalence thesis at the level of connotation. Considering arguments in favour of polyvalence at the level of connotation will inevitably involve coming upon reasons in favour of polyvalence at the level of denotation. As I hope will become apparent, when we are able clearly to see the variety of meanings of 'the' question, we are thereby enabled to see equally clearly that no one thing can be the answer to all of them. No one thing can be *the* meaning of life.[24] I shall start on this argument in the next chapter.

CHAPTER 3

In the previous chapter, I defined what is meant by a polyvalence view of the question of the meaning of life and its answers. In this chapter and the next, I am going to argue for a polyvalence view via three routes. First, I'm going to consider the two crucial words in the question apart from one another, focusing on the different meanings of 'meaning' and of 'life'. If I can establish polyvalence in connotation for either of these elements, the case will be made for polyvalence in connotation for the question that combines them. I believe I can do this for both elements. I'll start with 'life' and then move on to 'meaning' thereafter. We'll see at the end of this that already it's implausible to suppose that the different questions one is thus asking when one asks 'What is the meaning of life?' all have the same answer. So we'll already be getting some evidence for polyvalence at the level of denotation too.

After having done this, in the next chapter, I'll approach the same conclusion via a second route – I'll consider the question as a whole and offer up a list of what I hope will be seen to be plausible meanings that may be given to the question 'What is the meaning of life?' as a whole. That they are plausible will be evidenced to any particular reader primarily by how plausible they strike that particular reader as legitimate interpretations of the question. Secondarily, they'll be rendered plausible if we can find authors who have taken the question of the meaning of life in these senses. I hope that the reader himself or herself will provide the primary evidence. I'll provide the secondary evidence by way of referring to some who have interpreted the question in each way. This manner of arguing also does something to support polyvalence at the level of denotation, for again when we see the different meanings of the question 'What is the meaning of life?' we can see instantly that some of them just must – of conceptual necessity – have different answers from others.

And then finally, also in the next chapter, I'll talk about another line of argument – a third – that supports the polyvalence thesis. In essence this is the line that says the polyvalence thesis is supported by the successes and failures characteristic of extant theories of the meaning of life construed as meaningfulness-in-life as their proponents interact with one another, the successes being that each seems to explain many of our judgements about the meaningfulness of individuals' lives and the failures being that each seems to face persistent counterexamples. The best explanation of this, I'll contend, is the truth of polyvalence.

First then, let me consider the meanings of 'life' and 'meaning'. I'll start with 'life'. My claim here is that 'life' as it occurs in the question 'What is the meaning of life?' is a term with multiple meanings.

One might think that the broadest one is life as biological life per se – taking in, as it would, everything from the level of microbes up to that of people – and thus that this forms an outer limit for the focus of one's concerns when asking the question of the meaning of life. It certainly forms *a* focus. That it forms a focus for a part of one's concerns is indicated by the fact that one would not regard an answer to the following question as entirely irrelevant to them. 'Why is the world one with life in it, rather than entirely dead?' Theories that use the Final Anthropic Principle to answer this last question by claiming that the laws of nature are such as to require the evolution of observers (so that quantum wave functions may be collapsed) obviously speak to this. If it could be shown that, given that the laws of nature are as they are, an entirely dead world is not in fact possible, that question would be answered. And it seems to me that, in answering it, one would think that one had made at least some progress in answering the question of the meaning of life. The fact that one might well go on to ask why the laws of nature are as they are seems to me not to indicate no progress, but just insufficient progress to count the question under this interpretation as fully and finally answered. There would still be more to ask about. I hope then that it is plausible that a part of what one is asking when one asks about the meaning of life is whether or not there is any explanation – in terms of the laws of nature and/or in terms of something beyond them, God perhaps – for the existence of biological life as such. One part of the question of the meaning of life, then, is a metaphysical one (or a physical one if the right Metaphysics reduces it down to Physics). What is the correct explanation for physical reality existing so as to be conducive to life? Two things follow from this. First, under this sort of cosmic interpretation, the question 'What is the meaning of life?' has as its answer the correct metaphysical thesis (or perhaps correct interpretation of the ultimate physical theory). As such, it cannot have the same answer as 'it' has, for example, when it is interpreted as asking what contingent features of one's individual life will as a matter of fact give one a certain feeling – existential repletion, for example. Or in general to it when it is construed individualistically, i.e. interpreted as asking what constitutes meaningfulness in a life. The case for the polyvalence of the question 'What is the meaning of life?' at the level of denotation is thereby supported. Second, it follows that before we could answer the question as fully as it allows in principle, we would need to resolve the relevant metaphysical issues so as to be able to answer it fully under this interpretation. And this then may be predicted to be a source of dissatisfaction for us methodologically subsequent to the primary one on which I am focusing at the moment, in that metaphysical issues are seldom resolved completely satisfactorily and these ones seem likely to be no exception to that general pattern. We shall return to this point, which I shall call the 'waiting on metaphysics' point,[1] at several stages later, but it is important so I make it now as we pass by.

As I say, one might think that biological life per se must be the broadest sense of 'life' and thus form an outer limit to one's concerns when asking 'What is the meaning of life?' But it is possible to locate life in this broad sense within a yet broader context, the context of contingent things as such or even – broader still – things as such. It seems to me that something as broad as this is also in view – hazily in view perhaps – when one asks for the meaning of life – 'life' as meaning 'everything'. I say this as 'What, if anything, does it all mean?' and 'What's the meaning of it all?' are, it seems to me, variants of 'What's the meaning of life?'[2] One can argue that a concern for the meaning of *it all* must be a part of one's concern for the meaning of *life* if one allows that 'life' means at least in part biological life per se, for a part of what one is asking when one asks ostensibly about biological life's meaning is what meaning life in its broadest biological signification has in any yet-broader scheme of things and what meaning, if any, that broader scheme of things has. That takes one out to it all. Whether or not one does think this linkage holds may depend on whether or not one is attracted to the thesis that meaningfulness/meaninglessness (whichever is there) would spread from the top down. If one does incline to think that it would spread, then one naturally thinks that one cannot have a satisfactory answer to any question concerning the meaning of things lower down without there being a satisfactory answer to questions concerning the meaning of things higher up. Thus one will have to go as high up as one can – to the top – to answer any such question satisfactorily. Thus in asking about the meaning of life as biological life per se, one will have to consider oneself to be asking about the meaning of the stuff that forms the widest context of which biological life is a part – contingent stuff, and perhaps even necessary stuff (if there is any such). I say 'stuff' as it does on balance seem unlikely to me that one will consider abstract, rather than concrete, objects to be a focus of one's concern when one asks 'What is the meaning of life?' or 'What is the meaning of it all?' The domain in mind when one thinks about 'life' or even explicitly 'it all' is probably not *so* broad so as to include numbers, for example. Even if one does not have any sympathy at all with the fear that meaningfulness/meaninglessness would spread top down (so that any answer to the question of the meaning of life understood in some narrower sense must be 'taken under advisement' pending an answer to the question when life is understood in the broadest sense, and indeed when life in its broadest sense is placed in the broadest context of which it is properly a part), it seems to me one is nevertheless likely to concur that a part of what one is asking about when one asks 'What is the meaning of life?' is 'What is the meaning of it all?'[3] Even if one thinks that the question 'What is the meaning of it all?' is properly thought of as abutting, rather than overlapping, the question of the meaning of life, it's implausible to suppose that this border is as well marked and impermeable in most people's minds as it is in one's own. Often then, one should concede, 'What is the meaning of it all?' will make it across. It would after all be odd to think that someone asking the question 'What is the meaning of life?' was really intending (or could easily be persuaded to intend when the option was put to them) to ask something narrower than someone asking 'What is the meaning of it all?' Still, that is the outermost limit, it seems to me, of what one is asking for the meaning of, when one is asking for the meaning of life. And, more centrally,[4] it seems to me, one is asking about the meaning of life as biological life. Let's return then to that.

A relatively relaxed, biological, understanding of the meaning of 'life' would define it by reference to functional activity characterized by organic metabolic reactions. On such a definition, various 'lower' life forms – from bacteria to flowers, slugs, and snails – would non-problematically qualify as life. So would higher animals, including all humans and thus anybody able to ask a question concerning life's meaning. In practice, the biological understanding is usually made more restrictive than this in a variety of directions for the purposes of focusing biological investigation in more fruitful ways. Homeostasis, responsiveness to external stimuli, and growth and reproductive activity, for example, are things that are often included as definitional or quasi-definitional of life, with the resultant, if mostly unintended, exclusion from the land of the living of all those suffering from terminal decline in functionality, coma victims, the infertile, and so on. For our purposes at present we do best to take 'life as biological life' in the broadest sense.

We may redevelop a style of argument we've just utilized to meet the objection that, by taking life so broadly, we will have come up with an understanding of 'life' that is too all-encompassing to form a focus for any of our concern when we enquire into the meaning of life. It might be suggested that nobody, when asking 'What is the meaning of life?', has in mind the lives of bacteria or insects. However, such an appearance would be deceptive, if only because sometimes the apparent meaninglessness (or meaningfulness) of a life (that is counted as such only due to 'life' functioning in this broad biological sense) is taken to have implications for the meaninglessness (or meaningfulness) of individual lives such as our own, with which we are surely concerned if we are concerned with any life at all.

Consider these comments by Ludwig Feuerbach:

It is strange to tell, and yet it is the pure truth that it only took a flea to make me into a pagan. One day, whilst I was raising my folded hands to heaven … and was praying with great devotion, it bit me! Think of it! Right at the point of my most devout outpouring, right in the middle of the stream of prayer a flea took a healthy bite of my arm, causing me to pull apart my folded hands as fast as I could, to lose the thread of my devout prayer, and to pursue the infamous destroyer of my devotions until I had captured it and smashed it in a rage. Now the flea was dead, yet the painful wound that the blasphemer had inflicted on me still burned in my heart. 'Destroyer of devotion!' " Thus I spoke to the flea in my anger, "Who engendered you? What is your purpose in the world? You parasite, you blood-thirsty monstrosity, Did a wise sovereign, a loving Father who arranges all in His mansion for an intelligent purpose, Create you only to give others burdensome torments?" … And this objection catapulted me down to the dark abyss of titanic naturalism. Now, for the first time in my life, I really saw nature, saw how it produces from itself out of its own power, how it is its own ground and source of eternally struggling life, how it knows no laws beside those of its own being. So there! It was a flea through which I fell from faith; I would still be a believing Christian if there were no fleas in the world.[5]

It is difficult to turn Feuerbach's autobiographical ravings into an argument while retaining any assurance that Feuerbach himself would recognize and wish to claim ownership of the result. And it is difficult to make great advances in discussing any such argument without drawing on considerations of the meanings of 'meaning', which we have yet fully to develop. But we may perhaps hazard that Feuerbach would have had sympathy with the following argument.

This flea's life is obviously meaningless, as it serves no purpose that a God of the classical theistic sort could have. Were there a God of the classical theistic sort, then all elements of His creation would serve a purpose of His. Thus there is no God of the classical theistic sort. Thus we must conclude by catapulting ourselves into the abyss of titanic naturalism. I take it that may be translated as follows: we must think that life as a whole is devoid of meaning, at least in the sense of God-imposed purpose.

There are a number of points at which one might object to this argument. But as our purpose at the moment is merely to illustrate various meanings of 'life', let us, with that purpose in mind, look only at its first premise, that the flea's life is obviously meaningless in the sense Feuerbach has in mind – 'having a God-imposed purpose'. This is by no means certain. Perhaps God wished Feuerbach to become an atheist and was using the flea, effectively, if Feuerbach is to be believed, for this end. The flea's life is even very plausibly meaningful for some other understandings of meaningfulness. Imagine the following claims, as made by a companion of Feuerbach:

> It is strange to tell, and yet it is the pure truth, that it only took a vindictive human to make me into a pagan. One day, I observed a tiny flea, innocently drawing, in the only manner available to it, a very small amount of nourishment from the blood of my acquaintance, Ludwig Feuerbach – someone who had more than a sufficiency. Ludwig, who was thus mildly imposed upon, flew into a rage on account of it. Having been slightly incommoded, he smashed the poor creature in a rage. As he did so, I thought of him, 'Who engendered you? What is your purpose in the world? You vengeful, bloodthirsty monstrosity, Did a wise sovereign, a loving Father who arranges all in His mansion for an intelligent purpose, Create you only to destroy others who are trying to survive in the only manner that they can?' … So there! It was a human being through which I fell from faith. I would still be a believing Christian if there were no such people in the world.

We are freer to speculate here as to the suppressed argument, as we are inventing this companion to Feuerbach. So we may say that he believes that a life such as the flea's is one that is worth living for the creature living it and thereby meaningful in at least that sense of the term. It is Feuerbach's wanton destructiveness of such meaningfulness that our imagined observer of the incident thinks would be intolerable to the God of classical theism and hence forms in his mind the basis for an argument to God's non-existence that is, from that point on, structurally the same as that we have tentatively ascribed to Feuerbach.

Whatever one makes of these differing viewpoints on the meaningfulness of the life of a flea and the compatibility of the existence or destruction of such a life with the existence of a God and thus the existence of what, if any, sort of meaning it may be that He could provide were He to exist, we may see that the meaninglessness or meaningfulness of life at even the lowliest level is not something that should escape our attention when inquiring into the meaning of life. It may affect the meaningfulness of our human lives, something the meaningfulness (or lack of meaningfulness) of which is certainly central to our concerns as we ask 'What is the meaning of life?' Thus we can return all the more confident to the thought that the broadest biological sense of 'life' is a part of what one is asking the meaning of when asking the question of the meaning of life.

Before leaving this point, it will be informative to consider a passage from Taylor, in which he too discusses the apparent meaninglessness of the life of a lowly animal, in his case a glow-worm. This is what he says:

> Thus, for example, there are caves in New Zealand, deep and dark, whose floors are quiet pools and whose walls and ceilings are covered with soft light. As one gazes in wonder in the stillness of these caves it seems that the Creator has reproduced there in microcosm the heavens themselves, until one scarcely remembers the enclosing presence of the walls. As one looks more closely, however, the scene is explained. Each dot of light identifies an ugly worm, whose luminous tail is meant to attract insects from the surrounding darkness. As from time to time one of these insects draws near it becomes entangled in a sticky thread lowered by the worm, and is eaten. This goes on month after month, the blind worm lying there in the barren stillness waiting to entrap an occasional bit of nourishment that will only sustain it to another bit of nourishment until … Until what? What great thing awaits all this long and repetitious effort and makes it worthwhile? Really nothing. The larva just transforms itself finally to a tiny winged adult that lacks even mouth parts to feed and lives only a day or two. These adults, as soon as they have mated and laid eggs, are themselves caught in the threads and are devoured by the cannibalistic worms, often without having ventured into the day, the only point to their existence having now been fulfilled. This has been going on for millions of years, and to no end other than that the same meaningless cycle may continue for another millions of years.[6]

Taylor is drawing here on some themes that he has developed earlier on in the text from which this passage is abstracted. Cyclic or repetitious activity, exemplified *par excellence* by the case of Sisyphus's rolling the stone up the hill each day only for it to roll down again at night, evacuates the life which exhibits it of meaningfulness. The life of lower animals is characterized by this sort of activity and hence meaningless. But human life is not to be exempt from this charge. Taylor is not alone in thinking this way. Sartre had summed up the conclusion of similar thinking thus: 'Here we sit, all of us, eating and drinking to preserve our precious existence and really there is nothing, absolutely no reason for existing.'[7] And we have already looked at Camus. As Taylor goes on: 'This life of the world thus presents itself to our eyes as a vast machine, feeding on itself, running on and on forever to nothing. And we are part of that life.'[8]

There is more to Taylor's case than the following would suggest. At least a significant part of his thinking appears to be driven by the thought that through our status as animals, driven by our biological 'needs' to survive and reproduce for no purpose other than that later generations survive and reproduce, we find ourselves condemned to meaninglessness. But this 'more' seems to me easily convictable of the genetic fallacy: even if humans evolved out of creatures similar to glow-worms or fleas and even if certain of our biological properties are similar to those of these lower animals, that does not entail that humans per se cannot transcend these lower animals. We can assume to ourselves purposes beyond mere survival and reproduction, indeed purposes antithetical to our individual survival (though this is rare) and (and this is as frequent as contraception) reproduction. But whatever one makes of Taylor's argument here, he clearly speaks with his example of glow-worms to our concerns when we ask 'What is the meaning of life?'

As this discussion has already suggested, fleas and glow-worms are really of interest to most of us, human beings, only insofar as they affect us, human beings. Some people are able to get worked up, or at least pretend to get worked up, by ruminating on the case of parasitic wasps, these being creatures that do things to other creatures that would certainly be unpleasant were they to be done to us. They even feel able to conclude with confidence that the creatures parasitized thereby suffer to a degree incompatible with Theism. However, even were it not for their groundless speculative forays into the minds of insects, such examples must always be less gripping to us human beings as they never directly affect us in the ways that fleas – or wasps when they sting us – sometimes do directly affect us. A consideration of glow-worms similarly seems to us cogent to the issue of the meaning of life in the sense that most centrally concerns us only insofar as we can see our own lives as analogous in relevant respects to the lives that they lead and thus fear that we must draw over from a consideration of the meaninglessness of their lives a conclusion about the meaninglessness of our own. Terence could have said 'I am alive, so nothing that is alive fails to interest me'. But in fact he said, 'I am human, so nothing that is human fails to interest me.' And in this he echoed what is surely our main focus of concern as humans – ourselves. We are human beings and – for better or worse – it is thus human beings who concern us most. This is why such bracketing-off of cosmic interpretations doesn't seem to us – if we notice it at all – bracketing-off anything of great significance in addressing the question 'What is the meaning of life?' It is human life – at some level of specification – that we characteristically have in the forefront of our mind when we wonder whether life as such has a meaning. We shall then turn to that in just a moment, before looking at something more extensive in principle, even if we suppose it co-extensive in practice.

Consider then life in a very broad sense – sentient, conscious, morally significant life per se. This is a broad sense as it is not life in the sense of an individual's life, or even humanity's life – perhaps there are sentient, conscious, morally significant beings other than humans, on our planet (chimpanzees?) or on others (the sorts of beings that the crew of the *Starship Enterprise* often come upon). But neither is it life in the broadest of senses possible, for bacteria are alive but not included under this understanding. This is a sense of life that, I suggest, is a part of what one has in mind – or, perhaps better, can be brought to think one has in mind – to inquire about the meaning of when one asks

'What is the meaning of life?' Pending chimpanzees joining the debate or the discovery of the sorts of beings that the crew of the *Starship Enterprise* regularly come upon, we may though without fear of misleading ourselves call this an understanding of life as 'humanity's life'.

The precise delimitations of the human race over time are uncertain. (When did humans first emerge on the planet? When, if at all, will they become extinct?) Nevertheless, humanity, or mankind as it is sometimes called, is something to which one may refer and about the meaningfulness of which one may have concerns. It is no doubt this that is to at least some extent the object of some people's concerns when they ask about the meaning of life. Such people are asking whether the human race has a meaning. They are asking 'Why are humans here?' in addition to 'Why am I here?' It is obviously primarily humanity as a whole, for example, that Russell has in mind in the following passage when he speaks of 'Man'.

> That Man is the product of causes which had no prevision of the end they were achieving; that his origin, his growth, his hopes and fears, his loves and his beliefs, are but the outcome of accidental collocations of atoms; that no fire, no heroism, no intensity of thought and felling, can preserve an individual life beyond the grave; that all the labours of the ages, all the devotion, all the inspiration, all the noonday brightness of human genius, are destined to extinction in the vast death of the solar system, and that the whole triumph of Man's achievement must inevitably be buried beneath the debris of a universe in ruins – all these things, if not quite beyond dispute, are yet so nearly certain, that no philosophy which rejects them can hope to stand. Only within the scaffolding of these truths, only on the firm foundation of unyielding despair, can the soul's habitation henceforth be safely built.[9]

As with the comments of Feuerbach which we have just looked at, it is difficult to extract from this passage alone an argument or even a thesis that we may be sure Russell would have endorsed. But, combining this with what he says elsewhere, one may conclude with some confidence that Russell would claim that the life of humanity as a whole – that which he calls 'Man' – does not have a meaning where meaning is understood as purpose (and long-term consequence). Nevertheless, an individual man or woman can face up to this fact with 'unyielding despair' and thenceforward fashion for himself or herself a meaning, a purpose (and short-term consequence). Individual humans – men and women – can create meaning for themselves out of the meaninglessness of humanity's life. This is an interesting thesis.[10] For the moment, the point to notice is simply that in order to be able even to express the thesis we need to keep clear that there are two meanings of 'life'. Only thus can we say that Russell believes that life in one sense (humanity's life) is meaningless, even though life in another sense (life *qua* individual human's lives) is or can be made meaningful. Again, we are not at the moment concerned with whether or not such a position is one we have reason to adopt or reason to reject, just with giving ourselves a tool that would be needed to explore it – *viz.* the recognition that 'life' is ambiguous. And again we have with this recognition reason to endorse polyvalence at the level of denotation. If Russell's thesis is right, 'the' question of the meaning of life has two different answers. Under one interpretation, the answer is 'None'. Under another, 'Whatever we individually make of it'. But anyway, 'life' as a term has at least two different meanings.

Sometimes, the concern raised when considering the meaning of life is not so much with humanity in its entirety, but rather with the large bulk of it. One worries, for example, whether the life of 'the common herd' is or can be made meaningful. Is it perhaps that only a few supermen are able to triumph in the manner Russell suggests? From what he says elsewhere, Russell's view appears to have been that, in principle, anyone might create meaning for themselves and that if in practice this option is not open to all, then it is only contingent failures in the educational process or bad luck that have led to this result (though some suffering from serious mental disability are probably incapable of meaningful lives according to Russell). Nietzsche appears to have disagreed, thinking that the structures that enable the few to create meaning in an otherwise meaningless world inherently deny meaningful lives to the majority. So there is room for dispute here. That is to say, for a given understanding of 'meaningfulness', one may have different views on whether the life of humanity per se is meaningful or meaningless; whether the life of the majority of humans is meaningful or meaningless; and whether the life of individual humans is meaningful or meaningless. So again, we see that 'life' understood as the life of humanity as a whole and 'life' understood as the life of various proper subsets of humanity (e.g. 'the common herd', 'those alienated from the products of their labour', 'the leisured classes', 'Nietzschean supermen') are all in view when we ask 'What is the meaning of life?' Or at least all are in view if Nietzsche and the like are speaking to our concerns when we ask the question. And it seems to me plausible that they are.

The discovery that the life of humanity as a whole or some significant proper subset, even a subset of which one was a member, had a meaning, but one's own life did not, would be of limited comfort to one. The discovery that one's own life had meaning or could be made to have meaning, even if it came with the discovery that humanity's life as a whole did not have meaning and could not be made to have any, would be more comforting. Russell, as we have seen, is someone who drew comfort from this latter thought (if going through life with a self-conscious 'unyielding despair' is comforting; I incline to think it probably is, but I haven't – I confess – tried it). For Nietzsche 'strength', rather than 'comfort', would be his word of choice to describe what is arguably the same affect-cum-belief. It seems safe to say then that the sort of life the meaning of which we are *primarily* concerned with when we ask the question of the meaning of life is the sort of life that we as individuals asking the question are leading or could lead. We may not be hopelessly self-centred, but it is nevertheless primarily life of the sort we lead or could lead the meaningfulness of which concerns us most.[11] In practice, each of us would primarily like to know the answer to the question 'Can *my* life, as the human being I happen to be – limited in various ways because of that (generically: finite knowledge, abilities, and so on; and specifically: happening to be born in society *x*, class *y*; and so on) – nevertheless be, or be made by changes that it is in my power to effect, meaningful or more or less meaningful?' And what would that essentially involve (the philosophical question)? And what would it accidentally involve (the practical one)? Metz may overstate the case, but he makes a fundamentally true point it seems to me when he says 'Most of us care about whether the human species is significant, if at all, only insofar as it bears on the question of whether and how our own lives as individuals can be significant.'[12] Let us turn then to consider 'life' understood as the life of individual humans.

We find 'life' functioning in this sense in the following passages from Tolstoy.

> The truth was that life is meaningless. I had as it were lived, lived, and walked, walked, till I had come to a precipice and saw clearly that there was nothing ahead of me but destruction. It was impossible to stop, impossible to go back, and impossible to close my eyes or avoid seeing that there was nothing ahead but suffering and real death — complete annihilation. ... My mental condition presented itself to me in this way: my life is a stupid and spiteful joke someone has played on me ...

> One can only live while one is intoxicated with life; as soon as one is sober it is impossible not to see that it is all a mere fraud and a stupid fraud! ... Differently expressed, the question is: 'Why should I live, why wish for anything, or do anything?' It can also be expressed thus: 'Is there any meaning in my life that the inevitable death awaiting me does not destroy?'[13]

When Tolstoy says that the 'truth was that life is meaningless', it is obviously his life rather than anyone else's that he has in mind. Of course, in these passages Tolstoy tells us enough for us to hazard that he believes that the same considerations that lead him to conclude that his own life has no meaning (roughly, that death awaits him) would lead other reflective people to the same conclusion vis-à-vis themselves, that their lives are meaningless too. But it is from his own life that Tolstoy's concern starts. And, we may hazard, it would thus be, as it were, 'from the bottom, up', that he would run an argument for the meaninglessness of humanity's life or life per se. Russell, as we have seen, wished to assert the meaninglessness of life understood as humanity's life, but prevent a 'top-down inference' to the meaninglessness of the lives of individual humans. Tolstoy, starting with the meaninglessness of the lives of individual humans, would be, we might suspect, sympathetic to running an argument to the effect that the life of humanity, and indeed life per se, is made meaningless by the meaninglessness of the lives of the individuals who jointly constitute it, although in so speculating we obviously go beyond the evidence of the passages quoted. Regardless of whether it is Tolstoy's view (and in fact it was not the view to which he was ultimately drawn), this is another interesting position. Again, for the moment we are simply noting a few conceptual possibilities that we are enabled to mark using the notion of 'life' at different levels, thus justifying the polyvalence thesis. We are concerned with all of these. So it is 'life' in all these senses that concerns us when we ask 'What is the meaning of life?'[14]

I have said that it is our individual lives that are the main focus of our concerns when we ask 'What is the meaning of life?' A natural question to ask at this stage is whether each of our own individual lives considered as individual wholes is the 'narrowest' focus for 'life' as we express our concerns about its meaning when asking, 'What is the meaning of life?' No, it is not.

As well as considering an individual human life as a whole, we may consider aspects of an individual's life at a time or periods of time within an individual's life. So, for example, a friend might confide to you that he has come to see the marriage in which he remains for the sake of convenience as meaningless, in the sense of failing to give him any feeling of fulfilment, while he still finds meaningful in this sense his job as an accountant, in which he facilitates millionaires in limiting their tax exposure. Again it is difficult to say much with confidence until we have looked in more detail at the meanings of 'meaning'. But we've already seen enough to think that meaning as feeling of fulfilment with some aspect of one's life – existential repletion with a localized focus, as it were – is a perfectly legitimate use of the term. In the situation we are imagining, you have no reason to doubt that this sense of meaning is in use when your friend analyses both these two aspects of his life (there is no equivocation here). And thus – other things being equal (if you have no reason to suspect self-deception or similar things) – you should believe that he is probably right in his judgement of the relative meaningfulness of these aspects of his life in this sense of 'meaningfulness' (if not, you may be thinking, in other – more important – senses). It appears then that, in at least one sense of 'meaning', an individual life can have, at one and the same time and in the same sense of 'meaning', meaning in one of its aspects and not in another. One may wonder whether in such cases an overall judgement of 'net' meaningfulness of this sort is possible (ontologically if not epistemically). Perhaps it is, but, in any case, what goes to make up 'net' meaningfulness (or meaninglessness) of this sort is unevenly distributed over aspects of the individual's life. Thus we may truly say of one aspect of an individual's life that it is meaningful/ meaningless to a differing extent from another aspect even if a 'net' judgement is always available (ontologically if not epistemically) of the person's life as a whole. Similar considerations apply to periods in a person's life. Let's have a quick look at that.

The friend we are imagining might go on to say to you, 'So, those Wednesday evenings, which you may remember I took off from work last year to spend going to marriage-guidance sessions, well they didn't go anywhere; they were meaningless. However, the other evenings and the weekends, which you may remember I spent working in the office researching ever-more-ingenious ways around tax law, well they led to me now being a world authority; they were in that sense very meaningful.' A different sense of 'meaning' from earlier is being used now of course – meaning as leading to something that one believes to be valuable. But, at least provisionally (again it is hard to say anything more than provisionally prior to having unpacked the relevant meaning of 'meaning'), this seems like another legitimate sense. As different periods in one's life can differ in the extent to which they lead to things that one believes to be of value, so again we should think that in at least one sense of meaningfulness, some periods within an individual's life may be more or less meaningful than others.[15]

Overall, it appears that internal to an individual life, meaningfulness in at least some senses can be unevenly distributed both at one time (in which case we have spoken of it being distributed over aspects of the person's life at that time) and over time (in which case we have spoken of it being distributed unevenly over periods in that person's life). That being so, marking divisions internal to a life will be essential as we think about the meaning of life. There will be top-down and bottom-up inferences to consider too. For example, it is plausible that it is a necessary truth that if every aspect of a person's life is meaningless in the sense of affording that person no sense of fulfilment, then that person's life as a whole is, at least at that time, meaningless in the same sense, i.e. that this sense of meaninglessness allows an aspect-to-whole inference. Perhaps there are some senses that do not allow this; perhaps there are some that allow whole-to-aspect inferences; some that allow period-to-whole inferences and some that allow whole-to-period inferences.

Is there any even narrower sense of 'life'? It is possible to think about the meaningfulness (or otherwise) of actions within an individual's life. Levy: 'I shall not have the presumption to present a full and final theory of the meaning of life, but I will argue for something nearly as ambitious: an account of the structure that central activities in our lives must have, if they are to be ideally meaningful.'[16] Again the point here is not to decide these issues, just to notice them and by noticing them realize that all are cogent to our concerns when we ask 'What is the meaning of life?' because 'life' is a term with multiple meanings in that question.

We have drifted into talking about different meanings of 'meaning', but we have in this chapter so far primarily been looking at different meanings of 'life'. These have ranged from the broadest – biological life – to the narrowest – an individual human's life, and, within that, an aspect of or a period within an individual's life, or possibly even actions performed within life. We've even considered favourably the thought that in asking 'What is the meaning of life?' one may be asking in part a question that refers to something even broader than 'life' would ordinarily be taken to include, even in its broadest sense. One may be, probably is, asking what is the meaning of 'it all'? In the next section, we shall turn to focus on a couple of meanings of 'meaning'. In doing so, we shall have occasion to return to these various ways of unpacking 'life' and further explore some of the relationships between these various notions. But for now, I finish this section by expressing my hope that the various different meanings of 'life' I have unpacked have all been plausible to my readers as different – if related perhaps through e.g. top-down relationships – things the meaning of which they are asking about when they ask the question of the meaning of life and that it is very implausible to maintain that they are asking something about all the different referents of 'life' to which a single unitary value could be the answer. If that hope is well founded, then the case of polyvalence at the level of connotation and denotation is already made. Let us now turn from considering the meanings of 'life' to considering the meanings of 'meaning', in order to make the case that way too.

We shall start with a notion that we have just seen in play – meaning as mere causal consequence.[17] Sometimes, when people consider the meaning of an individual's life, they seem to be considering at least in part merely its causal consequences. In the same way that one might say, 'The Wall Street Crash meant misery for millions', intending simply to convey a belief that it led to misery for millions, so one might say 'The period of my life I spent training as a mechanic meant that I was able to secure the position I now hold with Honest Jimmy's Tyre and Exhaust' or 'Piero's life meant that artistic treatments of perspective would never be the same again', intending in these cases to convey simply the thought that a section of one's own life or the whole of Piero's caused various other things to obtain, a position in Honest Jimmy's business in one case and an artistic revolution in another. Thinking of the human race in its entirety, one might say 'Humanity's life means that other animal species now face a greater threat of extinction from another animal species than they ever have done in the past', intending simply to convey the belief that humans cause more species extinctions than any other species.

It is lack of causal consequence that forms at least a part of the grounds for some of the concerns people have about the meaning of sections of their lives, their lives as a whole, the life of humanity, or even life per se. Looking back in his or her retirement, a person might say 'Given that I spent the whole of my working life changing tyres at Honest Jimmy's, I now see that the several years I spent before then studying Renaissance art didn't mean anything for me, unlike the week I spent training as an automotive mechanic.' Stepping back a bit further, such a person might say 'Given that in a hundred years the effects of my life on the universe will be as if I had never lived, so my life as a whole has been (and what remains of it will be) meaningless.' Stepping back yet further and considering the life of humanity as a whole, someone might say 'Given that humanity as a species will one day become extinct, so humanity's life per se is without meaning.' And, finally, someone might say 'Given that all life will eventually be annihilated in the "heat death" of the universe, so life as such is meaningless.' These sorts of worries about the meaning of a section of a life, a life as a whole, humanity's life, or life per se, are premised then on understanding the meaningfulness of such things as being undercut by what one might *prima facie* characterize as lack of causal consequence. And this is how it is often characterized. However, upon reflection, the issue of concern here can be seen not to be with lack of causal consequence per se but with something a bit more specific. Let's focus down on the lives of individuals to bring this out.

Thinking at the level of molecules being disturbed in the paths they'd otherwise have taken by any given person's trajectory through space-time, then, while fatter people will trace wider spatio-temporal paths and relatively long-lived people longer ones, each person's life will have more or less the same causal consequences as everyone else's in purely quantitative terms. In four-dimensionalist terms, one person's 4-D worm is much the same as another. To have made this observation is to have placed ourselves in a position to see immediately that it is not primarily a concern about the sheer amount of causal consequences that underlies our concern that a section of a life, a life as a whole, or the life of humanity is, if it is without causal consequence, lacking in meaning.

In order to drive home this point, it will be useful to return to the case of Sisyphus, and some variants on it. Doing so will enable us to bring out how meaningfulness as mere causal consequence is a sense of meaningfulness that we do not think is very 'deeply' meaningful. But we think that it is a necessary condition for something that we do think of as deeply meaningful, which is why lack of causal consequence would undercut meaningfulness in a sense we care about deeply. This then will reveal a relationship of support between two sorts of meaningfulness, such relationships being ones that will be important later in the argument in establishing the amalgam (rather than grab-bag) version of the polyvalence thesis.[18]

Sisyphus, as we have already recounted, is a mythical figure who was condemned by the gods to spend eternity rolling a rock up a hill by day, only for that rock to roll back down the hill again at night. So, as Albert Camus – the person whose treatment of the story is the most famous one (or at least literary one; there is also a famous painting by Titian) – tells us, Sisyphus is someone whose 'whole being is exerted toward accomplishing nothing'.[19] There are variants on the myth, but, as it is usually told, we are led to think of this punishment as having started a finite amount of time in the past. Thus, although it will never cease, it will never actually be of infinite duration. And we are led to think of Sisyphus's world each morning as more or less the same as it was the previous one. Sisyphus finds one and the same rock that he rolled up the hill the previous day at the bottom of the hill the next, waiting to be rolled up again. The causal consequences of his actions each day are cancelled out each night. Thus it is that he accomplishes nothing with his daily efforts. Sisyphus then is someone whose life has no causal consequence (at least consequence that is carried over any one twenty-four-hour period). His life is hence devoid of meaning in the sense of causal consequence and it is no doubt feeling oneself in some respects like Sisyphus that explains some of the concerns one has about the meaningfulness of sections or even the whole of one's life, life as such, and so on. One tidies one's home and then, twenty-four hours later (maybe much less if one has children), it needs tidying again. What then was the point? None, it appears. That period in one's life spent tidying one's home was thus meaningless. But is not the whole of one's life, one then thinks, in this way pointless?

But it is not the mere lack of causal consequence that lies at the heart of our concerns.

To bring this out, let us alter two features of the original Sisyphus thought experiment. Consider an immortal, Andy, who has already spent an infinite amount of time at his daily activity and will spend all of eternity at it. His activity is, each day, to roll one more rock up to the top of a constantly increasing pile of rocks. Andy has then, *ex hypothesi*, already led a life of unsurpassable (as infinite) causal consequence. The world is already different in an infinite number of ways (mostly rock-related ways admittedly) from how it would have been had he never existed. The effects of each day's rock rolling are, in Andy's case, *not* cancelled out each night. Rather, they are carried forward into the next day and into the ever-increasing rock pile that he is accumulating. In the sense of meaning as mere causal consequence, we must thus say that Andy's life means more – infinitely more – than Sisyphus's. But in saying this and realizing how little we would nevertheless prefer to be Andy over Sisyphus (if indeed we would prefer to be so at all), we realize that having causal consequence is primarily valued by us not for its own sake. It is valued only as a *necessary condition* of something that we value for its own sake, having causal consequence in bringing about something significant[20] and positively evaluable.

We may imagine yet a third case, that of Bob. Bob is in the same situation as Andy, except that he rolls a different rock up the hill each day and uses the rocks not simply to make a pile, but as materials with which to construct an increasingly beautiful and elaborate (whilst never finished) building, something like Barcelona's cathedral. There can be little doubt that we would rate Bob as leading a more deeply meaningful life than Andy even were we to wish to count the mere causal consequences of their actions quantitatively as the same. Indeed, if we imagine a Charlie, who has been at a Bob-like task for only a finite amount of time and hence the causal consequences of whose actions are less, quantitatively, than Andy or Bob, we would nevertheless rate Charlie's life as more meaningful than Andy's.

What emerges from these considerations then is that while meaning understood as 'mere causal consequence' is a legitimate sense of meaning[21] and lack of meaning in this sense entails lack of meaning in at least some others, meaning in the sense of mere causal consequence is not something that we value for its own sake, which we care about in and of itself. Meaningfulness in this sense then is revealed to be not a very 'deep' sense of meaningfulness. We would happily trade in mere bulk causal consequence for other types of meaningfulness (choose to be sentenced to Charlie's 'punishment', rather than Andy's, thinking that by doing so we made our lives more meaningful overall). Bringing about significant positively evaluable stuff is plausibly a way of making a section of one's life or one's life as a whole meaningful in a deeper sense. As it's a necessary condition of bringing about significant positively evaluable stuff that one brings about stuff, so it's plausible to suggest that one's life having meaning in the sense of mere causal consequence is a necessary condition for its having meaning in the deeper sense that concerns us. When someone regards a section of his or her life as not meaningful because, as they incline to put it, 'it didn't lead to anything', their worry is not so much that it didn't lead to anything. (If they were shown that it actually led – via the whimsy of some angel – to an infinite number of things that they regarded as in themselves insignificant, this would not make them reverse their judgement.) Rather, their worry is that it did not lead to anything significant and positively evaluable. So, that's a couple of senses of meaning – meaning as causal consequence and meaning as significant and positively evaluable causal consequence – that are distinct but related to one another conceptually. One is a necessary condition of the other. That they are distinct is the point relevant to supporting the polyvalence thesis. That they are related this way conceptually is relevant to supporting the amalgam version of the polyvalence thesis. For now, let's turn to sketch what is obviously another sort of meaning that we are concerned with when we ask of an individual's life if it has meaning.[22]

As well as meaning as significant positively evaluable causal consequence, there's a sense of meaning as significant and positively evaluable causal *antecedence*. Sometimes our worry is not that our lives won't lead to anything significant, but that they haven't come from anything significant. This then is a sense of meaning that is particularly suitable to juxtapose with the one that we've most recently been discussing, as meaning as significant causal antecedence is pretty obviously going to be a different sense of meaning from meaning as significant positively evaluable causal consequence. Thus the case for polyvalence (at the level of denotation as well as connotation – that which comes before cannot be one and the same thing as that which comes after[23]) will be made.

Some people tend to downgrade the meaning of their lives when they learn that their conceptions were unplanned, that they arrived, as they may put it, 'by accident'. Some people think that were the Big Bang (or whatever it is that is the first event in the universe) to have been uncaused, then that alone would undermine the meaning that the universe might otherwise have had. It's the 'uncausedness' that worries them, or so they say. But again this cannot be quite right. One might become convinced that in fact the universe is of infinite age and entirely deterministic, so an infinite number of causes had led to one's creation. Nothing – including one's life – is in that sense an accident. This would affect one as much as were one to become convinced that indeterminism ruled to the extent that no event had a cause at all, including then one's life.

Again then, it is not sheer quantity of causal antecedents that determines meaning in the sense we are concerned with here but the significance of these causal antecedents. In particular, I would suggest, it's whether or not they were positively evaluable intentional states. This is why evolution is felt to be so threatening to our meaningfulness, both to us as a species and (thus) to us as individuals. 'At the centre of the Darwinian approach, as commonly understood, is the thesis that man owes his origins to a purely accidental chain of essentially blind natural forces.'[24] The question 'Why am I here?' is answered perfectly satisfactorily under one perfectly legitimate interpretation with 'Because your parents had sex.' But that answer does not begin to address the question of the meaning of one's life. One can see that one begins to address it if one goes on in answer 'And they had sex in order to conceive a "saviour sibling" for your older brother, someone to whom you could donate bone marrow, saving his life as a result.' That would touch on the question of the meaning of one's life, it seems to me.[25] And if a similar perspective was had from the point of view of eternity, it would speak to it all the more definitively as it would bring in what Seachris calls the 'ontological normative' element.[26] As Seachris well characterizes the worry behind Nagel's famous discussion of the absurd, on it, from the widest point of view possible, 'human existence and the existence of any particular person, appears to be radically contingent. There is no deep reason why you or I exist. Nagel seems to voice this worry in terms of the universe not caring. Such radical contingency … can be contrasted with a less "threatening" kind of contingency that, for example, characterizes the human race on theism … While our existence is contingent on theism, it is, nonetheless, grounded in the intentions and actions of a caring agent.' Theories of the meaningfulness of life that posit the right sort of 'antecedents'[27] thus speak directly to this concern. Finding one's place in an appropriate larger scheme of things (God's plan) then might be counted as finding one's life's meaning. This is certainly a part of what many people are asking about when asking what the meaning of their lives is – what's the purpose/point of them? – or, if asking about life or the universe *per se* – what's the purpose/point of it all? 'Where do I come from (and why)?' is for some no less related to the issue of the meaning of their lives than 'Where am I going (and why)?' Meaning as causal antecedence of the right sort – positively evaluable and purposive causal antecedence – is then a different meaning of 'meaning' from meaning as significant and positively evaluable causal consequence. Again then, we have reason to endorse the polyvalence thesis.[28]

So, I hope that these discussions of some of the various meanings of 'life' and of 'meaning' in play when one asks the question 'What is the meaning of life?' have been enough to show that the question is polyvalent and indeed that the answers are polyvalent too. As promised, I have a second line of argument for the same conclusion. In essence this argument consists of listing some plausible meanings of the whole question 'What is the meaning of life?' and offering them up for your approval as parts of what you are concerned with when you ask the original question. In the next chapter, I shall develop that argument. Naturally, there will be some repetition of some of the unpackings of 'meaning' and 'life' which I've just sketched. You will forgive me.[29]

CHAPTER 4

I shall start by listing but a few of the concerns that find their home in the question 'What is the meaning of life?'

As we have begun to see in the previous chapter, in asking 'What is the meaning of life?', one is asking what, if any, consequences there are of an aspect or period of an individual's life, the individual's life as a whole, humanity's life, or life per se (as seen, there is ambiguity in the word 'life'[1]). One is asking if any or enough of these consequences are significant and positively evaluable. One is asking what, if any, purposes are served (or exist whilst failing to be served) by life in one or more of these senses.[2] Is it here for something and as a result of someone's willing that it be here for that something; has it a teleos in that sense? One is asking what significance, if any, in a greater (potentially non-purposive) scheme of things life in one or more of these senses has.[3] 'What is the point of it all? Why does anything at all exist? Why are we here?' 'Why am *I* here?' One is also asking the less grand – 'how' – variant of these why questions: How do we come to be here? How do I come to be here?[4] One is asking what, if any, ideals are instantiated in an aspect or period of a life or life in one or more of the larger senses – 'What, if anything, does it "stand for"?' Is there some overarching goal or ideal for which a life stands or should stand even if as yet it does not? One is asking if there is a way of living that is objectively better than another way for oneself as an individual, or perhaps for humanity or life more generally.[5] One is asking what, within life in one of these senses, is desirable or valuable in itself. What – if anything – makes life worth living, worth going on with, for the individual[6] or group living it?[7] One is seeking in this way to engage with what Camus thought the prime philosophical question – what, if anything, is it about life that makes it rational not to commit suicide? One is asking whether or not life in one or more of these senses contributes positively to various sorts of extrinsic value in the world or beyond. Does it fit in in some appropriate larger scheme of things? One is asking whether it is emotionally or spiritually satisfying[8] or, more centrally, whether it is the proper object of such an emotion/mood even if it is not yet had.[9] Would it (or some temporal portion or aspect of it even if not the whole) appropriately ground the feeling of 'existential repletion', as I have been calling it, that Ayer and Wohlgennant characterized? One is asking whether it has an internal coherence, whether it has holistic properties of certain sorts.[10] Relatedly (but differently, for this is always to the good), one is asking whether it displays the sort of structural properties that Metz has in mind when he talks about one's life as a story, but a story with a certain value-infused direction. Most simply, do any bad parts earlier lead to good parts later (and good parts that it's implausible to suppose would have come about in any case or have been replaced by ones at least equally good had it not been for the bad parts).[11] What is the right story into which it fits?[12] To stay with Metz, one is asking 'Which ends intrinsically merit striving for, beyond one's own pleasure? How should a human person transcend her [sic] animal nature? What are the features of a life that warrant great esteem or admiration?'[13]

These are just some of the questions that find expression in 'What is the meaning of life?' I use them as illustrative of the diversity, not as exhaustive of it. While I have selected these as I incline to think they are the most central, I also believe there are many more questions of the meaning of life than these. At the moment, having only briskly listed some of the meanings of 'What is the meaning of life?', polyvalence is not justified by this second manner of arguing for it in anything but the most impression-istic of ways. To justify it more in this manner, I would need to do a 'literature review' of different authors and their different ways of taking the question and answering it, not just mention some in a few endnotes (as I have been doing). But I trust that even having done what little I have has been sufficient. I trust that each of these questions will have resonated with the reader in the sense that, in reading each of them, they will have elicited in him or her a thought that might gain expression in 'Yes, that *is* in part what I was asking when I asked, "What is the meaning of life?" Those authors you cited in the notes? While none of them seemed to capture everything I was asking about, they all addressed at least a part of it.'

Together then the two lines of argument developed so far – the first (the one that looks in turn at plausible meanings of 'life' and then of 'meaning'), in the previous chapter, and the second (the one that runs the two back together and looks at plausible meanings of the whole question 'What is the meaning of life?'), in this one – are the best argument for polyvalence at the level of connotation. And then, through that, they are the best argument for polyvalence at the level of denotation, as it will be immediately implausible that these various questions could all have one and same answer. If we look back to the various questions that I have just listed as sheltering under the question 'What is the meaning of life?', we will see that some of these questions *must* have different answers from the others. The way they are phrased just doesn't admit even the logical possibility that one and the same thing be the answer to all of them. The decisiveness of this last point in making the case for polyvalence at the level of denotation should not be belied by the brevity with which I have made it.

The sort of resonance that I've hoped to generate in the mind of the reader is the best evidence in favour of the polyvalence claim. One might think that this sort of resonance is the *only* sort of evidence that could be adduced, even in principle, for the claim of polyvalence at the level of connotation; this is the *only* argument for it. If we are dealing with what a question means, surely running a variety of putative meanings of its parts and of it as a whole past competent language users and seeing if more than one resonates in this way is all that can be done to support the claim that it means many things. But this is not so. There is, in addition, an argument in this area of which one might avail oneself. I shall sketch the general features of such an argument now. This then is the third line of argument in favour of the polyvalence claim that I promised. This argument is, it seems to me, less good as evidence, as it proceeds from premises that are less clearly true and via argumentative moves that are less clearly valid to the same conclusion. But that of course is not to say that it cannot contribute anything to one's rational assurance in the conclusion that there is polyvalence at the level of connotation (and then ultimately at the level of denotation too).

Let's again allow ourselves to focus on the individualistic interpretations of the question, i.e. the ones that inquire into the supposedly unitary property that is meaningfulness as it may be had by individuals' lives. In that context, the general style of this argument may be seen to be cumulative. It is built from multiple arguments, each of which one can construct as follows. One takes an extant theory of the meaning of life (as meaning in life) that one finds *prima facie* plausible – Wolf's, say, or Metz's – and one evaluates it as one would normative theories advanced in other domains. In its favour one counts those of one's first-order judgements – e.g. Gandhi's life was meaningful: Sisyphus's was not – that come out as true on it. Against it one counts those of one's first-order judgements that come out as false on it. The evidence is weighted by how confident one was in the particular first-order judgement in question. One then enters into some reflection – was whatever degree of confidence I initially had in a particular first-order judgement based on a prejudice or some such? Does the theory tell me of the judgements that it rules mistaken why I might have been confident in them even though they are mistaken, or does it leave such 'counterexamples' entirely unexplained? One may bear in mind other supposed virtues of the theory too – its simplicity perhaps. There is contention of course about how to weigh such factors. In any case, one reaches at the end of this a reflective equilibrium. If one does this with one or two of the extant theories, then I hazard one will find that persistent counterexamples remain – persistent in the sense that, even after such reflection, one will retain a high degree of confidence in the truth of the first-order judgement that the theory says is false. One will also find that persistent evidence in favour of the theory remains. It explains the truth of a lot of one's first-order judgements and it ties these truths together in intellectually satisfying ways. What is one to do? One analysis would be that there is one question and answer and that all the extant theories about that answer are wrong. The counterexamples prove the wrongness of all extant theories. The evidence in their favour is just plain misleading evidence. Another analysis would be that there are a number of questions correctly answered by articulating a number of properties, each going by the name 'meaningfulness', and these properties, while they often overlap, are not coextensive. Thus they must be different. The different theories have captured different ones of these properties more or less accurately. But of course no one theory has captured all of them. That analysis would explain *both* the evidence 'for' *and* the evidence 'against' each theory. The evidence 'for' in each case is evidence that the theory has captured a particular sort of meaningfulness accurately; the evidence 'against' is evidence that there's more than one sort of meaningfulness one was asking about and this particular theory hasn't captured at least one other sort. In that I take it one must take one's first-order judgements as evidence, insofar as no single theory remains counterexample free: but many have these other explanatory virtues, the hypothesis of polyvalence must be the hypothesis best supported by the evidence.

The earlier evidence – 'resonance' when one hears a certain way of unpacking 'the' meaning of 'life', of 'meaning', or of 'What is the meaning of life?' – was, as I said, impressionistic. This is even less – it's a suggestion of what impression one would get were one to go through all extant theories of life's meaning in the literature and deploy this method. But I cannot reasonably be expected to do more here. Looking in this way at all extant theories would be prohibitively time-consuming. Of course one could look in this way at some but not all. *That* wouldn't be prohibitively time-consuming – and, the more one looked at, the more evidence one would collect in this way for polyvalence. That is, in effect, just what I am doing by the by as the book goes on. So I hope that this line of argument has been and will continue to be buttressed as a side effect of my pursuing my main line of argument in this work. Before moving on from the point at this stage, it might be fruitful to consider what I would say was a parallel case. I shall have to treat the issue with rather broad-brush strokes.[14]

Consider the debates in moral normative theory between consequentialists, deontologists and virtue theorists. Consider them addressing the question 'What is it that makes something the moral thing to do?'[15] A consequentialist analysis is *prima facie* plausible and explains a lot of our intuitions, but famously there are counterexamples. Ditto for a deontological analysis. And for a Virtue Theoretic one. Perhaps there is a fourth normative theory just waiting to be discovered. But more plausible, it seems to me, is that there is no one property in virtue of which an action is the moral one. All of these theories capture properties that contribute when present to an action's being moral. An action might be moral in the sense of producing the best consequences; it might be moral in the sense of being well-intentioned; and it might be moral in the sense of being expressive of an estimable character. Moral goodness-cum-rightness is polyvalent.[16]

Assuming that this claim of the polyvalence of the question of the meaning of life is right at the level of connotation and at the level of denotation, we gain, as we have seen, at least the promise of a partial explanation of our sense of dissatisfaction with all the answers to 'the' question of the meaning of life as offered by sages, past and present; and that too is evidence in favour of polyvalence.[17] If there are indeed so many questions of the meaning of life, it is no wonder that no pithy formula, or even relatively long formula, could contain the answer to all of them. While multiple denotation is not entailed by multiple connotation, its possibility certainly is. If that possibility were actual – if these many different questions did in fact have many different answers – that would explain as right the attitude we have towards sages: our knowledge, even before they open their mouths, that we're not going to be fully satisfied with whatever comes out. And I think we should take that attitude as evidence. We should take ourselves to know what we think we know. And thus we do thereby gain support for polyvalence at the level of connotation and denotation.

When one realizes the polyvalence of the question and thus the answers to 'it', one must of course have some sympathy with the sages whose answers one has discarded as unsatisfying on coming to the point of this realization.

Consider the predicament in which a sage finds himself or herself when asked 'What is the meaning of life?' Insofar as he or she is able to make determinate sense of the question and not retreat into Delphic aphorism by way of answer (that itself being something that would be dissatisfying to his/her listener), he or she must disambiguate it in what strikes him or her as the most profound way and then answer it under that interpretation. Perhaps he or she then answers it correctly under that interpretation. But – be that as it may – as, depending on how it is disambiguated, 'the' question of the meaning of life is answered correctly with very different answers, so each particular answer proffered by a sage is likely to strike any individual hearer of it as at best only partial. And so it is that even when one thinks of a sage as having singled out something of value in life with his or her answer (perhaps even having singled out something of unsurpassable value), one cannot help but think that whatever he or she has described cannot be all that there is to making life meaningful – 'There must be more to it than that.' And so it is that this thought that one cannot help but have is right.

The polyvalence of the question of life's meaning also explains another thought that I hazard occurs with great frequency in response to the many answers proffered to it by sages: 'There's something in that.' Perhaps almost as frequently as one feels oneself dissatisfied with a particular answer, one thinks of the unsatisfactory answer as nevertheless having some cogent truth contained within it. If there is a God and He is as those who believe in Him characteristically suppose, the meaning of life is unlikely, one supposes, to have nothing whatsoever to do with finding union with Him. If ultimate reality instead consists of suffering inherent in a cycle of rebirth, then the meaning of life is unlikely, one supposes, to have nothing whatsoever to do with escaping from this cycle. Whatever one's religious views or lack of them, gaining in knowledge and wisdom, giving and receiving love, and a host of other things that have been offered by sages as keys to the meaning of life are, one will almost certainly believe, valuable and, believing this, one will suppose that it is unlikely that they are entirely irrelevant to the question of life's meaning. No answer to the question of life's meaning that has been propounded by sages of the past is wholly satisfactory, but few are wholly *un*satisfactory either. Again then, polyvalence of both question and answer explains how this is so.

From the vantage point of appreciating polyvalence, one can also explain (and one must also have sympathy for) those analytic philosophers in the last century who dismissed the question of the meaning of life as a mere expression of an emotion or a mood; a hopelessly vague formulation of some overly general scepticism about reasons for action; or an umbrella under which less lofty-sounding, but at least meaningful, questions were taking ill-advised shelter. That is how an ambiguous question and the partial answers to it could well look to philosophers who had been trained to sniff out nonsense masquerading as profundity. The truth though is different. One may say that it is not that the question of the meaning of life has too little meaning; it has too much.

The polyvalence also explains why a thousand flowers bloomed in answer to the question on the Continent even as Anglophone philosophers were doing their best to keep their lawns well weeded of them in Great Britain and the United States of America. In an intellectual culture where being clear what a question means is no prerequisite to starting to discuss it and where allowing one's thoughts to be moved along by what one admits are culturally generated associations of ideas (rather than insisting that they be passionlessly propelled by a universally applicable logic) is no bar to one's calling oneself a philosopher, we would expect discussions of a polyvalent question of philosophical significance to flourish in glorious and colourful confusion. Of course the exotic flowers that grew in such a climate could not be expected to appear anything other than spindly and sickly on closer inspection. Etiolated by their lack of exposure to the light of reason, they would far outreach the support provided for them by their roots, and their blooms would soon shrivel in our hands if we tried to pick them. But a puny plant may, by chance, reach as high as a more robust one. And this is exactly what we find. We have looked at a couple of examples already – some thoughts of Jean-Paul Sartre and of Albert Camus. While we would suffer acute embarrassment were we to be caught by even the most licentious Epistemologist claiming of any of these thinkers that they achieved knowledge of life's meaning (or meaninglessness), there are other things we may, with more boldness, say they achieved – insight, truth, and possibly even wisdom.

And finally, the polyvalence of the question both explains many features of the micro-structure of the quarrels between contemporary analytic philosophers and points the way to a more irenic future. I have in mind then the point that I have already talked about. A particular theory of the meaning of life (understood as being what makes for meaningfulness in a life) will be advanced by one philosopher – meshing with some of our pre-reflective intuitions about paradigmatically meaningful and meaningless lives. But then another philosopher will come up with a counterexample that appears decisive. On this first philosopher's theory, we can now see we'd have to say of a particular person, whose life may be taken without question to be meaningful, e.g. Gandhi, that his life was not meaningful. But obviously it is. That theory is thus beaten. A new theory is proposed. It is now the one to beat. And the cycle repeats. I should be clear that I do not think there is anything wrong with this methodology – which is just as well, as I shall be using it myself – but just that, as already indicated, its results are open to a non-standard interpretation. Rather than seeing the discussion through a Popperian lens of 'Bold conjectures, conclusive refutations', it could be – indeed should be – envisioned as one of 'Bold conjectures; partial confirmations and partial refutations'. The claim that *the* meaning of life just is x; therefore, all and only lives that exhibit x are meaningful and meaningful to the extent they exhibit x is indeed bold and most contributions to the debate are written in this bold style. But such bold conjectures are indeed refuted in their own terms by a single counterexample of a sufficiently robust nature (i.e. *prima facie* plausible and immune to reflective-equilibrium-undermining). And such counterexamples just keep coming. If one instead recasts the claim as 'The meaning of life in one particular and non-exhaustive sense of "meaning" and in one particular and non-exhaustive sense of "life" is just x; therefore, all and only lives in this particular sense that exhibit x are meaningful in this particular sense and meaningful in this particular sense just to the extent they exhibit x', that cannot be refuted in such a way. A putative 'counterexample' to such a claim would simply point the way to another sort of meaning and/or life, and further fruitful discussion. When each philosopher's theory of meaning is reconfigured as a theory of a particular type of meaning focusing on a particular type of life, conflict largely disappears.[18]

This 'irenic' perspective, as I have elsewhere called it,[19] follows from the polyvalence thesis. Metz finishes his book by saying that his theory is now 'the one to beat' – in many ways, a fitting end to a book that has been largely devoted to smashing up everyone else's theories. More irenic would have been to conceive of these other theories as ones with which to join forces.

So, that completes the case for the claim that, at the level of connotation and denotation, the question of the meaning of life is polyvalent. If the claim of polyvalence (in both connotation and denotation) is correct, then reaching as satisfactory an answer to the question of the meaning of life as possible will not be a matter of alighting on *the* correct answer and then spending our time adding sufficiently satisfying further detail to it and rationally compelling argumentation for it. The conclusion of our investigation will not come quickly – or even after much investigation – in the form 'Lo and behold, it was actually Sage *S* who got it right all along. Just to remind you, here's what Sage *S* said the meaning of life is: [**FORMULA PROVIDED**] And here are the arguments for believing that he got it right.' Given its commitment to polyvalence, this book then will be atypical in its construction.

Most books on the meaning of life have a final chapter that comes as the denouement, as it were, to their story. It always reminds me of the chapter at the end of the typical Agatha Christie novel, where the detective calls everyone together into the drawing room of whatever stately home a series of complex murders have been committed in and brilliantly reveals the true murderer. Having gone through various putative theories of the supposedly unitary property that is meaningfulness as it can be displayed in the supposedly singular thing that is life and found all these theories wanting, they conclude with a chapter that more or less begins with a sentence along the lines of 'So, what then *is* the meaning of life?' And then the supposedly right and hitherto elusive answer is presented – a new formula is given. Given my commitment to polyvalence, this cannot be the way I shall finish this book. If we know of polyvalence, we already know enough to know that there is no such thing as 'the right answer'. Indeed, this is the most important discovery that we have made in our investigations so far:

The correct answer to the question 'What is the meaning of life?' is not a correct statement of the meaning of life.

You can tell I think it's the most important discovery as it's the first sentence I've put in bold type and I gave it a paragraph to itself.

I won't spoil the surprise by telling you how I shall finish the book. But we can see how it must go on from here. Rather than being like the child on Christmas morning, impatient to open the present of 'the right answer', we shall have to be like the patient child ahead of Christmas, aware of the constraints operating on those who will give him or her gifts and spending time thinking about how best to structure the (rather long) wish list that is our question.

In other words, the methodology that must suggest itself to us in investigating the question of the meaning of life is as follows.

We should disambiguate the various meanings of 'meaning' and 'life' as they figure in our minds as we ask the question of life's meaning. We should show how, under the various interpretations of 'the' question we are hence enabled to disaggregate, we are or are not in a position to judge of life that it has meaning or does not have meaning and perhaps the extent to which it has or does not have meaning. And, finally, in those senses of the question where we are in a position to make judgements of the meaning of life, we should make those judgements and give the answers. This is the methodology that it will be necessary to employ in order to make as satisfactory progress as is possible on 'the' question 'What is the meaning of life?' But it will not be sufficient for a fully satisfactory answer, or even for as fully satisfactory an answer as is possible. As the rest of the book unfolds, we shall see a variety of reasons why it will be insufficient; what it is that we shall thus need to add to it; what it is that is needed but cannot be added by us; and what it is that not even God could add.

Before we get on to all those reasons for worry, in the next chapter I shall attempt to defuse a more basic worry that one might have with this methodology *per se*.

CHAPTER 5

The diagnosis that I have offered of the primary source for our dissatisfaction with particular answers to the question of the meaning of life does not present the problem posed by this question as, in this respect at least, an atypical one. In everyday life, situations frequently arise in which one asks a polyvalent question of someone and that person replies having missed at least some of the meaning one had in mind, resulting in one's feeling at least somewhat dissatisfied with his or her answer. Sometimes, of course, such a result is avoided by the person replying initially with a question of his or her own, designed to elicit clarification ('Are you asking a or b?'). One is able to reply in turn by stating that one is asking one, rather than the other. But sometimes the answer one would offer, if asked such a clarifying question, would be that one is asking both or, where one's initial question has more than two meanings, one would incline to say something like, 'All of them'. Such, in outline, is the case, I have been suggesting, with 'the' question of the meaning of life. But in the case of this question, there is another problematic feature. Again it is not unprecedented in everyday life. But it adds another layer of difficulty to the task of answering 'the' question of life's meaning. So we do well to be apprised of it.

As someone asking the question of the meaning of life, even asking it seriously and after much thought, it is unlikely one will have a secure and detailed prior grasp of the various different things one is asking. Were one to be given a list of possible meanings by the person of whom one was asking the question and asked by him or her to specify some or all of the meanings from that list as the meaning or meanings one already had in mind, one would not be able to compare the list one had just been given with a pre-existent list of one's own, and quickly tick off various meanings. One would not thus be able to respond speedily in the manner, 'Thank you. I am asking a, c, d and e, not b and f, as you have labelled them on your list. Now, please proceed to answer.' Rather, a more synergistic process would take place between the list one had been given on the one hand and one's own, somewhat ill-formed, prior thoughts on the other. One would find oneself saying things like 'You know, I hadn't really thought about it, but, now I see it there on your list, I think that meaning a is a part of what I was asking, or – perhaps better – a part of what I *now* wish to ask about when I put to you again the question of the meaning of life.' Look back at the list of questions that I briefly gave as illustrative of those that find expression in 'What is the meaning of life?' at the start of the previous chapter. I hazard you will have this sort of reaction to at least some of them.

A famous example of Wittgenstein's is cogent here.

> Our problem is analogous to the following: If I give someone the order 'fetch me a red flower from that meadow', how is he to know what sort of flower to bring, as

I have only given him a *word*? Now the answer one might suggest first is that he went to look for a red flower carrying a red image in his mind, and comparing it with the flowers to see which of them had the colour of the image. Now there is such a way of searching, and it is not at all essential that the image we use should be a mental one. In fact the process may be this: I carry a chart-co-ordinating names and coloured squares. When I hear the order 'fetch me etc.' I draw my finger across the chart from the word 'red' to a certain square, and I go and look for a flower which has the same colour as the square. But this is not the only way of searching and it isn't the usual way. We go, look about us, walk up to a flower and pick it, without comparing it to anything. To see that the process of obeying the order can be of this kind, consider the order '*imagine* a red patch'. You are not tempted in this case to think that *before* obeying you must have imagined a red patch to serve you as a pattern for the red patch which you were ordered to imagine.[1]

When being asked any clarificatory question about our original question 'What is the meaning of life?' ('Are you asking *a* or *b*?'), or when being provided with an answer to that question and thinking about its cogency to our concerns as we expressed them in the original question, we should consider ourselves as analogous to those who are asked to fetch a red flower from the meadow. We should not be tempted to think that, before hearing the clarificatory question and/or answer, there was a fixed fact about what we meant, which fact our being asked that clarificatory question/being given that answer has left entirely unchanged and merely uncovered to us. Rather, the fact about what we meant/mean is in part generated by what we incline to say in response to clarificatory questions and answers. Nevertheless, as long as we bear this Wittgenstein-inspired caveat in mind, we may usefully speak of a synergistic process taking place between our 'original' concerns when asking the question and anything a sage might offer us by way of a clarificatory question or an answer.

But one should consider the possibility of a different phenomenon from one's 'merely' getting clearer on the question or rather the questions one was first asking. One should consider the possibility of one's being led away from that question/those questions to another question/set of questions, led away from, but not so far away as to change the subject. It can be that, through reading a book on one topic, one becomes more interested in another topic. For example, one might read this book on the nature of the meaning of life and become more interested in the nature of the good life. But that is not the sort of change I have in mind here. I have in mind a change not in topic but in how one conceives of that topic. I have in mind a situation where one thinks that the person one is reading is definitely talking about the topic one was thinking about, but making one re-consider it quite fundamentally. 'I would have said I wasn't really asking about *p* until I read you telling me that any sensible person asking the question I was asking was really asking about *p* and I would still say now that I *wasn't* asking about *p*. But now I can see that you're right that anyone asking the question I was asking should really be thinking in terms of *p*, I'm going to change the nature (but not so much as to change the identity) of the question as I now put it.' Or perhaps, as a variant, 'I would have said I wasn't really asking about *p* until I read you telling me that any sensible person asking the question I was asking was really asking about *p*. But now I can see that I was already – admittedly perhaps in a rather inchoate and unreflective way – asking about *p*. My question then hasn't changed as a result of my reading of you, but my understanding of it has.'

The situation is yet further complicated by a fact to which we have already adverted in another context, *viz.* that, with notable exceptions, most philosophers to whom one might ask the raw question 'What is the meaning of life?', have extremely limited sympathies for any sort of polyvalence thesis. Thus they would be very unlikely to offer you such a list by way of reply in the first place. At best, they will answer the raw question with claims of the form 'People may naively have thought that the question meant *a*, but in fact, given that the only meaning that makes sense is *b*, then that is what we are really asking, if we are asking anything, when we ask it. Let me tell you then the answer to *b*.' Or – worse still! – this sort of assumption will never be explicitly stated. One will instead read their answer to 'the' question of the meaning of life as they have interpreted it and have to work out for oneself that they must be committed to the view that every interpretation other than the one they have given it does not make sense or for some other undisclosed reason is unworthy of consideration.

In order to address all these difficulties, if we are to answer the question of the meaning of life, we must adopt, at least initially, something of a 'come one, come all' policy towards the answers that have been given to it. Sometimes, assuredly, this is *not* the way to approach a philosophical question. 'Read the opinion pieces in newspapers. Read the most popular books on the topic. Listen out for it when it pops up as a topic on the radio.' Following that advice would serve one very ill indeed were one investigating the issue of whether we have on balance more reason to believe that a God of the sort Jews, Christians and Muslims worship exists than to believe that He does not. But that is because the God who is believed in by the adherents of these religions has been the subject of at least a couple of thousand years' reflection by philosophers. The concept of God – the classical theistic concept, as it is known – is well established. There are, as the need for a prefix 'classical' may suggest, dissenters from this consensus within what one might think of as still broadly theistic worldviews, but they are very much the minority.[2] That is what makes the God question different from ours. In our case, we are first and foremost trying to obtain clarity about what it is we're asking about, the meaning of 'meaning' and 'life' in the question of the meaning of life.

It is from the need for this sort of 'inclusive' policy that a worry might arise, the worry that we might thereby end up being *too inclusive*. For the methodology we are suggesting may appear to be to let anyone who asks and seeks to answer the question of the meaning of life approach the table and bring with them their interpretation of the question and their answer (or their understandings of what sort of thing could be the answer). Insofar as these seem different from those already represented at the table, we pull out for them a separate chair, allowing them thence to speak in turn. But we might then worry: is there then to be *no* limit to the meanings that people may give to 'the' question of the meaning of life? And were we forced to answer this question in the affirmative, it would be most implausible. The question of the meaning of life may, one may concede, have 'too much' meaning as we put it earlier; there are certainly other questions that investigation reveals to be polyvalent to a greater or lesser extent in the manner we are suggesting it is. But surely it would be ridiculous to think that we should make space at the table for all comers. There must be limits.

There are indeed limits on the interpretations that the question of the meaning of life may carry, limits imposed by quite general considerations concerning the nature of language and limits that we must therefore respect. As with all other questions, there are sorts of linguistic behaviour that someone might display in response to the question of the meaning of life that would be taken by all competent language users as indicative, not of having a particular – and perhaps unorthodox and therefore challenging – interpretation and thus answer to the question, but rather as indicative of not understanding it at all. So, we need not make space at the table for all comers, indeed we should exclude some. But how shall we decide whom to exclude?

First, and least controversial as a criterion for exclusion, the interpretations of the question and answers (or general description of the sort of thing that can be an answer) must be logically coherent before we consider them. There are many meanings to the question, but there are no meaningless meanings. That's the thing about meanings: they have to mean something. And that's the thing about logical incoherence: it fails even to mean something. We need not make space at the table then for those who tell us that they are going talk about the meaning of life but speak only gibberish thereafter.

While, as a criterion for exclusion, logical incoherence is uncontroversial, quite whom this criterion excludes when applied properly is sometimes controversial. Thus matters are not quite as clear-cut when it comes to applying this criterion in practice as one might initially have hoped given its clarity in principle. For example, Sartre contends that answers to the question of the meaning of life that involve God involve logical incoherence (because the concept of God is, he thinks, a logical incoherence). Thus, he would maintain, they need not even be considered. However, other serious thinkers contend that it is *Sartre's* answer to the question of the meaning of life that is incoherent and thus not needful of consideration. And we shall thus have to do some philosophical work to decide if either or both deserve a seat at the table in due course. (A spoiler: I shall argue that both do.[3])

Second, and potentially more controversial in principle as a criterion for exclusion, the interpretation of the question has to address at least an aspect of our concerns when we ask the question 'What is the meaning of life?' That is our reflectively accepted concerns as they find themselves after the synergistic interaction of which I have spoken just now. Of course, if the claim of polyvalence in connotation is right, any particular answer will address these concerns only partially and, in individual cases, we may believe that the answer speaks to the aspect on which it focuses entirely inadequately. But interpretations must at least address some aspect of our concerns in raising the initial question if they are to be considered further as interpretations of and putative answers to *that* question rather than, at best, answers to other questions which are beside our concerns when we inquire into the meaning of life. But if they do at least speak partially, inadequately, or even falsely, we suppose, to some of our concerns when we ask about the meaning of life, they *do* deserve a hearing, however partial, inadequate, or false we suppose their answers to be.

In thinking of examples of this criterion for exclusion in play, it will be fruitful first to imagine a couple of people who fail to identify the question and then, second, to imagine someone who succeeds in identifying the question but fails to answer it truly in such an obvious way that we would not wish to consider their answer further. The first two do not deserve a seat at the table. The third one does. First then, consider receiving this response to the question 'What is the meaning of life?'

'State of ceaseless change and functional activity, characterized by organic metabolic reactions.'

It's easy to see what's gone wrong here. What one was asking about wasn't anything to which that could be an answer, even a partial answer. Such a person has spoken to some other question, one that is beside one's concerns when one is asking about the meaning of life. They've told one the linguistic meaning of the word 'life'. So far, so easy. But there will be less clear-cut cases. Consider then the following response.

'To eat well; take exercise; and avoid too much drink.'

On balance, I'd incline to favour thinking of such a respondent as not having identified the question either. They seem instead to have been speaking to the question of what makes for a healthy life. Perhaps – just perhaps – they really are wishing to suggest that a necessary and sufficient condition on a life's being meaningful is that it be healthy because that is all that meaningfulness *is*. In that case they have identified the question after all and merely failed to answer it correctly. One would have to hear more to be sure. But it seems to me that that more might well lead one to think that they had failed to identify the question, failed in a less dramatic and obvious way than the first respondent, but failed nonetheless.

Now to an example of someone who clearly identifies the question, but equally clearly answers it with a falsehood. Let us consider someone holding a view that is so manifestly inadequate that it has in fact never been maintained as an answer to the question of life's meaning, except perhaps by fictional characters such as Ebenezer Scrooge. Nevertheless, it manages to address it, despite addressing it with an obvious falsehood. The view may be expressed thus:

'It's to make money – to die with the largest bank balance one can. It's not to pursue other purposes and maybe gain money along the way or to gain money as a means to other ends. The accumulation of money itself is the end, the only purpose of our existence.'

Someone propounding this view has obviously interpreted the question of the meaning of life as asking for the purpose of individual humans' lives, or at least of their lives since the invention of money. We no doubt think this answer to the question as so interpreted is wrong. But a person propounding this answer – should one ever be found – deserves a seat at the table. They have given the question an interpretation that we recognize captures at least some of what we were asking for an answer to when we were asking for an answer to the question 'What is the meaning of life?' The fact that we believe their answer to be entirely without merit does not detract from this earlier achievement of having identified a legitimate interpretation of the question.

I hope these examples serve to underscore then the distinction between not answering the question at all and answering it badly. Someone answering the question with a definition of the term 'life' as it might be found in a dictionary has simply failed to identify the question, has failed to answer it at all. Someone propounding the 'Scrooge' theory of life's meaning has answered the question, but with a falsehood. It's because we recognise the Scrooge theory as a falsehood as soon as we hear it that we can be led to think they've not answered it at all. (After all, answering a question with a falsehood and not answering it at all are both ways of failing to answer it with the truth and it's the truth we're ultimately after. So – naturally enough – we tend to lump together those who fail to answer at all and those who answer with a falsehood. Both are of no further interest to us.) But at this stage of our investigation, to repeat, we are doing the preliminary work of framing the question. And, for this preliminary work, those who we can recognise as answering it (albeit with an obvious falsehood) are of further interest to us for it may well be that we can learn from them more about what we are asking. So, from the Scrooge theory, one can learn that a part of what we are asking about is the purpose of life, if there is any.

Of course there are some who speak in response to the question 'What is the meaning of life?' whose 'blunders are too big', as Wittgenstein might have put it, to be thought of as comparable to either of the two sorts of people we've been considering so far. They do not speak cogently to some question that concerns issues other than life's meaning. Nor do they speak falsely to any aspect of our concerns when we ask the question of life's meaning. Such people may also be excluded from the discussion. Illustrative of this third group of people is the following story, as told by Nozick:

> A person travels for many days to the Himalayas to seek the word of an Indian holy man meditating in an isolated cave. Tired from his journey, but eager and expectant that his quest is about to reach fulfilment, he asks the sage, 'What is the meaning of life?' After a long pause, the sage opens his eyes and says, 'Life is a fountain.' 'What do you mean, life is a fountain?' barks the questioner. 'I have just travelled thousands of miles to hear your words, and all you have to tell me is that? That's ridiculous.' The sage then looks up from the floor of the cave and says, 'You mean it's not a fountain?'[4]

We may concede for the sake of argument that life itself may be compared in innumerable helpful ways to a fountain, but we know that the *meaning* of life cannot literally be a fountain. We recognize that no concrete object, such as a fountain, or indeed an abstract object, such as a number, can be an answer to *any* legitimate interpretation of the question of the meaning of life. Anyone who'd thought about the question of the meaning of life *at all* would know that these sorts of things cannot be answers. Thus the humour in hearing of a so-called sage who has as yet not worked out even this much for himself, or perhaps of hearing of a supercomputer, which has been working away at the question for thousands of years, telling us that the answer is a number. A similar story might involve a person asking a professional garden designer what water feature would make an attractive centrepiece for his garden and receiving in answer, '42'. The person asking the question would think on receiving this answer, not 'He must have mistaken my question for another close, but definitely distinct, one', or even 'Well, he may have understood my question, but that's just obviously not the right answer to it', but rather 'He must be joking with me', or some such.

Even with these criteria in play, setting some parameters on what will be acceptable as disambiguations of the question of the meaning of life, a worry may linger. The wisdom of individuals seeking a place at the table is not left unchallenged. Each has to be minimally coherent in the interpretation they give to the question and in their answer to it and the interpretation they offer has to address at least some aspect of the concerns of those of us who ask the initial question. But this still leaves unchallenged the 'wisdom of the crowds', as it were, the wisdom of the rest of us who are asking the question. Might we not worry then that we've set the table up in the wrong place, that the *real* meaning of the question 'What is the meaning of life?' is, for all we know, something entirely different from what we, the vast majority of competent language users, take it to be? Perhaps, unbeknownst to us in the crowd, the question 'What is the meaning of life?' really does mean 'What water feature might form an attractive centrepiece in a garden?' Thus, unsuspected by us, the sage Nozick talks about is offering a profound and indeed correct answer when he says 'A fountain' in reply. Or perhaps, if we really knew what we were asking about, a supercomputer telling us that the answer to our question was 42 would strike us as profoundly correct. But such a worry makes no sense. Such a thought gestures hopelessly towards no genuine possibility.

How can we be so sure? Because it is we, the crowd asking the question, who *create* the identity of the question with our concerns. They are our concerns and so we are authoritative over them and the question they form. Even in the case of a polyvalent question such as this, where there is no single hegemonic interpretation, but rather a family of legitimate interpretations, which of the potentially infinite number of interpretations count as legitimate members of the finite family is something that is determined by the reflective responses of the language users posing the original question. Words must mean what their users take them to mean and thus the question of the meaning of life, even if polyvalent, cannot mean something that it is obvious to every competent language-user it does not mean, even partially. And one thing that it is obvious, comically obvious indeed, to us that the question 'What is the meaning of life?' does not mean, even partially, is any member of the set of questions to which 'A fountain' or '42' might be an answer.

We, the crowd, are sovereign over the identity of question. But of course we are not sovereign over the identity of the answer to it, or at least it would require another and more controversial argument to establish that we were. Legitimate interpretations of questions are legitimate just in virtue of being taken to be so by competent language users. But correct answers to questions are not correct (or at least not usually correct) just in virtue of being taken to be correct by competent language users. This is why it has been important to distinguish between whether a putative answer addresses at least an aspect of our concerns when we ask the un-disambiguated question 'What is the meaning of life?' and whether we are tempted to think, even for a moment, that there might be something right about the answer given to the question as so interpreted. This is why in the Scrooge theory we looked at an example of an answer that did the first whilst not doing the second. We should insist that, if someone does the first, it is sufficient for the person giving the answer to have identified the question and given a legitimate interpretation of it and we should equally insist that even if we are not tempted for a moment to think that the answer they have given is correct, then that does not undermine the earlier achievement. But we should also insist that if someone does not do the first, they do not deserve a place at the table.

So, a failure to address (even inadequately) any aspect of our original concerns when asking the question 'What is the meaning of life?' is sufficient to exclude a person from a place at the table of people discussing it. Wherever they are best seated, it is not with us. Such a person might have given a correct answer to some other question. But such a person has not even begun to answer, even answer falsely, the question of life's meaning. So it is that the sage who says 'A fountain', in response to the question 'What is the meaning of life?' should not be allowed to sit down at the table of those discussing the question of the meaning of life. We should politely suggest that he plays with the supercomputer that is proffering up the number '42' whilst we go about our business.

All of this, it may be admitted, has painted the picture in rather too stark a contrast of black and white. There will be some seeking a place at the table who we can clearly see are speaking to an aspect of our concerns ('It's to grow in wisdom and knowledge'; 'It's to find union with God'). There will be some who we can clearly see are not ('It's a state of ceaseless change and functional activity characterized by organic metabolic reactions'). And there will be some who we can clearly see are just joking with us ('It's a fountain'; 'It's 42'). But there will also be those for whom the issue of in which category they should be placed is not determinate. Sometimes this indeterminacy will be epistemic, capable in principle of being removed by further interrogation of the person giving the answer. That would perhaps be the case with the person who answered 'To eat well; take exercise; and avoid too much drink.' But sometimes this indeterminacy will not be capable of being removed in this way. There will remain a certain amount of indeterminacy even after the most careful reflection and synergistic interaction with them that we can give, as a result of what we might call 'persistent residual vagueness' in our question. This is another source of dissatisfaction with answers to the question of the meaning of life.

Another example suggested by Wittgenstein is illustrative here. Imagine that you ask your young child to demonstrate her counting skills.

Case 1. She says, '1, 2, 3, 4, 5, 7, 8, 9, 10.'

She has answered your request imperfectly (look carefully: you will see that '6' is missing). 'Badly' might be rather harsh, depending on how old she is.

Case 2. She says, 'Red, Orange, Yellow, Green, Blue, Indigo, Violet.' She has not answered your question at all. Her blunders are too big. She does seem however to have answered another question, albeit one quite a long way away, in conceptual space, from the question one asked.

Case 1.1: She says, 'Red, 2, 3, 4, 5, 7, 8, 9, 10.'

Case 1.2.: She says, 'Red, Orange, 3, 4, 5, 7, 8, 9, 10.'

There is obviously a continuum of possible cases – 1.3. and so forth – 'morphing' between cases 1 and 2. Given that, we will be – rightly – tempted to conclude that somewhere along this continuum whether or not she is answering the question imperfectly (or even badly) or not becomes indeterminate. But, as Johnson famously observed, we should not let the existence of twilight confuse us into thinking we cannot distinguish night from day. It seems to me that the Scrooge theory, in responding to a purpose-of-life interpretation of the question of the meaning of life, has latched on to a quite central element of what we are asking about when we ask about the meaning of life. So this theory gets to be an answer to our question, albeit a bad answer to our question. The biological definition answer gets to be a quite good answer to another question, but not our question. The healthy living one probably gets to be counted along with biological one; 'A Fountain' and '42' certainly not; they are to be dismissed as jokes. So we can make some definite categorizations even though there are conceptual margins between all of these categories, ones that display this sort of continuum and, at the margins, others may call things differently from the way that I would call them.

In light of this persistent residual (residual as it will remain even after an idealized process of synergistic interaction) vagueness, to some sages we shall ultimately wish to say something along the lines of 'Well, that's "sort-of" an aspect of what I was getting at when I asked the question of the meaning of life.' Some interpretations of the question, we might say, seize on that which is central to our concerns when we ask it. Others, on what is more peripheral. And, at the outermost perimeters of the question, the border-lands of the concerns we express when we ask 'What is the meaning of life?' and thus the legitimacy of interpretations of it and the cogency of answers to it are not clearly marked. 'What is the meaning of life?' shares borders with 'What is it to flourish in life?', 'What is a good life?', and other questions. And these borders may appear somewhat different for different people, an issue to which we'll return in the next chapter.

While it undoubtedly complicates matters, in itself persistent residual vagueness is, as with the other features of the question we have just sketched, not unprecedented or even particularly troublesome. Persistent residual vagueness of a similar sort arises over many issues and to be forewarned about it is usually sufficient to be adequately forearmed against it. Indeed seldom do such matters significantly impede discussion or progress even when one is not forewarned.

By way of example, one may imagine initiating a discussion with someone over the extent to which Napoleon's intrinsic skills as a military strategist decreased with time, relative to the extent to which his decreasing success as a campaigner may be explained merely as a result of his opponents learning to cope with his strategies and the reduction in his own resources. (The correct response to his famous claim 'You cannot beat me.

I spend 30,000 men a month', would perhaps have been simply, 'Keep spending 30,000 men a month and, eventually, we will beat you.') One might profitably break this question down into others, which admitted of differing answers, and make progress that way. And, at every level, the discussion could no doubt be honed by reflective interchange: Are there not other possibilities? Is it not the mark of a great strategist to adapt his strategies to an adapting enemy? It is plausible to contend that there would be persistent residual vagueness in the crucial notion of what one is assessing when one is assessing skill as a military strategist even at the end of an idealized version of such a process of interchange. Yet progress could be made by such a process. Some facts could be revealed by it to be of determinately more relevance than others. Someone might point out, for example, that, throughout his life, Napoleon never developed anything but a rudimentary awareness of naval strategy, let alone tactics. This, while true, would be recognized as somewhat peripheral to what we were really trying to talk about. Naval operations had economic and political implications for him, but not direct military ones. Someone else might point out that, in the period immediately prior to his abdication, Napoleon performed amazing feats of arms with far-from-ideal forces, which fact – if admitted – would weigh more heavily with us. And so on. It is not even certain that a conclusive answer would not be forthcoming. But even if – as in this case one must suspect would happen – no conclusive answer was ultimately forthcoming, progress could nevertheless be made towards a well-grounded inconclusive answer. Such, we may reasonably hope, is the case with the question of life's meaning. Of course one may find oneself feeling dissatisfied with the prospect of the somewhat vague results that are all that could be obtained even after an idealized version of such an inquiry when dealing with a question that is shot through with persistent residual vagueness. But, insofar as one realized that this feature of the answer/answers was a function of persistent residual vagueness in one's original question, one would become satisfied with any dissatisfaction arising from this source. One would stop thinking, 'There must be more to it than that.' That then is the stage of satisfied dissatisfaction to which I hope you have been brought by my reflections so far.

'So is *that* it?' one might now ask. 'If we disaggregated the various legitimate meanings of the question of the meaning of life, legitimate by reference to appearing, even if only on reflection, to speak to at least some aspect of our concerns when we raised the original undifferentiated question of life's meaning; if we appreciated the centrality of the concerns raised by these interpretations relative to our reflective understanding of our concerns when asking the original question (taking into account persistent residual vagueness); if we discovered in turn the answers to each of the questions into which the original was thus "broken down" or discovered why answers to these sub-questions were not available to us; if we did all that, would we *then* reach a completely satisfying (or satisfyingly dissatisfying) answer to the question or rather then a list of answers to the list of questions, in any case something that didn't leave us thinking "There must be more to it than that"?' No, we would not. There would be more troubles ahead.

CHAPTER 6

In the previous few chapters, it has been argued that the question of the meaning of life is really many questions and it has been argued that these many questions have many different answers. Thus the view, popular in Analytic Philosophy until the past few decades, that the question of the meaning of life has no meaning, is mistaken – the truth is that it has too much. It was pointed out that this analysis would suggest to anyone trained in Analytic Philosophy a methodology: disambiguate the question and answer it in turn under its various disambiguations (or show why, under some disambiguations, it is impossible for us to answer it). I argued that this methodology is sound, and while I suggested that what I called persistent residual vagueness in one's original question sets limits on how determinate an answer to the question of the meaning of life one may reasonably hope to get using this methodology, I closed the previous chapter by suggesting that progress could certainly be made with it. Would that be sufficient to remove all dissatisfaction with the answer(s) to the question(s) of the meaning of life one thereby reached? Or rather, as I am putting it, sufficient to make one as satisfied with one's dissatisfaction as possible? Baggini approaches the question of the meaning of life in a similar fashion to that suggested heretofore, and indicates that he would be favourably disposed to the thought that this would indeed be sufficient. He says this of his approach:

> [It is] 'deflationary', in that it reduces the mythical, single and mysterious question of 'the meaning of life' to a series of smaller and utterly unmysterious questions about various meanings in life. In this way it shows the question of the meaning of life to be at the same time something less and something more than it is usually taken to be: less because it is not a grand mystery beyond the reach of most of us; and more because it is not one question but many.[1]

Baggini then is a pluralist in Metz's sense and mine – he endorses a grab-bag polyvalence. Schmidtz says at one point that 'there need be no particular feature that all meaningful lives share. There probably is no such thing as the very essence of meaning.'[2] He too then is a pluralist in Metz's sense as well as mine. One would need to read a fair bit more into this comment and what he says elsewhere in the piece from which it is abstracted to attribute to him a grab-bag polyvalence view, but, if I had to put money on it one way or the other, I'd say that that is his view. In any case, as already indicated, the thesis argued for in the current work is not one of grab-bag polyvalence, but one of amalgam polyvalence. And this makes for a crucial difference at least between Baggini and myself (possibly between Schmidtz and myself too). And it explains why I think, in a manner that Baggini does not, that the methodology suggested so far is insufficient for reaching as fully a 'satisfyingly-dissatisfying' answer as the question of the meaning of life permits. While Baggini is right that the question of the meaning of life may be broken down into other questions, he is wrong in a number of ways thereafter. Many of these other questions, we have already begun to see, are not in any significant way 'smaller' than the original question. Some at least are mysterious, most obviously, it seems to me, the cosmic ones. They seem destined to remain so for the foreseeable future. And there is sadly more work to be done than drawing up a chart with answers to all of them or blank spaces for the mysterious ones if we are to reach as satisfactory an answer to the question of the meaning of life as is possible. This is because polyvalence in the question, and the problems stemming from that as identified in the previous chapters (e.g. persistent residual vagueness), are not the only sources of dissatisfaction with the answers that have been offered to 'it' through the ages. Thus removing ambiguity and proffering various answers to the various questions into which 'it' is broken down, or explaining in particular cases why such answers are unknowable to us, will not remove all such dissatisfaction. To echo Baggini's terminology, having deflated the question, we shall need to re-inflate it again. Or, to switch metaphors, having broken the question down into its component parts, we shall find ourselves with good reason to suppose that these parts need to be put back together again; with reason to think that they need to be put back together again in the right way; and with reason to think that judging the right way is not going to be an easy task.

Let us skip ahead in our imagination to the end of the process of disambiguating the question and answering 'it' to see in more detail why this is the case and to start to locate sources of dissatisfaction other than the primary one – polyvalence – on which we have focused so far, and the persistent residual vagueness which we have talked about most recently. The next source of dissatisfaction arises from another part of the thesis argued for in this book – the need for amalgamation – and this is what I shall talk about more in this chapter.

Let us imagine then that we have in front of us a summary of our findings as they would be reached at the end of an idealized version of our investigation, laid out in the form of a chart-cum-list. Down one side is a complete list of the different legitimate meanings that can be given to the question 'What is the meaning of life?' – a, b, c, and so on. Alongside each one, we have either a philosophically satisfying explanation of why we are not in a position to answer the question as so interpreted, one that explains why it must remain in this sense mysterious, or a philosophically satisfying argument for why a particular answer is the one we have best reason to believe is the correct answer to the question as so interpreted. Over at least some sections of this chart the issue of persistent residual vagueness will have made itself felt. It is difficult to know how this should be represented in our imagination. Perhaps, as a first move, we might think of ourselves as writing certain sections in pencil rather than pen. Nevertheless, let us imagine that the chart has been completed and now stands in front of us awaiting our inspection. There are some general features of the chart that we can predict with confidence even before we have completed it. I shall discuss two now.[3]

First, while in advance of actually having conducted any part of the investigation that has led us to be able to draw up such a chart, we cannot be sure that each of the entries in it will not strike us as equally cogent to our undifferentiated concerns as expressed in our original question, 'What is the meaning of life?', we rightly suppose that they will not. As already mentioned, some of the interpretations of our question which we may, on reflection, have allowed through as legitimate, we may have done while nevertheless marking them down as less central to our concerns than others. We'll have said to some sages 'Well, that's a part of what I was getting at when I asked the original question, but not a big part.' These meanings of life will hence be ranked lower down the chart/list than the others.

I want to mention two quite general reasons for thinking the chart will be ranked and then follow these up with some supporting examples. The first general reason arises from our discoveries about the relative centrality of various meanings of 'life'. If we hold fixed a given meaning of 'meaning', more central to our concerns when we ask 'What is the meaning of life?' are those individualistic interpretations, *viz.* those that take 'life' to be referring to the individual lives of us who are asking the question. As I put it earlier, we may not be completely self-centred, but it is on our own selves that our concerns centre. So the disambiguation 'What is the purpose of biological life?' will be lower down the list than the disambiguation 'What is the purpose of our individual lives?' The second general reason is as follows. Our concerns when we ask our original undifferentiated question are desire-driven and the satisfaction of our desires is extremely unlikely to be indifferent to the desirability of the things for which it turns out on investigation they are desires. We are each of us individually likely to have a higher-order desire to regulate our lower-order desires by reference to the true desirability of their objects. Collectively then we are certain to want to regulate them and, as I shall explain in the next chapter, it is the collective view on this that is the cogent one. So, by way of illustration, let's focus down on life in the sense of individual life and suppose that there are in fact only two questions of the meaning of life and two answers – an individual's life may have meaning in sense x or in sense y. Suppose further that sense x is the sort of value it would be rational to prioritize having in one's life over many other sorts of values and certainly over having meaning in sense y. And suppose finally that, before discovering this, we would have said that each of senses x and y are equally central to our concerns as we asked the original question. Having made this discovery, we would wish to rank sense x higher than sense y, owing to the higher-order desire that I spoke about a moment ago.

Putting aside these two general reasons for a moment, brief reflection on a few examples suffices to establish the point that we shall wish to mark some meanings of life down by reference to their relative lack of centrality to our original concerns when we start constructing our list (and of course, the corollary of this, mark some senses up).

Consider, for example, the sense of meaning that we have in mind when we describe a certain person's life as having a meaning in the sense that it stands for a particular idea or value, in the manner that Lenin's life stood for the communist revolution; Gauguin's for the artistic imperative; Mother Teresa's for the relief of suffering; the Dalai Lama's for the religious and cultural values of Tibet; and so forth.[4] Metz says 'One argument is that since to be meaningful is just to be a symbol, and since life cannot be a symbol, life is not the sort of thing that can be meaningful. Although Gewirth[5] aims to show that life can be a kind of symbol, most reject this argument since there is no reason to believe that all senses associated with the term "meaningful" include the property of being symbolic (e.g. Smart 1999). After all, synonyms of "meaningful life" include phrases such as "significant existence" and "life that matters", which do not inherently denote something symbolic.'[6] But of course my view is that this is mistaken. Life can be a symbol – the lives of Gandhi, Nelson Mandela, Martin Luther King, and so on just are symbols of the ideas for which their lives stood. The fact that not *all* senses of meaningfulness as applied to individual human lives entail the property of being symbolic is by the by unless of course one has committed to Monism. On my view, these other 'synonyms' – of course that's not the best term for them[7] – of 'meaningful life' just point to other senses of meaning that a life may have, not reasons to think that this is not one.[8] So, I return to the claim that these persons' lives meant something in a manner in which, or at least to an extent to which, our own, rather more ideologically fractured, lives do not mean something. I talk about ideological fracturing here with the following sort of thing in mind.

In some moods I want my life to stand for a commitment to Philosophy above all else. Those moods don't last. It is not always laziness that overtakes them, though often it is that. Sometimes, it is my perception of other values – my obligations to my family, for example. I fail to continue work on some philosophical problem so as to be able to get home early and organize my daughter's birthday party. In general in life I am pushed by three desires: the desire to understand the world; the desire to improve the world; and the desire to enjoy the world. They do not always push in the same direction and I haven't committed myself to any one of them above any other. Nor even have I committed myself to a consistent way of balancing them against one another in cases of conflict, though candid introspection reveals to me that the last of the three wins out rather more often than not. Thus I speak of ideological fracture in my own case. My life doesn't stand for Philosophy in the way that it might were I more single-minded. Indeed, it doesn't stand for anything in the way that Lenin's, Gauguin's or Mother Teresa's lives stood for things. It doesn't have a meaning in that sense. Against this interpretation of my condition, one might say that my life doesn't have *a* meaning in the way that Lenin's did, but that it has three. It stands for three things: understanding, improving, and enjoying. Equally, one might say that it does have a meaning. It stands for one thing, *viz.* an inconsistent-over-time balancing of these three things. But neither of these ways of talking, it seems to me, reflects adequately the way this sort of meaning works. For one's life to have meaning in this sense, it must have *a* meaning. This is in virtue of the symbolic nature of meaning in this sense; if a symbol symbolizes too much, it stops being a symbol. There must be *an* idea – i.e. what is *genuinely one* idea – consistently ruling the rest in the way that there was what was genuinely one idea ruling the rest for Lenin, for Gauguin, and for Mother Teresa. The sort of meaningfulness under consideration here requires ideological purity. I just don't have it. Further, I hazard that most reading this won't have it either; they will be fractured as I am in this sense. Or, to put it in a manner that makes it sound like more of an accomplishment on our parts, most of us are not inclined towards monomania. Unlike Lenin, say, we have 'integrity' in the technical sense that Williams introduced when pointing out that having Utilitarianism as the overriding idea in one's life destroys one's integrity, though of course I am making the point that his argument generalizes from the case of Utilitarianism to any overarching idea in this sense.[9] In any case, however one puts it, we, I am supposing, don't have an overarching idea that shapes and regulates our commitments to lower-order projects. Lenin's, Gauguin's and Mother Teresa's lives had such; ours, I am supposing, don't. So their lives have meaning in this sense and ours don't. As L. J. Russell put it, 'Many people do not have a single dominant purpose: rather they have a variety of purposes, often with little relation to each other.'[10] And I am supposing that most of my readers will place themselves among the many as Russell describes them.

It is an interesting conceptual question – interesting to me anyway, in part because I cannot clearly see the answer to it – whether or not meaningfulness in this sense needs the person whose life is under consideration to have willed the thing for which their life stood. So, suppose – to put it in a rather question-begging form – a particular artist's life stood for the aesthetic imperative in the manner that Gauguin's did, but we know from his autobiography that this particular artist didn't really want to be an artist at all. He constantly willed himself to lead a life that stood for family values. He willed himself to stay at home and be a good husband and father. It was just chronic weakness of will in his case that led him to leave his family behind without any support and go off to some tropical island and paint wonderful pictures there. Would this dissonance between what this man intended his life to stand for and what it ended up standing for deprive it of meaningfulness in the sense that we are considering? Some would say so. Thus, Brogaard and Smith claim that 'if such an imposed shape or pattern is to contribute to meaningfulness, then it must be the result of the person's own efforts and his or her own decisions.'[11] I incline to think not (in this particular sense of meaningfulness – in other senses, certainly yes). The conflicting intuitions we may have here – I certainly have them – are explained in part by drawing on other senses of meaningfulness and in part by using the distinction between meaningfulness *simpliciter* and meaningfulness for the person concerned, the same distinction introduced in an earlier chapter. If, in the manner of the artist we have recently imagined, there is a dissonance between what the person concerned intended their life to stand for and what it actually ended up standing for, then its standing for what it did was sufficient to make the person's life meaningful *simpliciter* in the sense we have in view at the moment. But its not standing for what the person intended it to stand for was sufficient to make it fail to be meaningful *for them* in this sense. They did not appropriate to themselves the symbolic function of their life. If, as we have every reason to suppose he did, Lenin willed his life to stand for the communist revolution, and, as we also have every reason to suppose, it did so stand, then its doing so made his life meaningful *simpliciter* in the sense we have in view *and* meaningful for him in that sense.

There is another conceptual issue that we should consider at this stage as we pass by. Doing so adds to the case for the need to rank. Hitler's life stood for a particular worldview. He also intended it to do so. Did this then make his life meaningful *simpliciter* and meaningful for him in the sense we currently have in view? Or does this example show that there is some kind of constraint on the acceptability of the idea for which a life stands that a life must respect prior to its standing for that idea enabling meaningfulness of this sort?

There are many ways one might respond to this issue and I mention first the one that strikes me as the most *prima facie* plausible (even if *ultima facie* its plausibility comes second, after the view I shall end up endorsing). One way to respond to this example is to suggest that there *is* such a constraint, and if it is breached, while its being so does not prevent a given person's life being in this sense meaningful for that person, it does prevent it being in this sense meaningful *simpliciter*. That being so, we may say that Hitler's life was in this sense meaningful for him, but not in this sense meaningful *simpliciter*. That seems to square with the intuition I have that Hitler's life was meaningful for him in this sense, but accommodate the other intuition I have, which is that something has gone terribly wrong in his selection between the possible ideas for which a life can stand and that this wrongness should be reflected somewhere in one's account. But this logic is hardly compelling: I need to find fault with Hitler's life somewhere. This is somewhere; I'll find fault with it here. Audi says that a 'criterial element' of a life's being meaningful is that it be 'pleasing to God … on the uncontroversial assumption, anyway, that meaningfulness in a life is desirable overall.'[12] And Metz takes 'for granted … that meaningfulness … is desirable. More strongly, when I speak of "meaning" … by definition I mean something that is … valuable.'[13] And Cottingham says that 'meaningfulness is an inescapably evaluative notion; to describe a life as meaningful is at the very least to commend it as a good life.'[14] Well, if Audi, Metz and Cottingham are right, then Hitler's life can't have been meaningful in any sense. However, in the end, I incline to think that there is no moral constraint on this type of meaning (there is, of course, on others). Hitler's life was meaningful in this sense *simpliciter* and meaningful in this sense for him. It was so even though the idea for which it stood was one of the purest evil. To say it was displeasing to God (if He exists) and undesirable is to understate the issue. But that just shows that some sorts of meaningfulness can be displeasing to God (if He exists) and undesirable.

The lives of Lenin, Hitler, Gauguin, Mother Teresa and many more can be clearly seen to have the sort of meaning that is standing for an idea *simpliciter* (and of course often also for the people living them) even when we fail to see equally clearly that the ideas for which their lives stand are morally acceptable and fail to judge equally clearly whether or not their lives standing for these ideas is morally acceptable. A reason not to believe in the constraint then is that we can tell that people's lives are meaningful *simpliciter* (and of course often for them) in this sense before we know of the moral acceptability or otherwise of the idea to which they committed themselves or of their lives standing for that idea. One could have been convinced by Walter Pater (as one interpreted him) and think that the only value worth anything is aesthetic or by Plato (as one interpreted him) and think that all art is worthless or worse. In either case, one could still judge that Gauguin's life stood for the aesthetic imperative. A redacted biography of Gauguin (for example), one that omitted mention of the details that made his commitment to the aesthetic imperative morally questionable, would still be one from which we could judge of his life that it was meaningful in this sense, perhaps both *simpliciter* and for him. The fact that we will wish to judge that some people made their lives stand for ideas that they should not have made their lives stand for is, it seems to me on balance, best reflected *not* in denying that by making them stand for the ideas that they did they secured this sort of meaningfulness *simpliciter* (but instead perhaps only secured this sort of meaningfulness for them). Rather we should say that this sort of meaningfulness is not always a sort that is worth having. Sometimes at least – where the only idea that one is psychologically capable of making one's life stand for is as bad as that of Hitler, for example – it is very much worth avoiding. It would have been better for the world and for Hitler himself had he remained a failed artist in Linz, even though his life would not then have stood for anything and through not standing for anything would thereby have been less meaningful *simpliciter* and for him in the sense we are considering. Note the last bit of that sentence. No doubt his life would have been more meaningful in other senses had he stayed as a failed artist in Linz. And those could have been the senses that Audi, Metz and Cottingham had in mind when they talked of being pleasing to God, being desirable, and being commendable. My point is simply that it would certainly have been less meaningful in the sense we are considering at the moment – it wouldn't have stood for an idea. Leading the most meaningful life that one can *in this sense* may not be leading the best life that one can.[15]

All of this being so, when we consider meaningfulness in this sense, we may ask of ourselves which of the following is more central to our concerns as we ask 'What is the meaning of life?' Is it simply meaningfulness in this sense *simpliciter* or is it more basically meaningfulness in this sense for us? And consideration of our own ideological fracturedness, as I have put it; how we're probably rather contented in our own fracturedness; and the case of Hitler, might lead us to wonder about how central either of these are to our concerns when we ask 'What is the meaning of life?' I hazard that upon synergistic reflection one will find that they are not both equally central and that both are somewhere near the periphery. (Probably both somewhere near the periphery as we'll have been more concerned about the sorts of meaningfulness the having of which in a life can be guaranteed to make that life better than we are about any sort of meaningfulness that doesn't bring that sort of guarantee with it.) The answer to the question 'What is the meaning of life?' that one might express with the words 'It's to find one idea and commit yourself to it so fully that everything else becomes subordinate, so that one's life as a whole stands for it' has some truth in it. Doing that would certainly give one's life a meaning in the sense we are considering at the moment, a meaning *simpliciter* and a meaning for oneself. But that seems unlikely to be the sort of meaning or meaning for us that we most care about having. After all, as reflection on our own ideological fracturedness and on our contentment with it shows, we don't consistently *want* to be the sort of people who are ideologically pure and thus have meaningfulness in this sense as we recognise the disvalues (loss of integrity) that such monomania brings. And, after all, as the case of Hitler shows, it's not that we can rely on meaningfulness in this sense being something the having of which would in itself or in consequence make the world or ourselves better off. Plausibly then it is other sorts of meaningfulness – ones that we would like our own lives to have and ones that seem to be inherently positive values – that are more *apropos*. And this is all, I submit, evidence that it is very unlikely that we will find that each of the two modes, as we may put it, of this sort of meaningfulness (the meaningfulness in this sense *simpliciter* and meaning-fulness in this sense for us) is equally central to our concerns as we express them in the initial question, 'What is the meaning of life?', equally central to one another and equally central to all our other concerns.

Another example illustrating the need to rank is the following. Consider first the sense of meaning in life that we discussed earlier as being all that there is to it according to Ayer and Wohlgennant: a life's being such as to generate in the mind of the person living it (at suitable reflective moments) a peculiar feeling of existential repletion. That seems to me a perfectly legitimate meaning of meaning. It seems to me clearly to speak to an aspect of our concerns when we ask the question 'What is the meaning of life?' So far, so good. But the 'spoof eulogy' that we looked at earlier – where you were asked to imagine yourself being described in your eulogy as someone who had managed to have this feeling despite leading a life that was entirely unworthy of it – led us to consider favourably a more objectivist spin on the same idea. This then is another sort of meaning, the sort of meaning that a life has by being such as to be an appropriate ground for such a feeling in the person living it even if that feeling is not yet had by that person. Again then, that seems to me a perfectly legitimate meaning of meaning. It seems to me to speak clearly to an aspect of our concerns when we ask the question 'What is the meaning of life?' And the objectivist spin on the idea seems to me to speak to concerns that are more central than those that are spoken to by the subjectivist spin on the idea. If you could only have one, which would you choose – to have a life worthy of this feeling even though you would not feel it, or to have a life you felt worthy of this feeling even though it was not? I know which answer to that question I myself would give. Even if you would give a different answer, reverse the ranking relative to me, that in itself is evidence for the claim I'm currently trying to support, which is merely that you will incline to give a ranking, i.e. you will on reflection see that one of these is more central than the other to the concerns you had in mind as you asked the original question 'What is the meaning of life?'[16]

This is not, incidentally, another place to deploy the distinction between meaning-fulness in whatever sense is under consideration *simpliciter* and meaningfulness in that sense for the individual concerned. The difference between the objectivist spin and the subjectivist spin on the idea of grounding the feeling of existential repletion is not that difference. To illustrate that it is not, consider the following example. Suppose that Wittgenstein devoted himself to Philosophy and did rather well at it. On the (to me, plausible) assumption that doing well at Philosophy is appropriate grounds, object-ively, for the feeling of existential repletion, then Wittgenstein's life was meaningful in the sense of meaningful given by the objectivist spin on the Ayer/Wohlgennant view. It seems that it was also meaningful in this same sense *for him*. He chose this life for himself knowing what he was doing. He appropriated this purpose to himself. But he may well, despite all that, not have had the feeling of existential repletion as he reflected on his life as a whole. He may have been always frustrated – frustrated, but continued with it nonetheless under the 'Better-to-be-a-dissatisfied-Socrates-than-a-satisfied-fool' principle. So, he'd have the objective meaning (*simpliciter* and for him), but not the subjective one. That reveals then that the objective meaning is not the *simpliciter* mode of a sort of meaning and the subjective one the for-the-individual-concerned mode. As Smuts puts it 'Merely knowing that one's actions have value does not make them satisfying to perform. Wouldn't housework be better if it did!'[17]

Of course most of us would, in most cases, if we recognized or merely believed ourselves to recognize our lives to have those features that would appropriately ground a feeling of existential repletion, then go on to have that feeling as we reflected on them. But we might not and some activities are such as to make one's not having the feeling more likely and predictably so. We might, on committing ourselves to a particular form of life – being a philosopher, say – know that we would not get the feeling of existential repletion even if our lives became worthy of it. Yet, on the Better-to-be-a-dissatisfied-Socrates-than-a-satisfied-fool principle, we might commit ourselves nonetheless.[18] We might want the sort of meaning described by the objectivist spin on the Ayer/Wohlgennant view more than we want the sort of meaning described by Ayer's own subjectivist spin on it and we might realize of ourselves that we weren't the sort of people who'd ever be as self-satisfied as Ayer himself was able to be as he reflected on his philosophical achievements. One of the reasons that might make us want the objectivist sort of meaning rather more than the subjectivist one is that we think it more worth wanting and as such more central to the sorts of concerns we had when we asked about the meaning of life. We wanted our lives to be more meaningful in the deeper senses even if they had to be less meaningful in the less-deep ones. That's what made us judge them more central. Our concerns are not indifferent to the desirability of the objects at which they direct themselves. For what it's worth, as my readers will have already discerned, that much is true of me. And, as I have said, in having this sort of higher-order desire, I am typical. So, as most of my readers will be able to discern, that much is true of them too. Again, we shall wish to rank.

So, even in advance of actually drawing it up, we are in a position to know that we shall wish to rank entries in the chart/list, at least roughly (persistent residual vagueness will prevent a completely determinate ordering). We might think of those higher up the chart as being the senses of the question that are determinately more central to our concerns as we ask the original question than are those that are lower down. And we are in a position to know that this task, while not effortless, is not entirely impossible. We have already begun it by considering a few examples and I have ventured how we might rank them.

There is an element of subjectivity to all of this of course, and we do well to note it before moving on. As has perhaps already become apparent owing to your differing in your intuitive rankings to the ones I have suggested would be mine, two people, each of whom are perfectly competent users of the language, might, if left to their own devices, construct two differently ranked lists. And, presumably most often at the bottom end, things on one list mightn't appear at all on the other. So, when I have been talking of the list that 'we' would have drawn up by the end of an idealized application of this method-ology, which list did I have in mind? Yours, mine, somebody else's? In short, none of them.

It seems to me very plausible that there is enough commonality in the concerns expressed across the community of competent language users who ask 'What is the meaning of life?' to set up an intersubjective list; we may call it the standard list. The standard list then might not be the list that is had by any actual individual. It is this list that I have had in mind when I have been talking of the list that 'we' would draw up. Why am I so confident from the armchair as it were (not having actually done the drawing up that I've been talking about) that there will be enough commonality in our concerns for such an intersubjective standard to emerge? Certainly that there is this commonality cannot be known entirely *a priori*. My main ground for this confidence is the cohesion of the literature on the topic of life's meaning. Certainly, we find in that body of literature many occasions when one author speaks past another, or has apparently altogether different concerns from another. But, it seems to me, we find more occasions – many more occasions – when one author speaks to another; has only slightly different, or even exactly the same, concerns as another. We may be able to – significantly, I haven't actually been able to do this – find two books that are nominally about life's meaning but yet that have no overlap at all in the concerns they address. But we certainly can easily find pairs of books that have considerable overlap and differ more in the relative impor-tance they assign to those concerns. The remarkable overlap obtains between works written in very different philosophical traditions – the analytic and continental, for example. Indeed, I think it would not be too much of an exaggeration to say that there is no greater difference in the concerns across those two traditions than there is within either one of them. The difference (which is assuredly great) is in the style of discussion in which these traditions treat of these shared concerns. This is not so in other areas. So, by way of contrast, 'the' topic(s) of personal identity as it (they) is (are) understood in the analytic tradition and as it (they) is (are) understood in the continental tradition has (have) widely different concerns, not just different styles of discussing the same concerns. The reading list for the topic as it occurs in a course in analytic metaphysics not only would have no overlap with the reading list for its namesake as it occurs in a course in continental metaphysics, but there'd be a very good reason behind that fact. If you tried to put the two into discussion, you'd see that they may, now and again, be using the same terms, but they have no significant common conceptual content. They are not asking the same questions, but approaching them differently. They are asking completely different questions. That is not, it seems to me, the case with literature on the meaning of life. In short, we may all be asking slightly different things when we ask 'What is the meaning of life?' But we are also all asking similar things and there's more similarity than there is difference. That's what's 'kept the topic together' in the way that metaphysics hasn't been kept together.

Having drawn up the standard list, a decision needs to be made about how to use it. Presumably (as it is very plausible that all of us, considered individually, will deviate from the standard somewhat), we shall wish to use the standard list in such a way as to allow that most deviations from it are linguistically permissible (that is, they do not signify a failure to understand the question). Using the standard list in this fashion is of course compatible with using it to say of some linguistically permissible lists that they are nevertheless determinately wrong. So, consider a list that has on it all the elements on the standard list, but inverts the order given to them by the standard – so that which would standardly be taken to be most central to our concerns (i.e. highest up the list) becomes least (i.e. at the bottom), that which would standardly be taken to be least central becomes most. Such a list is then permissible in the sense that a person who drew it up as indicative of his or her concerns when asking the question would not be showing by such a ranking that he or she had failed to understand the question. But, nevertheless, such a ranking would be determinately wrong by reference to the standard.[19] The standard then will be one by which some deviants can be said to be determinately mistaken in taking one sort of meaning to be more central than another, though equally some will not be able to be so shown. There will be indeterminacy here as elsewhere. This then is another case of the vagueness of the question, the dissatisfaction arising from which I have already discussed. So I will not go over that ground again.[20]

I said I would talk about two features of the chart-cum-list that may be predicted even prior to us having completed it. The first is that it will need to be a ranked chart/list of the meanings of life, ranked by reference to how central they appear (on synergistic reflection) to our original concerns in asking the question. The more central (and, on reflection, judged deep meanings of life) will be higher up. The second feature that I am about to talk about is that this ranking will need to be redone in a sense; there'll need to be what I shall call a second ranking or a re-ranking. While it is helpful to separate this second ranking out from the first conceptually – for the need for it arises for different reasons and generates different issues – the second ranking is not temporally or even procedurally secondary to the first ranking.

While in advance of actually conducting at least some part of the investigation that has led us to the results contained in such a chart, we cannot of course be sure that these answers to the question will not be completely separate – metaphysically and concep- tually – from one another, we rightly suspect that they will not be. This suspicion is well grounded. And this issue generates more difficulties than the first. It is what drives us to an amalgam polyvalence thesis, rather than a grab-bag one. These connections lead to 'clustering' on the list.

It is, we readily believe, a mere accident of language that the word 'bank' has two meanings – 'financial institution of a certain sort' and 'steeply inclined area of land'. We would thus not be at all surprised if the question 'How do you avoid ending up in a bank?', when disambiguated into 'How do you avoid ending up working in a financial institution of a certain sort?', as asked of his tutor by a student of Economics in his final year of study, and 'How do you avoid running your punt into the land at the edge of the river?', when asked of a friend by the same student in more carefree days, yielded two answers that had nothing whatsoever to do with one another. However, even before conducting our investigation into the various meanings of 'the' question of the meaning of life, it is hard to believe that it is a mere accident of language that has resulted in all these meanings being carried by what is, on the surface, one question. And, if we were to conduct the investigation, as I say, we would see that this suspicion is well grounded. We shall conduct the investigation to establish this in just a moment. For now, let us speak to what follows from it.

As we unpacked these various meanings, we would discover various sorts of relationship between the ways in which life in one of its senses may or may not have meaning in one of its senses. These relationships mean that the original question cannot be broken down into other questions the answers to which are then left floating entirely separate from one another, to be ordered in the chart merely by reference to their centrality to our original concerns when raising the question of life's meaning, or rather – as we should prefer – our original concerns after they have undergone a bit of reflection as a result of dialogue with the concerns of others and consideration of their relative deepness. As we looked down a chart drawn up using just that principle, we would find relationships such as the following: an individual's life can only have meaning in sense p if it also has meaning in sense q; but it can only have meaning in sense q if humanity's life in general has meaning in senses q and r. And so on. These sorts of relationships would pull these meanings of life into clusters. A new iteration of what we have called the 'synergistic' interaction between question and answer would need to be undertaken as a result of one finding oneself wanting to say things like 'I would have said that meaning in sense p was not very central to my concerns, whereas meaning in sense q was really central, but now I realize that one's life having meaning in sense p is a necessary condition of its having meaning in sense q I shall need to revisit that issue.' Indeed 'revisit' seems unlikely to be quite the right term; 'visit' seems likely to be more appropriate. There is likely to be even more persistent residual vagueness at this stage in the process of reordering the chart than there was at the first, as it is even less likely one will have a clear prior idea of how important and thus immovable by synergistic interaction and discovery of clustering one regards the centrality or lack of centrality of the various meanings of life one now finds conceptually and metaphysically related to one another.

This process will of course be complicated yet further by considerations of how the chart that one would have constructed if left to one's own devices is affected by one's accumulating knowledge of the charts that others would have constructed if similarly so left, by the need to reach the standard list. And, in this connection, an added complication is the need, when it comes to this second ranking, to give more weight to the charts of those who – like oneself – have discovered the connections between different meanings of life. At the first ranking, one will find oneself wanting to say things like 'I would have said that meaning of life p was not very central to my concerns, whereas meaning of life q was really central. However, now I see that, for the vast majority of people, meaning of life q is much less central than meaning of life p, I shall need to pull down q, relative to p, in constructing, as I am aiming to do, the standard list for the first ranking.' And, at the second ranking, one will also find oneself wanting to say things like 'I would have said (and still will say) that one's life being meaningful in sense p is made more important than I'd otherwise have thought by its being a necessary condition on its being meaningful in sense q, and, although most people wouldn't rate p as being as central to their concerns as I consequently do tend to rate it, I can see that that's only because most people haven't found this connection. Among those who, like me, have found the connection, the joint verdict is different. So I won't let the views of the majority on this issue count against my re-ranking in line with the minority who, like me, have spotted the connection and thus drawn the two senses closer together into a cluster.'

Of course, all of this will be difficult. However, on the plus side, some of the vagueness that was persistent at the earlier stage might be removed during this ranking. At the first ranking, one will find oneself saying things like 'I would have been very vague about how high up the list to put meaning of life a, but now I see that almost all people place it very high up, that helps me to see that I should place it very high up too.' And, at the second ranking, one will find oneself also saying things like 'I would have been very vague about how high up to put meaning of life q, but now I see that it's a necessary condition of meaning of life p and I was always very sure where to place p, that removes at least some of that vagueness.' So, for reasons of this sort, there will be vagueness lost as well as vagueness gained. While the vagueness gained in itself might leave one feeling dissatisfied anew with the results as they now found themselves reordered on the chart, again, as at the earlier stage, reflection on the source of this (vagueness in one's original question) should lead one to feel satisfied with any dissatisfaction so arising. And, as well as the loss of some vagueness, there is another reason for encouragement at this stage.

We are, by discovering these connections, edging over from the task of understanding our question to answering it, for we are moving from thinking uncritically about the relative centrality of various meanings of life to our collective concerns as we first asked the question 'What is the meaning of life?' to thinking critically about what should have been central to them. For we are now – when we move from what I am calling the first ranking to what I am calling the second ranking – counting for less the rankings of people who seem to be misinformed about the connections between the different senses. We are starting to understand the relative deepness of the various meanings of life. And, what is more, we are starting to appreciate the reasons for endorsing amalgam polyvalence over grab-bag polyvalence. For it is these connections – the logical and metaphysical ones – that make the amalgams. How so? To that question I now turn.

CHAPTER 7

At the end of the previous chapter we had reached the stage of imagining ourselves having completed what I called the second ranking of the chart-cum-list that we have been thinking of as representing our final answer to the question of the meaning of life, i.e. the most definitive answer that we can reasonably expect we could – in an idealized case – achieve. I suggested that at this stage we would be finding ourselves with reasons to endorse amalgam polyvalence. It has been a chapter or so since I defined amalgam polyvalence. Forgive me then if I start this chapter by repeating what it is. It is the view that while there are genuinely distinct meanings of life, i.e. genuinely distinct sorts of meaning that an individual life or life in one or more of its other senses may have, at least some of these meanings of life are non-causally related to one another in what we might call supportive or inclusive ways. (Grab-bag polyvalence is the view that they are not related at all, other than perhaps causally.) Thus, on our chart/list as it appears after what I am calling the second ranking, some meanings cluster together. By 'supportive' or 'inclusive' relationships, I mean relationships such that having one sort of meaning of life entails – either logically or metaphysically – something positive about having another. The clearest sort of relationship of this sort would be logical implication, e.g. where an individual life's having meaning in sense a strictly implies that it has meaning in sense b. (And then there's the metaphysical correlate of this – e.g. where an individual life's having a meaning in sense x metaphysically necessitates that it have it in sense y.) But there are weaker sorts of support than this. For example, if a life's having a meaning in sense p was a necessary, but not a sufficient, condition of its having meaning in sense q, that would be a supportive relationship as I am understanding it of p to q (obviously this is an entailment in the other direction, from q to p).

Assuming then the case for polyvalence has been made in previous chapters, the case for amalgam polyvalence is thus made in part by revealing non-causal relationships of the right sort, ones that entail support between differing sorts of meaning or meaning of the same sort when held by life at different levels of generality (a period or aspect of an individual's life, an individual's life as a whole, humanity's life, or biological life per se). Discovering supportive connections of the logical/metaphysical sort then forms one part of the case for eschewing a grab-bag polyvalence and endorsing in its stead an amalgam polyvalence. (The other part, which I shall come to in a moment, is discovering relationships of mutual undermining.[1])

We've already seen some examples of supportive relationships in passing. But some further examples would be helpful at this stage, I think, both to illustrate the substance of the claim and justify it yet further. Of course, technically even one example suffices to prove it. I'll give three or four in what follows. I like to be thorough.

One concern we have about an individual's life when we ask about its meaning is whether or not there is something in that life that is desirable or valuable in itself, a thing that makes that life worth living, worth going on with, for the individual concerned. That is, I hope it can be seen without argument, a sort of meaningfulness that is quite central to our concerns when we ask the question 'What is the meaning of life?' It's a sort of meaning that is quite desirable or – as I have been putting it – deep. So, it'll be quite high up the chart/list we are imagining as representing our final answer to the question 'What is the meaning of life?'

Taylor, in discussing the case of Sisyphus, says that 'Even if we suppose, for example, that the stone is but a pebble that can be carried effortlessly, … not the slightest meaning is introduced'[2] to the life of Sisyphus. It is not the pain attending the physical effort that makes Sisyphus's life meaningless (although if we suppose pain, it certainly makes it worse). But it is the fact that it never comes to anything. As Taylor goes on, 'if we supposed that these stones, instead of rolling back to their places as if they had never been moved, were assembled at the top of the hill and there incorporated, say, in a beautiful and enduring temple, then the aspect of meaninglessness would disappear. His labors would then have a point, something would come of them all, and although one could perhaps still say it was not worth it, one could not say that the life of Sisyphus was devoid of meaning altogether. Meaningfulness would at least have made an appearance, and we could see what it was.'

Taylor supposes that if Sisyphus had instilled in him an unquenchable desire to push stones up hills, one thus perfectly satisfied by his daily toil, this would be 'merciful'; 'his life is now filled with mission and meaning'. But Taylor actually qualifies this claim almost as soon as he has made it: Sisyphus's life 'has now gained not the least shred of meaningfulness'. As he goes on, 'an existence that is objectively meaningless, in this sense [achieves no purpose], can nevertheless acquire a meaning for him whose existence it is' (affording him pleasure).

Taking our cue from Taylor, the idea of meaning as being something about one's life that makes it worth going on with can then be given an objectivist spin or a subjectivist one, marking out two different sorts of meaningfulness. I shall argue that they are two different sorts by showing that either can be present without the other. That having been done, I shall then argue for a relationship of support between them, in this case the relationship is that having one is a necessary condition of having the other. ('Huh?' I can almost hear my reader thinking. An immediate question will be how, if either can be present without the other, one can *possibly* be a necessary condition of the other. The answer, to give away the trick by which I'll pull this particular rabbit out a hat, is that when one is present in one mode it is a necessary condition of the other; when it is present in the other mode, it is not. It is in that second mode then that one can be present without the other. Obviously a lot turns on this, so I'll go into it in more detail later. But I wanted to say something of it now so that I could at least acknowledge the thought behind the 'Huh?' and provide some reassurance to my reader now that those worries will be addressed.)

The objectivist spin on the idea is of the sort of meaningfulness that a life gets in virtue of having something in it that is desirable (even if not desired) or valuable (even if not valued) in itself, a thing that does make that life worth living (even if it is not perceived to do so), worth going on with, for the individual concerned. Good candidates for features that can give a life meaning in this sense are the sorts of things one might find oneself wishing to draw to the attention of a friend who one finds contemplating suicide on the ledge at the top of a tall building. 'You've got everything to live for!' one shouts. 'Like what?' he replies. The list of things in his life that one would then give is the list of things that ground, one supposes, this sort of meaningfulness in his life. Perhaps he has a happy family life, including young children who love him and need him. Perhaps he is rightly admired by colleagues and friends for his many virtues. Perhaps he is on the cusp of some amazing discovery – the answer to the question of the meaning of life, say (after all, he has a copy of this book in his possession; all he needs to do is come in and read it). And so forth. Your friend's life is already meaningful in this objectivist sense then, even though he doesn't at the moment realize that it is. And your hope is that you'll get him to realize that it is by giving him this list, thus making what are sometimes called 'objective reasons' for him to live what are also sometimes, by contrast, called 'subjective reasons' for him to live. There is also then a subjectivist spin on the idea.

The subjectivist spin on the idea is of the sort of meaningfulness that is lacking in the life of the suicidal friend we have just imagined and what you're trying to generate in him by your telling him what he has to live for. It's the sort of meaningfulness that a life gets from its appearing to the person living it to be desirable or valuable in itself (whether or not it really is desirable or valuable in itself), a thing or things that makes or make that life appear to be worth living, worth going on with, to the individual concerned (even if it or they do or do not in fact make that life worth living, worth going on with, for him or her).

If one is even moderately optimistic about the human condition, one believes that most people have a meaningful life in this sense in the objectivist sense. It's not that suicide is a choice towards which the majority should be positively disposed, or even indifferent. However, one's knowledge that a very great number of people suffer from depression of a sufficiently deep sort to make suicide attractive to them is sufficient for one also to know that sadly far from everyone has a meaningful life in this sense in the subjectivist sense. We have imagined a friend who had an objectively meaningful life in this sense but a subjectively meaningless one already. A good candidate for a life that has meaning of this sort in the subjectivist sense but not in the objectivist one can also be imagined.

Consider an obsessive collector of miniature teapots. He is insular, friendless; he spends his days in his warehouse-like home trawling the internet for miniature teapots to add to his collection. The only other ornament amongst the shelves of miniature teapots in his home is a small plaque on which he once carved his motto: 'Whoever dies with the most miniature teapots wins!' He thus – as a means to the end of collecting as many miniature teapots as possible – keeps himself fit and healthy; he eats well; he exercises; and so forth. Occasionally, so as to recharge himself for more collecting, he writes a bad-tempered letter to the editor of the magazine *Miniature Teapot Collector*, making some pedantic point about an article or some such in its previous edition.

Such a person's devotion to the task of amassing the greatest set of miniature teapots possible *ante-mortem* obviously gives his life meaning in the subjective sense we have characterized. It appears to him that there is something in his life that makes it worth going on with, *viz.* collecting miniature teapots. His 'philosophy', if we may honour the principle articulated by his motto with that name, propels him from bed each morning to spend his days assiduously doing the only thing he thinks ultimately worthwhile – collecting miniature teapots. He gets no enjoyment from any of this, but he persists with it nonetheless. After all, as his motto tells him, it's not whoever dies having most *enjoyed* having had a collection of miniature teapots who wins, but rather whoever dies with the most miniature teapots who wins. But while this person thus has a meaningful life in the subjectivist sense, he does not seem to me to have it in the objectivist sense. There is in fact nothing in his life that makes it worth going on with, or, if there is, it is the very 'thin' fact that he could change – it's worth his continued living because he might one day do something that makes his continued living worthwhile. But, as I say, that seems to me very 'thin', and not enough if in fact the potential is never actualized. If in fact he gets to the end of his life and has never really done anything but collect miniature teapots, I would say his life will have been completely meaningless in the objectivist sense we have just characterized. It will have been so whilst being very meaningful in the subjectivist sense, more meaningful indeed in this sense than the average and thus I hazard most of my readers' lives.

At one stage, Dilman says this: 'Sometimes it seems to one that there is not much meaning in another person's life though one knows that the person himself doesn't think so. Here one may be inclined to attribute this appearance to one's own short-sightedness and arrogance and to make what the person himself thinks and says the criterion of whether there is meaning in his life or not. Yet it may well be a mistake to follow this inclination. Could one not, in all humility, say to another person, "If I know you at all, if you are the sort of person I think you are, you are really wasting your life and you don't like it yourself. You don't get much out of the life you lead, you don't put much into it. The way you spend your time must seem rather futile and pointless to you, however unwilling you may be to recognise it"? Socrates may have talked to Alcibiades along these lines. As Alcibiades puts it in the Symposium: "He compels me to realise that I am still a mass of imperfections and yet persistently neglect my own true interests by engaging in public life. So against my real inclination I stop up my ears and take refuge in flight …" But, of course, one's suspicions may be unfounded, he may not be the sort of person one thought he was. Or one may have dismissed the way of life as meaningless without regard to the person whose life it is. What one should have said was: "To me that way of life would be meaningless. I couldn't live that way." But this is not to say that the other person's life is meaningless. So our idea that if a person thinks that his life is meaningful then we cannot have reason to think otherwise is false though it contains an important truth. That truth is that we cannot separate a life from the person whose life it is and judge the life by our own personal standards—standards that we apply to our own life.'[3] Now, one doesn't have to agree with all of this to see truth in the point that one can suppose that of some senses of meaningfulness, at least, a person's self-reports

– however sincere – of their life's being meaningful may be mistaken. And such is the case, I think we'll agree, with the obsessive collector of miniature teapots. He certainly has subjective meaning. He certainly believes himself to have objective meaning. But, in his belief that his life has objective meaning, he is mistaken.

These then are two sorts of meaningfulness; that they are two is shown by the fact that I have just illustrated – a life can have either one of them without having the other. Now I need to make the case for there being a relationship of support between them. Indeed I have said that I will make the case for one being a necessary condition of the other. To return to the immediate question that must be raised of me at this stage: how *can* I hope to do this (given that I've already shown that a life can have either one without having the other)? Had I merely shown that a life could have say the first without having the second (but not that a life could have the second without having the first), then the way would be open for me to argue that the first was a necessary condition of the second. But I have not done that. I've shown that a life can have either one and at the same time not have the other. So surely, I'm hoisted on my own petard now. As already briefly indicated, the answer comes with the mode distinction that I introduced earlier.

In order to make this argument persuasive, first then I need us to note that the distinction between the objective sort of meaning just characterized and the subjective one is not a case of a sort we have already considered – there being one sort of meaningfulness that can be had in two 'modes', as I have been putting it, *viz.* the *simpliciter* mode and the for-the-individual-concerned mode. I need us to note that it is not that objective meaning in this sense is the *simpliciter* mode of a given sort of meaning and subjective meaning is the for-the-individual-concerned mode of that same sort because I need these to be accepted as two different sorts of meaning (not thought of as one sort being had in two modes) for my argument that then links them to support amalgam polyvalence. We are in a position to note this now as it is shown by the fact that you can have subjective meaning without objective – as the case of the obsessive miniature teapot collector shows – whereas in the case of a sort of meaning that shows this sort of modality, one cannot have meaning in the for-the-individual-concerned mode without having it in the *simpliciter* mode. The obsessive miniature-teapot collector believes he has objective meaning in the for-the-individual-concerned mode, but we see from the outside that he is mistaken. So this is not just another case of there being one sort of meaning that is capable of being had in two modes. Nevertheless, we can see a place for the deployment of the 'mode' distinction again.

The objectivist sort of meaning comes in two modes, the *simpliciter* mode and the for-the-individual-concerned mode, and, in that second mode it is a variety of the subjectivist sort of meaning – in the way that knowledge is a variety of belief. So, we can then say that one's life having meaning in the subjectivist sense of this sort of meaning just characterized (its seeming to the person concerned that there is something in it that makes it worth going on with) is a necessary condition of its having meaning in the objectivist sense in the for-the-individual-concerned mode (its *correctly* seeming to them that there is something in it that makes it worth going on with). Suppose one's life is meaningful in the objectivist sense and one comes to believe this of it. It then becomes meaningful in this sense for one, which will entail its becoming meaningful in the subjectivist sense too. But, as already mentioned, the example of the miniature teapot collector shows that one's life can become meaningful in the subjectivist sense without its having meaning in the objectivist sense at all, so subjectivist meaning cannot simply be objectivist meaning in the for-the-individual-concerned mode – there is no objectivist meaning at all in that case. That then shows a logical relation between two sorts of meaning. Objectivist meaning in the for-the-individual-concerned mode entails subjectivist meaning, though subjectivist meaning does not entail objectivist meaning either in the for-the-individual-concerned mode or in the *simpliciter* mode. As I said earlier, one instance suffices to prove the point: the different sorts of meaningfulness are not then all entirely separate as grab-bag polyvalence would assert. At least two are tied together in this way. Some version of amalgam polyvalence must be true.

Now it could be argued that this is all an artefact of my choosing to talk of certain types of meaning as being unitary yet displaying two different modes (the *simpliciter* mode and the for-the-individual-concerned mode), rather than of these as cases of two types of meaning and that talking of two types of meaning in these cases would better carve reality at the joints. If that is right, then my argument above falls apart. To that I have no need to object and, in this context, this alternative way of thinking would actually help me in making the case for amalgam polyvalence (albeit not via the argument I've just sketched, which would indeed, as I concede, fall apart). If meaningfulness of a particular sort *simpliciter* and meaningfulness of that sort in the for-the-individual-concerned mode, as I have been putting it, would in fact best be thought of not as one sort of meaningfulness being had in two modes, but rather as two different sorts, then we already have an amalgam of two different sorts of meaningfulness whenever we come across what I am calling one sort that is capable of displaying these two modes. We already have it because, to keep putting it in my terms, having a given sort of meaning in the *simpliciter* mode is a necessary condition of having it in the for-the-individual-concerned mode. There are several sorts of meaningfulness that are capable of displaying what I am inclining to call these two modes (we've already looked at enough to know this), so there are several amalgams.[4] In other words, my way of talking earlier (and which I am sticking with now) makes my case for amalgam polyvalence (and indeed for their being multiple amalgams, which case I would also be happy to make [though it is inessential to my developing argument]) harder to make than would the alternative way of talking. One way or another then, the case for amalgam polyvalence is made.

Now consider another sort of meaning, one that we have already briefly sketched – the meaning that some individuals' lives have in the sense of their standing for a particular idea. I take it that this is obviously a sort of meaning that an individual's life might have that is a different sort of meaning from any of those just spoken about. However, equally obviously, for a life to be meaningful in this sense for the individual concerned, it must be meaningful in the subjectivist sense of the sort of meaning we have just characterized. The person living it must feel/believe it worth going on with. If so, the subjectivist sense of meaning just characterized is a necessary condition of meaning in the sense of standing for an idea in the for-the-individual-concerned mode. Now it is important as always in this context to note that this is not causal dependency/necessity. It's not that, as a contingent matter of fact, one cannot cause oneself to commit to an idea in this sort of way if one cannot cause oneself to want to continue on with life at all (although something in this area is probably true, or as true as psychological generalization ever gets to be). But the truth to focus on here is that not even God could make one and the same person be a person who commits their life to an idea to such an extent that it shapes all other commitments and thereby makes their life meaningful in the sense of standing for that idea and meaningful in this sense for them, yet also not be a person who feels/believes of their life that there is something in it such that it makes their life worth going on with and thereby be a person whose life has meaning in the subjectivist sense of meaning we have just discussed. Of course one can die for an idea, but we are talking now about living for one. We are talking about one's life standing for an idea, not one's death standing for an idea. And so it is conceptually necessary that to have meaning in the sense of one's life standing for an idea, in the for-the-individual-concerned mode, one's life must have meaning in the sense of there apparently being something in it that makes it worth going on with for one. As I just said, one's life having meaning in the sense given by the subjectivist sense just characterized is a necessary condition for one's life having meaning in the sense of standing for an idea. This then is another instance of support between two different sorts of meaningfulness. If a life is meaningful in the one sense, it must – of logical necessity – be meaningful in another. One instance is enough to prove the point and we now have two. The different sorts of meaningfulness are not all entirely separate as grab-bag polyvalence would assert. Rather, some version of amalgam polyvalence must be true. At the risk of laying it on too thick, here's a third case.

Consider these two sorts of meaningfulness that an individual's life may have: first, meaningfulness in the sense of fulfilling a purpose in an appropriate larger scheme of things and, second, meaningfulness in the sense of knowing one is fulfilling a purpose in an appropriate larger scheme of things.[5] Again, this is not the place to deploy the meaningfulness *simpliciter* and meaningfulness for-the-individual-concerned distinction. And again it is important that it is not. If it was, then, given the way I have been setting these things up, we would be considering an example of one sort of meaningfulness in two different modes, the *simpliciter* mode and the for-the-individual-concerned mode. And again I want this to be an example of two genuinely distinct sorts of meaningfulness so that, when I show how they are related conceptually so as to be supportive, we get once more reason thereby to endorse amalgam polyvalence over grab-bag polyvalence. Again though, I should stress that I can meet the counterargument that these results are only obtained as a consequence of my adopting a manner of speaking of various sorts of meaningfulness being unitary whilst yet being capable of being had in different modes and that a manner of speaking that would better carve value reality at the joints would have it that these are really cases of two distinct sorts of meaningfulness. I can concede that (for the sake of argument), for, if it is right, then we can already see we have as many different amalgams as there are sorts of meaningfulness that have this sort of modality, as I'm calling it. Proceeding then in the manner of talking that I favour, let me spend a moment or two first showing that it is not a case of the distinction between a given sort of meaningfulness *simpliciter* and that same sort for the individual concerned. Then I'll show that it is a case of an amalgam. And then, to top it off, I'll make this third example into a fourth. I'll show that a supporting relation holds between it and the amalgam we've already introduced.

Consider the following scenario. You are a soldier fighting on the right side in a just war. Whilst out on patrol, your commanding officer wisely judges that the military necessities are such as to require one soldier to go ahead in front of the rest of the platoon towards, it is supposed, the enemy. That way, if the enemy are there, they will reveal their position by firing on that soldier. The rest of the platoon will be safe and able to respond appropriately. Your commanding officer explains all of this to you and then tells you that you are to be that soldier. So, your walking ahead of the rest of your platoon has a meaning in this sense; it has a purpose in an appropriate larger scheme of things. Your doing this will be making your life more meaningful in this sense than it would have been if you hadn't been chosen, *ceteris paribus*. (This is revealed by the fact that if you die doing your duty here, we would not say of your death that it was a meaningless one and would cite the military function you were performing in support.) It has this sort of meaningfulness *simpliciter* then. And you know this about it, so it has meaning in the sense of knowingly fulfilling a purpose in an appropriate larger scheme of things. But that seems to me *in*sufficient for its having meaning in this sense for you. And, that being so, knowingly fulfilling a purpose in an appropriate larger scheme of things cannot be fulfilling a purpose in an appropriate larger scheme of things in the for-the-individual-concerned mode. To see this, let us further suppose that you are in fact a coward. You know your side is the right side and the war is just, but you – quite naturally, if not commendably – just don't care about any of that. All you care about is saving your own life. That then would, I think, prevent your contribution to the military success of your platoon being meaningful for you. You would not be able, as I have been putting it, to appropriate to yourself the meaning-giving purpose that your commanding officer had assigned to you. You could still go forward as ordered (perhaps only if your commanding officer pulls out his pistol and points it at you telling you he'll shoot you himself on the spot for cowardice unless you go forward). But you couldn't, by going forward under such threats, be counted as appropriating to yourself your C.O.'s purposes; it would be your purpose (of saving your own life) that would still be behind your doing whatever it is you end up doing.

Obviously one can have the sort of meaningfulness that is fulfilling a purpose in an appropriate larger scheme of things without having the sort of meaningfulness that is *knowingly* fulfilling a purpose in an appropriate larger scheme of things. In the example as given, the commanding officer explains his rationale to you before sending you forward, but there is no necessity that he do so. He could just send you forward with no explanation whatsoever and you not work out his meaning-giving purpose yourself. With such an alteration to the example, it would then be the case that your walking ahead of the rest of the platoon would give your life meaning in the sense of your fulfilling a purpose in an appropriate larger scheme of things but not give your life meaning in the sense of your knowingly fulfilling a purpose in an appropriate larger scheme of things. However, obviously, one cannot have the sort of meaningfulness that is knowingly fulfilling a purpose in an appropriate larger scheme of things if there just *is* no purpose one is fulfilling in an appropriate larger scheme of things. The second conceptually requires the first; knowledge conceptually requires truth. These then are two sorts of meaningfulness with a conceptual connection – one's a necessary condition of the other. Here then is an amalgam. Two examples were twice the number needed to make the case. Now we have a third.

It is worth pausing to note an issue that has perhaps been slightly misrepresented (or at least underrepresented) in the case as presented thus far. I have spoken of a situation in which you as a soldier fulfil a purpose in an appropriate larger scheme of things and of your doing that as your making your life meaningful in that sense. More precise would have been had I said that your doing that made that period of your life in which you were doing it meaningful in that sense. Even more precise would have been had I said that it made that aspect of that period of your life that was your fulfilling this military function meaningful in that sense. (It didn't, after all, make meaningful your wearing the particular underpants that that you happened to be wearing during the same period but which, I am taking it, had no connection with your military function.) Whether or not your life as a whole is meaningful in the sense of fulfilling a purpose in an appro-priate larger scheme of things is left undetermined by the fact, which I am assuming, that the relevant aspect of this period of your life is made meaningful in this sense. To see this, suppose that you are in fact a coward because you are the obsessive miniature-teapot collector characterized earlier. There are just no teapots at issue in this war, only things that threaten teapots and your ability to collect them. Your life as a whole then, very plausibly,[6] is overall meaningless in the sense where to be meaningful one must be fulfilling a purpose in an appropriate larger scheme of things, even though that aspect of that short period of your life you spend doing this is not meaningless in that sense. So, that an aspect of a period of a life has the property of meaningfulness in this sense doesn't entail that the whole of the life does so. But it seems to me it supports the whole of the life doing so in a weaker way than entailment. We can see this by reflecting on the fact that the more aspects/periods of your life that get meaningfulness in this sense, the stronger the case will be for the whole of your life having meaningfulness in this sense, and stronger by virtue of logic, not causality. Other senses of meaningfulness also clearly allow this sort of support between the level of an aspect of a period of a life and the level of the whole of a life.

So, return to the sort of meaning that is its appearing to one that one has something in one's life that makes it worth going on with, worth living. Again, it seems to me that having that sort of meaning – that feeling – for just a fleeting moment or two in one's life is insufficient for making one's life as a whole meaningful in the sense that it characterizes. By way of illustration, consider a pupil of mine who suffers from clinical depression and has done so all of his life. He has never felt that there was anything in it that made it worth continuing with *except* for five all-too-brief minutes when, during a tutorial, I entertained him with an anecdote concerning academic life. For those five minutes, it did appear to him that there were lots of things in his life that made it worth continuing on with. But then our conversation moved back to the topic of the tutorial and he was left back where he'd been beforehand. When we consider the life of such a person as a whole, it seems to me, it cannot be truly said to have been meaningful in the sense of seeming to be worth going on with for the person concerned, even though five minutes of it were. However, parts of one's life having this sort of meaningfulness are supportive of the whole having it in that if there are enough of them, then they add up to give the whole this sort of meaningfulness too – and add up to this effect of logical necessity. If *every* waking moment of a given person's life is meaningful in this subjective sense, then the whole *has* to be so too, of logical necessity. So here's another sort of supporting relationship, this one tying together not two sorts of meaning-fulness but meaningfulness of one sort when present in a period of an individual's life to meaningfulness of the same sort when present in the individual's life as a whole. It doesn't seem to me to be a fallacy of composition to reason that if every moment of a given individual's life is subjectively worth going on with to them, then their life as a whole – as the aggregate of such moments – is subjectively worth going on with to them. So that's another sort of connection that will draw together into a cluster senses in which life in one or more of its senses can be meaningful in one or more of its senses.

Another example of the same phenomenon. Perhaps I am destined with this work to make a meaningful contribution to Philosophy; I like to think so. If so, then that makes what would be in themselves meaningless minor tasks, each of which makes a negli-gible contribution to completing it – looking up an inessential yet worthy-of-inclusion quotation in someone else's work; fine-tuning an endnote, so that it best expresses a small but correct caveat to a point made in the main text – become meaningful as they contribute to this project. Individual five-minute periods within my working life become meaningful when they would not otherwise have been so because they are included within that section of my working life that is devoted to completing this book. An individual five-minute period of my working life of this sort might be such that it can only have meaning if it is in this way included in a meaningful larger part. If I spend five minutes finding a reference for a quotation that in the end I don't use, that five minutes remains meaningless. Sometimes then, the meaningfulness of shorter periods can be generated by the larger whole. This is another case of amalgamation – a conceptual connection between meaningfulness in one sense when had at one level of life (a period) and meaningfulness in that same sense when had at another level (the whole or a larger period).

Indeed the lives of artists whose work is unappreciated in their lifetimes, but who, perhaps many years after their death, are recognized as geniuses, gain meaningfulness by this *post-mortem* recognition. Van Gogh is often mentioned in this connection. Not all sorts of meaningfulness then are what we might call 'hard facts'; some are 'soft'. Whether or not it is true of me now that I have more than a hundred thousand hairs on my head is a hard fact, made to be as it is by the state of my head now. Whether or not it is true of me now that I have more than a hundred thousand hours left to live is by contrast is a 'soft' fact, depending on what happens in the future. Whether or not the minutiae of scholarly activities that go into writing a book have meaning depends on the final text. Whether or not my life now has meaningfulness in the sense of significance depends on what happens later.

It is worth pausing to note that the amalgam on which we've latterly focused is conceptually related to the one discussed in the first two examples. Fulfilling a purpose in an appropriate larger scheme of things is, it seems to me, sufficient for (though not necessary for) there being something in life that makes it worth going on with for the individual concerned in the objectivist sense. (It's not sufficient for it in the subjectivist sense, as the example of the thought experiment of you as the cowardly soldier shows.) That then is another example of a connection arguing in favour of amalgam polyvalence over grab-bag polyvalence. One example would prove the point. We're now up to at least four or five. I really am laying it on thick. I should move on.

Given that all the meanings of life we've looked at in our examples so far in this chapter amalgamate together, one might naturally wonder if *all* the meanings of life amalgamate together. If they do so, then the danger of monism arises[7] – so, naturally, I shall deny that they do so. But an alternative – compatible with polyvalence – is that all that cluster, cluster into one amalgam, leaving the rest separate outside. Again, prior to completing the chart/list that we have been imagining as representing the least unsatisfactory answer to the question of the meaning of life as is possible, it is hard to address this issue definitively. But I wish to canvass the possibilities at this stage. Amalgam polyvalence per se allows that there could be just one cluster, but it also allows that there could be several. My own view is that there are several. It is not that a certain number of the different meanings of life cluster together, reflecting an amalgam as I am putting it, and that the sorts that do not fit in there are each left unconnected to each other except perhaps causally. To establish that there are several amalgams I'd need to go through another example showing amalgamation and then show the lack of conceptual or metaphysical connection between that amalgam and another, say the amalgam I've already discussed. And I won't do that now. For now then, I'll leave the issue, by merely pointing out two things. First, it is implausible that all cosmic meanings of life will amalgamate (at least with individualistic ones). Second, nothing in my argument turns on whether or not single-amalgam polyvalence turns out to be true rather than multiple-amalgam polyvalence. Of course, to repeat, my view does commit me to the view that not *all* the meanings of life amalgamate into one, because – as already indicated – for that to happen would be for polyvalence to be shown to be false and monism true. But I can show that that doesn't happen without showing multiple amalgams. I can show it in the manner of the next chapter, by showing that some meanings of life – even some of the individualistic ones – just can't be amalgamated with others.

In closing this chapter, let us go back to imagining ourselves with the chart/list of all the various questions of the meaning of life that we have broken our original question into and, besides each question, its answer or an explanation of why we are not in a position to know the answer. And let us imagine ourselves having completed what I am calling the second-ranking stage of constructing this list of the meanings of life. We are now in a position to see that, at the second ranking, some of the relationships we will have become aware of will draw together into clusters senses in which life in one or more of its senses could be meaningful in one or more of its senses, leading us to pull certain meanings of life together and move them collectively up or down the list. In this chapter I hope I've done enough to show that there is at least one such cluster, reflecting there being at least one amalgam of meanings of life. (And latterly I have suggested – but not argued for – the thesis that there are several.)

As well as some of the conceptual and metaphysical relationships between the different meanings of life pulling some of them together, some would do the opposite. They would drive wedges between differing senses in which life in one or more of its senses could be meaningful in one or more of its senses. It is from this point – that some would do the opposite – that yet another spring of potential dissatisfaction bubbles up. As we redrew the chart at the stage of the second ranking, we would realize that there is no way for life in every sense of that term to be fully meaningful in every sense of that term and this is a qualitatively new source of dissatisfaction, in that it is dissatisfaction stemming from one's appreciation of features *of meaning* and *of life*, not a feature of the question one is asking about them. To become satisfied with one's dissatisfaction with answers to the question of the meaning of life as they emerge from this source then would require a quite different move from any canvassed heretofore. Fortunately, such a move can be made. But these are issues that we need to spend a moment or two appreciating, and appreciating what follows from them, if we are ever to be satisfied with the dissatisfaction that stems from them. We shall turn to this task in the next chapter.

CHAPTER 8

The sort of issue that I closed the previous chapter by discussing is, I think, best illuminated by returning to consider the issue of what God brings to the party and what he takes away.

There are obviously three broad views possible on the relationship between Theism and the possibility or actuality of meaningfulness in human lives. We have come across the first two already. The first I am calling 'optimism'; it is the view that Theism's being true contributes (or, assuming it is false, would contribute) to meaningfulness. The second, I am calling 'pessimism'; it is the view that it detracts (or would detract). The third I have not discussed. One may call it 'neutralism'; it is the view is that it doesn't (wouldn't) affect things either way either because it doesn't/wouldn't affect it at all or because the effects do/would cancel out. It is worth stressing again that these are very broad views and that there is consequently much potential for nuance internal to each of them. One variant of the optimistic view that is worth drawing out for attention once more would have it that God not merely contributes to meaningfulness, but is necessary for there to be any at all. Another variant, which I'll come to in a moment as the majority view among theists, is that, absent God, we might yet have some shallow or transient meaning in our lives, but we couldn't pass a threshold or obtain the type of meaning that we have most reason to care about.[1] As well as the potential for nuances internal to each of the three broad views, there is the potential for nuanced combinations. So, one might hold the view that Theism's being true would contribute for some but detract for others.[2] Or one might be drawn to the view that I myself will argue for: while a net contributor to the meaningfulness of all human lives, Theism's being true contributes more to the meaningfulness of some people's lives than it does to others and it actually detracts in certain senses of meaningfulness from the meaningfulness of all. Having pointed out the potential for nuance, it is also worth noting that this potential is not fully actualized in the literature at present and it's hard to find anyone who argues (at least at length) for neutralism. The majority writing in the field have in fact been drawn to one of the simpler and more extreme views: Theism's being true is (or would be) an unqualified contributor to meaningfulness for all or it is (or would be) an unqualified detractor for all. Having argued in the previous chapter, via several examples, for amalgamation of various meanings of life, in order to meet the challenge that all meanings of life amalgamate and hence Monism (rather than Pluralism as I define it, aka Polyvalence) is true, I need now to show that one at least does not amalgamate. That's what I'll do in this chapter and the meaning of life I shall start with in this context is the one that I started this book by discussing.

Let us return then to the philosopher whose views we sketched briefly at the beginning of the book as paradigmatic of the pessimistic school of thought, Sartre. I now wish to outline Sartre's view in a bit more detail in the hope of rendering a more modest variant of it plausible.

In his lecture 'L'existentialisme est un humanism', Sartre contrasts the way in which a paperknife gets its meaning, *viz.* from the purpose had by its creator in creating it, with the way in which we humans may give our own lives meaning, by choosing for ourselves which purposes to adopt. We only have this freedom, he suggests, because we live in a Godless universe. The following is a famous passage from that work in which he outlines the view:

> If one considers ... for example ... a paper-knife ... one sees that it has been made by an artisan who had a conception of it ... Thus the paper-knife is ... an article ... which ... serves a definite purpose. ... Let us say ... that its essence ... precedes its existence. .... When we think of God as the creator, we are thinking of him ... as a supernal artisan. ... God makes man according to a ... conception, ... as the artisan manufactures a paper-knife ... [The] essence of man precedes ... existence ... [On the other hand,] if God does not exist there is at least one being whose existence comes before its essence ... That being is man ... Man is ... that which he makes of himself. ... [He] is [thus] of a greater dignity [than a paperknife] ... If ... it is true that existence is prior to essence, man is responsible for what he is. Thus, ... [atheistic] existentialism ... puts every man in possession of himself as he is, and places the entire responsibility for his existence squarely upon his own shoulders.[3]

It seems to me that in this passage – and elsewhere in his writings – Sartre hits upon an important sense in which a person's life may have more or less dignity, by which I shall be taking it he is most charitably[4] interpreted as meaning be more or less meaningful in a particular sense. It has it according to the degree of self-creative autonomy he or she enjoys. And Sartre makes a true point about it, *viz.* that, in this sense of meaningfulness even if no other, God detracts – were He to exist, would detract – from the meaningfulness of our lives. As Cottingham puts it when he discusses the view, none 'of us wants the meaning of our lives to depend on a superior agent whose purposes are at least partly opaque to us. For better or worse, we want to determine our own conditions for meaning; we want the right to map out the direction of our lives by reference to our own "conception of the good", not someone else's, however benign they may be.'[5]

As a prelude to defending a variant of Sartre's view, I should concede a little bit of ground: he rather overstates his case – here and elsewhere – in two ways.

First, Sartre overstates his case by suggesting that our lives can only be meaningful at all if we live in a Godless universe. Sartre assumes that, were God to exist, we would be reduced to the status of paperknives (or – my own preferred analogy – to the status of Junior Widget-Affixers). As already mentioned, this might be true if one adds to bare Theism a 'meticulous providence' view of God's plans for His creatures. On such a view, at its extreme, God has a plan for every aspect of our lives and a preferred option for every choice that faces us, however small. His purpose for us is that we have no area in which we may exercise self-creative autonomy whatsoever. All of our essence precedes our existence, as Sartre might have put it.[6] But there is obviously scope for adding to bare Theism an understanding of God's providential plan for us which is 'looser' than this and indeed such a looser understanding is commonplace. God's very purpose for us is in part that there be areas in which we may exercise the sort of self-creative autonomy that Sartre sees as essential for a certain type of meaningfulness. Many theists hold that, in his terms, the essence that precedes our existence is in part one whereby our existence precedes some of our essence. The extent of the 'looseness' within God's purposes for us is of course precisely the extent to which the theist may hope to mitigate the problem Sartre diagnoses without challenging its fundamental logic. Indeed, a peculiar sort of Deism, whereby God, though causally responsible for initiating the universe, created on a whim and has never had any purposes whatsoever for any of His creatures, would evade Sartre's problem entirely.

Second, Sartre overstates his case by suggesting that there are no other senses of meaningfulness that we may reasonably care about (if only by omitting to mention the possibility of other senses) and which God, were He to exist, might help us in achieving rather than limit our chance of achieving. Sartre seems to suppose that the sort of dignity generated by acts of self-creative autonomy is the only legitimate meaning of life. But of course I have argued that there are other senses. For the moment then, I wish to make the point that these two concessions – though cogent – should not be taken to detract from Sartre's achievement in hitting upon a sense of meaningfulness in human lives from which God detracts or – as Sartre would have preferred it – would detract were He to exist. God's existence, should He exist, is not unqualifiedly good news from the point of view of our lives being meaningful even if it is on balance good news. His existence is, one might say, a mixed blessing. This is the modified Sartrean thesis that I wish to defend in this chapter.

Let us ground ourselves in a mundane situation to see this Sartrean sense of meaningfulness in operation. Doing so will do two things. First, it will render in more vivid colours and thus make clearer the sort of meaningfulness that Sartre is talking about. Second, it will render it plausible that we value this sort of meaningfulness. Both of these are important because, as we have already seen in the case of Hitler, some sorts of meaningfulness we do not value (or at least do not value much) and I wish to forestall the thought that all positive sorts of meaningfulness amalgamate (leaving only neutral or negative ones behind). Were that to have been so, a good case could then have been made for saying that only very peripheral meanings of life fail to amalgamate and hence it would have been plausible to maintain that the ones that don't amalgamate may be discounted when considering the 'true' meaning of life, which true meaning hence can be considered monistically.

Imagine then that a friend of yours works at a car factory and that, one day, he says to you this: 'I'm resigning from my position as Junior Widget-Affixer, as it is a meaningless position, meaningless in the sense that I'm given no responsibility for designing any significant aspect of my role; all those details are laid down by Management.'

You would understand fully what your friend was saying to you and indeed think that, if the situation was more or less as he had described it, he was right in his analysis. His job really is meaningless in the Sartrean sense. The plans of others have limited his scope for permissible self-creation to vanishing point, at least in the workplace. You might of course wish to argue your friend out of his decision to resign. You might say, for example, 'But think of what the job means for your family – it means a roof over their heads and meals on the table.' However, in bringing this consideration or similar considerations forward you would, it seems to me, have to be doing one of two things, neither of which would fundamentally undermine Sartre's case.

The first thing you might be doing is using Sartre's sense of meaning, but disagreeing with your friend that the job really is meaningless in that sense. It might be that your friend's taking and staying in the job of Junior Widget-Affixer, while appearing meaningless if considered merely in its own terms, is a manifestation of a role over which he has taken responsibility in designing significant aspects, the role of provider for his family say. Thus, when described in these terms, it can be said to be meaningful. If so, then, from a larger perspective to which your friend may switch without self-deceit, the job may be said to be meaningful in the Sartrean sense even though if seen only from a narrower perspective to which he may also switch back without self-deceit, it would be said to be meaningless in that same Sartrean sense. That seems to me quite possible. Before moving on to consider the second thing you might be doing, it is worth reflecting on what one then goes on to do with the observation that it is possible as there are a number of ways of accounting for its possibility.[7]

One way of looking at what might then be going on is to think that the job's apparent meaninglessness in Sartre's sense in the smaller context is just that – merely apparent meaninglessness. It would have managed to be genuine meaninglessness were it not for the meaningfulness in Sartre's sense that it has in the wider context. The wider context 'overwhelms' the narrower one. It could be that what you are doing with your comments is simply encouraging your friend to switch to considering this wider context so as to realize this, to realize that he is just plain wrong.

Another way of looking at what might be going on is to think that perhaps there is no overpowering in the sense just sketched – the wider meaningfulness leaves the narrower meaninglessness intact. All you can be rightly doing is encouraging your friend to switch to viewing his situation from the wider context and see that it has wider meaningfulness in the Sartrean sense (even though it continues to have narrower meaninglessness in that same sense). In addition, you can be asserting that this wider meaningfulness has greater depth – is more to be desired – than the narrower meaning-lessness is undesirable. It doesn't nullify the narrower meaningfulness ('overwhelm' it, as I have been putting it), but it outweighs it. We don't need to decide between the two to make progress, so let's leave each on the table as possibilities for the moment.

The second thing you could be doing is using a different sense of meaning to the Sartrean sense that your friend had employed – meaning as significant positively evaluable consequence, perhaps. I have already argued that this as a plausible meaning of 'meaning'. So I will not repeat that argument. But if the meaningfulness of an action and thus an aspect or period of a person's life can be a matter of its bringing about valuable effects, then meaningfulness in a life in that sense can, it seems to me, be present to extents that are not perfectly correlated with meaningfulness in a life in Sartre's sense. Someone who does community service under duress (as a punishment) and someone who volunteers for the same community service may well produce the same evaluable consequences and in that sense then their efforts may be equally meaningful. But for one these actions have Sartrean meaning and for the other they do not. We can also see that this is a different sort of meaningfulness by adding details into the thought experiment concerning your friend, such that this sort of meaningfulness too becomes either determinately absent from or determinately present in that case as we imagine it, and by seeing as we do so that we do nothing to affect the degree of Sartrean meaninglessness present. (All of this is of course adding – by the by – to the case for polyvalence.) Let us then add such details.

First then, let us suppose that you happen to know this about the factory in which your friend works. After your friend has affixed widgets to the things that pass him on the conveyor belt, these things pass into another room where an equally depressed Junior Widget-Remover takes them off. Were you to know that, you would know that there was an added sort of meaninglessness (absence of significant positively evaluable consequence) to your friend's role, added that is to the sense of meaninglessness that Sartre has in mind. Second, let us suppose that instead you happen to know this about the factory. The widgets your friend is attaching are actually crucial parts of the cars to which he attaches them, cars that go out into the wider world and are used as small ambulances, being instrumental in saving many lives. That fact, were it to obtain, would seem to add this sort of meaningfulness to his activities, but it would not thereby affect the meaninglessness of his role in Sartre's sense.

So, if you are using a sense of meaning that equates meaningfulness with significant positively evaluable consequence, it seems to me that you might well be speaking truly when – using your sense – you say that the job is meaningful and yet your friend be speaking truly when he – using Sartre's sense – says that it is not. You are simply speaking past one another. Of course the fact that in the situation we are imagining you think it cogent to make your claim suggests the possibility that you suppose that yours is a sort of meaningfulness that outweighs, or perhaps even 'trumps' (is somehow lexically prior to), the Sartrean meaninglessness of your friend's job. But even so, you should not think that your friend's job having meaning in your sense makes it any less meaningless in Sartre's sense. In encouraging your friend to stay in his job in this fashion (in contrast to the first) you are not in any sense challenging the accuracy or fullness of his analysis of its meaninglessness in the sense of meaninglessness that he is using. You are just challenging its completeness as an analysis of its meaningfulness in all senses, by drawing on another sense of meaningfulness. Of course, as a defender of the polyvalence thesis, I think that this sort of talking-past one another is quite often the correct diagnosis of disputes concerning life's meaning. But it is worth noting that, even if it is, the disputes can still be substantial as they, on correct diagnosis, can turn out to be disputes about which sort of meaning is more desirable or, as I am putting it, 'deeper'. Be that as it may, it seems to me that we have seen no reason to think that there's not a determinate sense of 'meaning' that Sartre has hit upon, Sartrean meaning as we may call it, and that it is absent from your friend's current job in the car factory, assuming it is as he has described it to you. And I think, further, that we are in a position to see that it is a sense of meaning that we value in life. To see that we value it, let us suppose your friend continues as follows: 'By the way, I've been offered the position of Executive Vice-President on the senior management team at the company; were I to accept, I'd be in charge of long-term strategic planning and "blue skies" thinking. The pay and other conditions – pension and so forth – would be as with my old job as Junior Widget-Affixer.'

In that case you would surely unqualifiedly encourage your friend to resign from the first job and take up the second. This new job would mean the same in the sense of 'meaning' you were using – roof over family, meals on table – and, in addition, mean more in Sartre's sense. But that you'd encourage him to make this move, rather than be neutral with respect to him doing so or staying in his current job, suggests that you do value meaningfulness in Sartre's sense of meaningfulness, even if not much (if you'd have happily seen it trumped by meaning in the 'significant positively evaluable consequence' sense). So, one's life's having meaning in the determinate sense of meaning that Sartre has hit upon is, one thinks, its having something valuable. Of course one thought experiment and our imagined reactions to it are hardly proof of such claims, but they are, I think, indicative.[8] We do value meaningfulness in this Sartrean sense; we do value, as he puts it, existence preceding essence.

Sartre presumed that we live in a Godless universe. As already mentioned, this presumption appears to have been buried so deep in his psyche that he never felt the need to support it with anything but the briefest (and flimsiest) of arguments. We may disagree with him in this presumption and we may have argument on our side when we do so. But, even if we do, I contend that we should admit that the fact that we don't live in a Godless universe means that our lives are not as meaningful in the sense that Sartre has well marked out, not as meaningful in this sense as they would have been if, *per impossibile* then, Sartre had been right in his Atheism but everything else have been as close to the actual as is logically possible. As already conceded, if there is a God, then our positions mightn't yet be akin to that of paperknives, or even Junior Widget-Affixers. They might be more akin to those of Executive Vice-Presidents and thus we still have at least some – to some tastes, more than enough – meaning in Sartre's sense of meaning. And, as already conceded, it may be that the sorts of meaningfulness that God helps us achieve outweigh the loss in the Sartrean meaningfulness that, even with the loosest sort of purpose for us (short of the peculiar Deism I have mentioned), He cannot but force us to incur. The point is simply that we cannot have as much meaning in Sartre's sense as if Sartre had been right in his Atheism. And that, in itself, is bad for us. We won't be 'self-employed', as it were, free to style ourselves as President, Chairman of the Board, Chief Executive Officer, and anything else that might catch our fancy. At the most fundamental level – like it or not, realize it or not – we will be 'working' for someone else in the sense that there will be a God who has at least some purposes for us that are not as they are as a result of our choosing them for ourselves, but rather are as they are as a result of His choosing them for us. At least some of our essence will precede our existence.

This lack of ultimate self-creative autonomy is not something that theistic religions can fairly be accused of having hidden from us as an implication of their worldview. Jews would define themselves as the people who follow the will of God as revealed in the Torah and other authoritative teachings, the Talmud, Midrash, *et cetera*. Christians are those who seek to follow Christ, but follow him in what way? Not in his manner of dress or by speaking Aramaic, but rather in doing God's will. Muslims are, quite literally, 'those who submit' to the will of God, that will being taken to be revealed most authoritatively in the Koran, but also in the Hadith. Following a law one believes to have been written by God on tablets of stone thousands of years before one's birth; following someone one believes to have been the perfection of that law, the incarnation of God, and, as such, a model for all thereafter; humbly submitting oneself to the commands of God as revealed to, and in the life of, His messenger: none of these could strike one, even for a moment, as manners of living in which, as Sartre might have put it, one's own existence is being supposed to precede one's essence. Rather, each overtly supposes that a pattern has been laid down for us by another, God. This may not be a pattern for every detail of our lives. But it will be a pattern for at least significant areas of our lives, areas of our lives we may well find ourselves wishing we were more free over, indeed areas that, such religions are also unanimous in teaching, it is in our (at least post-lapsarian) *human nature* to wish ourselves more free over.

For example, each of these religions has a slightly different understanding of how marital relations are to be conducted and each allows significant elements of choice to families and individuals, over whether or not to marry at all; over whom individuals may marry, if they marry anyone; and over how individuals arrange themselves and their responsibilities within any marriage they enter into. But these religions speak with one voice on the issue of adultery. It is impermissible. It has not been left up to us to construct for ourselves, should we so choose, an essence whereby we are adulterers, the religion only instructing us to 'live authentically' by whatever choice on this issue we may happen to make. This is, of course, not the case on Sartre's view. Should one so choose, one could go in for some 'blue skies' thinking, indeed behaving, in this area as in all others. Man being responsible only to himself for his life, he is free to create for himself the essence of an adulterer and live accordingly. Such freedom is denied to those who subscribe to one of the theistic religions and thus very natural human urges will, on occasion, lead such people to feel alienated from certain aspects of the way of life they believe themselves to be compelled to lead. Furthermore, these aspects can be very significant to one's sense of self and to one's well-being as it is related to one's sense of self. This then is something that God takes away from the party.

I do not think, as some who follow Sartre do, that the problem arises from other-imposed purposes and their consequent constraints on our powers of self-creative autonomy being inherently *degrading* to the person imposed upon and constrained. This is why I have considered myself charitable in translating Sartre's worries about our dignity into ones about our lives' meaningfulness. Indignity and degradation seem to me to be notions that mischaracterize what it is that God threatens (would threaten were He to exist). I have already briefly addressed this point, but it is instructive in this context, I think, to consider in a bit more detail the extent (if any) to which other-imposed purposes are inherently undignifying or degrading to the person imposed upon and whether any such indignity or degradation inevitably vitiates them of meaning-for-the-individual-concerned value. I shall argue that they are not inherently undignifying or degrading and that, in any case, indignity and degradation doesn't necessitate vitiating other-imposed purposes of meaning-for-the-individual-concerned value.

As we have already seen, Baier suggests that it is inherently degrading to a person to have some purpose imposed on their lives, or even a period of their lives, by another.[9] He says this:

> To attribute to a human being a purpose in that sense is not neutral, let alone complimentary: it is offensive. It is degrading for a man to be regarded as merely serving a purpose. If, at a garden party, I ask a man in livery 'What is your purpose?' I am insulting him. I might as well have asked, 'What are you for?' Such questions reduce him to the level of a gadget, a domestic animal, or perhaps a slave. I imply that we allot to him the tasks, the goals, the aims which he is to pursue; that his wishes and desires and aspirations and purposes are to count for little or nothing. We are treating him, in Kant's phrase, merely as a means to our ends, not as an end in himself.[10]

This strikes me as so confused that it is difficult for me to know where to start with it, but it does contain some element of truth – if not an important truth, then a relevant half-truth. First, let us consider the issue of offending one of one's host's servants by asking him his purpose at a garden party. *Contra* Baier, it is not at all inherently offensive to suppose of a man whom one has securely identified by his manner of dress as a domestic servant on duty at a party that he has some function there. How could one *avoid* supposing that he served (or at least was intended to serve) a purpose having thus identified him? Nor is there anything inherently offensive then in asking him what this purpose is, *assuming one asks the question in the right fashion.*

Baier's imagined manner of posing what is potentially an inoffensive question is itself so artlessly brusque as to be verging on the offensive, we may agree. But this is in large part through its carrying with it a double implication, each part of which *would be* offensive to any right-thinking domestic servant. First, there is a 'conversational implicature' as it were that the person asking the question is doubtful that the person of whom it is asked has any purpose at all. Baier's manner of putting the question would make it natural for the person of whom it was asked to think that a suppressed '... because, frankly, you don't seem to be serving any purpose to me' clause was in the questioner's mind. Second, and relatedly, it is offensive owing to the fact that it would be a matter of pride on the part of a good domestic servant serving his master's or mistress's guests that these guests did not *need* to ask him his purpose, for, if he is serving it properly, they should be able to tell it instantly from looking at him, for he would be constantly performing it. If his purpose were to serve drinks, for example, he would have an apparently never-emptying tray of drinks in front of him offering them to the person who might otherwise not be sure what his purpose was.

Thus it is that if the issue of what purpose is served by a particular domestic servant has arisen in one's mind, it is indeed a delicate one to raise with the servant himself or herself – delicate, but not of insuperable delicacy. One might say, for example, 'Excuse me, I take it you're the butler? If so, may I ask if you'd be kind enough to …' In any case, none of the delicacy arises because it is inherently offensive to suppose that a person is a servant or that as a servant, he or she serves, or is intended to serve, some purpose. What might be offensive would be to suppose that a person is a servant and that, nevertheless, he or she is not serving the purpose that he or she is intended to serve. The person to whom Baier is contemplating asking such a question assuredly serves as some sort of functionary. He is in livery, after all. And, one must presume, on application of the principle of charity towards him, that he wishes to fulfil his function. Thus, insofar as one can avoid giving him the impression that one is of the belief that he is not fulfilling it now by asking him what it is, he will be glad to answer any such question.

In general, asking people what they do, even if not in general asking members of the domestic staff what they do, is *de rigueur* at parties. That being so, it might be considered offensive *not* to express such an interest if one found oneself for a relatively prolonged period in the company of a member of the domestic staff whose function one could safely assume he would not be offended one had not as yet identified. The Queen, after all, famously asks 'And what do you do?' of her subjects when she meets them. They are, almost universally, flattered that she has taken, or at least troubled to feign, this interest. Of course in this context to reply with 'And what do *you* do?' *would* be offensive. But having answers to questions such as 'What's your role in our company?'; 'What's your job description?'; 'What's your function in this office?'; and 'What's your purpose in the team?' does not in any way degrade one. Nor is there any implication in asking such questions of people that the person to whom one is asking them is to be treated merely as a means, and not also as an end in himself or herself. Of course there is an implication that he or she may be considered as a means, but not *merely* as a means.

So, assuredly, Baier has overstated his case. But we should be careful not to overcorrect in response. Perhaps, in the case that we have followed Baier in imagining, there is in fact, *contra* Baier, nothing offensive in supposing that the person has a purpose, but that is only because we are, in the background as it were, supposing that the purpose is chosen in part by the servant himself. We are blithely assuming that the person in livery would say to us something like the following, were we to get into extended conversation with him.

'I've chosen to go into domestic service and, pursuing my career in the fashion with which I'm most comfortable has led me to offer myself as a general manservant to my master, your host today. Today, at my master's instruction, I am serving you as wine waiter. That is my purpose. And, all of that being so, it would be my very great pleasure were you to allow me to serve you a drink.'

Such a conversation would reveal that the servant has a purpose decided on by his master. But it would indeed seem strange to think of it *imposed* on him by his master, and thus as detracting from his dignity. This is in part because it is one to which the servant has freely acquiesced. He has chosen to put himself in a position where his purpose may be determined by another and he could choose to resign and thereby escape from under this purpose at any moment. Hence his dignity is secured. Any of us who have taken on a job have done something similar. Our intuitions would change if we imagined that the man in livery instead replied with the following.

'As a new-born child, I was sold by my parents to my master, your host today, sold into a life of slavery from which the law prevents me escaping. Today, at my master's instruction, I am serving you as wine waiter. That is my purpose. And, all of that being so, I am eager – snivellingly so – to be allowed to serve you a drink. I pause only to tug my forelock.'

Baier may suggest that our situation were we to have a God-imposed purpose would be more akin to the second of these cases than the first. We were not milling around a careers fair, approached God's stand, asked him his terms and conditions, and then freely signed up to Him as our master. He brought us into existence with these terms and conditions. We were thrust into the world as Heidegger puts it. Even allowing the point made earlier, that God need not be depicted as (and is usually not depicted as) having given us a meticulously planned purpose and even allowing that God need not be depicted as (and is usually not depicted as) having left us no freedom to choose not to acquiesce to His purpose in at least some respects, it must be admitted that He has planned some aspects and He hasn't left us free not to acquiesce to all aspects. And, even putting all that to one side, we just are – most fundamentally – in the role of servants, *regardless of our wishes*. It's only up to us how good or bad as servants we choose to make ourselves. This is the point about God's authority over ours constraining permissible acts of self-creation. The Queen does not degrade us when she asks us, her subjects, what role we play in her United Kingdom. But it would be foolish for us subjects to suppose an equality between ourselves and our monarch or that we are subjects because we chose so to be and she our Queen because we chose that. The Queen is of course merely an earthly monarch, so there is a perfectly respectable and morally important sense in which she is our equal. Indeed, our living in a constitutional monarchy makes for a legal sense in which she is our equal. And we live in a democracy and could, collectively, change ourselves into a Republic. But, as it stands, she is our ruler and, if we are temperamentally inclined towards Republicanism, that fact will be irksome; irksome, but it seems to me not inherently degrading. Someone's life can have a non-degrading purpose imposed on it by another, even when that purpose is one that the person would not themselves have chosen and that non-degrading purpose can add to the meaning of their lives. Consider the case of Anne Frank.

Anne Frank's life has great meaning, even though we have every reason to believe that large parts of it and its overall trajectory did not serve the purposes that she had.

Her life serves a purpose that is of value (the purpose of the Anne Frank Foundation – interestingly then a purpose that was only assigned to her life after it had ceased), a purpose that is larger and more significant in terms of positively evaluable consequence than any purpose her diaries reveal her to have had during her lifetime. This example serves for me to illustrate the fact that giving someone's life a purpose that they did not choose, even when it is one that the evidence suggests they would not have chosen (in her case, the evidence is provided by her diaries and the ambitions and girlish hopes for herself that she outlined there), does not necessarily detract from their dignity. Indeed, it seems to me that Anne Frank obtains dignity through the purpose-giving activities of the Anne Frank Foundation. So we are left to conclude that Baier and Sartre misstate and rather overstate their case; God need not threaten us with indignity or degradation at all and He may well add meaning to our lives by giving us purposes, even ones that would not be of our own choosing. But – despite all that – they are right in maintaining that there is a certain valuable sort of meaning that the God of Theism[11] just cannot help but detract from; we have called it Sartrean meaning.

The issue of whether 'bootstrapping' meaning in Sartre's fashion is really possible needs further investigation before we can rest content with this conclusion. Some believe that Sartre's account of meaning is logically incoherent. As my discussion of his view will already have suggested, this seems to me too hasty, indeed wrong. It seems to me that if Sartre is wrong, he is wrong of necessity, but the sort of necessity in virtue of which he is wrong is a metaphysical one, not a logical one. If Sartre is wrong, he is wrong for metaphysical reasons (there just is a God and He is the metaphysical ground of all value), not logical ones (that his view does not make sense, that there is no logically possible world in which it is true). Nevertheless, it will be instructive to spend a moment or two looking at how an argument against Sartre's logic might best be made and how it might best be met. Looking at this will enable us to state the modified Sartrean thesis more fully and more powerfully.

The most plausible line to take against Sartre's logic is – it seems to me – not to deny that he has hit upon a sense of meaningfulness and that in general individuals' lives can be more or less meaningful in this way in proportion to the amount of responsibility they have for deciding on certain of their contents – in proportion to the extent to which, as one might put it, their existence precedes their essence. Rather, it is to insist that, in the limiting case, where essence did not precede existence to any extent whatsoever, this general relationship would break down. In other words, the most plausible attack on Sartre's view would be to allow that one may generate meaning in the sense that Sartre discusses, but insist that this is only so in cases where there is some wider context of meaningfulness already in place. And, if God is necessary for this wider context, then it's not the case that we could only fully have this sort of meaning in a Godless universe. On the contrary, we could only have any of it in a Godly one. Thus Cottingham: 'Reflection shows that meaningfulness must arise from the value antecedently possessed by the objects of our choice, not merely from exercise of the choice in itself. The mere adoption of "projects" cannot by itself confer meaning.'[12] If God is needed of logical necessity for this antecedent value, then Sartre must be mistaken of logical necessity. But it seems to me that He's not – even if my Platonism is wrong of necessity, the necessity in virtue of which it's wrong is not a logical one; Platonism about value at least makes sense.[13]

The example of the factory worker, at least as presented so far, does not do anything to undermine this challenge to the modified Sartrean thesis, as, were the friend, the Junior Widget-Affixer one is imagining, to move to the projected position on the senior management team, there would still be, above any of his individual meaning-generating choices, an overarching structure of meaningfulness into which those choices needed to fit. He would still be on the senior management team of a car factory, in charge of – presumably then with some responsibility to other members of the board and/or the shareholders for – long-term strategic planning. His role wouldn't leave him free to choose to sack all the workers and leave the factory the largest piece of 'ready-made' art ever created or to decide not to think about anything that might happen more than five minutes in advance of whatever board meeting he was on his way to attend. One might argue that if we try to think-away this sort of background altogether – think-away those parts of his essence that would still precede his existence in this new job – no possibility of meaning-creating choices of the sort Sartre has identified would survive. On one occasion, Kant entertained the whimsy that a bird might reflect on the nature of the air through which it moved in flight and decide that it would fly even faster were it to find itself in a complete vacuum. But we of course can see that such a thought would be mistaken – an understandable mistake perhaps (especially for the bird-brained), but a mistake nonetheless.

In this vein, let us imagine your meeting your friend from the car factory again after several years. This time, he says to you this:

'Since we last spoke, I've been promoted to the top of the firm – "God", as I like to style myself now. Now I'm not responsible to anyone, no shareholders, nobody at all. If I like, I could turn the company from car production to the production of something else entirely, or to the production of nothing at all. I could spend my days just twiddling my thumbs if I chose, and to no one, other than myself, would I be responsible for such a choice. I am able, if you like, to rewrite my job description in any fashion I wish, as and when it appeals to me. And thus I am always maximally deserving of the 'Employee of the Month' badge, which I thus regularly award to myself. Do you know what? I find this position just as meaningless as I did my original position as "Junior Widget-Affixer".'

It must be conceded that the last sentence of this would not come as a complete surprise given what had gone before. And this might be taken to provide some support for the anti-Sartrean argument I am trying to articulate. But I think we would do better to interpret what is going on in this imaginary situation not as your friend finally failing to be able to secure meaningfulness for himself in Sartre's sense as he reaches the top of the ladder, but rather as the friend losing meaningfulness in another sense of meaningfulness while still having increased meaningfulness in Sartre's sense. The 'God' job really is more meaningful in Sartre's sense of meaning than the job as part of the senior management team, which in turn really is more meaningful in this sense than the job as Junior Widget-Affixer. However, your friend's positions in the company as he has moved through to the 'God' job, while becoming more meaningful in Sartre's sense with each move, have, at least at the end of this process, become less meaningful in at least one other – perfectly legitimate, but different – sense. Thus, when he now considers the overall meaningfulness of his current position in the 'God' case, he inclines to describe it as 'just as meaningless' as his original position. A good contender for this sense of meaningfulness is knowingly fulfilling a purpose in some appropriate larger scheme of things. Again, as I have argued for it already, I don't wish to defend the claim that this is a legitimate sense of meaningfulness. On this occasion, I just offer it up in the hope that it will be obvious that it is a legitimate sense of meaningfulness. Once your friend finds himself in the 'God' job, he no longer has any of this meaningfulness left and he is decrying this loss in what he is now saying to you.

The correct conclusion seems to be then that Sartre's is a sense of meaningfulness that it is logically possible for a human life to hold fully.[14] Whether or not it is metaphysically possible for our lives to be or be made fully meaningful in this sense depends, obviously, on metaphysics. If Classical Theism is true, then they certainly are not and cannot be made so. God's life would, of course, then be fully meaningful in Sartre's sense. If there is no God of the classical theistic sort, then perhaps this logical possibility is a metaphysical possibility for us. But perhaps it is not, even then. Some other issue in metaphysics may prevent it.[15] In any case, the type of impossibility in which generating meaning in Sartre's sense of meaning by one's choices would be impossible were it not the case that one's essence already preceded one's existence to at least some extent is, I would suggest, if it exists at all, a metaphysical impossibility, not a logical one. Sartre's position at this point is a logically coherent one.[16] In some logically possible worlds, some of us do fully[17] have meaningfulness in Sartre's sense, though of course these logically possible worlds are not metaphysically possible if God exists. To make that point is just to state one part of the modified Sartrean thesis that I am arguing for, *viz.* that God makes it logically impossible for us to have fully meaningful lives in the Sartrean sense of meaningful. Given that if Theism is true, God's there of metaphysical necessity, so it's metaphysically impossible for any of us to have fully meaningful lives in the Sartrean sense and that is, in itself, bad for us.

Even though arguments against the logical possibility of ultimately 'bootstrapping' meaning for oneself in the Sartrean way do not work, such arguments do reveal again the truth of the polyvalent understanding of life's meaning that I have argued for on independent grounds earlier. Sartre's is a perfectly legitimate sense of meaning, but there are other, equally legitimate, senses – fulfilling a purpose in some appropriate larger scheme of things, for example. Possibly these arguments even reveal that we care more about our lives being meaningful in one or more of these other senses of meaningful than we do about them being meaningful in Sartre's sense, or at least that we do so once our lives are past some, perhaps vague, threshold of meaningfulness in Sartre's sense. We might think the arguments do this if we imagine that we would encourage the friend, if the opportunity arose (and surely he could make it arise), to resign from the 'God' job and go back to the job on the senior management team. We might even find ourselves thinking that God, if He does exist, leads a less overall meaningful life than we do, even while having meaningfulness in Sartre's sense to the maximum extent possible, for God's life has no purpose in an appropriate larger scheme of things, there being no appropriate larger scheme of things into which He fits. If we give the sort of meaningfulness that Sartre talks about a lexical priority over other sorts, we'll resist this thought. But if we give the 'fulfilling-a-purpose-in-some-appropriate-larger-scheme-of-things'-sort of meaningfulness lexical priority, we'll be unable to resist it.[18] These sorts of considerations are obviously germane then to the task that I have called the second ranking.

In any case, it has emerged that God, if He exists and is not either maximally meticulous or the peculiar deistic God that I have mentioned in passing, has had – of logical necessity – to strike a balance in what He has given us between two sorts of meaningfulness. These are meaningfulness as Sartrean self-creative autonomy and meaningfulness as having a purpose in some appropriate larger scheme of things (with obvious knock-on effects then for meaningfulness as fulfilling a known purpose in an appropriate larger scheme of things). The more He gives us the former, the less He can give us the latter. This is because there is an inverse relationship between these two sorts of meaningfulness. Those, if any, who do achieve a life of full meaningfulness in the Sartrean sense – perhaps some of us do so if Atheism is true (Sartre himself perhaps?); God alone does so, if Atheism is false – cannot have any meaning in the sense of fulfilling a purpose in an appropriate larger scheme of things. And a life that has a purpose in a larger scheme of things cannot be fully meaningful in Sartre's sense as there will be some purposes laid down for it by that larger scheme. If there is a unique way in which the balance between these two sorts of meaningfulness is best struck for all of us, God in His perfection will of course have selected that. If there is not, other possibilities open themselves.

After considering a final objection to the modified Sartrean thesis I'm defending, we'll explore the issue of whether there is plausibly a unique place to strike the balance best for all of us and (spoiler alert) what follows from there not being one. But for the moment I just wish to underscore the simpler point that is the conclusion of this chapter so far. If we assume for ease of exposition a single right spot to strike it, then in striking the balance there (in not being either a maximally meticulous God, on the one hand, or the peculiar deistic God, on the other), then – whatever the overall goodness of His striking the balance there – God has done as Sartre insisted He would have to do. He has made our lives less meaningful in the Sartrean sense, less meaningful than He would have done had He struck the balance a bit closer to the peculiar deistic end of the spectrum. Of course again I must stress that to have struck the balance a bit closer to the peculiar deistic end of the spectrum might have been to have made our lives overall less meaningful. But that is not the point. The point is that however overall less meaningful it would have made our lives, it would have made them more meaningful in the Sartrean sense, a sense of meaningfulness that in and of itself we rightly value. It may not be the deepest, but it's not shallow. If you complain to the doctor that the medicine he is giving you tastes terribly bitter and the doctor explains to you how making it even the tiniest bit sweeter would have had inevitable side-effects such that it would have been, all-things-considered, worse for you, then you should indeed stop complaining. But what you were complaining about – it's being terribly bitter – was in and of itself a bad feature of the medicine (even though, in having, it, the medicine was overall better for you than it would have been had it not had it).[19] These two types of meaningfulness then are goods and cannot be amalgamated. So the 'threat of monism', raised in the manner expressed at the end of the previous chapter (that all the individualistic meanings of life [or at least all the good ones] amalgamate into one) is avoided.[20]

I now wish to consider a way in which one might seek to block this conclusion. It might appear that we can 'reclaim' this loss of meaningfulness in Sartre's sense simply by appropriating to ourselves God's purposes for us. If your friend had found himself inescapably in the role of Junior Widget-Affixer, shouldn't he just have reconciled himself to that? Very plausibly, yes. Wouldn't his doing so have made this role more meaningful to him? Very plausibly, yes again. Wouldn't its making the role more meaningful to him be its reclaiming the meaningfulness in Sartre's sense that he had been in danger of losing? I shall argue not. It would simply be his gaining in meaningfulness in the sense of felt satisfaction at willingly and knowingly fulfilling a purpose in an appropriate larger scheme of things. Similarly, it seems to me, appropriating to oneself God's purposes for one is not reclaiming in any sense the Sartrean meaninglessness engendered by God's having these purposes for one. It is simply fully availing oneself of the possibilities that God has generated for meaningfulness in human lives by striking the balance, as I am putting it, wherever He has struck it. It's making the best of things, things that remain in one respect less than the best they logically could be.

We may, if we come to believe in God and learn of His purposes for us, appropriate these purposes to ourselves and thus they become purposes of our own choosing. Indeed, reacting in this way would seem the only rational thing to do in the light of such revelations. But (a) this will not in fact happen for all of us, at least *ante-mortem* (some, after all, remain atheists) and it will not happen perfectly for any of us *ante-mortem*. And, more importantly, (b) even if we did perfectly appropriate these purposes to ourselves (as, on Theism, we will do *post-mortem*[21]), this would not make it the case that the purposes were as they were because we had chosen them. Rather, it would be us choosing them because we recognized them to be inescapably as they were. And this second point is sufficient to defend the modified Sartrean thesis against the line of attack that I have in mind, *viz.* that we may simply reclaim meaningfulness in Sartre's sense by appropriating to ourselves God's purposes for us. Seneca may have said 'The wise man escapes necessity by willing that which necessity will force upon him.' It's certainly the sort of half-truth that pervades Stoicism. But it is a half-truth: you don't really escape necessity this way; you are just, perhaps, enabled to fool yourself into thinking that you have escaped it. Similarly, the sort of meaningfulness that a purpose gets for a person solely in virtue of its being most fundamentally a purpose of his or her own choosing is not added to by a person choosing to appropriate to himself or herself the pre-existing purpose for him or her that is had by someone else. This is so even if the wise thing to do is to appropriate it to himself or herself; even if it is ultimately inescapably what he or she will do because his or her nature is such as to necessitate it; and even if, by appropriating it to himself or herself, he or she gains another sort of meaningfulness, as he or she may well do (and would do in the case of God's purposes, at least ultimately), *viz.* a certain sort of satisfaction. It is helpful in this context to draw-in the notion of alienation, for I think we can use it to help those of us who are theists understand why it is that the claim that on Theism we are, in one sense if not others, alienated is one the truth of which will inevitably be hard for us to believe, or – better – hard for us to feel.[22]

In the case of your imagined friend, the Junior Widget-Affixer, one may think that the meaninglessness of his job was generated by his being, as Marx might have put it, alienated from the product of his labour. One thing Marxists are keen on pressing is that one must not interpret the notion of alienation as it is deployed in such claims merely as a psychological state of dissatisfaction. The alienation of your friend is, at least in part, his having no responsibility for designing the objects that pass him by on the production line and having no responsibility for deciding on even the smallest details of how he contributes to them or how they go on to be used. If he took the job on the senior management team, at least some of this lack of responsibility would disappear. Thus the greater meaningfulness of the second position in Sartre's sense. Less of his essence would precede his existence, one might say. He would become less alienated. Conversely, if your friend was simply hypnotized so that he (falsely) believed of himself that he had designed the objects that passed him by and decided the smallest details of how he contributed to them and how they went on to be used or if he simply took a pill so that he became entirely satisfied with the facts as they were, while, in either case, his appreciation of his level of alienation might decrease, possibly even vanish entirely, in neither case would his true level of alienation be affected. Being a theist is analogous to having taken the latter route, which is, I hazard, why those of us who are theists find the Sartrean/Marxist claim that Theism alienates us so *prima facie* implausible. We certainly don't feel alienated by our Theism. Indeed, the more we take ourselves to have succeeded in appropriating to ourselves God's purposes for us, the more satisfied – at one with the universe, our fellow man, the supernatural order, and everything else of value – we feel. But of course if the Sartrean/Marxist claim is true, feelings won't be a good guide here.

Marx famously characterized religion as the 'Opium of the Masses' and it seems to me that as a theist one should concede that the analogy is at least somewhat apposite. If Theism is true, belief in it offers an opiate to this sort of alienation. While its being true makes the sort of appropriation to oneself of the purposes of God the only object-ively rational response and the only response consonant with our deepest and most fundamental desires, this appropriation does nothing to remove our alienation from these purposes in the Sartrean/Marxist sense. They are still fundamentally as they are because of God's will, not ours. But we can make a virtue out of a necessity here. I'm reminded of perhaps the most famous saying attributed to someone who certainly wasn't a Marxist. Henry Ford reportedly said 'Any customer can have a car painted any colour that he wants so long as it is black.' As a customer, on hearing this, the most rational thing for you to do might well be to reconcile yourself to having your car painted black. But even supposing complete success in this – you perfectly appropriate to yourself Ford's choice of colour – your car is black not because you choose that it be black, but rather because Ford chose that it be black. The choice of colour was most fundamentally his, not yours. You are still in this way alienated from it however good you feel about it. This would remain so even if Ford genetically engineered prospective customers so that their most natural and deepest desire was for black even before they discovered that this was the only colour cars came in. So, it's not that one can object to the conclusion that if God exists our lives must have less meaning in Sartre's sense by pointing out that we can simply appropriate to ourselves God's purposes for us and thereby reclaim meaning in Sartre's sense. It's not simply that we cannot point this out because in fact none of us do (*ante mortem* at least) perfectly appropriate to ourselves God's purposes for us, but rather and more fundamentally because, even if we did, that would be at best us perfectly 'opiating' ourselves to the alienation that we nevertheless continued to undergo.

The situation here is assuredly made more complex by the fact that appropriating to ourselves God's purposes for us isn't simply opiating ourselves to this alienation. It is also to add to the meaningfulness in our lives. Indeed it is the felt satisfaction at this adding that is doing the opiating. The point to stress though is similar to one made before. Appropriating to ourselves God's purposes for us adds to the meaningfulness of our lives in a different sense of meaningfulness from the way that these purposes being as they are because God chose them, rather than because we chose them, detracts from the meaningfulness of our lives. It adds by adding to the meaningfulness of our lives both in the sense of willingly and knowingly fulfilling a purpose in some appropriate larger scheme of things and (probably) in the sense of felt satisfaction at willingly and knowingly fulfilling a purpose in some appropriate larger scheme of things.

Let us suppose, for example, that God has a special purpose for me and this special purpose is that I do my best to contribute to philosophical understanding of the meaning of life. If so, then, as discussed earlier, my life is being made more meaningful in some sense of meaningful (fulfilling a purpose in an appropriate larger scheme of things) by my writing this book than it would have been had I been doing something else. I'm writing this piece and thus aligning myself with the purpose that God has for me. It seems to me that this alignment is best construed as contributing to the meaning-fulness of my life in this sense even if I don't know it is happening. Be that as it may, the fact that God has this purpose for me can contribute all the more to the meaningfulness of my life if I do realize it (then it'll bring meaningfulness in the sense of knowingly fulfilling a purpose in the appropriate larger scheme). Even more so if I appropriate it to myself, making the alignment part of the description under which I will myself to continue on in the activity of writing this piece. Then it'll bring meaningfulness in this sense *for me*. If I am psychologically normal, it will also bring meaningfulness in the sense of a peculiar sort of felt satisfaction at willingly and knowingly fulfilling a purpose in an appropriate larger scheme. This last, it seems to me, is the same feeling as the existential repletion of which Ayer/Wohlgennant spoke, albeit focused in this case on the one activity, not on one's life in general. This felt satisfaction may indeed – I am suggesting – be described as 'opiating' one against one's persisting alienation in the Sartrean/Marxist sense, though 'opiating' would need to be stripped of any pejorative overtones, but so be it. If a worker finds himself in a particular job in the factory as a result of some prudent decision by the Managing Director, then his being there, rather than anywhere else, has a meaning-giving purpose. But it will only fully have meaning for him – the particular worker – if he realizes this and willingly assents to it. His subsequent known and wilful alignment with this purpose will probably bring felt satisfaction, one that could be described as an opiate. But it need not make him oblivious to the fact that the purposes for himself that he has now fully appropriated to himself are as they are because the Managing Director chose them, rather than because he chose them. And thus reflections of this sort need not make us, if we are 'opiated' theists, oblivious to the fact that the modified Sartrean thesis about our continuing alienation is true.

So, again we see God's 'dilemma'. If God is meticulous enough in his providential purposing for me so that His purpose for me is that I write on this topic rather than any other, then that adds to my life's meaning and I can in principle add still further by coming to know that purpose and appropriating it to myself. If He reveals that this is His purpose for me, for example, then I can will myself to continue on writing on this topic rather than any other because of this and thus gain the sort of meaning that comes from my knowing of this aspect of what I am doing that it is wilfully fulfilling a purpose in an appropriate larger scheme of things. No doubt I shall gain in addition an extra sort of satisfaction thereby with the activity. And perhaps increased motivation to persevere with it. And perhaps other goods too. All to the good. But then my scope for permissible self-creative autonomy will have been reduced relative to what it would have been had God simply had for me the purpose that I write on any philosophical topic that interests me. More of my essence will precede my existence. If, by contrast then, God is not so meticulous, His purpose being merely that I write on any topic in Philosophy that interests me, then the particular nature of the topic on which I am writing is meaningless in the sense where to be meaningful something must fulfil a purpose in an appropriate larger scheme of things. Any philosophical topic in which I was equally interested would have done as well. So, I cannot, by willing myself to continue on writing on this topic rather than any other, gain the sort of meaning that comes from my knowing of this aspect of what I am doing that it is fulfilling a purpose in an appropriate larger scheme of things. And thus that peculiar sort of satisfaction will be denied me on this point. Less of my essence will precede my existence. It's instructive, I think, to step back for a moment and see the continuum somewhere along which God must have struck the balance, so as to re-enforce the point that at either extreme and at all points in between there is something good and something bad. Just how meticulous do/would we want God to be?

'In a hundred years' time, who's going to care?' This question is usually asked in a context where it is supposed that the correct answer is 'No one'. Let us grant for a moment that this supposition is correct, so as to aid reflection on what would follow from its being so.[23] This being the correct answer could be depressing, uplifting, or neutral. A reason to find it depressing would be the worry that then nothing we do can matter. Nothing can matter unless it matters for someone who lasts forever; nothing matters for someone who lasts forever; so nothing matters. But this is of course prone to multiple objections. Nagel famously responds to this by saying that 'it does not matter now that in a million years nothing we do now will matter'.[24] Perhaps the most obvious objection is simply that things can matter without mattering to someone. As Metz says in a fabulous piece of understatement, 'Philosophers have yet to sort out the role of standpoints in appraising lives; it is still a live issue'.[25] And of course there is the more usual objection, that things can matter without mattering forever.[26] One reason to find the fact that nothing we do will matter to anyone in a hundred years' time uplifting – liberating even – is that it would give us some reason to hope that at least life was not 'too meaningful', that not everything we did was serving a crucial purpose in some appropriate larger scheme of things. If every little thing one did, from brushing one's teeth in the morning to brushing them at night, was going to matter to someone in a hundred years' time, that would seem at the least too burdensome and also perhaps to threaten our freedom. I think this is the sort of concern that Sartre had about God. If we're not Sartre, we perhaps tend to ignore the possibility that a life might have too much meaning in a given sense (i.e. that there may be senses in which life could be meaningful and even in which it was rational to want it to be at least somewhat meaningful, but in which, past a certain point, one it was rational to want to stop adding to), because the greatest danger for most of us in the affluent West appears to us to be not that we might lead too-meaningful a life, but the opposite. But at least in one sense – mattering to someone[27] – we on reflection probably do not want our lives to be as meaningful in all their details as it is logically possible they could be. We probably don't want – say – God to have meticulously planned which way we brush our teeth and for it thus to matter to Him that we conform to His plan in this particular. But, on the other hand, nor do we want nothing we do to matter ultimately, do we want for God, if He exists, to be the peculiar deistic God mentioned earlier. If we're not Sartre then, we will want God – if He exists – to be somewhere in the middle and we'll want God (or something functionally equivalent) to exist.

If we do think that God exists, then, unless we go for either the maximally meticulous view or the peculiar deistic view of God's purposes for us, we are construing one of God's purposes for us as being that we get to choose for ourselves what purposes to have within certain parameters. In Sartre's terms, we are saying that we do indeed have an essence that precedes our existence, but a part of this essence is that over some areas our existence precedes our essence. If we believe in God, we are only disagreeing amongst ourselves over where God has struck the balance.

This looseness in God's providential plan for us only makes sense, I think, given the sort of Pluralism about 'the' good life that I mentioned briefly at the start of the book. But such a Pluralism is very plausible on independent grounds. Again it is worth noting that this sort of Pluralism is a different sort from the Pluralism about life's meaning that I have spent some time arguing for. Pluralism in the sense operative now is the thesis that the good life for humans may be made up of a variety of different goods in different combinations.[28] I want to conclude my most recent line of argument by suggesting that, given it, God's existence adds more to the meaningfulness of some people's lives than it does to others. A number of lines of argument support this conclusion. The first is a pretty straightforward one.

Some people devote their lives to Philosophy; others to Music; others to promoting education; yet others to ministering to the sick; and yet others to scientific discovery. And of course most of us split our time and energies between a number of such goods. According to a plausible Pluralism about 'the' good life, each of these ways of living is potentially a good way of living and, in many cases even if not all, not capable of being ranked relative to the others. As will have become apparent, it seems to me that on Theism we should think of God as having in general left it to us which of the sets of values internal to these activities we choose as our 'area(s) of specialization', as it were, as long as we maintain a minimum standard in various 'areas of competence', if you like – that is a morality. As some of these ways of living as they particularize themselves in individuals are more meaningful in a Godly universe than in a Godless one and some are more in a Godless one than a Godly one, so – straightforwardly – God's existence will make some people's lives more meaningful than it will make other people's. So, for example, two values internal to the discipline of Philosophy are following one's reason wherever it leads and reaching important truth. That being so, theistic Philosophers of Religion who are in other respects like atheistic Philosophers of Religion are leading more meaningful lives than their atheistic peers if they live in a Godly universe. They are leading less meaningful lives if they live in a Godless one. Meaning-wise, God's existence then, even if overall a blessing for all, is a blessing that falls unevenly on philosophers of religion per se. We have come across this argument before, in the introduction. There are other lines of argument that lead to the same conclusion.

It seems to me that there are a number of different ways in which God could have permissibly struck the balance between the two sorts of meaningfulness on which we have been focusing most recently, that is the meaningfulness than an individual life may have in the sense of its being a product of permissible autonomous self-creation, and the meaningfulness it may have in the sense of its fulfilling a purpose in an appropriate larger scheme of things. One way to justify this claim would be to point out that these two sorts of meaningfulness, while related conceptually to one another such that one can only have one to the extent that one lacks the other, seem to be in an important sense incommensurable. From this alone it might seem to follow that there would have been a number of ways of striking a balance between them that would not be incompatible with God's perfect goodness.[29] That being so, He may have struck it differently for different people or differently for one and the same person at different times.[30] Then the extent to which, meaning-wise, God's existence is a blessing will vary between these different people or vary for the same person over time or at least not be determinately invariant. In addition, in that another sort of meaningfulness[31] is generated by the extent to which this balance is struck as one would oneself have chosen to strike it, this generates the possibility for either a consonance or dissonance between this last sort of meaningfulness and the choices that God has made for one in this particular. This again makes His existence more or less of a blessing, meaning-wise, for different people or for one and the same person at different times. And then finally, there is a certain type of 'interference' in our life-plans that God, it seems to me, is probably obliged to engage in and which will spread meaningfulness around unevenly. Let me say a bit more about that.

The sort of Pluralism about 'the' good life that I sketched previously applies generally. But, in the case of particular people, God, in His perfect goodness, may find Himself required to interfere and make certain sorts of lives that would otherwise have been permissible, indeed good, bad for the people who had hitherto been leading them. There is thus potential for a certain type of bad luck[32] to fall on those people with whose lives He does have to interfere for these moral reasons. It is potentially bad luck in that it potentially makes God's existence less of a blessing, meaning-wise, for them than it is for others who are in relevant respects otherwise like them. This is so because God is plausibly required by His perfect moral goodness to strike the balance in different places for different people or the same person at different times so as to achieve His overall purposes for us collectively.

For example, suppose that it was particularly important in the Divine Economy that one of two brothers, Jonah and Jonas (the latter of which you've never heard of, for good reason), go and preach to Nineveh, but that either brother would have fulfilled the purpose equally well. God, in His perfect goodness, had to choose one and let us say that it was as the text would suggest: He chose Jonah. That was in a sense bad news for Jonah. He had to work whilst his brother was free to go on holiday to a place they'd often talked about as 'the perfect getaway location', Tarshish. Jonah – who may well have quite-permissibly committed himself to a vision of the good life involving holidaying in Tarshish – found that, of a sudden, more of his essence was being made prior to his existence, as Sartre would have put it. That wasn't where he'd have struck the balance. That God chose Jonah to be the Prophet threatened Jonah's enjoyment of another sort of meaningfulness as well. One legitimate sense of the term 'meaningful' has been argued to be given by the Ayer/Wohlgennant view, i.e. to be such that in that sense a life, an aspect, or a period within a life is meaningful just to the extent that, in his or her most reflective moments, the person living it feels in a certain way content with it when he or she considers it. Jonah had less of this meaningfulness whilst he was three days in the belly of the big fish than his brother, Jonas. Jonas was simultaneously spending those three days sitting on a beach with his jug of Sangria. It's just hard to feel content with anything when you're in a belly of a fish (I'm guessing); it's just easy to feel content with everything when you're on a beach with a jug of Sangria (I know). But in another sense God's choice was bad news for Jonas. He didn't get to be a Prophet; to use his next few months to knowingly fulfil a purpose in some appropriate larger scheme of things; to gain ultimate satisfaction from that. (Not that it's obvious from the text that Jonah gained ultimate satisfaction from his knowingly fulfilling a purpose in an appropriate larger scheme of things either, but I like to think that he did.) Jonas just spent these months drinking Sangria on a beach and has since been forgotten about entirely. Jonah's name lives forever. So, each has lost out, in various senses, by God's making the decision that he has – striking the balance in two different places for the two different brothers. And, in other senses, each has gained by His doing so. It is implausible to maintain that these differences cancel out and leave the brothers equally blessed, meaning-wise. Of course, given incommensurability, it is perhaps equally hard to maintain that one life may be determinately ranked above the other meaning-wise. If we do suppose that, as it stands, God's existence is, in terms of meaning, an equal blessing, net, to both brothers, we can
· see how it could easily have been an unequal one by varying contingent features of their

circumstances in our imagination. For example, we may posit that in fact Jonas found his Sangria a little bit too sweet for his liking and thus found that he couldn't, whilst drinking it, feel quite as satisfied as originally posited with his life when considered as a whole. Contingent features like this seem unlikely to be as finely balanced as they'd need to be across the whole of humanity at any one time and over time to mean that God's existence contributes evenly to the meaningfulness of all. And, if that's so, it's an extra reason to suppose that God's existence is, as I am putting it, more of a blessing for some than for others. And this is of course even absent considerations about different sorts of meaningfulness, consideration of which would multiply our reasons for thinking that overall meaning would not be distributed evenly.

The question of how 'fine-grained', as I put it, God's purposes for us are seems to matter too. Only on the maximally meticulous providence view does God have a purpose for each aspect of our lives; that might seem then to make everything potentially meaningful in the sense of potentially fulfilling a purpose in an appropriate larger scheme of things (down to whether I brush my top teeth before my lower or vice versa). But – by doing so – it threatens to flatten out meaningfulness (at least of this sort). My brushing of my teeth is no less potentially meaningful in this sense, but also no more, than my giving of a tutorial. My life as a whole is no less or more potentially meaningful in this sense than that of Mother Teresa. For these and the reasons sketched earlier, we don't actually either believe that God is or want God to be that meticulous. But if He's not, then surely there will be some unevenness in the distribution of meaningfulness in the sense of possibility of fulfilling a purpose in an appropriate larger scheme of things.[33] And some unevenness in other sorts too. If God tolerates – probably even directly brings about – unevenness in meaningfulness, might some people be 'victims' of the meaning system and to what extent? To illustrate the issue: suppose that someone has to live an overall meaningless life as an example for the rest of us to use in cautionary tales and thereby avoid overall meaninglessness ourselves. In that their life will be a useful example to the rest of us, it will thereby ironically fail to be entirely meaningless. It will in fact bring about significant positively evaluable consequences – the rest of us not leading overall meaningless lives like this one. And of course it will stand for something – meaninglessness – and thus have, ironically, that type of meaning that is standing for an idea. But one might nevertheless think that one's life getting meaning in this way will not be its getting as much or as valuable a sort of meaning for oneself as it would have got had one's life got meaning through, say, one's leading the free world in the struggle against Nazism. Or consider Judas as he is portrayed by Christianity. He played a more important role in the economy of human salvation than pretty much anyone other than Jesus. Did he therefore have a more meaningful life than the rest of us? He is a cautionary tale, a facilitator, a piece of nomenclature, and more.[34] I only raise these questions; I do not answer them.

By way of summing up: as we have observed, at least as a Junior Widget-Affixer, the factory bell rings and one can go home; engage in leisure pursuits of one's choice; and so on. Junior Widget-Affixer may be a meaningless job in Sartre's sense, but it is only a job. A Junior Widget-Affixer has, we may suppose, a life outside work. As we have seen, it is indeed from this that there emerges scope for argument to the effect that even in Sartre's sense of meaningfulness, there may be a wider context in which what is or seems meaningless in a narrower context becomes meaningful or may be seen as such. The Junior Widget-Affixer is assuredly alienated from the product of his labour *qua* worker, but he is perhaps not *qua* provider for his family. Be that as it may, the most inescapable product of one's labour, alienation from which is thus alienation of the most inescapable sort, is one's life itself. One has no life outside one's life. So, if one has the same sort of relationship to an aspect of one's life as a whole as in the thought experiment one's friend has towards his role as Junior Widget-Affixer, there is no respite for the alienation one is under, unless that is one is free to redesign that aspect so that it better accommodates one's wishes. On Theism (in contrast to Atheism or the peculiar sort of Deism that has been mentioned now and again), there just are limits to the extent to which one can permissibly redesign one's purposes, limits imposed on us by our creator's purposes for us. And so we just *are* alienated in this sense to at least some extent. We have conceded that there is perhaps still respite for the feeling of alienation. As well as 'disreputable' opiates (one might, for example, get drunk or in other ways dull one's sensibility to the relevant facts), there is the more 'reputable' opiate of a theistic religion, reputable in that it need not dim one's awareness of the Sartrean/ Marxist alienation one continues to undergo. It adds meaningfulness of different sorts to counterbalance this alienation, plausibly more than counterbalance it. The possibility that one might become reconciled to one's 'job' – the plan for one's life that God has – is not then, as we have seen, incompatible with the modified Sartrean thesis I have been advancing. Alienation is not dissipated by one's appropriating to oneself the purposes that God has for one even if appropriating to oneself God's purpose for one does add to the meaningfulness of one's life in perfectly legitimate (if different from Sartre's) senses of meaningfulness. It adds to it in the sense of allowing one to see aspects of one's life as fulfilling a part in some appropriate larger scheme of things. And it adds to it in the sense of allowing one to find a meaningfulness for oneself in these purposes, and indeed (probably[35]) to feel a certain sort of satisfaction from fulfilling these purposes. But the extent to which one can gain meaningfulness in these senses is the extent to which one does not have meaningfulness in Sartre's sense. So God's existence is a mixed blessing, even if it is on balance a blessing for all of us. And God's existence is more of a blessing for some of us than it is for others.

So, in conclusion, even if God is a net contributor to the meaningfulness of all our lives, God cannot help but detract in one sense from the meaningfulness of all our lives (the modified Sartrean thesis) and He cannot help but contribute more to the meaning-fulness of some of our lives than He does to that of others. As I have been putting it, His existence, even if overall a blessing for all of us, is a mixed blessing for all of us and one that's mixed differently for some of us. (I have admittedly yet to establish that it is overall a blessing for all or even any of us; I shall do that in the next chapter.) Of course we are not left entirely impotent bystanders to all this. We have it in our hands to make ourselves into the sort of people to the meaning of whose lives God can contribute as much as metaphysical necessity allows and we may reasonably hope and pray to avoid bad luck in regard to meaning, as reasonably as we hope and pray to avoid other sorts of bad luck. If there is a God, He wishes that we do just this for ourselves. He knows our hopes and He hears and answers our prayers. So, in this respect as in many others, the meaning of our lives is dependent on the choices we make.

CHAPTER 9

So, assuming He exists, the Lord giveth and the Lord taketh away. He giveth and He taketh away differently from different people and differently from the same people at different times. But can we, despite all that difference, make out some general truths about how He affects things at their most fundamental, overall, and how He affects things at this level for us collectively and for us as individuals? Does the Lord giveth more than He taketh away? Or does He taketh away more than He giveth? I said in the introduction that I would answer this question in favour of the view that He giveth more than He taketh away, the view I labelled 'Optimism'. I shall put forward the argument for thinking that this is the right answer in this chapter. First, I'll look at what contribution God might make to the cosmic meanings of life. Second, I'll look at what contribution He might make to the individualistic meanings of life, though, as we shall see, these two ways in which He might contribute cannot be fully separated out from one another.

First then, let us return to the cosmic interpretations of the question 'What is the meaning of life?', interpretations such as the following: What is the meaning of it all? Why is there anything concrete at all? Why is the concrete stuff that there is as it is? In particular, why is there life and why is there life of a morally sentient and significantly free sort, such as we take ourselves to be?[1] If we assume for a moment that there is a God, then He provides answers to these cosmic questions and in doing so He brings to the party. For cosmic questions I can't see any sense in which He might be argued to take away from the party, although the issue – to which I'll come in just a moment – of whether or not He brings to the party more than would otherwise have been there is not an easy one to address (it is not even an easy one to formulate, as we shall see). In any case, for the moment, if we allow ourselves to assume that Theism is true, the following questions get the following, entirely standard, theological answers. As they are entirely standard and this is not primarily a work of Philosophical Theology, I shall simply state these answers briefly.

Question: Why is there anything concrete at all? Answer: There had to be – God exists and is a metaphysically necessary being, so there is no possible way that there could have been nothing. Question: Why is there anything contingent at all? Answer: Because God chose to create something other than Himself; that stuff thus had to be contingent on Him. Question: Why is there the particular contingent stuff that there is? Answer: Because God chose to create that particular stuff, rather than any other sort. Question: And why life, in particular life of our sort? Answer: Because God wished to create life and life of our sort (rather than a lifeless universe or one in which the only sort of life was microbial, for example). A reason for His preferring creating us over creating nothing or over merely creating microbes may well have been that we are morally sentient and significantly free; we would be able to enter into certain intrinsically valuable relationships with Him that lifeless stuff or merely microbial life would not. So, as I say, all these more cosmic questions get their traditional theological answers.

I think that it is obvious that, presuming He exists, God adds many meanings of life in this way. And I think it is also obvious that He doesn't take away any meanings of life in this way, or at least He doesn't by His choices. This is unlike, I have argued in the previous chapter, what is the case with certain individualistic meanings of life (e.g. those that depend on His choice over where to strike the balance for us between being meticulous and being deistic, as I have put it). In those latter cases, He affects things contingently and inevitably to the detriment of some sorts of meaningfulness in our lives; He taketh away as well as giveth. He does that at the individualistic level, but not at the cosmic level. At the cosmic level, He giveth but doesn't taketh away at all. Well, I say that, but we might nevertheless wonder whether if God exists, then, even if not as a result of choices He makes, He might add fewer meanings of life at the cosmic level than there would have been had He not been there at all. This then would not be something that He could have affected. But it might be argued to be something that we could nevertheless regret. And thus it might be argued to be a ground for Pessimism. Might we not say that God taketh away through, by existing, preventing what would otherwise have been the right metaphysics and metaethics – ones that would have provided greater meaning – from being right? This is a difficult question to understand and thus address because, to continue at it from the perspective that presumes Theism is true, it requires us to consider how we should think about what would have been the case had that which is necessary (God existing) been different and thinking about the impossible, even if not itself impossible, is no easy task.

As it is no easy task, I would like to sidestep having to engage in it at all. Sadly I cannot. I cannot entirely sidestep it, but I can sidestep it to some extent for reasons that will become apparent, and that I shall endeavour to do later on. For the moment then, I shall attempt to engage with the issue.

I have addressed the issue elsewhere, in two papers.[2] In the second, I sum up how I think one should approach questions of this sort as follows: 'the only way to ground judgements that it would be better or worse were situations which obtain of metaphysical necessity to have been different is to portray metaphysically possible and impossible worlds as a proper subset of logically possible worlds. On this picture, we have the actual world as our centre of focus, naturally enough. Around it in logical space, we have metaphysically possible worlds (which are also, of course, logically possible). And then we cross a significant boundary, into a 'doughnut' of worlds that are logically possible yet metaphysically impossible. Value judgements of a merely counter-factual sort – Would it have better had Hitler died in his crib? – involve comparisons between worlds all of which are in the centre of this doughnut. Value judgements of a counterpossible sort (where the sort of possibility 'countered' is metaphysical in nature) – Would it have been better had I used a time machine in order to kill Hitler in his crib?[3] – involve comparisons between worlds that are in the centre of the doughnut and worlds which are in the doughnut itself. Only by thinking of the modal landscape in this way can we make both metaphysically possible and metaphysically impossible worlds available to us in logical space for evaluative comparison and thus only by thinking in this way can we say of some metaphysical necessities that it would be better, not worse, were they otherwise and say of others that it would be worse, not better. (Thinking this way means that we do not need to say of every metaphysical necessity that it would be *both* better *and* worse were it otherwise – we avoid the counterintuitive consequences of the Lewis/Stalnaker semantics for counterpossibles, *viz.* that they are all true'.[4])

Rather than repeat the general arguments of either of these papers, let me just sum up the methodology they suggest one employ in assessing such issues as they pertain to God and the cosmic meanings of life. When, from a theistic perspective considering what would have been the case had Theism been false, one should look into the nearest world in logical space as reached when travelling out from the actual world along the Theism/Atheism axis. The first world one comes to as one then passes over from Theism being true to Atheism being true is the right comparator world. The comparator world will be judged logically, but not metaphysically, possible, and – hopefully – one will find oneself able to evaluate it for the cosmic meanings of life it contains and determinately find it to be either better or worse overall (and perhaps – at a greater level of detail – differently so for different cosmic meanings of life) by reference to that criterion. That having been done, one can then address the question of just how much God brings to the party at the cosmic level relative to what would have been at the party had He not been there to do any bringing. The same method may be employed *mutatis mutandis* by the Atheist in seeking to assess the issue as they will think of it. How much cosmic meaning God would have brought to the party had He been there, given that in fact He is not? They'll travel out from the actual world as they conceive it along the Atheism/Theism axis and find their comparator world that way. It won't be the same comparator world as the theist's of course, but it may nevertheless be evaluable in the same manner and thus – potentially – theist and atheist (and agnostic indeed) can agree on the truth on the Optimism/Neutralism/Pessimism issue even if they'll of course continue to express that truth differently, inflected as it will be by their respective Theism, Atheism or Agnosticism.[5]

So much, so hopeful. However, I have also argued in those papers that judging the nature of the right comparator world is no easy task and – significantly – theists and atheists will disagree as to relevant aspects of its nature. I don't want to repeat the arguments of those papers, but the reason for this difficulty is easy to guess at even without argument. When travelling in the land of metaphysical impossibility, we have very little to guide us. When trying to travel in this land and keep together a group of people who disagree over its topology, it's going to be even more difficult. All of this makes the comparative question one to which it is difficult to reach an answer that will prove agreeable across the theist and atheist divide. I pause to note that this then could be argued to be a new source of dissatisfaction for us in thinking about the meaning of life, new as it stems from difficulties in considering the Optimism/Pessimism issue which are peculiarly generated by its requiring us to consider how to evaluate what we must take to be metaphysical impossibilities. But this is the same – 'waiting on

Metaphysics/Metaethics' – reason for dissatisfaction that we have already come across, diagnosed, and thus done our best to make ourselves satisfied with. And we don't want to double-count. Anyway, I refer readers interested in pursuing the matters further to the arguments of these two papers. For present purposes, it comes as some relief to realise that we do not need to get into the difficulties these papers draw to our attention (but do little to resolve) for the following reason.

Whatever view we ultimately have reason to endorse here won't matter much. This is because, whether or not we should say that God contributes to or detracts from (as we'll put it if we're theists; 'would contribute to or detract from were He to exist', as we'll put it if we're atheists) cosmic meanings of life, these cosmic meanings of life themselves just don't matter much in the context of our asking 'What is the meaning of life?' That is to say, the cosmic meanings of life are not central to our reflectively endorsed concerns when we ask 'What is the meaning of life?' They are not central unless that is they have conceptual or metaphysical links with meanings of life that are, in their own right, central. Given that, after all the rankings have been completed, these cosmic meanings of life – whatever they are – would tend of their nature to sink down the chart/list of meanings of life. They'd need pulling up by some such link, into a cluster with something that is naturally more buoyant, an individualistic meaning of life. Even if is correct to say – as it seems to me it would be correct to say – that, putting it in the theistic way that appeals to me, God brings more cosmic meanings of life than would have been around had He not existed, in so bringing to the party, He's not bringing much. Any case for Optimism grounded on cosmic meanings alone thus won't be very strong. Of course, it may turn out that by bringing the 'not much' of cosmic meanings of life to the party, God – for some logical or metaphysical reason – is also bringing one or more individualistic meanings of life to the party too and that latter may amount to 'a much'. In that case we have this derivative reason to be interested in the cosmic meaning of life after all. But my point is that cosmic meanings of life per se are not that deep in the sense of deep we have been using. It is perhaps *prima facie* surprising[6] that God, in contributing meanings of life at the cosmic level, is contributing little.[7] But it is not *ultima facie* surprising – our concerns start from where we are, ourselves.

In short, I conclude – though much of the argument for this has remained off stage, in the two papers – that if there is a God, then He does contribute many meanings of life at the cosmic level, through taking centre stage in the correct metaphysics and metaethics, He brings more than He takes away at this level. And He brings more than would otherwise have been there at this level. This is, I would concede, a reason to favour Optimism. However, it is not a conclusive reason (a) because those arguments that are off stage for the latter half of this are inconclusive and, more definitively, (b) because the sorts of meanings of life God thereby contributes are not intrinsically very deep ones in the sense we have been using the word 'deep'. There is a reason arising from their intrinsic nature to think that they will not feature high up on the list of the meanings of life in the chart/list that we have been imagining as constituting our final answer to the question of the meaning of life (although extrinsic links could bring them up). So, one way or the other (either because they remain naturally low down or because they are pulled up by being linked to individualistic meanings of life that were 'already' higher up) God's contribution to the meaning of life in terms of contributing cosmic meanings of life is rendered insignificant or parasitic upon His contribution to individualistic meanings of life. One way or another, the issue of which of Optimism, Neutralism, and Pessimism is right will thus turn on how much God brings to the party for us individually (or would bring if He were to exist). We need then to consider those meanings of life that are intrinsically higher up the list, the more individualistic meanings of life.

Second then, in turning to the individualistic meanings of life, my task in defending Optimism is the task of defending the thesis that we may provisionally put as follows (we'll make it more specific in a moment). If we presume Theism, God adds more to the meanings of our lives than He takes away.[8] For the atheists, the issue will be configured differently, as atheists of course think that God isn't there and thus think of themselves as being asked to reflect on a counter-possible. For the atheist then, the Optimism that I'm defending is better expressed as the thesis that were Theism true, God would add more to the meaning of our lives than He'd take away. Now that we can justifiably concentrate on Optimism as a thesis about how God affects (or would affect) things for us individually, we are enabled to avoid – at least to the maximum extent it can be avoided (more on this in a moment) – the complications of needing to consider comparator worlds that can only be hesitatingly characterized in the relevant respects prior to deciding which of Theism or Atheism is true, the problems that stymie attempts to reach agreeable answers to the more cosmic questions.

So, for the theist, two worlds need to be considered. First, the actual world (as he/she conceives it) needs to be considered and the score chart, as it were, for what God brings and takes away drawn up. Second, the theist must consider (as he/she conceives it) a counter-possible comparator world. But – and this is the crucial point for avoiding at least some of the problems of which I have spoken recently – at least certain of its characteristics will be fixed by the way all individualistic questions are framed. We'll have to be taken to exist in the relevant comparator world for it to be a viable candidate for being the right comparator world. It seems fair to take it to be a world such as the atheist thinks the actual world to be.[9] For the atheist, the same applies *mutatis mutandis*. Two worlds need to be considered. First, the actual world (as he/she conceives it) needs to be considered and the score chart, as it were, for what reality (which he/she conceives of as *sans* God) brings and takes away drawn up. Second, he or she needs to consider what he or she will conceive of as a counter-possible world, the world where things are as theists believe and the score chart drawn up for there. But this counter-possible world that he or she must consider is not as problematic a counter-possible world to characterize as some, again because we must exist in it. In particular then, it's not as problematic as those that would need to be characterized were he or she instead to consider the question of how much more (or less) cosmic meaning there would be were Theism true. That – cosmic – question would require the atheist to consider the issue of whether, if there were a God, we'd still exist at all. Perhaps, he or she might maintain, we wouldn't, for perhaps he or she has been led to his or her Atheism by reflecting favourably on the thought that if there were a God, He wouldn't have created a world like ours at all, with creatures like us in it at all. If so, then he or she will reasonably argue that the nearest world in which there is a God is one in which none of us exist. But we are now – in turning from cosmic questions to individualistic questions – able to bypass all such problems. Assessing the Optimism/Pessimism issue as it pertains to individualistic questions of the meaning of life requires of the theist/atheist merely that they consider how much more (or less) meaning there is, relative to our world, in a world that is the same as our world in as many respects as is logically possible – in particular in having all of us in it – given that in it Atheism/Theism is true.

For many, the argument of this chapter heretofore will have seemed entirely redundant. They would have accepted from the get-go that there's nothing of insuperable difficulty in imagining two worlds, *W1* and *W2*, which are identical to one another in all the properties that theists and atheists can agree our world has (in particular each contains each of us) and differ solely in the properties that theists and atheists disagree over our world having – one, let's say *W1*, being the one where Theism is true, and the other, so let's say *W2*, being the one where Atheism is true. And they would have accepted from the get-go that we should think that the right answer to the question of which of Optimism, Neutralism and Pessimism is true turns on a comparative judgement of the meaningfulness of our lives in these two worlds – cosmic meanings of life are by the by. If *W1* comes out as the one in which our lives are overall most meaningful, then Optimism is true; if *W2*, then Pessimism; and, if neither, then Neutralism. All I can say to such people is, well done; you got from the get-go to where I've had to get to from somewhere other than the get-go. I'm sorry to have wasted your time. I won't waste any more. I'll just go on and argue for Optimism at the individualistic level.

I believe that a number of lines of argument may be used to support Optimism at the individualistic level. I have sketched some already, in the introduction. I shall at this stage draw out a selection for further discussion. The selection is by no means exhaustive of the lines of argument that converge on the optimistic conclusion and nor will my treatment of each line be exhaustive of all of its nuances or of the extant (let alone possible) objections to it. Nevertheless, my discussion will, I trust, be sufficient to make the case and draw out some common themes in the lines of argument that support Optimism. The main themes I shall draw out I shall call the quantitative point and the qualitative point.

One way in which my discussion will be incomplete is that it will assume various things that are in themselves controversial about what Theism and Atheism are best taken to entail, in particular what they are best taken to entail for each of us about any afterlife. I shall be assuming in my argument as I develop it that Theism entails a heavenly afterlife for all of us and that Atheism entails no afterlife of any sort for any of us. Both of these assumed entailments are controversial and the second one is certainly not a logical implication of Atheism. In essence, I'm just going to be assuming that the sort of atheist who is of most interest in this debate is the one who thinks that this – *ante-mortem* – life is all that there is, not the sort who believes in Atheism but also in some form of afterlife. Prior to developing the argument from these starting assumptions, a brief exploration of how things would play out differently were one not to grant them is in order, I think.

If you're a theist who thinks that there is no afterlife at all awaiting any us,[10] then my argument will carry less weight for you, assuming as it does that you're wrong in this regard. Less weight, but not no weight. Some strands of my developing argument – those that focus on what *ante-mortem* meaning God might be able to create for us with His purposes for us *ante-mortem*, for example – might still carry weight, though you'll need to unpick these strands from those with which they'll be interwoven in my argument, those that do suppose that His purposes for us extend with us into a *post-mortem* future. If you're – as is more common – a theist who believes that, while a heavenly afterlife awaits some of us, a hellish afterlife (or plain annihilation) awaits others, then again my argument will carry less weight. Though it will carry a bit more weight than it does for the theist who believes in no afterlife for anyone. And, in addition to the argument I am going to develop, as mentioned in a previous note, you will be able to add an argument of your own for Optimism. The precise form of this additional argument will depend on the criteria you suppose God will use finally to separate those destined for Heaven from those destined for Hell/annihilation. Suppose, for example, that you hold that it is only those who come *ante-mortem* to believe in some particular doctrine concerning God – presumably one of those ways in which your own religion characterizes Him – who get into Heaven.[11] On such a supposition, you would correctly reason that the view on this doctrine to which one comes *ante-mortem* is far more meaningful in the sense of having significant evaluable consequences than it is on my view.[12]

As I said, I shall also be assuming that Atheism entails no afterlife for any of us. If you are an atheist who believes that a trans-dimensional super-being, or perhaps a future trans-human person or robot at an Omega point,[13] will in fact give us all an afterlife that – let's say – will be a near simulacrum of the sort of Heaven that Universalism suggests awaits all of us, my arguments will again carry less weight; again, less weight, but not no weight. In that God would give us genuine Heaven rather than the 'ersatz Heaven' you believe us to be destined for, a case for Optimism should, it seems to me, still carry some weight for you. How much weight, it seems to me, will depend on how close you conceive your 'ersatz Heaven' to be to what God would give us were He to exist. If identical, then indeed the some weight will shrink to zero weight. Most atheists reading this though need not trouble themselves with these thoughts. Most atheists reading this will think that our *ante-mortem* life is all the life that there is. So, assuming they agree with me in my assumption that Theism entails Universalism, they'll agree with me in my starting presumptions that the relevant comparison is between how much meaning our lives have in a world in which this – *ante-mortem* – life is all that there is (the actual world as they'll see it) and how much meaning our lives have in a world in which this *ante-mortem* life is but a small part of all that there is or rather will be, because each of us lives on *post-mortem* in a heavenly realm. These then will be agreed to be the *W1* and *W2* that need to be compared with respect to our lives' meaningfulness for the Optimism/Pessimism issue to be resolved.

Once these assumptions are in place, we can see more clearly that the claim to be defended in defending Optimism is not the claim that God makes/would make our *ante-mortem* lives more overall meaningful than they would be/are if He didn't exist/

given He doesn't exist (though I think this could in fact be defended). Rather, it is the claim that God makes/would make our lives considered as *ante-mortem* plus *post-mortem* wholes more meaningful than our *ante-mortem* lives alone would be/are if God didn't exist/given that God doesn't exist. And having stated the assumptions, we are already in a position to see a key resource that the Optimist may draw on in defending this view. The overall *ante-mortem* plus *post-mortem* life, the package, as I put it earlier, that Theism predicts for us is *much bigger* – potentially infinitely bigger[14] – than the package, just *ante-mortem* life, that Atheism[15] predicts for us. This will prove key at a number of stages. I call it the quantitative point. In short, while life is meaningful in many senses – and many deep senses – regardless of what, if anything, happens to us after death, in giving us the right sort of immortality – Heaven – God makes our lives as finite *ante-mortem* plus potentially infinite *post-mortem* wholes more meaningful overall (than our lives would have been had they simply been our finite *ante-mortem* lives). He does this by adding quantitatively to the overall total meaningfulness. But have we not already come across arguments for immortality making our lives – even when considered as *ante-mortem* plus *post-mortem* wholes – meaning*less* through being boring? We have, and I shall not give them as detailed a treatment as they deserve. But my conclusion with respect to them may be anticipated: they just don't work.

It is true that several philosophers have argued that the afterlife, were it to exist, would make life less meaningful, or – more modestly – have suggested that it would detract from the meaning of life in some sense of meaning or even several other senses. Of course, to this more modest claim my thesis – endorsing polyvalence as it does – may bow. Indeed, this *should* be conceded. My own endorsement of Optimism is ultimately somewhat tempered by such a concession. But the real issue is where this concession leaves us with regard to assessing the overall, net, contribution God makes/would make. Even given that if there's a God and the afterlife, it is a mixed blessing, is it still, on balance, a blessing? And I shall argue that it is. If it's not a blessing, it's certainly not because Heaven will be boring.[16]

One of the questions that philosophers discussing the issue have, to my mind rather-misguidedly, focused on is whether or not Heaven would be boring. We have mentioned Williams in this context already, but there are others.[17] Of course as a first response to claims that Heaven would be boring, it is perfectly adequate to point out that boredom is a psychological reaction to one's state; God is omnipotent; and thus He could stand in the way of such causation. There's no non-causal necessity that anything, even the most boredom-worthy activities possible, actually generate boredom in the minds of people. Williams himself addressed this move by saying that to suppose that God 'magics away' our boredom is to suppose a diminution in our condition, not an improvement. But again, a perfectly adequate first response is to say that it would not be to do that were the activity that might otherwise have threatened to become boring not boredom-worthy. And surely worshipping God in the full glory of the beatific vision would not be boredom-worthy.[18] And Metz makes the good point that 'it might also be worth questioning whether boredom is truly sufficient for meaninglessness. Suppose, for instance, that one volunteers to be bored so that many others will not be bored;

perhaps this would be a meaningful sacrifice to make.'[19] And there are also arguments
of the sort Donald Brukner discusses,[20] though – as with Metz's point – some of these
rely on imperfections, e.g. humans tending to forget what they've done – imperfections
that we'd need to be freed from for our Heavenly afterlife to be maximally desirable,
as I take it we must view it (by definition). That is to say that they avoid the boredom
objection but only at the expense of making immortality less than perfectly desirable
on other grounds.[21]

Metz says this at one stage: 'One way to sum up these points is by viewing them as
contending that Heaven is ultimately impossible. Supposing that the word "Heaven"
is defined as a maximally desirable existence that lasts forever … these critics are
maintaining in effect that it cannot exist; eternity is incompatible with a maximally
desirable existence.'[22] This seems to me a good way to sum it up, good in part as it allows
us to see where the burden of proof lies. Why think it's impossible? The burden of proof
is usually thought to need to be shouldered by those who say of things that they are
impossible. Those who maintain that a given thing – especially perhaps when it's a thing
that has been believed to be actual by billions – is possible, aren't usually considered to
have to shoulder it. (Note: we are talking about possible truth here, not actual truth.)
And think about Metz's last sentence here – Heaven is defined as a maximally desirable
existence (I would say, 'the maximally desirable *post-mortem* existence'). How could a
maximally desirable existence not be one that it was desirable to continue? And would
that not entail its being everlasting? If Heaven is a mode of existence such that for every
period in it, its continuation is desirable, then it's desirable that it continue forever. If
it's a mode of existence that is maximally desirable, therefore it will continue forever.
Otherwise at least one period in it, its last, would have the undesirable feature that it
was its last. Taylor considers the fact that if Sisyphus rolled stones uphill to make a great
temple, which he one day – perhaps only after much toil – finished and then sat back to
appreciate, 'infinite boredom' would thereby become his lot.[23] It is interesting that Taylor
imagines Sisyphus's relationship to his temple as one of 'contemplating it', rather than
using it to facilitate his contemplating the divine. That, I think – especially if combined
with the never-endingness of the construction (again, think Barcelona's cathedral) –
seems to me likely to make quite a difference. I think that the boredom objection to the
desirability of immortality may be dismissed.

One argument for Optimism that seems to me to work is based on 'purpose theory',
as it may be called.[24] As we have seen, if there is a God, then – unless He is the peculiar
deistic God who has been mentioned from time to time – He has purposes in creating
us. He has purposes for us generally – that we be morally good; that we exercise
significant free choice *ante-mortem*; that we come to know and love Him perfectly (a
purpose to be achieved fully only *post-mortem*). And He has purposes for at least some
of us that are peculiar to us as individuals – e.g. that Xavier be a missionary; that Yaro be
ordained; that Zoe be a philosopher. Contrary to some, it seems to me that God's having
these purposes for us gives our lives meaning in the sense of having a role in an appropriate larger scheme of things even if we don't conform to these purposes to any extent.[25]

So, to revert to my example of a Managing Director placing a certain person on the factory floor in the role of Junior Widget-Affixer. That the Managing Director has made this person Junior Widget-Affixer gives his being where he is on the factory floor, rather than somewhere else, meaning in the sense of purpose; it is a role in an appropriate larger scheme of things.[26] It is an other-imposed purpose, but, as we have seen, that doesn't stop it being a meaning-giving purpose. It has meaning in this sense *simpliciter* and meaning in this sense for the Managing Director. It has this even if the Junior Widget-Affixer entirely fails to perform the function for which he is there. Even if he entirely fails to fulfil this purpose and even if it has none of this meaning for him. Perhaps he is just sitting by the conveyor belt on strike, using his being there as an opportunity to try to convince any other 'worker' who comes by to join him in his strike. If so, he is actually using his being where he is to further a purpose contrary to that of the Managing Director (who wants the factory to run smoothly).[27]

Similarly then, I would suggest that these general purposes that we have in a Godly world and do not have in a Godless world make our lives meaningful in this sense *simpliciter* – they are what we're here for – and they make our lives meaningful in this sense for God. They do this even if we completely fail to fulfil any of them to any extent, or even assign ourselves a purpose at odds with them.[28] But that they do this is controversial. Many would say that for such other-imposed purposes to convey meaning on our lives, then it is necessary that these purposes be fulfilled to at least some extent in our lives and/or necessary that we appropriate them to ourselves. So, for this reason if no other, it would not be prudent for me to put much weight on my claim that neither purpose fulfilment nor appropriation is in fact necessary for meaning generation. And I need not put any weight on it, for these God-imposed purposes can be fulfilled. They often are *ante-mortem* and, on Theism, those that God has for us *post-mortem* are all perfectly fulfilled then. And they can be appropriated. They often are *ante-mortem* and all of those that God has for us *post-mortem* will be perfectly appropriated then. So, at the level of God's generic purposes for us, we just do face morally significant choices *ante-mortem* and thus fulfil that purpose – there's just no getting away from that. And at the general and particular level, these God-imposed purposes can also make our lives meaningful for us (assuming we come to know of them and appropriate them to ourselves, as some of us at least are able to do to some extent at least *ante-mortem*). *Post-mortem*, we will all come to know of God's purposes for us and perfectly appropriate them to ourselves if Theism is true.

At one stage Metz says that if 'we can step back from the purposes of individual life and doubt their point, we can step back also from … the kingdom, power, and glory of God, and put all these things into question in the same way.'[29] Indeed, in a sense we can; it's not a full-blown category mistake to do so. But doing so is nevertheless misguided if we are asking about God's general purposes for us in the same way that it would be misguided to ask for a proof of axioms. God's general purposes for us – e.g. being moral *ante-mortem*; enjoying everlasting blissful perfect communion with Him and our fellow man *post-mortem* – are necessarily worthy, 'pointy' if you like. While we can ask what the purpose of being moral is; what's so good about the *summum bonum*; and so on, we shouldn't expect any answer beyond that. By contrast, God's particular purposes for us are more sensibly questioned, albeit that we shouldn't take our ability to question them sensibly as evidence that there isn't a point to them. Suppose God tells Jonah to go to preach to Nineveh. Jonah can sensibly wonder what the point of his going there is. Wouldn't his brother, Jonas, have done the job equally well? Won't God forgive them anyway? But if it is genuinely God who is telling Jonah to do this, then there will be answers to these questions, perhaps not ones available to Jonah, but answers nonetheless. So we can sensibly question the point of our particular vocations, if we have them, but shouldn't take our failure to spot the point as evidence of there not being one.

In all of these ways then, our lives in Godly worlds are more meaningful than they are, *ceteris paribus*, in Godless worlds. How much more? Potentially infinitely, as the *post-mortem* period is potentially infinite. Initially, it might seem that we should say that quite how much meaning in the sense of purpose God adds/would add depends on what our world is like, as we may say, 'lower-down the order of being'. But I shall argue that in the end we need not in fact take such considerations into account.

To get to the conclusion that God adds a lot it might seem that we must suppose that there's nothing relevantly similar to God 'lower-down' the order of being already adding quite a lot. So, suppose that in fact our world is one where vegetarian Martians genetically seeded our planet many millennia ago with the intention that, when they returned from their round-the-galaxy trip for a celebratory meal, there would have evolved on the Earth creatures, as it turned out us, who would be suitable conversation partners at the feast. They would be people with whom they could share what they had learned and then go on to live with in peace and harmony, through their life-extension technology giving us each an average lifespan of several millennia. If that is in fact what our world is like, then there's already much more of this sort of meaning generated by things lower down the order of being than God. More of it, that is, than most of us suspect we have if God's potential contribution is bracketed-off from consideration (most of us not suspecting that things like these Martians are behind our evolution). It is difficult to know quite how to articulate exactly how much more there is given these Martians, but let us say that there's quite a 'goodly dollop' of this sort of meaning-giving-purpose already in the universe in virtue of them. Thus, if there's a God, He won't be increasing the total of meaning-giving-purposes as much as He would be if ours had been a world in which these Martians weren't already adding this goodly dollop. But this point is ultimately rather moot for a variety of reasons, the most obvious of which is that none of us believe that ours is a world like this, but the most fundamental of which is that, even if it were, God would still be adding potentially infinitely by giving us an everlasting afterlife. The Martians may extend our *ante-mortem* lives by several millennia. But (a), they can only do so, I am supposing, for those of us who haven't yet died by the date of their return; the generations that preceded their return will have come (and more cogently gone) too soon to benefit. And (b), even the meaning that can be enjoyed in a lifespan of several millennia will ultimately amount to a small dollop when compared with that enjoyed everlastingly *post-mortem*. And again, given that the afterlife is potentially infinite, so any finite dollop will diminish in relative size, tending to nothing over time.

So, my reader will have detected that the line of argument pushed here (and elsewhere) is in essence as simple one. God makes our already-meaningful lives more meaningful by prolonging them with their meaningfulness, heightening it in intensity (we'll come to this more later) and prolonging it potentially infinitely. Thus, this addition to the meaningfulness of our lives is potentially infinite.[30] This is a simple point, but no less decisive for that. We may call it the quantitative point. We have made it of the sort of meaning that is having a purpose in an appropriate larger scheme of things, in this case God's plan (or that of the Martians), and in the sense of ultimately (*post-mortem*, if not before) fulfilling that purpose having perfectly appropriated it to ourselves, so that it becomes meaning-generating for us. But the same quantitative point can be made of other sorts of meaning too.

Consider then the Ayer/Wohlgennant view that meaning in life is existential repletion. We considered their own subjectivist spin on the idea – where one's life is meaningful just if one does have this feeling towards it – and, more favourably, an objectivist spin on the idea – where one's life is meaningful just if it would be the worthy object of such a feeling. According to my Pluralism, both are legitimate meanings of life. If there's a God and thus a heavenly afterlife for us, that *post-mortem* life will be one of perfect existential repletion infinitely extended. Thus God will add potentially infinitely to the meanings of our lives in both of these senses. Turning to other contemporary naturalist writers, we find Frankfurt, as noted, arguing that meaningfulness involves losing oneself in an awareness, activity or relationship. Again, my Pluralism allows me to think that that may well be right in the sense of capturing a sort of meaningfulness that an individual's life may have. If so, and Theism's right, then our heavenly afterlives will be more meaningful at any time in virtue of having it at a greater intensity at all times than any period in our earthly lives. God thus adds and adds again potentially infinitely in virtue of this benefit being extended in duration without limit. Or consider Wolf, who – as we have also noted – claims that loving what is worth loving constitutes meaning in life. If Theism is true, what is more worth loving than God?[31] If Theism is true, then in our *post-mortem* state we will be brought fully and finally to love God (with perfect intensity at any one time, more perfect than any achieved *ante-mortem* [except perhaps for fleeting moments by some mystics]), and we will continue to love Him at this intensity forever. Again then, if Theism is true, God adds potentially infinitely to the meaning of our lives in Wolf's sense. Or finally Levy, who contends that meaning-fulness in life lies in progressing towards goals that can never be completely realized as one's understanding of them changes as one approaches them.[32] If there is a God, then it is possible to imagine our *post-mortem* communion with Him involving this sort of progression-without-end in our understanding of facets of Him – the contents of His omniscience as it pertains to certain areas. I could add yet more examples to illustrate the quantitative point, but I think what I have said will be sufficient. It may perhaps be summed up in some words attributed to Stalin: quantity has a quality all of its own.

As well as the quantitative point in favour of Optimism, there is also what we may call the qualitative point: God adds qualitatively to the meaning to our lives. Let me turn then to developing that line of argument.

As we have been quick to point out, life is meaningful in some senses regardless of what, if anything, happens to our achievements and us after our death. My argument now is that it would be even more meaningful if we are going to get (the right sort of) immortality because then our actions will continue to have what I shall call significance meaning. In that they will continue to have it everlastingly in the ultimate context in which they are placed, I shall call this ultimate significance meaning. In that they will continue to have it for us – as we will exist to appropriate it – I shall call it ultimate significance meaning for us. This is a quality of meaning that our lives don't have on Atheism and it is a relatively deep meaning. I shall argue that were God merely to add ultimate significance meaning in the *simpliciter* mode, He would not be adding a very deep sort of meaning to our lives. But the fact that He will/would add ultimate significance meaning in the for-the-individual-concerned mode is/would be His adding a relatively deep sort of meaning to our lives. And thus Optimism is supported. So, what is this sort of meaning?

Let us return to consider a passage from Tolstoy's autobiographical 'Confessions', a passage where, in telling us of a searing moment of self-realization in his own life, he implicitly reveals a certain understanding of what would be required (and yet is – he believed at this stage in his life – absent) for life to be meaningful.

'I had as it were lived, lived, and walked, walked, till I had come to a precipice and saw clearly that there was nothing ahead of me but destruction. It was impossible to stop, impossible to go back, and impossible to close my eyes or avoid seeing that there was nothing ahead but suffering and real death — complete annihilation. ... I [had] lived for thirty or forty years: learning, developing, maturing in body and mind, and ... having with matured mental powers reached the summit of life from which it all lay before me, I stood on that summit — like an arch-fool — seeing clearly that there is nothing in life, and that there has been and will be nothing. ... Differently expressed, the question is ... "Is there any meaning in my life that the inevitable death awaiting me does not destroy?"'[33] And Tolstoy, at this stage in his life, inclined to answer this question 'No'.

It is futile to pretend that Tolstoy has not hit on a nerve with these observations. Yet futility has never been a bar to the pretensions of Philosophy. Flew tells us this:

Tolstoy was one of those inclined to hold, as if this were a necessary truth, that nothing can matter unless it goes on forever; or, at any rate, eventually leads to something else which does. But there really is nothing at all ineluctable, or even especially profound, about this particular value commitment.[34]

My response may be anticipated. Flew is right that things can be meaningful in several perfectly legitimate senses (for example, fulfilling a purpose in some appropriate larger scheme of things) even if they do not last forever or do not lead to things that do (the larger scheme might not require such results).[35] But Flew is wrong if he thinks, as he seems to think, that there is *no* sense of meaning at all in which death – if it is the permanent cessation of existence – detracts from life's meaning. Consider this passage from Craig:

'If each individual person passes out of existence when he dies, then what ultimate meaning can be given to his life? Does it really matter whether he ever existed at all? It might be said that his life was important because it influenced others or affected the course of history. But this only shows a relative significance to his life, not an ultimate significance. His life may be important relative to certain other events, but what is the ultimate significance of any of those events? If all the events are meaningless, then what can be the ultimate meaning of influencing any of them? Ultimately, it makes no difference.'[36]

Craig's view is more nuanced than Tolstoy's and thus nicely sidesteps Flew's sweeping dismissal. Craig acknowledges that death as complete annihilation would not eliminate all meaning in the sense of bringing about significant positively evaluable consequence. Craig calls what would remain 'relative significance'. But he points out that were *everything ultimately* to come to nothing, this would remove 'ultimate significance', would in that sense render all that had gone before it meaningless. In a similar vein, Dilman considers how one may come to see one's life against the background of impending death and he says of such a perspective that it is:

'As if two people playing chess were to be told that someone would come along and upset the pieces before the end of the game. It is understandable that they should feel that they may as well pack up—since it makes very little difference now what moves they make. I am not, of course, saying that all those who carry on and who manage to find a point in their lives are oblivious of this.'[37]

Similarly, Goetz asserts 'that if we are to believe that life is ultimately meaningful or nonabsurd (and by "ultimately" I mean roughly "in the end, when all is said and done"), then we will be rationally driven to admit that God exists'[38] and that God will arrange for us an afterlife in which, as Goetz puts it, 'morality and happiness embrace'.

Flew is impatient with all thoughts of this kind. Of Tolstoy, for example, he says that 'what began as clinical autobiography is developing pretensions to a wider insight into the depths of the supposedly universal human situation'. He continues:

'Tolstoy is sliding from the merely autobiographical: "there were no wishes the fulfilment of which I could consider reasonable"; to the ostensibly objective conclusion that suffering and mortality really must withdraw all reasonableness from every attempt to satisfy any ordinary human desire.'[39]

Flew would, presumably, similarly inveigh against Craig, Dilman, and Goetz. He would insist that for most of us, not knowingly being on our deathbeds, our situation is more akin to the following:

We are told, having played numerous games of chess and being in the middle of quite an interesting one right now, that at some stage in the future, perhaps after this and many more games have been completed, someone will come along and upset the pieces during a game. In such a circumstance, perhaps one would be licensed to conclude that the *last* game to be started will be one in which it makes little difference what moves one makes. But unless one has reason to suppose this particular game – the one being played now – *is* the last one, this does not make it any less interesting or the moves one makes within it any less significant in the context of this particular game. A certain move may still be clever, another stupid, another winning, and so on. As Trisel puts it, 'if we adopt a reasonable standard for judging whether our efforts are "significant" it will not matter whether humanity will persist for an extended time.'[40]

The issue, one might suggest, is one we have already come across – the issue of contexts and our perspectives on them. For example, even if something appears, indeed *is*, transient from a broader perspective, that does not stop it appearing, indeed *being*, long-lasting as seen from a narrower perspective. A house built from straw is, if tales of wolves huffing and puffing are anything to go by, likely to be less long-lasting than one built from brick. The fact that even a house built from brick will eventually be eroded into sand does not prevent us saying truly in the ordinary senses of the terms that a house built from straw is a temporary structure, whereas one built from brick is permanent. A similar logic may be discerned, Flew is free to suggest, behind the use of words such as 'significant' and 'meaningful'. A particular bundle of straw may be very significant within the context of building a house of straw, but the house of straw itself be insignificant in the context of the development of a sheltered housing project for little pigs. Or perhaps the house of straw itself may be significant in this wider project, if only through being, through its disastrous collapse, an example of the sorts of easily avoidable, and in that sense meaningless, deaths that can befall little pigs if they are not properly accommodated in brick-built houses. Perhaps it is an example that is then crucial and thereby very meaningful in motivating more brick-built houses for little pigs in future. In turn, sheltered housing projects for little pigs may be very meaningful to little pigs in the sense that these little pigs care a lot about them, even if, in some yet-wider scheme of things, their concerns mean little. Perhaps the little pigs are in fact bred and kept merely so that the eating of them can provide some incidental amusement for wolves on weekend hunting trips and house-wrecking parties.

It seems that there are various senses of meaningfulness in which things can be meaningful in one context even whilst, at the same time, they are meaningless in another context. 'Significance meaning', as we may call bringing about significant positively evaluable consequences, is certainly one of these. Craig would do well to accept all of this, as, far from deflecting us from following his course, accepting such points is itself making *progress* along his course. For the same pattern of thinking that leads us to think that various things have significance meaning in one context (are 'relatively significant', as Craig would put it) while being significance-meaningless, as we may put it, in another, should lead us to think that, in the widest context of all, all of life fails to have significance meaning (is 'ultimately insignificant', as Craig would put it). *Unless* of course that widest context incorporates some mechanism for extending at least some of what is valuable in life to this widest context. In other words, the same sort of reasoning that leads us, with Flew and perhaps *contra* Tolstoy, to see how things can retain significance meaning in a narrower context even whilst they have none in a wider one, should lead us to think that, unless the widest context of all has a particular religious character, then life as a whole; *a fortiori*, human life; *a fortiori*, the life of any individual human, has no significance meaning in the widest context in which it finds itself. *Ultimately*, unless the widest context has a particular religious character, life – in all its senses – is meaningless in this sense of meaning – significance meaning (not, *n.b.* and perhaps *pace* Craig, all senses of meaning). God can give our lives ultimate significance meaning and thus we have the grounds for Optimism, of which I have spoken.[41] There's a unique sort of meaning – ultimate significance-meaning that God can provide.[42]

'Most crucially, the counsel of despair typically is grounded in an observation that our lives are not of cosmic importance. Therein lies the beginning of a fundamental error. The question is not whether we can identify something (e.g. the cosmos) on which your life has no discernible impact. The question is whether there is anything (e.g. your family) on which your life does have a discernible impact. The counsel of despair typically is grounded in a determination to find some arena in which nothing is happening and to generalize from that to a conclusion that nothing is happening anywhere.'[43] There is some truth in this, but it doesn't capture the force of the argument for Optimism or hence meet it. Nobody is seriously worried that their life might not have meaning because they discover that there are parts of our universe (beyond our light cone, say) that it is physically impossible they will ever be able to affect, or by being led to believe – perhaps by reflecting on cosmological fine-tuning – that there are probably innumerable parallel universes. The worrying discovery is that the things we *do* affect are proper parts of a larger whole in which they have no significant effect (or at least have no significant effect unless that larger whole has a particular religious character). We find out that we're spending our time spinning wheels that are connected to proximate bits of the machine, but that these bits in turn are – more ultimately – disconnected from the larger machine of which they are a part (again, unless that is that larger machine has a particular religious character). The worry comes from thoughts such as the following, which – as I said earlier – one may not in fact find purely worrying: In a hundred years' time, who's going to care?

As Taylor puts it:

> Our achievements, even though they are often beautiful, are mostly bubbles; and those that do last, like the sand-swept pyramids, soon become mere curiosities while around them the rest of mankind continues its perpetual [Sisyphus-like] toting of rocks, only to see them roll down. Nations are built upon the bones of their founders and pioneers, but only to decay and crumble before long, their rubble then becoming the foundation for others directed to exactly the same fate. The picture of Sisyphus is the picture of the existence of the individual man, great or unknown, of nations, of the race of men, and of the very life of the world.[44]

It does seem to be only with something of a jolt that one moves from considering the significance of a certain action with regard to a portion of one's life – perhaps the likely

149

effects on those immediately around one at home and at work of a decision to take a holiday at one time of the year, rather than another – to considering the insignificance of any such choices in the whole span of human history. But that is not the jolt of moving from a context in which one's own life forms a part to moving to no such context. It is moving to a wider context, in which one realizes that one's life is located and in which one realizes that one's life as a whole is as insignificant as the most insignificant details of one's life are to one's life as a whole. Some might urge 'You don't need to think that way!' True, but you don't need not to think that way and thinking that way is very natural and directs one towards a sort of meaning, ultimate significance-meaning that we may well lack.

So Tolstoy, Dilman, and – perhaps in a more nuanced way – Craig have hit upon a sense in which individual humans' lives, if they are permanently terminated at death and their only effects are those that they have in this world, are meaningless. They've hit upon a sense – ultimate significance-meaning we have been calling it – in which human beings, when they are seen in some of the wider contexts in which we may quite properly place them, lack meaning unless a particular religious hypothesis is true. We may or may not be worried by the possibility of meaninglessness in this sense in this context – 'in the long run' or at 'the ultimate level', where it manifests itself. We are perhaps less likely to be worried by it when we appreciate, with Flew and contra Tolstoy, that it does not deprive us of meaningfulness in this sense in the short run or at a less-than-ultimate level. But significance-meaninglessness is a sense of meaninglessness. It is one we value reducing in our day-to-day lives. It is one that can only be eliminated entirely if it is eliminated at the ultimate level. And it can only be eliminated at the ultimate level if a certain type of religious hypothesis is true. It could be eliminated there, for example, were there a God such as the one that Jews, Christians and Muslims worship, a God who preserves and magnifies into eternal life all that is most valuable in our lives as led this side of the grave. This is indeed the answer that Tolstoy ultimately gave to his question. He became a Christian and thus believed he'd found this sort of ultimate meaning in his life.

So, I return to the claim that if there's a God, our lives have ultimate significance-meaning. While it's not effortlessly knowably true that if there's not a God, they don't have ultimate significance-meaning, I am, it will be recalled, assuming for the sake of argument that the atheists who are worthy of debate here do not suppose e.g. an alien giving us an afterlife. The issue now, in deciding whether God is bringing more to the party than He's taking away, is deciding just how deep a sort of meaning this is (or would be). How high up it is on the chart/list we have been imagining as representing our answer to 'What is the meaning of life?' If it's high up, then Optimism is justified. If it's low down (a fortiori if it's not on it at all), then it's not. (If it's not on it at all and in fact if, on reflection, we could see that it would be a sort of meaning we'd be best off without, then Pessimism could be justified by reference to it. But I think I've done enough already to show that this can't be right.) So, where is it?

Sadly, on this crucial issue, I find it hard to make definitive progress. The literature seems to divide neatly between theists, who think it very high up, and atheists, who think it very low down.[45] What God would certainly secure for us is ultimate signifi-cance-meaning (and I'm taking it that the atheist we're debating would concede that his/her Atheism does not give us that). But that ultimate significance meaning is a deep meaning of life is less certain. Thus it remains uncertain whether or not we may build a case for Optimism on its foundations. As already indicated, the claim that it is high up becomes even less certain once we accept, as it has been argued we should accept, that there is not a problem of top-down spread of significance-meaninglessness should our lives when placed in their ultimate context be significance-meaningless. That is to say, we've conceded that, even if there's not a God, our lives may well have – most of them surely do have – significance meaning in certain lower contexts. The fact that they don't have it at the top doesn't adversely affect that.[46] And if one realizes that one doesn't have a 'top-down-spread' reason to fear ultimate significance-meaninglessness, one's reasons to care one way or another about it diminish it seems to me to a matter of temperament. Does one actually care much about it? And here, as I say, the literature seems to divide neatly into theists who say 'yes' and atheists who say 'no'.[47] This is at least somewhat worrying epistemically. But we can find some common ground I think. Ask yourself 'Do I really care much whether that which I care about in my quotidian life is cared about by ultimate reality?' I venture that you will find that of some things you care about in your quotidian life, you don't care whether or not anything more ultimate cares about your caring about them. Something may be significant to me – a whimsical desire that, while recognizing its whimsical nature, I nevertheless feel strongly: say that I manage to beat my personal best on a computer game – but I may not care if it is insignificant in a wider scheme of things. Do I care about beating my personal best? Yes, certainly. Do I care if nobody else cares about my beating my personal best? No, not at all. But I venture that we probably do want other things we do to be significant in the wider scheme of things; we care about them and we care that others care about them and that reality 'cares' about them in the sense of not being structured so as to erase them altogether. And that seems proper. Of course, I shouldn't want someone to care about which way I brushed my teeth the last time I brushed them (absent gerryman-dered conditions). But it seems to me that I should want someone to care about other things – things that are objectively more important than which way I last brushed my teeth. Taylor's 'sufficient unto the day' approach I can't and shouldn't take about some of the things I care most deeply about – the well-being of those who I love. I learn that a meteorite will instantaneously destroy all life on earth tomorrow. The fact that the day after tomorrow then – bracketing-off God – nobody will care doesn't make me more sanguine. It makes things worse. All that humanity has accomplished and all the people who I love will be gone. 'In a hundred years who's going to care?' someone asks. 'Well, quite. Nobody. That's what makes it such a disaster' is my reply. But *how much* should we care about this?

Consider Achilles' choice between a long and comfortable life, but one of purely local significance-meaning (being quickly forgotten about after his death), or a short and dangerous life, but one that will be remembered for thousands of years and thus have more ultimate significance-meaning. Some would not choose as Achilles chose.

I say 'some', but in fact I'd hazard that most people are like that. That's why Achilles is exceptional rather than the norm. And thank goodness for that; imagine what the world would be like if Achilles was the norm. Most of us show by our choices that while we do quite often care to 'buy' less-ultimate significance-meaning at the expense of other goods, we do not so often care to 'buy' more-ultimate significance-meaning at the expense of other goods. Once we see that ultimate significance-meaning is not necessary for non-ultimate significance meaning, we see that these meanings of life do not cluster. They are separate and our best guess as to their place on the chart/list can thus only be given by reference to our own intersubjective reactions.[48] And these do not on balance seem to me unequivocal in favour of the principle 'the more ultimate the significance-meaning, the higher up it is'.[49] Thus I think that Nagel's response to this probably has *some* truth in it. We can realize that – absent God (or a functional equivalent in the relevant respects) – nothing we do ultimately matters. But we should also realize that the fact that – absent God (or a functional equivalent) – nothing we do ultimately matters doesn't matter. But then again most of us do have some desire for the ultimate significance-meaning of some of what we care about. Even if we wouldn't choose as Achilles chose, we recognize something of value in Achilles' choice. So Nagel's view has some falsity in it too. The case for Optimism grounded on God's giving us ultimate significance-meaning *simpliciter* seems then to be there, but weak.

We can best see the strengths and weaknesses of the case, it seems to me, if we consider non-traditional models of the 'afterlife', ones that give us ultimate significance-meaning simply by having God perfectly remembering for eternity our *ante-mortem* lives and see how attractive (or otherwise) we find them. This is the model that Hartshorne found sufficient to sustain him:

> 'One might say that we mould the picture which forever will hang in the divine mansion. God will make as much out of the picture in beholding it as can be made; but how much can be made depends partly upon the picture and not merely upon the divine insight in seeing relations and meanings. The true immortality is everlasting fame before God.'[50]

Hartshorne's view has not won many adherents in the theistic community. But I would suggest that this failure to win support is not due to a failure of the model to provide ultimate significance-meaning to our lives. It is rather due to its failing to provide ultimate significance-meaning *for us*. And I'd suggest that its failure to win support is evidence that we do not regard ultimate significance-meaning *simpliciter* as in itself a very deep sort of meaning even if we're theists. That's why the case for Optimism grounded on it alone is weak. It is only deep owing to its being a necessary condition of ultimate significance-meaning for us.[51] This, I think, we can conclude is relatively deep and thus the case for Optimism grounded on God's giving us ultimate significance-meaning *for us* is stronger. Let's go over that ground now.

Were there to be a God who remembers for all eternity everything about every life lived, then that would be sufficient for every individual's life, no matter how insignificant it may be in any other context, to have in what is metaphysically the most fundamental context possible, significance. Whatever other meaning it lacked or lost, one's life would unchangeably mean something by meaning something to God who unchangeably has the right attitude to it. As already discussed, one may worry in fact that one's life having ultimate significance-meaning to this extent – all the way down to this level of detail, as it were – would be for it to mean *too much*. God, being omniscient, would preserve in his memory every detail of every (otherwise insignificant) aspect and period of one's life. Nothing, no matter how trivial one had supposed it to be (or perhaps *hoped* it to be), escapes his gaze, a gaze that in turn is fixed intently on it for all time. As one contemplates how one brushed one's teeth last, this is a matter of indifference. But as one contemplates some of the more shabby choices of one's youth, this may a discomforting thought. Be that as it may, on this model each detail of our lives will lead to something that lasts forever, God's memory of that detail of our lives. The chessboard will be kicked over and the pieces destroyed by time. But every move of every match we ever play will be recorded faultlessly. And not simply recorded in some dusty volume that in turn sits unread on a shelf, but rather in one that is being continuously pored over by the most attentive and interested chess grandmaster possible. That is Hartshorne's model.

However, preserving the memory of a person is not preserving that person. Nor, I think we would all agree, is it as good for the person as preserving that person. As mentioned, on Hartshorne's view, at death our *ante-mortem* lives, while retaining significance meaning for God, lose significance meaning for us. And there do seem to be senses of meaninglessness in which death as permanent cessation of the person would make life meaningless even if the memory of the person were preserved beyond it. Expanding on our reflections on the meaninglessness for oneself that death threatens, at least a part of what one may worry about when one worries about a feature of one's life being meaningless is that it has no significant effects for *one's own* life. It is, as it were, a wheel that is unconnected to the mechanism bringing about a future *for oneself*. If death were the end of the future for oneself, then ultimately all the wheels within wheels that we spend our time building and spinning would become disconnected in this way *for us* as there would cease to be any us to whom a connection could be made. Hartshorne may say that 'our welfare is appreciated and immortalized in God, along with the welfare of all those we care about'.[52] But what we want – and it seems to me reasonably want – is that *we* be immortalized by God, along with all those who we care about. What would it really matter to us that He appreciated and immortalized our welfare if He wasn't appreciating and immortalizing us? Next to nothing now and of course literally nothing by then; we would no longer be there for it to matter for. To bring this home, imagine the differing attitudes one would have in the following two situations. In each, one is in a lifeboat along with all those one loves, desperately undernourished and under-watered, on the brink of death. Suddenly a large ship is spotted. One waves frantically and the ship alters course to intercept. In case A, the ship provides a straightforward rescue – food, water, medical care, all are judiciously provided to one's loved ones and oneself. In case B, the ship provides a team of journalists who reassure one that they intend faith-fully to document the last moments of the lives of one's loved ones and oneself and to make their footage the closing moments of 'biopics' which they'll upload to the internet, documentaries then that will appreciate and immortalize the welfare of one's loved ones and oneself.

We want meaningfulness (of positive sorts) for us. This is why Hartshorne's picture hasn't won converts. That our lives have ultimate significance-meaning – have it for God – is of less deep concern for us than that they have it for us. But that they have it for us is – I think – of deep concern for us and that is what makes the traditional picture of the afterlife – one where it's an afterlife for us, not just for memories of us – appealing. As Nick Waghorn has reminded me, Woody Allen said 'I don't want to achieve immortality through my work. I want to achieve immortality by not dying.' What I want is not just that my finite life means something for God for infinity. I want it that my life means something for me for infinity. Of course best would be if it means something for God for infinity and for me for infinity. And if the fact that it means something to God for infinity means something for me for infinity and the fact that it means something for me for infinity means something for God for infinity. But that second package of things that I want – I suggest – we do all want and we have no reason to think that that desire is not responsive to the desirability of that to which it is directed in this case. And thus if God exists, then, in giving us that, God gives us quite a bit. 'In order for an immortal life to be desirable, it must be able to sustain one's categorical desires; it must be able to support the desire for significance.'[53] Indeed, and Heaven does this. As Cottingham puts it: 'the ultimate meaningfulness of our actions, on the view advocated here, comes from their taking their place, *sub specie aeternitatis*, as actions that eternally matter: where whatever spark of good they contain is a source of joy to a being of supreme wisdom and love. This amplifies, as it were, confirms the meaningfulness that they already had on earth, and protects them against the erosions of time and contingency, shielding them against the backdrop of impermanence against which nothing in the long term matters very much. And if we add to this the doctrine of individual post-mortem survival, then the blessed who have led good lives, or received the grace of redemption, will share personally in that eternal meaningfulness, and the joy that crowns it.'[54]

Before we conclude our consideration of this line of argument for Optimism, which we have called the qualitative point, we need to consider what 'costs' come with God's giving us ultimate significance-meaning for us. The sort of meaning that is ultimate significance-meaning for us – that our lives continue to be significant to us, our actions to us, because we're around – can only be 'bought' at the expense of our lives, or rather individual periods and actions within them, not having meaning in the sense of bringing about significant and evaluable effects on our lives as a whole. For in keeping us around in the ultimate context so that these meanings can continue to be ones for us, the whole of our lives is constantly being added to *ad infinitum* and thus the contribution made to its evaluable aspects by any one period is constantly being diminished as that period retreats into the past. This then is another 'trade' issue that God would have to have addressed. We can imagine him doing so in conversation with us. What we would find ourselves wanting to say to God gives an indication of where we will think the balance lies with regards to the considerations we've presented so far in making the qualitative point. Does it in fact favour Optimism. as I have supposed, or Pessimism? Imagine then the following:

God says to you as a pre-incarnate soul, 'Alright, it's up to you. I can either give you *ante-mortem* life alone, in which case your actions and some of the things that happen to you can have meaning in the sense that they'll significantly affect in some evaluable way what happens to you thereafter. As the thereafter for you will be finite, so some of your actions and some of the things that happen to you will have significant evaluable consequences on your life as a whole. Or I can give you a finite *ante-mortem* life plus a potentially infinite *post-mortem* afterlife where you'll be with me in Heaven, in which case your life as you live it will then have ultimate significance-meaning. In the most ultimate context in which it finds itself (finally with me in Heaven), it will be significant and not just for me, but for you, because you'll be everlastingly living it. But nothing in your life will have anything but short-term (relative to the whole – this might of course be, in more 'absolute' terms, quite a long time, 10,000 years or so) consequence in terms of affecting the evaluable aspects of the whole. You choose.'

What would you choose? Personally, I'd choose immortality. That of course is compatible with immortality being worse overall meaning-wise than mortality, but – meaning being just one value – nevertheless better overall. (It's also compatible with me just mistaking what would be best for me.) But, insofar as I try just to think clear-headedly of the values that feature on the chart/list of the meanings of life and choose by reference to those so as to make my existence as overall meaningful as possible, I retain a relatively high degree of confidence that I'd be choosing correctly if I chose immortality. I think Sartre would choose mortality – better to reign in finite far-from-Hell than serve for eternity in to-me-hellish Heaven. I fear we may be down to a temperamental difference again, that in this argument we have reached the bedrock and our spade is turned.[55]

It is perhaps ironic that the reason – if it is a reason – to doubt that our lives being finite would threaten their meaning can be readily 're-purposed' to provide a doubt that our lives having ultimate significance-meaning for us would threaten their meaning. At one stage, Craig dramatically poses the question: if everything we do is ultimately going to be erased in the Heat Death of the universe, what's it matter what we do? And his implied answer is that it doesn't. As discussed, I don't think that the implied answer follows or that Craig himself is most charitably interpreted as thinking that it follows. But a similar point can be made about our lives as we will be leading them in Heaven. If everything we do on any one day in Heaven is ultimately going to be levelled down in its effects as the millennia in Heaven pass by so that, say, 100,000 years after it'll not make any difference what it is we do on any particular day in Heaven, what's it matter what we do on any day in Heaven? And thus we see why we are most charitable to Craig – who believes in the traditional afterlife as I do (though he's not a universalist) – if we don't allow the implied 'It doesn't' to stand.

At this stage, my theistic co-religionists who, unlike me, think that some of our *ante-mortem* choices determine whether or not we get to Heaven might interject that their model – summarily dismissed by me at the start of my investigation – is more attractive than the one I have been defending as it gives some of what we do *ante-mortem* meaning in the sense of significant evaluable consequence on the whole. On one such model, as noted, the potentially infinite whole takes on a positive or negative character depending on what one's managed to do in one's *ante-mortem* life with regard to developing saving faith in Christ. Either one ends up in Heaven or one ends up in Hell.

There is actually theoretical room within my universalist model as I have specified it so far to accommodate everlasting effects for *ante-mortem* actions. A simple way of seeing the space is to consider the fact that one might argue that the intensity of the hedonic tone with which one will experience Heaven at any one time (how pleasurable one will find it) could be fixed somewhere along a continuum (at a point within the positive range of course) depending on one's *ante-mortem* choices. So, for example, one might say – compatible with Universalism – that whosoever gets their *ante-mortem* Theology right in some particular respect enters Heaven to enjoy it at twice as intense a level as those who get there having got their *ante-mortem* Theology wrong in that particular respect. Each of us will get into Heaven then and each of us thus has a potential infinite pleasure to look forward to. But we'll be – as it were – approaching that potential infinite at two different speeds, the *ante-mortem*-theologically astute at twice the rate of the *ante-mortem*-theologically backward. So my model has space for such an addition (we don't need to abandon Universalism to make space for it). But I don't myself think that this sort of differentiation within Heaven is compatible with our clearest vision of how a loving God would arrange things. Nothing for my main line of argument turns on this, so I'll leave it to my readers to decide. What is much more plausible is that there is a Purgatory awaiting some after death but prior to Heaven, and what one does *ante-mortem* (and in that *post-mortem* purgatorial state) affects how long one spends there and its character. That addition to the model – which I think is to be favoured on independent grounds[56] – won't make the diminishing-meaningfulness-with-time point go away. It just kicks that particular can down the road. Eventually we'll all get into Heaven, so the fact that Hitler spent – say – 10,000 years in purgatory before he got there and Mother Teresa – say – ten seconds, won't make any difference to the quality of life they enjoy in Heaven (though as I say one could maintain that it would). But even if, as seems to me on balance best to maintain, it won't make a difference to the quality of life they'll enjoy in Heaven, it will make some difference to the total quality of afterlife they have enjoyed. And that difference in total will track with them *ad infinitum* – Hitler will always be behind on the total (and, though the gap will shrink without limit with time, on average) quality of afterlife. But then we would have to accept something along those lines on the model *sans* Purgatory, given that people have different qualities of *ante-mortem* life.

So, we do have a loss in a certain type of meaningfulness with Theism, but it seems to me (a) a relatively minor loss and (b) one that, if you regard it as more significant than I do, you could ameliorate by exploring the space in my model that I sketched in the previous paragraph so as to make my model, thus adapted, more plausible to you. Are there other sorts of losses that are more major and less easy to get around? It seems to me that there is one.

It is of course a point so obvious that it could easily be overlooked: our *post-mortem* life will be very different from our *ante-mortem* life. I have argued elsewhere, and do not wish to repeat in detail the case here, for us retaining in Heaven no free will over choices where there is an objectively best way to choose.[57] We'll have no self-creative autonomy to fashion ourselves in anything other than the best way (or one of the joint best if two or more are equally good, as is I think plausible). In essence, for the reason that we cannot be allowed to mess up our afterlives (for ourselves or for others), God will have to strike the balance, as I have been putting it, a lot closer to the meticulous end of the spectrum in the next life than He has struck it in this life. In the next life, we will not be free over choices between any options where there is a difference in objective value (as to be so would be for us to have the chance to mess up Heaven, and Heaven is by definition unmessable-up[58]). So we'll have a lot less Sartrean meaning in our *post-mortem* state. Once we're in Heaven, all of our essence as it pertains to objectively evaluable choices will precede our (heavenly) existence, as one might put it.[59] This fact about our *post-mortem* selves though will be the result of our own choice. In the Last Judgement (after which, on my model, we all get to Heaven), we choose to have our essences in future (as they pertain to objectively evaluable choices) 'precede our existences' as it were, i.e. our *post-mortem* existences. We choose to be changed into perfection, from which then we shall never be able to fall again. But that choice having thus been made, we shall from that moment on be without Sartrean meaningfulness with respect to any objectively evaluable (as different) elements of our continuing life. And of course if there are any of us who would not choose to be so perfected (I doubt that there are), then my Universalism commits me to thinking that some will end up being perfected in Heaven solely because God has chosen that they be so, not to any extent involving them choosing it. Again, my temperament makes me sanguine about this, not least because we will retain meaning in Sartre's sense for dimensions of our afterlives where there is no objectively best thing for us to do/be. But I think someone of Sartre's temperament would feel differently and again I find it hard to advance arguments that I can think of as rationally compelling for people of different temperaments.

One discovery which we've made so far is that the question 'What is the meaning of life?' is one the answer to which we cannot see clearly this side of the grave, and that in itself is unsatisfactory. God could let us see it clearly the other side of the grave. He could convey to us the relevant part of his omniscience as it were. Although it would take us on too long a detour to get into the details here, I think that we have good reason to suppose that He would do this. In essence, it's of a piece with his perfecting us with regard to our making the best choices whenever there is an objectively best choice to make. Let's suppose then that God will give us this in our *post-mortem* lives. Will that in itself make our *post-mortem* lives more meaningful? Yes, it seems to me that it will, but it seems to me that it won't make them much more meaningful. If I'm right in what I've been saying in this book and you've been believing me/following the reasons for it, you already know more about the meaning of life than the vast majority of people. But your life hasn't been made appreciably more meaningful by your coming to this understanding than it would have been had you instead devoted the time and energy to some worthy social project. And this perfecting of our knowledge of the meaning of life won't remove all dissatisfactions either. It will remove the problems that a gap between what's subjectively reasonable and what's objectively reasonable can generate, and that will do rather more to help with our lives' meaningfulness. And it will have other knock-on benefits. One will be more existentially replete and so forth – all the sorts of things that come 'as standard' with a Heavenly afterlife anyway, as we have been discussing. So, though it won't remove all dissatisfaction, coming to know the meaning of life as fully and finally as God knows it does seem to add to the meaning of our lives and thus the case for Optimism gains some support from this consideration too.

God's existence, and the sort of afterlife that goes with it, is a logical possibility. It may or may not be a metaphysical possibility. If there is a God, then the fact that there is a God is a metaphysical necessity. If there is not, then the fact that there is not is a metaphysical necessity. But whether or not there is a God is not something that can be decided by logic alone. Neither arguments that seek to show that the concept of God is incoherent, and thus of logical necessity not instantiated, nor ontological arguments, which seek to show that the concept of God is of logical necessity instantiated, work. This and the possibility of life after death are substantial issues; I have devoted a doctoral thesis, a book and thirty or so papers to them in the past myself. We cannot afford to digress into them now. Sadly, considerations of space mean we must pass by.

We may conclude that if there's a God and a Heavenly afterlife for all, that makes our *ante-mortem* lives more overall meaningful and it makes our lives (as *ante-mortem* and *post-mortem* lives) more meaningful than our lives (as purely *ante-mortem* lives) would have been had Atheism been true. It does so in a number of ways. The most obvious is quantity. We just get more of the meanings of life than we would have done had death been permanent annihilation (*a fortiori* on balance if it had meant Hell). But there are qualitative ways too. The relative deepness of some of these ways is unclear, which is no doubt unsatisfactory. But at least one seems relatively deep – ultimate significance-meaning for us. And so we may conclude that, in the debate between optimists and pessimists, the optimists are right. We may conclude it, but – as I have latterly signalled – I am aware that those of other temperaments, as I have called them, may call things differently here and I am aware I have no arguments that I can think of as showing them to be inconsistent, just out of sync. with my own set of intuitions. But this is ultimately the way every such issue ends up – a conflicting set of intuitions. For myself, I conclude God brings more to the party than He takes away. He brings by keeping the party going, and keeping it going for us.

For those who are atheists but of my temperament then this will be a further source of dissatisfaction. There'll be something that is logically possible (God) which sadly – owing to the way metaphysics unfolds – cannot exist and thus cannot do the overall meaning adding that, *per impossibile*, it would have done had it existed. Those who are theists, by contrast, will find here a source of satisfaction. Those who are agnostics, as indicated earlier, will find it unsatisfactory that they cannot know whether they should be dissatisfied or satisfied on this point. This though is the 'waiting on metaphysics' source of dissatisfaction with answers to the question of the meaning of life, which we've already diagnosed and are trying not to double-count. Let us move on.

CHAPTER 10

We have seen in previous chapters that, *whatever our religious beliefs or lack of them,* we have reason to conclude that no single individual's life can, by dint of some of the relationships between different sorts of meaningfulness, be fully meaningful in *all* the senses that we may separate out from one another and reasonably care about. This inescapable feature of life may be unsatisfying to us. But in that – as we have now seen – it is a feature that not even an omnipotent being could remove (*even in a heavenly afterlife for us or even from his own life*[1]), we should be satisfied with any dissatisfaction arising from our awareness of it. If there is a God of the sort Jews, Christians and Muslims worship and we one day find ourselves with Him in a Heaven of the sort that they imagine awaits at least some of us, we will not be able justifiably to complain to Him that He did not give us the full measure of Sartrean meaning that we would have been able to enjoy, had, *per impossibile*, He not existed but the universe and us done so on our own. If there is no God of this sort, then we cannot justifiably complain to Reality that God does not exist and that, by not doing so, we've thus been denied at least some of the chances we'd otherwise have had of fulfilling a purpose in an appropriate larger scheme of things or complain to God that, by not existing, He's denied us the chance of an afterlife that would have added, potentially infinitely, to our lives' meaning (our lives then being rightly considered to be *ante-mortem* and *post-mortem* wholes). Beckett's 'He doesn't exist, the bastard' is as incoherent as it sounds – though of course it expresses a profound truth (or rather, if Theism's true, it expresses what would have been a profound truth had Atheism been true). In the previous chapter we saw that, despite all that, we may reasonably conclude that if God is there, then our lives are overall more meaningful than if He is not. God brings more to the party than He takes away – the thesis we have labelled Optimism. He brings and He keeps on bringing, through keeping the party going, keeping it going infinitely, and keeping it going for us.

We have seen that the cosmic meanings of life that God provides are not that deep in the sense of deep we have been using. They will not naturally feature high up in the chart/list of the meanings of life that we have been imagining as articulating the final answer to the question of the meaning of life. Individualistic meanings of life are deeper – rightly of more concern to us. We have illustrated the tension between different ways in which an individual life may, potentially, be meaningful by reference to several senses of meaning. There are other senses that we could have focused on and that would have generated similar tensions. That being so, let us express at a more abstract level a question that now raises itself as we consider the individualistic meanings of life on which our concern focuses and turn to the practical task of living in the light of what we have discovered to date concerning the meaning of life.

If an individual's life may have more meaning in a particular sense, x, only at the expense of its having less meaning in another sense, y, is it the case – sometimes or always – that these senses – x and y – may in principle be ranked and it be determined that, say, a life fully meaningful in manner x is, despite that, less deeply meaningful than one only partially meaningful in manner y? Now, while I have indicated my belief in incommensurability, I have also indicated at numerous points in the argument to date, that, nevertheless, for *some* values of x and y, we have reason to suppose that there *is* in fact a determinate ranking. We have reason to believe that some lives, which are only partially meaningful in one sense, *are* more deeply meaningful than others, which in turn are fully meaningful in other, perfectly legitimate, but – our reflective intuitions tell us – shallower senses.[2] We discussed several such cases in making the argument earlier for the chart/list being a ranked chart/list. So, for example, I would maintain that our lives being fully meaningful for us in the Tolstoy/Craig sense (meaningful in this sense at the most ultimate level) is their being more deeply meaningful than they would have been had they been fully meaningfully in Sartre's sense. But some would disagree.

Holding in mind the thought on which we can agree though – that there is at least a partially determinate ranking – let us return to consider the chart/list that we have been imagining detailing the findings reached at the end of an idealized investigation into 'the' question of life's meaning. And let us go back over the ground that we have traversed, to recapitulate where we are and how we've got there. This will help us, I think, in seeing where we need to go next.

It will be recalled that we are thinking of the chart/list as having one column representing the various legitimate interpretations of 'the' question, the various questions into which the raw question 'What is the meaning of life?' may be broken down. And, beside this, another column, which contains, for each entry in the first, either an explanation of why the question as so interpreted is one we are not in a position to answer[3] or an answer to the question as so interpreted. Initially we thought of the chart as being roughly ordered by what, on some reflection, appears to us to be the centrality of these interpretations to our raw concerns when asking the original question of the meaning of life (roughly ordered, as there is some persistent residual vagueness in this ordering as a result of this sort of vagueness in our original question). Despite any vagueness, if each person were left to their own devices, perhaps some people's charts would end up determinately ordered in different ways by this process from those of others. If we were considering merely the centrality of interpretations of the question to the individual people asking it, then, as in general each person is himself or herself the greatest authority on what concerns him or her, so we would appropriately have demurred from saying that at most one of these determinately different orderings was right. But, as we saw, we need to move beyond our own individual devices to generate the list with intersubjective validity. That then leads to further complications, leading us ultimately to replace what I called the first ranking by what I called the second ranking, which requires us to reorder into clusters the meanings of life that form amalgams as a result of connections of a conceptual or metaphysical sort. Connections of these sorts being troublesome to know of (at least some of them) makes this second ranking more troublesome than the first – or troublesome for different reasons anyway. We have what might be called a further reason for controversy, though it is really to be classified alongside those pertinent to the second ranking. Having moved to the issue of deepness, we need to be yet more prescriptive. This is because the most central concern (or really overarching 'uber'-concern) that we have is the concern to discover the deepest sense of meaning. That being our most central or 'uber'-concern, we will wish to have our other concerns as reflected in the ranking of the items on the list restructured if necessary in the light of this discovery. This is a bit rough – 'the deepest'? Better perhaps would be to say 'the deeper over the less deep and the overall over even that'. Be that as it may, the issue of how to rank by reference to deepness is another vexed one. It seems, we saw in the previous chapter, that deepness itself is affected by metaphysical/metaethical issues and thus that – pending a resolution of these issues – we would not be able to fully determine (or even as fully determine as the indeterminacy allows) the right ranking. But it is clear that if we suppose we had resolved those issues, the chart/list would be one ranked by reference to deepness.

So it is that by this stage in the process of investigation the reflective (but philosophically uninformed) centrality of an interpretation of the question to one's concerns when first asking the question will have been definitively displaced by the reflective (and philosophically informed) deepness of the interpretation and answer to the question, by what one now believes one has good reason to suppose *should* concern one in asking the question. Centrality to one's (or even our collective) raw concerns or even our reflectively accepted concerns and clustered meanings of life will be displaced by relative deepness of these clusters of meanings of life as the principle of ranking in the final version of the chart/list of one's findings. This we might then call the third ranking, though just as the second was not likely to be temporally posterior to the first, so this is not temporally – or indeed methodologically – posterior to the second. The third ranking is likely, I posit, to reorder things less than the second as, I posit, we would often find between different meanings of life that we judge them different but do not judge them different in deepness. The 'difference but no difference in deepness' verdict though will not be universal; sometimes the verdict will definitely be 'different and different in deepness'. Given that we will all have started the investigation with some thoughts about which of the various meanings of life are deeper than others and started by caring more about what we thought were the deep ones than what we thought were the less deep ones, we will have already been using deepness – or at least our not-fully-thought-out impressions of deepness – as a principle of ranking even at the first ranking. All that I am saying is that at this stage of finalising the chart we will wish to return to it, or rather to using our most-well-thought-out understanding of deepness as the principle of ranking.

As indicated at the start, it seems to me that the most-well-thought-out understanding of deepness is desirability, though one may ask to whom – to oneself as an individual, to us collectively as humanity, to us collectively as morally sentient significantly free creatures (which set may be coextensive with humans but may not), to God? The answer is not clear and its being not clear is another reason for dissatisfaction. But it seems to me on balance that our concerns being primarily for individualistic meanings of life as we ask the question anchors the relevant sense of deepness as what is desirable for us as individuals. It is from our own lives that our question starts, and thus that our most well-thought out understanding of what is desirable for us as individuals will form our most-well-thought-out understanding of deepness. If God asks 'What is the meaning of life?', then it will of course be what is most desirable for God that forms the criterion for ranking. But then we'd expect the answer to the question 'What is the meaning of life?' as posed of His life by God to be structurally different from the answer to the question as posed of our lives by ourselves. And it's really the question as posed of our lives by ourselves that we are primarily asking when we ask 'What is the meaning of life?'

This being the case is the reason why we need to 're-inflate' the question of the meaning of life. The methodology of 'deflation' is necessary, but on its own insufficient for as fully a satisfying answer as life permits. But now a problem arises, or rather re-arises. When it was just centrality to our reflective, but philosophically uninformed, concerns, we could in general merely defer to the reflective intuitions of competent language users to resolve such issues insofar as persistent residual vagueness allowed them to be resolved. As we moved on to the second ranking, we had to move on from this, to doing some Philosophy. And now we are discussing deepness for the third ranking, we again need to do Philosophy. The answers to the various questions into which 'the' original question of life's meaning may be deflated are related in various ways and some of the ways in which they are related depend on various metaethical and metaphysical issues. So we cannot, until we have settled those issues, know quite how we should re-inflate the original question. Certainly the reflective intuitions of competent language users are not guide enough. And even if we reached clarity on how the clusters formed, the ranking of these clusters is another issue over which there is and will continue to be controversy. So again we cannot know – pending a resolution to these issues – quite how to re-inflate the original question. The deepest question of the meaning of life is one the precise identity of which and one the answer to which thus also waits on metaphysics and metaethics and waiting on getting our first-order evaluative judgements of desirability right (though – as I have indicated – we must take as a methodological presumption that we intersubjectively get them right if we're to proceed at all). That being so, pending the conclusion of substantive work in these areas or revelation making such work unnec-essary, we have another reason to expect to continue to be dissatisfied with the answer(s) to the question(s) of the meaning of life. These answers will need to be left related to one another by links that are in some cases hypothetical (e.g. 'If Consequentialism is true, then y is a deeper sense of meaningfulness than x; if not, then ...; 'If there's a God, then x is a deeper sense of meaningfulness than y; if not, then ...'; and so on). There are huge issues in metaethics (as well as metaphysics and at the level of our first-order judge-ments of desirability) that will have an impact here.

So, for example, I myself think of the relationship between God and value in a Platonic way – roughly, the most fundamental structures of value precede God's act of creation. That being so, I think that the nature of the deepest sort of meaning of life is relatively invariant across logical space as one moves between Godly and Godless worlds.[4] (Of course whether or not that relatively invariant value is instantiated varies considerably.) If you've had this sort of issue in mind, you may have spotted me presupposing a Platonism of this sort as I've set up some of my examples. However, someone who took a different horn to the Euthyphro dilemma as it pertains to meaningfulness from me, thinking that what gets to be the deepest form of meaningfulness depends on God's choosing it to be such (not that God chooses it because He recognises it as so independent of anything He might do about it) will not think as I do about the invariance of this across logical space. And thus the identity of what is deep meaningfulness in our universe will wait on the question of whether or not Theism is true.[5] And what *is* the correct solution to the Euthyphro dilemma? Another huge issue. All in all then we find ourselves with reason to suppose that, having broken the question of the meaning of life down into what we hoped were smaller and more tractable component parts, we now need to put them back together again; and they need to be put back together again in the right way. But which is the right way depends on which is the right metaethics and which is the right metaphysics. And finding out the right metaethics and right metaphysics is no trivial task. The question of the meaning of life then has its share of the dissatisfactions of metaethics and metaphysics. All of this we have seen in the previous chapter. And of course, as always, we await fully satisfactory answers to many of the relevant first-order value questions. Is this waiting on metaethics and metaphysics (and the definitively right first-order value judgements) then the final reason for our dissatisfaction with answers to the question of life's meaning? It is not.

Let us suppose for a moment in our imagination that all that we have so far talked about as being necessary for answering the question of the meaning of life has been accomplished. We have seen metaethics and metaphysics *sub specie aeternitatis* and reordered our findings accordingly. We – for example – have decided to push up or pull down meanings of life, ones that appeared to have a certain place in the list to us at an earlier stage but now we believe can be seen to be determinately above or below their original position. We have seen clearly all the conceptual and metaphysical links between senses, so the clusters have stayed together as we've done our reordering. And we have now reordered solely according to the principle of deepness, allowing our earlier judgements of centrality to be in some cases misguided, given that our primary purpose when asking the question of the meaning of life was to ask the question of the deepest meaning of life or rather to care more about the deeper meanings than the shallower ones. Some clusters have consequently moved up and some clusters have moved down in the third ranking. As we return to look down the chart now, noting the incompatibilities between different meanings of life, we may put an issue that faces us as one of our noticing that some meanings of life can only be 'bought' at the expense of other meanings of life and thus we may wish to think of 'trade-offs' between differing meanings of life.[6] Some of these trade-offs will have been determined in advance of any choices we may make. For example, the trade-off between our lives being meaningful in Sartre's sense and their being meaningful in the sense of serving a purpose in an appropriate larger scheme will already have been fixed by whether or not there is a God (or something functionally equivalent in the relevant respects) and to what extent this God (or His equivalent), if He (it) exists, has fixed our essences, as Sartre would have put it, prior to our existences and thus choices. It will depend on where he has 'struck the balance', as I put it in a previous chapter, between being meticulous and being deistic. But, unless the fact is that there's a God (or some such) who (which) has micro-managed us down to the level of paperknives (as not many theists actually believe), other trade-offs will be dependent on choices that we remain free to make.

Situations may arise then that raise in one's mind the practical question of how in one's own life one would be best advised to trade off meaningfulness in one sense for meaningfulness in another. The chart we are now imagining ourselves in possession of will of course be ranked with the deeper senses of meaningfulness higher than the shallower ones, respecting the correct clusterings. But it would be implausible to say that it was worth sacrificing any amount of a shallower sort of meaningfulness in order to achieve any increase in a deeper one, however slight. This is a point worth stressing.

One might be forgiven for thinking first that any amount of shallower meaning-lessness is worth sacrificing for any amount of deeper meaningfulness (at least if the only evaluative respect in which the choices differ is in terms of meaningfulness). But that thought does not withstand scrutiny. An analogy suggests itself with Mill's distinction between higher and lower pleasures and his own view that it is always worth sacrificing any amount of a lower for any amount of a higher. So, for example, one would be rational in eschewing an anaesthetic whilst having one's appendix removed if one could, as a result of doing so, whilst in considerable (but only sensuous, i.e. non-intellectual, i.e. lower) pain, nevertheless read a work of Philosophy and thus gain somewhat in intel-lectual, i.e. higher, pleasure. That just seems absurd. We are more concerned with deeper meaningfulness than we are with shallower meaningfulness. But we are concerned even more so with what we might call overall meaningfulness when overall meaningfulness may be defined as getting the balance right *vis-à-vis* trading different sorts of meaning-fulness in our lives when they need to be traded.[7] So, we must now consider what we might call *overall* meaningfulness and consider how best to construct this notion out of the materials to hand. One natural thought to have when considering how to represent this would be to wonder whether it might be done mathematically. Perhaps there is some formula describing a function that appropriately weights the different sorts of meaningfulness, giving heavier weightings to the deeper sorts, and thus combines them into a quantity that we then do best (by the standards of making our lives as overall meaningful as possible) to maximize. (Obviously the danger of Monism presents itself again; even though in this case it is only a danger of Monism as a theory of the property of meaningfulness as had by individual humans' lives.) But, on reflection, one will wish to resist this natural thought for the following reasons. (That one will wish to resist it means that again the danger of Monism may be avoided.)

First then, we must recognize that the meanings of life on this chart/list concern senses of life other than life as an individual human life, so again we can't raise the practical question sensibly about all trades. Second, if we confine ourselves to the meaningfulness-in-life answers, i.e. the answers on the list that pertain to individualistic interpretations of the question, and if we confine ourselves to trades that it is in our power to make (i.e. that exist after any decision God may have made) and for which then we may in principle sensibly ask the question about trades (and admittedly it is these that concern us most, after all synergistic interaction and multiple rankings, and thus it is going to be these – we may reasonably predict – that will be higher up the chart/list); even then, while, despite certain issues of incommensurability, some 'trade-offs' between differing sorts of meaningfulness in life may indeed be understood more or less straightforwardly mathematically, some sorts of meaningfulness in life seem to require the eschewing of a strategy of maximization altogether and the notion of overall meaningfulness is, I suggest, one.[8] We may make this point more forcefully by utilizing some of the points that Williams has made in discussion of the 'integrity' objection to Utilitarianism. (We have already come across the position in connection with our discussion of the sort of meaningfulness that a life gets from its standing for an idea.) Williams introduced to the philosophical literature a quasi-technical understanding of what it is for an individual's life to have 'integrity'. Roughly, we may say that an individual's life has integrity in William's sense just if he or she is *un*willing constantly to subject his or her everyday commitments to a higher-order principle that instructs him or her to maximize something, the good. Drawing Williams's points over to our context, the thing in question would be the individual's life's overall meaningfulness, rather than the good. Williams points out that to see oneself as compelled by morality always to maximize the good would be to hold any other 'obligations' or commitments only provisionally. It may not be obvious how a lack of integrity in Williams's sense threatens a life's meaningfulness. This is because a life led in such a way, would, it must be conceded, have an overriding and unifying worldview, and thus be very meaningful in one sense, the symbolic sense. As already discussed, an individual's life *is* sometimes said to have had great meaning just in virtue of its having had some dominant aesthetic, moral, ideological or religious goal, an overarching long-term project that – by acts of the will on the part of the individual concerned – selected and ordered the lower-order projects to which he or she committed himself or herself. Even if we look for our examples to a Utilitarian on whom Williams's original point would be most pressing, we could concede that in Williams's sense, his life has no integrity, while also accepting that it has more symbolic meaning through its unwavering commitment to Utilitarianism than the rather more morally feckless, or – as I put it earlier – ideologically fractured, lives led by the rest of us. But two points may be made here. First, Williams would surely argue that such a life would be one from which the person living it was inevitably alienated and would thus, at the same time as being meaningful in the sense of having a unifying overarching project, fail to be meaningful to the person concerned in other senses. (This is the point made before, using his 'integrity' discussion.) Second, this alienation would be all the more pressing an issue were there to be no ideology overarching one's life choices other than the determination on one's own part to make these choices in the manner that led to one's life being the most overall meaningful that it was possible for it to be. There is a parallel to be drawn here with the Paradox of Hedonism. Those who tried in each of their choices to maximize their lives' overall meaningfulness would end up leading less overall meaningful lives than at least some of those who directly aimed at something else. 'The mistake is akin to the one you would make if you were so dedicated to writing your autobiography that from an early age you decided to do nothing except write the autobiography. What would there be to write about?'[9] This is a substantial point, but, as I take it to be obvious, I merely assert it. This being the case, it is at least possible that the notion of overall meaningfulness, even for one who has all epistemic barriers removed – seeing all relevant metaphysics, metaethics, and first-order values *sub specie aeternitatis* – would not yield a determinate answer for at least some 'trade-off' issues and this could well be an additional source of dissatisfaction for us. But we have of course faced the issue of indeterminacy before in investigating the meaning of life, and we face similar issues every day. So again we don't want to double count and again we should be satisfied with any dissatisfaction arising from this source.

What is perhaps more troublesome than any of this is that there is another source of dissatisfaction with answers to the question of the meaning of life which stems from a regrettable feature of our condition that we have repeatedly swept to one side in our imagination as we have been proceeding so as to be able to see other features more clearly: this side of the grave at least, we never *can* reach the position of viewing all the relevant aspects of reality *sub specie aeternitatis*.

So far, when we have noticed it at all, we have observed our ignorance merely as a phenomenon that puts epistemic distance between us and the correct chart/list. But it is a phenomenon that actually affects the chart/list too or at least it affects it *ante-mortem*. *Post-mortem* (assuming we live on *post-mortem* and God acts as He may reasonably be expected to act so as to close this epistemic distance) it won't be there to affect the chart/list. But that then makes for another significant problem, albeit it is an instance of the general 'waiting on metaphysics' kind. The *ante-mortem* chart/list of the meanings of life is different from the *post-mortem* chart/list (assuming we have a *post-mortem* life), and thus we may say that the meaning of life changes over our lives if our lives are considered as *ante-mortem* and *post-mortem* wholes. Given this, we should go back to the start of synergistic interaction, as we called it, and ask of ourselves whether, in asking 'What is the meaning of life?' and focusing solely on the individualistic interpretations of that question that we may be giving it, we mean the meaning of our *ante-mortem* lives; of our *post-mortem* lives; or of our *ante*-plus-*post-mortem* lives. Naturally, in responding to ourselves asking this question, the most likely answer will be: 'You know what? I hadn't really thought about it.' We are back again with all the problems with which we started. But let's not repeat our discussion of that. Let's instead reflect on how is it that this epistemic distance from the list affects the list itself.

One of the ways in which an individual's life can be more or less meaningless for him or her is the extent to which he or she is disabled by circumstances not of his or her own choosing from doing what seems to him or her reasonable given the beliefs that he or she has. So, let us consider by way of example two men, A and B, both of whom are sitting one morning in their common room having coffee and reading the newspapers. This room is on the ground floor of a building which is in fact on fire. As a result of this fire, the common room will fill with fatal fumes within the next twenty seconds; the only escape would be via the window. A has yet to realize any of this and is thus sitting blissfully unaware, in his armchair reading the paper and idly sipping coffee. B has just realized it and is thus about to throw his coffee and newspaper to one side and jump through the window. He is only considering whether or not to delay in order to save A. A has objectively as good a reason to jump out of the window as does B, but subjectively he has no good reason. If A were forced from his chair by B, having his coffee and newspaper snatched from him as he was propelled through the window, this event would be meaningless for him in several senses, at least at the time. Later on, we may suppose, B would seek to explain himself to A. But let us stipulate that circumstances are such that an explanation of this sort could never present itself to A. That being so, the event of A's being grabbed from his armchair, having his coffee and newspaper torn from his hands, and being pushed out of the window by B would be and remain entirely meaningless, not in the sense that it would in fact serve no purpose that he had, for A probably does have the purpose of preserving his life (at least in the dispositional sense in which one usually has such purposes), but in the sense that it would not appear to him to serve any purpose that he has. Indeed it would appear only to thwart A's purposes. There is then, absent the epistemic advantages of B, a tension in A's life between different sorts of meaning. Thus, even if we suppose that there is in fact one correct ranking (even if it be partially indeterminate) of differing meanings of life; even if we suppose a determinate ranking within it of all the meanings of life that pertain to meaningfulness in life; and even if we suppose we can discover it and that two people agree on this ranking, even then, between these two people, if they do not have access to the same facts about the world, there can arise tensions of this sort between different sorts of meaning. And failing us becoming effectively close to omniscient, there will be this sort of tension for us whatever God does about it *ante-mortem*. *Post-mortem*, my presumption is that if there is a God and an afterlife, then as He will be able to clear this up for us (and no longer have countervailing reasons not to do so). So – one way or another – after we've died, this will no longer be a source of dissatisfaction for us. Whether or not dying is in this respect something to look forward to then will be an issue on which theists and atheists will part company – will our questions finally disappear from our minds because we'll disappear or will they disappear because they'll be answered?[10]

By this stage, one is likely to be at least somewhat discouraged. Rather exhaustedly, one might ask 'Is *that*, at last, it? If we disambiguated the question; got our metaethics and our metaphysics straight (of course, this is impossible for creatures of our epistemic abilities [at least *ante-mortem*, absent special divine revelation]), so we could clearly see the chart/list of all the meanings of life; if we got all the relevant facts right (of course this is impossible for creatures of our epistemic abilities and thus there will be problems of the sort generated by differing things making some lives meaningful [in the sense of being subjectively reasonable by reference to the value of overall meaning for the persons living those lives] from those that make it meaningful [in the sense of being objectively reasonable by reference to the value of overall meaning], at least *ante-mortem*); if we had ranked our chart, not by reference to how central these senses of meaningfulness were to our concerns when asking the original question, but rather by reference to how, on philosophical investigation, these senses could be seen to cluster (the second ranking) and then ultimately how deep these various clusters of meanings of life were revealed to be (the third ranking); if we looked at all the trade-offs internal to issues of life's meaningfulness, i.e. all the answers that pertained to individualistic interpretations of the question, i.e. 'What constitutes meaningfulness in individual humans' lives?'; if we worked out, as determinately as the issues allowed, formulae with which to maximize meaningfulness for those internal trade-offs where the notion of maximization was appropriate (whilst appreciating that maximization would not be the right notion to employ at the highest level, for 'integrity'-type reasons, when trying to understand what the overall meaning of life is and when trying to achieve a life with overall meaningfulness); if we did all that (some of which we can't do without dying and finding a God [or something functionally equivalent in the relevant respect] there to help us do it), would we *then*, at last, find as completely satisfying an answer to the question of the meaning of life as life and this question about it permits?'

Yes, we would.

You can tell I count that as an important point as it's only the second sentence in the book that I've put in bold. Sadly, it's a 'Yes, but ...' The 'but' comes as we would not be finished with reasons for dissatisfaction even then. We would, finally, have found as completely a satisfying answer as the question and life permitted, and thus the dissatisfaction that we would continue to feel would not now take as its proper object the answer that we had in front of us; it would refocus itself on the question.

The reason for our final dissatisfaction is that, once all the above work had been done, we would realize that the question of the meaning of life is not as significant a question as we had hoped it to be, for us individually, which – as I have been saying – is really what interests us most individually, or indeed for us thinking less self-interestedly. Metz indeed supposes his answer to the question of the meaning of life to be 'the holy grail'. But it isn't. There are many things we rightly wish to discover about reality that are far less grand and all-encompassing, but no less important, than the correct answers of the question of the meaning of life in its cosmic interpretations. And there are many things in our lives that we rightly value alongside and in some circumstances above its meaningfulness, even above its overall meaningfulness. Thus the correct answers to the question of the meaning of life in its individualistic interpretations are not always of most cogency to our lives. We have already seen the issue of trade-offs arising internal to considerations of meaningfulness (trading meaningfulness in one sense for meaningfulness in another). But this raises the issue of trade-offs of a qualitatively new kind. It may be better for us, not just if we trade off some meaningfulness in one sense in order to achieve greater meaningfulness in another, deeper, sense, for example, but if we do not lead all-things-considered the most overall meaningful lives that we can lead. Wolf says at one point that 'it is unclear, whether, beyond a certain point, it matters whether one's life is more meaningful. A meaningful life is better than a meaningless one, but once it is meaningful enough, there may be no self-interested reason to want, as it were, to squeeze more meaning into it.'[11] In fact, of course, my view is that it is clear that even before one reaches the point where one's life is overall meaningful, it may be self-interestedly better to abandon the pursuit of meaningfulness and pursue other goods. And of course if one brings in the interests of others, the reasons to abandon overall meaningfulness as a significant life-goal multiply. An overall meaningful life may well be worse for a person than an overall meaningless one, given the costs that may come with meaning in terms of other goods. And it may well be worse for other people, which fact may give the person even weightier reasons not to seek overall meaning. Van Gogh's life was worse for him than that pictured by P. G. Wodehouse as being enjoyed by Bertie Wooster, but Van Gogh's life was more meaningful in every sense of the term than Wooster's. (Wooster's was overall meaningless, it seems to me.) Nevertheless, if faced with a choice for one's life – Van Gogh or Wooster – I think self-interest alone would dictate one pick Wooster.

We can develop a thought experiment to illustrate trades between meaning in life and other values, one that shows we – somehow if only sometimes – balance these incommensurables in judging which would be the overall best life for ourselves. (Again, of course, there is indeterminacy and again I am adopting the Johnsonian principle that the fact of twilight should not disable us from thinking we can distinguish night from day.) So, suppose that you are offered your pick of a life along a continuum of possible lives. At the one extreme is a Van-Gogh-like life – a tortured genius with great artistic achievement; at the other, a Bertie-Wooster-type life – carefree japery with no achievement or anything meaning-generating at all.[12] Plausibly we would all plump for something in the middle. But quite where would vary for each of us. And we need not suppose there is a correct spot at which we should balance, correct that is for all of us. What's correct for one may be incorrect for another. That's in part because a part of the overall meaningfulness of one's life is generated by one's life being about as overall meaningful as one would like it to be, not more or less. Some people just want meaning more than do others and there's no determinate standard to say of some of them that they are right or wrong to want it more than these others. You've read almost to the end a book of Philosophy devoted to the question of the meaning of life. You are atypical – probably even atypical among those who've started reading this book. Most don't want meaning as much as you do. Most going about their day-to-day lives are content with relative meaninglessness if it comes with comfort, or even lack of discomfort. My point is they may not be going wrong in this. Indeed, if we are to trust our intersubjective reactions, we've reason to think they are going right in this.

When people first ask the question 'What is the meaning of life?' they characteristically presume that a full and correct answer, were one forthcoming, would carry in its wake answers to all the further questions of life – what sort of people they should be and how they should live. It seems to them impossible that someone might genuinely know the meaning of life in the deepest sense or perhaps overall, as I put it, and yet not know the projects to which he or she did best to commit, and so on. 'Crucially, to know the meaning of life is to know how to live'.[13] It is the dissonance between this presumption and a second one, the one that has guided us (namely that no answer-capable formulation will be satisfying), which explains much of the humour we find in popular jokes concerning the meaning of life. For example, towards the end of the, rather hit-and-miss, film, *The Meaning of Life*, the following lines occur:

'Well, that's the end of the film. Now, here's the meaning of life. ... Well, it's nothing very special. Uh, try and be nice to people, avoid eating fat, read a good book every now and then, get some walking in, and try and live together in peace and harmony with people of all creeds and nations.'[14]

Despite such jokes told at the expense of the question, we tend to persevere with the presumption that the answer to the question of the meaning of life would be in a sense a formula (more complex to be sure than that frivolously offered by Monty Python, but in essence of the same type), and a formula that would give us the answers to *all* the questions that face us in life.[15] 'Why have we not yet got the right formula?' we naturally wonder. 'Well, it must be very hard to get at' we suppose in reply. And it must be very hard to get at because – once got at – there's nothing else that's worth getting at, for everything else of importance about life is derivable from it. This supposition no doubt explains in turn why stories that involve people finding life's meaning characteristically involve them doing so only having done difficult things, travelling to difficult-to-reach places such as the Himalayas, for example. And it explains why stories about people who have found the meaning of life always show them as somehow floating above the practical concerns of the world with a zen-like calmness and wisdom, effortlessly leading in every respect the good life. It's impossible to imagine that someone who knew the meaning of life could be late getting the kids to school; have forgotten to brush their hair (or his); miss a deadline for a paper that he's promised (for someone to whose conference he'd been kindly invited to present it at; accepted; and then realized he'd double-booked himself for; so had to back out of anyway); and so on. Be that as it may, the reality is far different: as well as there being no formula (for reasons given at length), the presumption that someone who came to the point of genuinely knowing the meaning of life as much as is possible *ante-mortem* would thenceforward ineluctably lead the good life is wholly mistaken. The person who – *per impossibile* – *ante-mortem* completes the chart we're imagining as giving the answer to the meaning of life might lead no more meaningful a life than that led by the rest of us. Indeed someone who completed it to as great an extent as *ante-mortem* human limitations allow quite probably would have led a less meaningful life than the rest of us, as drawing up this chart to this extent would have needed to occupy them to the exclusion of more meaning-generating things they might have otherwise been doing. This is because the meaning of life is not primarily to know the meaning of life as fully as it can be known and thus this person would not have been engaging in as inherently a meaning-adding activity in getting to this stage as some others, others in which we may speculate he/she might have been engaged instead.

The question of the meaning of life is an important question, but it is not the only important question. It may be in some sense an ultimate question, but it is not the only ultimate question in the sense that the answer to it dictates the answers to all other questions of importance. As the meaning of life is not to know the meaning of life, so even someone who did know the meaning of life better than another might well end up leading a less meaningful life than that other. What is perhaps more surprising, but is also the case, is that a person who knew the meaning of life might end up rationally *choosing* to lead a less overall meaningful life than that other. This is because the truly wise try first and foremost not to lead meaningful lives, but to lead good ones. And, if what I ventured earlier about goodness in life also being polyvalent is correct, so the spiral of dissatisfactions that I have charted for meaningfulness in life would replicate itself were one to investigate that notion.

CONCLUSION

First, let me sum up. This book has primarily sought to answer the question 'Why is it so hard to answer the question "What is the meaning of life?"' Only secondarily (and very partially and inconclusively) has it answered the question 'What is the meaning of life?' My hope for it is that it has answered its primary question as completely and conclusively as the nature of the secondary question and our world allows and that I'll hence have enabled us to feel as fully satisfied as possible with the dissatisfaction that the secondary question engenders. Or at least my hope is that by coming to appreciate – as I hope I have facilitated us coming to appreciate – certain structural features of the answer to the question of the meaning of life, we shall have become satisfied with the dissatisfaction that a knowledge of these features enables us to predict will be generated however reality fills in that structure.

I took as one starting point for my investigation something that I suggested is a characteristic response to the various answers to the question of the meaning of life proffered by sages of the past or present – dissatisfaction. And throughout the book I have been seeking to explain why people who ask the question 'What is the meaning of life?' characteristically feel dissatisfied with the answers that have been and are given to it. And why they know they are going to be dissatisfied with any answer that is going to be proffered to it in the future. In doing so, I introduced the recent history of the question in Anglo-American philosophy and the key themes of the book, as well as, as the book went on, reaching conclusions about the structure of 'the' right answer to 'the' question and the various sources of dissatisfaction that the question, its answers, and life permit. Some key discoveries are as follows:

First, there are several legitimate meanings of 'What is the meaning of life?' In the question, 'What is the meaning of life?', 'life' may be taken to have several meanings. These differing meanings of 'life' range from the most inclusive, biological life per se; through humanity's life (the life of the human species, or 'mankind' as it is sometimes called); to the least inclusive, the life – or an aspect or period of the life – of the individual who is asking the question. It is even possible to locate the broadest sense of life – biological life per se – within a yet broader context – the context of contingent – or even broader (perhaps), concrete – things, as such. 'What's the meaning of it all?' is, it seems, a variant of 'What's the meaning of life?' and a part of what one is asking when one asks ostensibly about life's meaning is what meaning life – in its broadest signification – has in any broader scheme of things and what meaning, if any, that broader scheme of things has. As well as 'life' being polyvalent, there are several meanings of 'meaning'. Thus, when one asks 'What is the meaning of life?' one asks an assemblage of largely overlapping, but significantly different, questions at once. 'The' question and 'the' answer are polyvalent, as I put it. There are many legitimate questions of the meaning of life and many more-or-less correct answers to them; there are many meanings of life. This, I have argued, is a big part of the explanation for why we're dissatisfied with every answer that has been given to the question and every answer that will be given or can be given to it.

Second, there are various sorts of relationships of a conceptual and metaphysical kind obtaining between the different senses in which life in each of its senses may or may not be meaningful, between the meanings of life that we would find on the chart/list of meanings of life that we may imagine would constitute the least unsatisfactory answer that could be given to the question. Some of these relations are ones of support, as I put it, entailing we endorse an amalgam version of the polyvalence thesis, rather than a grab-bag version. But some of these are the opposite. It is in virtue of some of these being the opposite that we have reason to suppose that a single individual's life cannot, by dint of these relationships, be fully meaningful in all the senses that we can separate out from one another and reasonably care about. And there's nothing God could do about some of these issues. And that's another source of dissatisfaction, this one with life (taken in its broadest sense – reality as such), not the question one is asking about it. But nevertheless it's a source of dissatisfaction with any answer that can be provided to the question of the meaning of life. We might reasonably want to be completely free in a Sartrean sense – to have to its fullest the sort of meaning that would come from being responsible to no one other than ourselves for how we live our lives and being able to create what meanings for them we choose, without any external authority constraining us in any way. We might reasonably want to have a role in an eternal plan; to be here for a divine purpose and to have the sort of meaning that could come from that – knowingly fulfilling a purpose in an appropriate larger scheme of things. But we can't have both these things we reasonably want to the fullest extent we might reasonably want each of them if we considered them individually. And that is dissatisfying too.

Some meanings of life are 'deeper' than others – more intrinsically desirable. Even if one focuses down solely on the deepest – some of the individualistic ones – there's no 'formula for a meaningful life' that will give one's life meaning in all senses of the term. There's no formula for determinately ranking by reference to deepness all the various individualistic meanings of life. Even if – *per impossibile* – there were, we have reason to think we'd be most rational in pursuing overall meaningfulness, rather than deeper sorts at the expense of shallower sorts in all cases. There's no formula for overall meaning-fulness either. And again, even if – *per impossibile* – there were, we have reason to think that we'd not be most rational in pursuing overall meaningfulness to the exclusion of other values. First, it would be self-defeating. Second, there are many things in a life that we rightly value alongside and in some circumstances above its meaningfulness, even above its overall meaningfulness. So we might rationally choose not to make our lives as meaningful as we could. Even a perfectly good God would *not* be a meaning-maximizer for us. Obviously, this is more plausible as true if one's already granted that Consequentialism is false and thus God needn't be a value-maximizer at all. But it is equally true if God is required to be a value-maximizer given that meaningfulness is not the most important value. There is a danger – philosophers who reflect on meaning are, as a result of their trade, peculiarly susceptible to it – of supposing meaning to be the supreme value, possibly even the Holy Grail, but to be forewarned of this danger is to be forearmed against it.

So, even God, who does know the meaning of life better than anyone else and is omnipotent and omniscient as well as perfectly good, might well end up not choosing to assist us as much as He could in making our lives meaningful. This adds a qualification to the overall 'optimistic' thesis argued for in the second half of the book. The view argued for has been that, especially through giving us a Heavenly afterlife, God adds more meaningfulness than He'd have to subtract, that – as I have been putting it – He brings more to the party than He takes away. The new qualification is that He mightn't choose to bring as much as He could, either *ante-mortem* or *post-mortem*. *Post-mortem*, I can't see any reason why He wouldn't at least remove our epistemic distance from the correct chart/list. But also – through removing from us the freedom to make less than optimal choices (we can't be allowed to mess up Heaven) – Sartrean concerns would become more cogent. What we do in Heaven will be a lot more meticulously planned (and controlled) than what we do on Earth. Still, through giving our lives – construed as *ante-mortem* and *post-mortem* wholes – potentially infinite meaning in various senses, including especially ultimate significance-meaning for us, God does giveth more than He taketh away. Thus the thesis I have called 'Optimism' is the one that we have most reason to endorse.

Regardless of one's religious beliefs or where one falls on the optimist–pessimist spectrum of opinion, there is still an encouraging 'Take Home' message at the practical level. The practical conclusion of the book is still an 'upbeat' one: your life is already meaningful in some valuable senses; your life can be made meaningful in others. If there's a God, that's even better (net), though not unqualifiedly good news. The book's also relatively encouraging about death regardless of one's religious views. The inevitability of death and death itself when it comes certainly doesn't destroy all meaning. If there's a God, it destroys less. So much for the practical level. At the philosophical level, things remain less than encouraging. For all the reasons discussed, the question of the meaning of life is one that can never be answered entirely satisfactorily. Even dying won't remove all dissatisfaction (unless that is it permanently removes us, and that observation is itself rather dissatisfying). All that we can do is understand why this is so and why not even God could make it otherwise. Thus understanding, we may become satisfied with our dissatisfaction. That state of satisfied dissatisfaction is all that I promised I would facilitate us in progressing towards. But I hope I will be counted by now as having done at least something towards that end. In any case, I have done as much as I am able and thus it's time for me to stop. If there is a God, then, on the other side of the grave, He will complete for us the journey on which we have started.

NOTES

Introduction

1 N. Rescher, *Human Interests*, Stanford: Stanford University Press (1990), 154.

2 This reveals an interesting suppressed premise in Sartre: distributing meaningfulness-for-a-life is a 'zero-sum game'. Our lives being meaningful for God (in that He'd given them a purpose or purposes in such a way as to make them meaningful for Him) would stop them being meaningful for us (as it would stop us giving them a purpose or purposes in such a way that those purposes made our lives meaningful for us). That premise is not obviously true. Why is there an internecine relationship between purpose-giving-and-thereby-meaningfulness-for-people-generating agents? And, even if there is, why would God's putting meaning in our lives 'trump' our doing so, rather than the other way around? I'll come to articulating and, what is more, defending what I take to be the most plausible Sartrean view later. For the moment I note that as well as not needing to accept the 'zero-sum game' premise, one need not accept the 'God's authority trumps ours' premise (it need not be accepted even by those who accept the 'zero-sum game' premise). Certain passages of Camus suggest to me an alternative within a broadly Sartrean zero-sum-game view. In a Godly world (i.e. one in which Theism is true), one is able – despite God having chosen a purpose or purposes for one – nevertheless to create meaning for oneself by simply scorning God's authority. Scornfully rejecting authority enables one to escape from under it. I think that this is to misrepresent how authority (necessarily) works and thus think that this way is not navigable, but that's only because I have a much more absolutist conception of authority than the historical Jean-Paul Sartre had.

I am here rejecting without argument then a view discussed by Wolf in her paper 'The Meanings of Lives' (in J. Perry, M. Bratman and J. Fischer [eds], *Introduction to Philosophy, Classical and Contemporary Readings*, Oxford: Oxford University Press [2012], 837–48), the view she characterizes as asserting that a 'life can be meaningful only if it can mean something *to* someone, and not just to *someone*, but to someone other than oneself and indeed someone of more intrinsic or ultimate value than oneself ... if there is no God, then human life ... must be ... meaningless, because if there is no God, there is no appropriate being *for whom* we could have meaning' (845). It seems to me that there would still be someone – oneself – and that the sorts of meaning that need to be for someone just need someone to be for, not someone other than oneself to be for.

3 Jean-Paul Sartre, *Existentialism is a Humanism*, P. Mairet (trans.), London; Methuen & Co. (1980 [orig. 1946], 29.

4 Well, 'unlimited' might be a bit strong – 'we have no purposes that we can think of assigning ourselves that are ruled out by being at variance with those pre-assigned by an authority' would be a more precise way of putting it. There will be some limits to the purposes we can think of, of course.

5 T. Nagel, *The Last Word*, Oxford: Oxford University Press (1997), 130–1.

6 The notion of absurdity as Nagel deploys it is not related in any simple way to the issue of meaningfulness, though it seems to me there are connections. The original paper under discussion here is T. Nagel, 'The Absurd', *Journal of Philosophy* 68.20 (1971): 716–27. It is reprinted in his *Mortal Questions*, Cambridge: Cambridge University Press (1979), 11–23.

7 The most plausible Nagelian thesis seems to me an epistemic one: we cannot know that Absurdism is false. (Absurdism is variously understood as the notion of absurdity is variously understood. Leaving it under-specified at this stage then, let me simply say that Absurdism is the thesis that reality is fundamentally absurd.) It is true that the actual Nagel seems in certain passages committed to a stronger thesis than the one I find most plausible: Absurdism is true, indeed it is knowably true. Thus perhaps 'Nagelian' should have scare quotation marks around it in the main text wherever it occurs.

8 Nagel, unlike Sartre, is ultimately an objectivist about such values; he just fears that we cannot know with certainty that values are objective.

9 T. Nagel, 'The Absurd', as reprinted in his *Mortal Questions*, Cambridge: Cambridge University Press (1979), 23. This passage in itself reveals some tensions in Nagel's thought. Duncan Pritchard discusses Nagel's view and points to problems with it and ways to reinterpret it so that it comes out more coherent in his 'Absurdity, Angst, and the Meaning of Life', *The Monist* 93.1 (2010): 3–16. I am basically in accord with Pritchard.

10 B. Russell, 'A Free Man's Worship', in his *Mysticism and Logic*, Bungay: Penguin (1953), Chapter 3.

11 A. Flew, 'What Does it Mean to Ask: "What is the Meaning of Life?"', in his *The Presumption of Atheism and Other Essays*, London: Elek Books (1976), Chapter 12.

12 E. D. Klemke, 'Living Without Appeal: An Affirmative Philosophy of Life', in E. D. Klemke and S. M. Cahn (eds), *The Meaning of Life: A Reader*, Oxford: Oxford University Press (1999), 172.

13 G. Kahane, 'Should We Want God To Exist?', *Philosophy and Phenomenological Research* 82.3 (2011): 674–96, 681.

14 One thing that I never intend to mean by it is the thing that is most commonly meant by it in the wider literature of Philosophy, the thing that is sometimes called 'Political Pluralism', *viz.* the thesis, roughly, that the state should not seek to impose any particular vision of the good life on its citizens. The thing that I intend to mean by it in the main text here is what is sometimes called 'Value Pluralism'. The sort of Pluralism I shall endorse later (and prefer to call 'Polyvalence', as the word 'Pluralism' has already been 'spoken for' in the relevant literature) could be considered in part a localized form of Value Pluralism. That's because it is – in part – a pluralism about what I shall contend is the 'oft-times-but-mistakenly-supposed-to-be-unitary' value, meaningfulness, that individual human lives may have. It is in part that, but it is not solely that as my view is also a pluralism about the connotation and thus denotation of the phrase 'the meaning of life', which allows that some of the things one refers to with that phrase are none of the plural values (and indeed at least one non-value thing) that go up to make meaningfulness in individual human lives. I call these the cosmic interpretations of the question 'What is the meaning of life?' Nevertheless, it would come as no surprise, if one had read to the end of the book and not noticed me endorsing it explicitly, that I do endorse a more global Value Pluralism, which is what I aim to refer to with the term in the main text here, and it is thus not misleading to think of me as following the Value Pluralist tradition of Berlin, Williams et al., and of what I am doing in this book as in large part applying this tradition to meaning-in-life issues.

15 This is a bit rough as a definition. I myself later maintain that sometimes it is not up to us how to choose between incommensurable values in the sense that despite their

incommensurability there can be a determinate objective ranking. The doctrine of 'Value Pluralism' to which I aim to refer here is subject of extensive debate and it would be misleading of me to represent it as having a stable definition, shared by all those who would self-identify as value pluralists. Isaiah Berlin is often credited with originating the idea, though he himself cites predecessors. Bernard Williams is the other *locus classicus*. The most fully developed and well argued for variant of it that I find most plausible is given by M. Stocker in his *Plural and Conflicting Values*, Oxford: Clarendon Press (1990).

16 This example assumes that privacy has a value that remains more or less fixed across logical space as one moves between Godless and Godly worlds that stay the same in other respects. And this assumption could be rejected. One could think that in Godly worlds privacy is less of a value than it is in otherwise similar Godless worlds. Thus, although threatened, not so much of value is threatened by God. On that view, I concede, so much the worse for my example. I move in my next example to a case that does not seem to me quite so open to this objection. However, I should admit that a certain 'Platonic' solution to the Euthyphro dilemma must be accepted for any examples to work along these lines. If one thinks that all value ceases to exist as one moves from Godly to Godless worlds in logical space, for God is necessary to undergird it, then God's existence cannot coherently be thought to threaten any values at all except in the – rather odd – counterpossible way that I shall discuss later in the book. We shall come to the view that God is needed to undergird value per se in the main text in the moment.

17 There are issues that are being swept under the carpet here somewhat to do with whether or not the person should be said to exist in both *W1* and *W2*. We'll return to these in the main text in due course and speak to them then.

18 I used the terms 'pessimism' and 'optimism' in this technical sense first in my survey piece 'Recent Work on the Meaning of Life and the Philosophy of Religion', *Philosophy Compass* (2013). Confusingly, Edwards calls those atheists who think that life has no meaning as there is no divine cosmic scheme and no eternal life 'pessimists' in his 'The Meaning and Value of Life', in E. D. Klemke and S. M. Cahn (ed.) *The Meaning of Life: A Reader*, New York: Oxford University Press (1981). These pessimists, in Edwards' sense, are optimists in my sense; they are those I call nihilists in the main text.

19 Optimism in the sense spoken of here has some affinities to the view that Metz labels 'Supernaturalism' (e.g. in his 'New Developments in the Meaning of Life', *Philosophy Compass* 2.2 [2007]: 196–207, but he uses the same terminology in numerous places elsewhere). 'Supernaturalism' is defined there by Metz as the view that 'life is meaningless if the only world that exists is the one known by physics' (T. Metz, 'Could God's Purpose be the Source of Life's Meaning?' *Religious Studies* 36 [2000]: 293–313, 196). Having defined it thus, he then divides supernaturalist views into what he calls 'God-centred views' and 'soul-centred views'. It is left unclear where certain Buddhist views would fit in this taxonomy, those that would seem to be supernaturalistic in Metz's sense, yet would deny both Theism and the existence of the soul. But I deviate from Metz's terminology for other reasons. First, while some theists do maintain that life would be entirely meaningless if the only world is the one described by physics (see discussion in the main text in a moment), a larger number claim that if Theism were false, individuals' lives might still have some meaning – shallow or transient meaning, it might be called – but would not have another sort of meaning – deep or eternal meaning, it might be called (and indeed is called, e.g. R. Audi, 'Intrinsic Value and Meaningful Life', *Philosophical Papers* 34 (2005): 331–55, 350; and P. Quinn, 'How Christianity Secures Life's Meanings', in J. Runzo and N. Martin (eds), *The Meaning of Life in the World Religions*, Oxford: Oneworld (2000), 53–68, 55. Such theists then would not count as supernaturalists on Metz's understanding and that seems odd to me. Further, the

distinction between God-centred and soul-centred views seems somewhat redundant. The majority view amongst theists is that God and an afterlife jointly are needed to make for this deep and eternal meaning; neither on their own would be sufficient. So, I submit, we have reason to prefer my terminology over Metz's. Metz himself argues that this 'accommodation' with naturalism – allowing that even *sans* God there might yet be some meaning in human lives – is not the right move for supernaturalists, as he understands them, to make. 'To see this, suppose that a religious thinker … maintained the weaker view that while a relationship with God would make our lives more meaningful, it would not be necessary for meaning. The problem is that virtually no naturalist would dispute this claim … Naturalists emphasize that God's existence is irrelevant for meaning, that for a life to be meaningful there need not exist a spiritual person who grounds the universe. Therefore, for religious thinking to carve out a distinct and interesting position, it must maintain that God's existence and a certain relationship with Him are necessary for life to acquire significance' (T. Metz, *Meaning in Life*, Oxford: Oxford University Press (2013), 108). But this does not seem right to me. We've already seen some prominent naturalists – Sartre, Nagel, Russell, Flew, Klemke, and there are others – who would do that which Metz assures us virtually no naturalist would do. And, as it is the majority opinion amongst actual theists, telling them that they should abandon it simply because it is not 'distinctive' enough relative to some other (less plausible as committing oneself to more) position seems, in any case, misguided.

20 E. Wielenberg, 'God and the Meaning of Life' in his *Value and Virtue in a Godless Universe*, Cambridge: Cambridge University Press (2005), 17. The view then is the extreme one that Wolf discusses in the passage in note 2. This is just one variant of the view though.

21 I talk here of the 2003 Cottingham. His views have undergone modification; I am not sure he would still hold to the position attributed to him in the main text. Still, as a place-marker for a set of views if not for other reasons, the 2003 Cottingham is preferable to the current Cottingham. The only theist I am aware of who currently holds to the extreme view explicitly is W. L. Craig, in his 'The Absurdity of Life without God', in *Reasonable Faith: Christian Truth and Apologetics*, 3rd edn., Wheaton, IL: Crossway Books (2008), 65–90. However, it seems to me that it is his commitment to a particular way of solving the Euthyphro dilemma that in turn commits him to this more extreme view and many other contemporary theistic philosophers are also committed to this particular way of solving the Euthyphro dilemma and thus are, it seems to me, implicitly committed to the more extreme view.

22 J. Cottingham, *On the Meaning of Life*, London: Routledge (2003), 64.

23 J. Cottingham, *On the Meaning of Life*, London: Routledge (2003), 72–73.

24 J. Cottingham, *On the Meaning of Life*, London: Routledge (2003), 67. As Brogaard and Smith point out, one would be foolish to rule out such luck by stipulation, rather as a Kantian might stipulate-away moral luck. 'One might stipulate that the meaningfulness of a life must be such that luck never plays a role. This, however, swiftly leads to nihilism about meaning. For if none of our achievements are without contingency, and if luck can play no role in determining how meaningful a life is, then our lives will have no meaning.' (B. Brogaard and B. Smith, 'On Luck, Responsibility and the Meaning of Life', *Philosophical Papers* 34 [2005]: 443–58, 454). This is a little bit quick of course; a worldview where a meticulously provident God created a deterministic universe would be one with no luck, but I think Brogaard and Smith are in essence right here.

25 There is a 'third' way, briefly mentioned in note 2, but I do not mention it in the main text as it does not seem to me plausible. One might deny the premise that God's meaning trumps ours. Even if God has assigned one a purpose, one can assign oneself a purpose at variance with that and this second purpose then become the purpose of one's life in such a way as to give one's life its true meaning. Here, briefly, is why I would dismiss this. It seems

to me that if I am working in a factory fixing widgets to the things that go past on the conveyor belt because that is what the Managing Director has decided that I should do for the purpose of making cars, then that is my purpose in being there. If I assign my activities my own purpose – perhaps it is easiest to imagine that I do this if we imagine that I am in ignorance of why I'm really there – then I just get to be mistaken about why I'm there. I do not get to change why I'm there and thus I do not get my self-assigned purpose to be the real meaning-giving purpose of my being there. The real meaning-giving purpose of the Managing Director trumps any attempt at meaning-giving purpose-assigning by me. So, for example, I might, in the situation we are imagining, say of myself that my purpose in affixing the widgets is to perform a dance. My thinking of my repetitive movements in this way might well make them appear more meaningful for me. Given that we are imagining that I do not know why I am really there, it probably would. Now ask, if we should say that my doing that would actually make what I am doing more meaningful *for me*. I confess to *some* temptation to say that it would. But I resist it in the end and would suggest instead that the misnamed 'meaning for me' that I have in such a case managed to generate is rather a subjective (mis)perception of fulfilling my objective purpose, not the subjective correct perception of fulfilling my objective purpose. (It is the illusion of 'meaning for me', not the real thing.) To see this, let's recall the fact that it is clear (clear to us thinking about the case from the outside, not clear to me as I exist in the situation we are imagining) what the objective purpose of me being there really is. That is, it is clear what the answer to the following question is: Am I really there to make cars or to dance? Clearly, the former. That being so, if I had realized this and appropriated it to myself, that would have been in part my subjective correct perception of my fulfilling my objective purpose, and thus that would have been that meaning-giving purpose adding meaning for me. But we are instead considering a case where I, in ignorance of my objective purpose, seek to assign myself a purpose and then think of myself as fulfilling the purpose that I thus think of myself as now having. That then is not for that pseudo-objective-purpose to give my life this sort of meaning for me. It is at most for me, in ignorance of its pseudo-status, to take it to be giving my life this sort of meaning for me. That, it seems to me, is the way authority works; see note 2. The Managing Director just does have authority over me. As I said in note 2, I have a much more absolutist conception of authority than some.

26 Metz says this at one point: 'There is an *a priori* connection between meaning and purpose, at least in that "purposive" is one synonym of "meaningful"' (T. Metz, 'The Concept of a Meaningful Life', *American Philosophical Quarterly* 38.2 [2001]: 137–53, 140). I do not agree with him in that I take 'meaningful' to be far broader in meaning than 'purposive' – purposive is not *the* meaning of 'meaningful' and thus not a synonym of it, but I do agree that it is *a* meaning of 'meaningful'.

27 Natural, but not universal. Levy obviously does not feel the pull at all. He dismisses theories of the meaning of life, which ground it in God's purpose thusly: 'I shall have little to say about these accounts, except to note that they do not satisfactorily explain how it is that our connecting up with God's purposes is supposed to make our lives meaningful. If we are to play a role in God's plan, that He has prepared for us, and which He could carry out without our help, how does that confer meaning on our lives? Children do not have meaning conferred upon their lives when they play a part in projects carefully prearranged for them by adults' (N. Levy, 'Downshifting and Meaning in Life', *Ratio* 18 [2005]: 176–89, 179). Even allowing that there are ways – quite standard ways – of unpacking God's relationship to us such that His purposes cannot be fulfilled (except in the minimal sense of the outcome being in accordance with His permissive will) without our help, and ways which Levy could have explained to him, it seems that he would not be at all inclined to sympathy for the thought that God's having a purpose for us could be relevant to the question of life's meaning. Of

course, this is inconclusive. That Levy dismisses a caricature of the mainstream theistic view is not conclusive evidence that he would dismiss the real thing were it presented to him. But his remarks are, I think, indicative.

28 S. Goetz, *The Purpose of Life: A Theistic Perspective*, London: Continuum (2012), 174.

29 Note these last two words, 'for us'. It seems it obviously would add to the meaning of our lives for the Martians. The point is that the Martians' purposes for us would not be appropriated to ourselves by us (I am assuming), as they would be rightly judged by us too degrading.

30 There are other senses in which they do not make for meaningfulness in the slave's life. Indeed, there are some significant senses of meaningfulness in which they detract from the meaningfulness of the slave's life. But these other sorts of meaningfulness are not ones *for them*. Perhaps then this just shows that, *contra* for example Klemke in the passage quoted earlier, it is not really meaningfulness *for us* that we are solely interested in, or should be solely interested in if we cannot be sure our psychologies are perfect.

31 It is not just God who can perform this sort of transfiguration. In what is almost the final scene of the film, *Angels With Dirty Faces*, the lead character – a tough gangster, called 'Rocky' – has put to him by the priest who visits him on Death Row a choice. Face his imminent execution as would come naturally to him – heroically – and thus continue to be idolized by his youthful followers. That would mean that his followers could be predicted to follow him yet further down the path of criminality and no doubt some of them end up in due course on Death Row themselves. Or degrade himself, by feigning cowardice as his jailors take him to his execution. Then his erstwhile followers would be disgusted by him and turn from his path. As he is subsequently led to his execution, we see Rocky change, very suddenly, from square-jawed, level-eyed toughness, to screaming, pleading and clawing at a radiator in an apparent attempt to stop himself being dragged to his death. Suppose that Rocky did choose his reactions (the film leaves the matter uncertain). If so, he turned his final degradation into his most glorious moment. Or consider another 'Rocky', Saint Peter, who, if tradition is to be believed, was crucified upside down as a result of telling his executioners that he was unworthy of being executed in the same manner as Jesus. Again, his degradation was his most exalted moment. These then are grand examples. But in each of our lives we can find less grand ones – whenever, in order to make someone feel more comfortable at finding something difficult, for example, we point out that we ourselves found that thing difficult the first time we came across it (rather than hide that fact from them) or in general whenever we choose for similar motives to reveal a weakness, rather than conceal it. Our bringing such minor 'degradations' on ourselves for these reasons transfigures their value for us. Acts of humility do not humiliate the person who makes themselves humble for noble ends, and that is no less true of little acts of humility than it is of grand ones.

32 J. Cottingham, *On the Meaning of Life*, London: Routledge (2003), 22.

33 Of course it may be that Cottingham is intending with his talk of meaningfulness to an agent to pick out the same relationship as I am doing when I talk of meaningfulness for an agent, in which case then I agree with him (at this point – at others, e.g. in his Monism, his belief that this is the only sort of meaning that there is, I disagree).

34 This example and the notion, though not the precise term, is suggested to me by Cottingham. See e.g. J. Cottingham, *On the Meaning of Life*, London: Routledge (2003), 69.

35 Some theists claim that the afterlife is irrelevant to Theism's being true adding to life's meaning, but the consensus has been and remains that it is not. See e.g. J. Cottingham, *On the Meaning of Life*, London: Routledge (2003), 74ff.

36 For a dissenter, see J. Kekes, 'The Meaning of Life', *Midwest Studies in Philosophy* 24 (2000):

17–34, 30ff., who says that 'It follows from the possibility that immoral and non-moral projects may give meaning to lives that the moral answer is mistaken in regarding successful engagement in morally good projects as a necessary condition of meaningful lives' (31). My own view is that certain sorts of meaningfulness do require moral engagement; others do not. Kekes, being a monist (of which more later [he calls himself a pluralist]), does not see this.

37 It is argued to be so, for example, by William Davis in his 'The Meaning of Life', *Metaphilosophy* 18 (1987): 288–305.

38 S. Goetz, *The Purpose of Life: A Theistic Perspective*, London: Continuum (2012), 6.

39 L. Pojman, 'Religion Gives Meaning to Life', in E. D. Klemke and S. M. Cahn (eds), *The Meaning of Life*, New York: Oxford University Press (1981), 28.

40 W. James, 'Is Life Worth Living?' in his *The Will to Believe and Other Essays*, London: Longmans (1897), 57, originally published in *International Journal of Ethics* 6.1 (1895): 1–24.

41 This is not quite right. For example, I might have the desire that I be spoken of in glowing terms in the eulogy at my funeral. That is, on some understandings, an I-desire, but one that – obviously – I am not going to be around to see satisfied (if it is satisfied).

42 As Waghorn puts it, 'that I will eventually die seems to rob my life of at least some of its meaning, namely those meaningful activities I could have engaged in had I lived longer' (N. Waghorn, *Nothingness and the Meaning of Life: Philosophical Approaches to Ultimate Meaning Through Nothing and Self-reflexivity*, London: Bloomsbury [2014], 1).

43 Of course, this is not true of all atheisms. I paint in broad strokes at this stage.

44 B. Williams, 'The Makropulos Case: Reflections on the Tedium of Immortality', in his *Problems of the Self*, Cambridge: Cambridge University Press (1973), 82–100. See also M. Nussbaum, in her 'Mortal Immortals: Lucretius on Death and the Voice of Nature', *Philosophy and Phenomenological Research* 50 (1989): 303–51. She endorses Williams' 'fork': either it will not be us who live forever or there'll be something inherently undesirable (in Nussbaum's analysis, a failure to be able to display certain virtues – courage, for example) about our doing so.

45 For example, C. Belshaw, *10 Good Questions about Life and Death*, Malden, MA: Blackwell (2005), 82–91; and J. Ellin, *Morality and The Meaning of Life*, Fort Worth, TX: Harcourt Brace College Publishers (1995).

46 Despite what I say in the main text here, I actually think that there *is* a sense of meaningfulness that we do care about things in our lives having (but ultimately should not and will not) that requires mortality. This is the meaningfulness of an action or a finite period of one's life as a function of its ultimate significance on the whole. Actions or periods that we take to have greater evaluable causal consequence on one's life as a whole are judged to be more meaningful in this sense then than those that – even if they have greater short-term consequence – we suppose ultimately make little or no difference. Immortality (of the right sort – right for the other purposes I've discussed already) eliminates the meaningfulness in this sense of our actions/*ante-mortem* lives or at least reduces it without limit over time (these are different ways of configuring the issue, but I can run them together for my present purposes) and indeed it does so for our heavenly actions and finite periods spent in Heaven too. By the time one has spent a million years in Heaven, pretty much everything that one did on Earth seems likely to me to have been rendered of negligible meaningfulness in this sense. For any action or period of our *ante-mortem* life to have meaning in this sense then requires one of two things. Either mortality (a cut-off point, so that the whole is not constantly being added to and thus the contribution to its

evaluable aspects made by earlier decisions reduced (either to zero or without limit; as I say, one could configure things differently here)). Or the wrong (wrong by reference to other considerations) sort of immortality (e.g. one in which whether or not one gets to Heaven or Hell depends on what one does *ante-mortem*). There is a parallel here with a discussion by Quentin Smith in his 'Moral Realism and Infinite Spacetime Imply Moral Nihilism', in H. Dyke (ed.), *Time and Ethics: Essays at the Intersection*, Dordrecht: Kluwer Academic Publishers (2003), 43–54. He argues that if the world contains an infinite degree of value, then nothing we can do can add to it (infinity plus any amount is still infinity). Of course it is not an exact parallel. On Theism minus the pre-existence of the soul (which is the standard view) we will never have had an actually infinite life. We just have a potentially infinite one ahead of us. But 'the law of diminishing meaningfulness-with-time' point still stands with respect to the sort of meaningfulness that is having an evaluable causal consequence on one's life as a whole as made with regard to actions or any finite period within one's potentially infinite life. We'll come back to this point later in the main text.

Of course, as Brian Leftow has pointed out to me, that a shorter life is not more meaningful does not entail that having some finite length to one's life is not a necessary condition of meaningfulness.

47 Another approach would be to suggest that immortality (at least if known about with certainty) would deprive us of reasons for doing things at any time and thus at all times, and this would detract from – possibly even evacuate all meaning from – our existence. Victor Frankl (in *The Doctor and the Soul*, Alfred Knopf: New York [1957], quoted in R. Nozick, *Philosophical Explanations*, Cambridge, MA: Harvard University Press [1981], 579) writes that 'death itself is what makes life meaningful. What would our lives be like if they were not finite in time, but infinite? If we were immortal, we could legitimately postpone every action forever. It would be of no consequence whether or not we did a thing now ... But in the face of death as absolute *finis* ... we are under the imperative of utilizing our lifetimes to the utmost.' I do not think this view is worthy of substantive discussion however. Things that are inherently worth doing are things one is *prima facie* reasonable in doing now just in virtue of that inherent worth. One needs countervailing reason to *delay* doing them, not reason (beyond their inherent worth) for doing them. And it is things that are inherently worth doing that are just the sort things that we are traditionally pictured as doing in Heaven – living in perfect communion with God and our fellow man; worshipping God in the full glory of the beatific vision; and so forth. Leon Kass, in *'L'Chaim and Its Limits: Why Not Immortality?' First Things* 113 (2001): 17–24, says that mortality is necessary for motivation and appreciation, but similarly I am not convinced.

48 Again, I am painting with broad strokes – an atheist might hold that we do get an everlasting afterlife, provided for us by some trans-dimensional (but non-divine) super-being. I shall continue to ignore such people; my apologies to them.

49 See note 46 for one sense of meaningfulness indeed in which I think it is definitely true.

50 L. J. Russell, 'The Meaning of Life', *Philosophy* 28.104 (1953): 30–40, 34, says this: 'If we feel that [someone's suffering in] their present life is merely an infinitesimal part of an eternally prolonged existence, we may be less likely to want to do something about it.' Indeed, we may be. Of course, we may equally well not be. As I say, much depends on temperament. Certainly, the thesis that it would be rational for us to care less needs argument, argument that is seldom given. That is not to say that it cannot be given. Arguments that suggest that value-maximizing forms of Utilitarianism, for example, cannot cope with infinite utilities, seem to me to have much going for them. But, then again, I am not a value-maximizing Utilitarian, so I do not have a horse in that race. Nor do many theists.

51 See e.g. B. Trisel, 'Human Extinction and the Value of Our Efforts', *The Philosophical Forum*

35.3 (2004): 379–91, 384–5, for an analysis of how this can certainly happen (but need not do so).

52 B. Clack and B. Clack, *The Philosophy of Religion*, Cambridge: Polity (2008), 178–9.

53 R. Audi, 'Intrinsic Value and Meaningful Life', *Philosophical Papers* 35 (2005): 331–55, 344.

54 W. James, 'Is Life Worth Living?' in his *The Will to Believe and Other Essays*, London: Longmans (1897), 62.

55 N.B. 'Pluralism' is being used in a different sense now to that in which it was used in the main text earlier. I shall go into more detail in the next chapter but, briefly, in the main text earlier I was using it to refer to the view that usually goes by the name value pluralism. Now I am using it to refer to a view that is focused solely on the plurality of the meanings of life.

56 I talk predominantly of polyvalence rather than ambiguity primarily as 'ambiguity' seems to me to carry pejorative overtones, whereas polyvalence, if anything, carries positive ones.

57 My paternal grandfather, in case you had not guessed, led, by the standards of his time and culture, a relatively ordinary life.

58 I think that the usage I am about to outline and hereafter deploy better reflects what is going on in the untutored judgement of deepness that we make day to day. Whether or not I am right in that will be for my reader to judge as he or she reads on and sees my usage at work. But if he or she fails to be convinced by this claim of consonance with everyday usage, it is of no matter for my argument. He or she may take my usage then as a stipulated technical usage of the term 'deepness' and its cognates, one adopted to enable me to articulate a part of the structure of meaningfulness as 'a' property that individuals' lives may have.

59 I know this is not the most widely recognized translation of the relevant passage from *The Book of Job*; the King James version actually reads, 'The Lord gave, and the Lord has taken away'. But it occurs in the 1559 *Book of Common Prayer* in the Order of Service for the Burial of the Dead and I prefer it. It is how I would myself translate the motto of this book, given in its original Hebrew on the title page.

Chapter 1

1 E. M. Adams, tells – and tells tellingly – of hearing 'a distinguished analytic philosopher confess rather apologetically, in his presidential address to the American Philosophical Association, that once in a time of weakness and lapse of judgement he wrote a paper on the meaning of life' (E. M. Adams, 'The Meaning of Life', *International Journal for Philosophy of Religion* 52 [2002]: 71–81, 71).

2 'Meaningfulness is a central but, at least in contemporary secular moral theory, hitherto relatively neglected aspect of well-being,' says Antti Kauppinen, in 'Meaningfulness and Time', *Philosophy and Phenomenological Research* 84.2 (2012): 345–77, 345. I do not actually agree with Kauppinen in locating meaningfulness here – some sorts of meaningfulness contribute to well-being, but some do not (or at least do not have to do so). I am going to argue later that Hitler's life was meaningful in the sense that it stood for something (a particular ideology), but its doing so did not add to his well-being (or that of anyone else).

3 Metz has some interesting lines of explanation for why the area is, as he puts it, 'frankly something of a backwater' in his 'Recent Work on the Meaning of Life', *Ethics* 112.4 (2002): 781–814, 782.

4 It occurs to me to reflect that if I did not have a tenured position from which I anticipate never desiring to move on, I would be chary of writing on the topic myself.

Notes

5 S. Wolf, 'The Meanings of Lives', in Joshua Seachris (ed.), *Exploring the Meaning of Life: An Anthology and Guide,* Malden, MA: Wiley-Blackwell (2013), 304.

6 W. Davis, 'The Meaning of Life', *Metaphilosophy*, 18, 3/4 (1987): 288–305, 290.

7 I have put the bits that he didn't quite say in square brackets in the quotation.

8 I (dimly) remember (or I may be imagining it) that when I first heard that the ratio of a circle's circumference to its diameter, i.e. pi, was not a rational number, I was similarly dissatisfied. I wanted the world to be different in this respect (and perhaps quite reasonably so – although counterfactuals with impossible antecedents are tricky, one might argue that if it had been 3, say, then that would have made my maths homework easier). But in coming to see that it was a mathematical necessity that pi not be rational – it was something not even God could have made come out differently – I became in the end satisfied with my dissatisfaction. That is the sort of transition I hope to facilitate here.

9 It is philosophically illuminating to ask quite when the question 'What is the meaning of life?' was *first* posed and why it was first posed then. Obviously one can find concerns that – even if not using the term 'meaning of life' or terms that can uncontroversially be supposed to be its cognates – are similar to those in mind when one asks 'What is the meaning of life?', in ancient sources. *The Book of Ecclesiastes* is usually mentioned in this context. And, in addressing themselves to what makes for the good life, the founders of Western Philosophy – Plato and Aristotle – could plausibly be argued to be engaging with it too. But a case can be made that the determinate question 'What is the meaning of life?' really arose only in the past few hundred years, possibly even later. As will be obvious from the main text, I think I can detect the question in James, just over a hundred years ago now. Metz, writing in 2013, says that 'it is only in the last 50 years or so that something approaching a distinct field on the meaning of life has been established in Anglo-American philosophy, and it is only in the last 30 years that debate with real depth has appeared.' (T. Metz, 'The Meaning of Life', in *Stanford Encyclopedia of Philosophy* [first published online Tuesday 15 May 2007; substantive revision Monday 3 June 2013). Obviously one cannot detect the question in Anglo-American philosophy before there was Anglo-American Philosophy or in Analytic Philosophy before there was Analytic Philosophy and quite when these things started is another issue that may be fought over. But others claim to detect the question in sources still earlier than any plausible starting dates for them. Thus Iddo Landau, wrote in 1997, under the title 'Why has the question of the meaning of life arisen in the last two and a half centuries?', *Philosophy Today* (1997): 263–9. The usual argument for not tracing back further than this is roughly that it was only with the so-called 'Death of God' that the question arose, because prior to His demise, everyone had been satisfied with the answer He provided. Thus Alisdair MacIntyre in 'Comments on Frankfurt', *Synthese* 53 (1982): 291–4, 291: 'There are concepts that are able to appear on the cultural scene only when some other older concept or concepts have been displaced in such a way as to leave cultural space for them. So it is only in a post-theological age such as our own that the concept of the meaning of life is able to appear and to flourish. For the question "What is the meaning of life?" fills the space left vacant by the question "Does God exist?"' Or, as Baggini puts it, 'All would agree that the "discovery" that there is no God has created a crisis of meaning for human life. The reason for this is that we assumed that purpose and morality had their source in something outside of ourselves. When this assumption was overturned, we lost the source of life's meaning.' (J. Baggini, *What's it All About?* London: Granta [2004], 10). While I think that there is some truth in claims such as these as generalizations, explaining why the question rose to prominence in Western culture when it did, such claims cannot be plausible if presented as explaining what was genuinely the first occurrence of the question. In general, the claim that the question could only arise after the so-called Death of God because prior to His demise everyone

uncritically accepted that He was the answer to it suffers from numerous objections, even if one ignores its oddly Euro-centric perspective (what were the Chinese doing all this time?). First, atheists were around long before the so-called Death of God, and were obviously wrestling with it – Lucretius, for example. Second, theists – prior to the so-called Death of God – seem to have been thinking about the nature of the answer God may be taken to provide and thus wrestling with it – Aquinas for example. Third, it is a very odd thesis that holds that the question does not arise before *t* because prior to *t* everyone had been satisfied with the answer God provided to it. What was it that they were satisfied with this as an answer to if they had not yet posed the question to which it was the answer? And then, fourth, the dissatisfaction of which I am speaking in the main text is not a culturally/ temporally contingent matter, so it will have predated the so-called Death of God; even the theists who accepted that God was the answer will have felt that that cannot be all that there is to be said about it. So, the answer to the question that I would give is that the question 'What is the meaning of life?' was first posed some time in prehistory and it was posed then simply because humanity had at that stage evolved enough to be able to pose it. It has been posed ever since. It will be posed until the human race becomes extinct.

10 William James, 'Is Life Worth Living?', in his *The Will to Believe and Other Essays*, London Longmans (1897), 34. Interestingly, James seeks to locate the psychological source of the problem by looking in diametrically the opposite direction to Moritz Schlick, a philosopher to whose opinions we shall come in a moment. James says that the 'sovereign source of melancholy is repletion. Need and struggle are what excite and inspire us; our hour of triumph is what brings the void. Not the Jews of the captivity, but those of the days of Solomon's glory are those from whom the pessimistic utterances of in our Bible come' (W. James, in his *The Will to Believe and Other Essays*, London Longmans [1897], 47). (It is not at all obvious, of course, how this squares with the thought in the passage from James quoted in the main text earlier.)

11 If his essay 'What Makes a Life Significant', in his *Talks to Teachers on Psychology, and to Students on Some of Life's Ideals*, New York: Henry Holt (1899) is anything to go by, he would not have counted such people as leading significant lives. Though that text too is unclear, it seems to me that James is of the opinion that for significance one must have a particular sort of attitude – variously characterized as joy, delight, enduringly-finding-novel – towards what he calls an ideal, where ideals are construed as 'relative to the lives that entertain them'. His view, in essence, seems close to that of Frankfurt, to which we will come in due course.

12 A. Flew, 'What Does it Mean to Ask: "What is the Meaning of Life?"', in his *The Presumption of Atheism and Other Essays*, London: Elek Books (1976), 167.

13 This is a bit rough and ready as a characterization of Logical Positivism, but nothing turns on its inaccuracies.

14 L. Wittgenstein, *Tractatus Logico-Philosophicus*, C. Ogden (trans.), London: Routledge & Kegan Paul (1988), 187 (6.52 and 6.521).

15 P. Quinn, 'The Meaning of Life According to Christianity', in E. D. Klemke and S. M. Cahn (eds) *The Meaning of Life*, New York: Oxford University Press (1981), 35–41, 35.

16 N. Uygur, 'What is a Philosophical Question?', *Mind* 73.289 (1964): 64–83, 75.

17 These were the diagnoses of Moritz Schlick (in his 'On the Meaning of Life', *Philosophical Papers II*, D. Reidel Publishing Co. [1979], 112–28) and John Wisdom (in his 'What is There in Horse Racing?', *The Listener*, 10 June 1954) respectively. In each case, as with James, the problem of the meaning of life is taken to be a psychological one in the mind of the person asking about it, a problem to be removed by refreshing 'the spirit of youth' (M. Schlick, in his 'On the Meaning

of Life', *Philosophical Papers II*, Dordrecht: Reidel Publishing Co. [1979], 128) in the person and/or persuading them to engage in intrinsically enjoyable activity, such as horse racing was for Wisdom. That having been done, no genuine philosophical problem requires anyone's further attention. One of Wisdom's pupils, Michael Wolf, recalls that Wisdom practised what he preached in this regard. 'Wisdom was … a fanatic about horse-racing. He had an upturned chair in his rooms with a saddle on top of it and once, when we went to his lecture, he had scrawled in chalk on the blackboard, "Gone to Newmarket", the famous race-course not very far from Cambridge' (http://www.roangelo.net/logwitt/mwolff.html [accessed 22 July 2008]).

18 J. Cottingham, *On the Meaning of Life*, London: Routledge (2003), 19.

19 R. M. Hare, 'Nothing Matters', originally published as '"Rien n'a d'importance": l'anéantissement des valeurs est-il pensable?' in *La Philosophie Analytique*, L. Beck (ed.), Paris: Editions de Minuit (1959/60); reprinted in English as '"Nothing Matters": Is "the Annihilation of Values" Something That Could Happen?', in his *Applications of Moral Philosophy*, London: Macmillan (1972), Chapter 4.

20 A. J. Ayer, 'The Meaning of Life', in his *The Meaning of Life and Other Essays*, London: Weidenfeld & Nicolson (1990), 189. Ayer also pays a backhanded compliment to the more cosmic interpretations of the question; in his debate with Copleston (P. Edwards and A. Pap (eds) *A Modern Introduction to Philosophy*, 2nd edition, New York: The Free Press 1965), he says – *pace* Copleston – that science can handle all why questions (as long as those why questions are intelligible) and thus those aspects of the question of the meaning of life, insofar as they are intelligible, may be hived off for scientists to deal with. (We shall define 'cosmic interpretation's in a moment.)

21 R. Wohlgennant, 'Has the Question about the Meaning of Life any Meaning?', repr. in *Life and Meaning: A Philosophical Reader*, O. Hanfling (ed.), Cambridge: Basil Blackwell Inc. (1987), 34–38 (originally Chapter 4 of his *Philosophie als Wissenschaft*, Chicago: Open Court (1911).

22 A weaker claim – chanced by Williams – may well be true. Williams says at one point that 'one good testimony to one's existence having a point is that the question of its point does not arise, and the propelling concerns may be of a relatively everyday kind as certainly provide the ground for many sorts of happiness' (B. Williams, 'Persons, Character and Morality', in A. Rorty (ed.), *The Identities of Persons*, Berkeley: University of California Press [1976], 197–216, 208, *cf.* 209).

23 Theirs is a subjectivist view and while I have been playing a bit fast and loose with making alterations to their view so as to make it more plausible than the one(s) that, as a matter of the history of ideas, it is more credible they actually held, to alter it so as to be objectivist seems to me a step too far if one wishes to call the resultant view by their names. In the main text later, I therefore call the view an 'objectivist spin' on the Ayer/Wohlgennant view.

The same problems of being too subjective arise for Berit Brogaard and Barry Smith's view, as articulated in their 'On Luck, Responsibility and the Meaning of Life', *Philosophical Papers* 34 (2005): 443–58. They defend an intersubjectivist theory of meaning in life – meaning is engaging in whatever activities are ranked highly by one's society. But what if one's society is wrong? And how to identify one's society? All the problems of intersubjectivism in value theory and of cultural relativism flood in. And the same goes for Wai-hung Wong's view as articulated in his 'Meaningfulness and Identities', *Ethical Theory and Moral Practice* 11 (2008): 123–48. He says that if a person's identity is valued in certain of its facets for its own sake by that person and others, it is thereby meaningful. Consider the eulogies spoken of Reinhard Heydrich. They reflected just the sort of approval by his fellow members of the SS that would make his life meaningful on these accounts, which shows clearly that something is missing from these accounts.

24 J. Kekes, 'The Meaning of Life', *Midwest Studies in Philosophy* 24 (2000): 17–34.

25 A. J. Ayer, 'The Meaning of Life' in his *The Meaning of Life and Other Essays*, London: Weidenfeld & Nicolson (1989), 178–97, 196–7.

26 I owe my knowledge of this story to my colleague Peter Kail. Ted Honderich tells a similar tale. He witnessed Ayer second in the queue behind another gentleman, waiting to be buzzed in to an exclusive private members' club in London. The first man buzzed and the voice at the other end of the intercom asked him to identify himself. He said quietly 'Harold Macmillan'. He was let in. Ayer buzzed next and, on being asked the same question, declared 'I am Sir Alfred Jules Ayer, Professor of Philosophy at the University of London and Fellow of the British Academy'. The only wonder is that Ayer allowed himself to be second in the queue.

27 Stephen Darwall, Berit Brogaard and Barry Smith (S. Darwall, *Impartial Reason*, Ithaca: Cornell University Press (1983), Chapters 11–12; and Brogaard and Smith, 'On Luck, Responsibility and the Meaning of Life' *Philosophical Papers* 34 [2005]: 443–58) occupy a middle ground. As mentioned of Brogaard and Smith in a previous note, their view is that there is an inter-subjectively valid standard of meaning, generated by what we would all agree upon from a certain collective ideal observer standpoint. (See also again Wong, 'Meaningfulness and Identities', *Ethical Theory and Moral Practice* 11 [2008]: 123–48.) As also mentioned already, personally, I am not convinced for the same reasons that people generally have if they fail to accept intersubjectivism as objective enough when it comes to accounting for moral value.

28 A. Camus, *The Myth of Sisyphus*, J. O'Brien (trans.), London: Penguin (2005 [orig. 1942]). Camus is rather hard to interpret. One permissible reading of him would seem to me to be that he thinks along the same lines as Sartre, Nagel, and Klemke: it is only 'objective', other-imposed, meaning that is lacking; we can still fashion subjective, self-imposed, meaning for ourselves, by acts of 'absurd creation'. However, in the main text, I prefer another reading: life is meaningless *tout court*; what we best do in the light of that is react with scorn.

29 A. Camus, *The Myth of Sisyphus*, J. O'Brien (trans.), London: Penguin (2005), 117.

30 As Wolf puts it, 'I am inclined to accept the standard view that there is no plausible interpretation of that question [What is the meaning of life?] that offers a positive answer in the absence of a fairly specific religious metaphysics' (S. Wolf, 'The Meanings of Lives', in her *The Variety of Values, Essays on Morality, Meaning, and Love* Oxford University Press [2015], 91). But, nevertheless, she maintains that, absent such a metaphysics, we can characterize what it is to have meaning in life. Metz sometimes calls the questions of 'whether the universe has a meaning or of whether the human species does', 'holistic' or 'cosmic' questions: '[I] set aside such holistic understandings of the question of life's meaning, so as to make progress on the individualist construal' (T. Metz, *Meaning in Life*, Oxford: Oxford University Press [2013], 3). And, as Metz puts it in a recent survey piece, 'most recent discussions of meaning in life are attempts to capture in a single principle all the variegated conditions that can confer meaning on life' (T. Metz, 'The Meaning of Life', *Stanford Encyclopedia of Philosophy* [first published online Tuesday 15 May 2007; substantive revision Monday 3 June 2013]). And by this he means to capture what property it is that is meaningfulness in individual humans' lives. Similarly, in another survey piece, in his first sentence, Metz says, 'In this article I survey philosophical literature on the topic of what, if anything, makes life meaningful,' (T. Metz, 'New Developments in the Meaning of Life', *Philosophy Compass* 2.2 [2007]: 196–217, 196). He then goes on without further comment to talk solely about philosophers addressing what makes individuals' lives meaningful. Why so narrow? Why not survey those who discuss what (if anything) makes humanity's life meaningful, or what makes life understood as biological life meaningful? Why not discuss

philosophers who address the question in its most 'cosmic' sense, such as, What is the meaning of it all? The answer is that Metz's survey piece does its job well – it surveys the field accurately and the field is united in its presumption that we can get on and answer the question, as posed, of an individual's life, the question of what within it will contribute to its being meaningful, without needing to discuss wider senses of life and the more cosmic questions of meaning that one might ask of them. I think this presumption mistaken for reasons that will become clear as the book goes on. In essence, if roughly, we cannot separate out the questions of the meaning of life under its cosmic interpretations, as we may call them, from those under its individualistic interpretations, as we may call them, and think that in answering just the last set of questions we have answered the original question. First, we will have failed to do so as most people are asking both sets of questions and, second, we will have failed to do so as how one answers each set of questions has implications for how one answers the other. At least some arguments proceed from the top-down, e.g. 'Given that the universe and humanity has no purpose: no purpose we can assign to our lives individually can give our lives meaning.' That argument can be tackled – and many do tackle it – solely at the level of validity. But it can also be tackled at the level of the truth of its premises. In any case, any treatment of the question that brackets off aspects of it must remain incomplete and the cosmic aspects, it seems to me, just are aspects of the question as it occurs in the minds of most people asking it. Metz himself tacitly concedes this when he calls holistic/cosmic 'understandings' that, understandings of the question. He does not call them misunderstandings of it.

However misguided, the widespread presumption that the question 'What is the meaning of life?' under its cosmic interpretations and the question under its individualistic interpretations can be decoupled and that one can answer the last without any commitments to any particular type of answer to the first has had one important and beneficial consequence. That it is a widespread presumption has helped the question 'What is the meaning of life?' gain in respectability, as were the question still to be believed to be married to questions about, for example, in Wolf's terms 'fairly specific religious metaphysics' (as I believe it is married), it would have to share the disrespect that religious metaphysics continues to be given in Philosophy generally. Waghorn expresses a similar point: 'Metz's narrowing down of the question of the meaning of life … has the advantage of allowing us to debate … the meaning of life for an individual and so avoiding the predominating thought of not so long ago that the question of life's meaning was ill-formed' (N. Waghorn, *Nothingness and the Meaning of Life: Philosophical Approaches to Ultimate Meaning Through Nothing and Self-reflexivity*, London: Bloomsbury [2014], 167).

31 The word 'cosmic' is standardly used to refer to issues surrounding the meanings of some entity larger than an individual human's life – humanity's life; life as a whole in its biological sense; 'it all'. But it is worth noting that Wai-hung Wong uses 'cosmic' slightly differently in his 'Meaningfulness and Identities', *Ethical Theory and Moral Practice* 11 (2008), 123–48. He says there (page 128), that 'Three distinct but related questions can be asked about the meaningfulness of one's life. The first is "What is the meaning of life?," which can be called "the cosmic question about meaningfulness"; the second is "What is a meaningful life?," which can be called "the general question about meaningfulness"; and the third is "What is the meaning of my life?," which can be called "the personal question about meaningfulness".

32 P. Singer, *Practical Ethics*, Cambridge: Cambridge University Press (1979), 219. Singer himself seems to think that a general (though not universal – there are psychopaths) truth about humans is that they will in fact only find this sort of fulfilment by aiming at reducing avoidable pain (P. Singer, *How are We to Live? Ethics in an Age of Self-Interest*, Oxford: Oxford University Press (1997)). Interestingly, Williams contends (in 'Persons, Character and Morality', in A. Rorty [ed.], *The Identities of Persons*, Berkeley: University of California

Press [1976], 197–216) that meaning in life is to be identified with the reasons we take ourselves to have to continue living, which reasons – he maintains – are often in tension with the sort of impartial morality that, according to Singer, is precisely the sort of thing to which wholeheartedly committing oneself is necessary if one is to give one's life meaning (psychopaths and the like aside). Lawrence Thomas also argues that 'the moral person is favored over the immoral person to lead a meaningful life' for psychological reasons (in his 'Morality and a Meaningful Life', *Philosophical Papers* 34 [2005]: 405–27, 406). Another view (worth mentioning at this stage as it may sound similar but is in fact quite different in its objectivism about meaningfulness) is that of Aaron Smuts. He argues (in his 'The Good Cause Account of the Meaningful Life', *Southern Journal of Philosophy* 51.4 (2013): 536–62, 536) that 'one's life is meaningful to the extent that one promotes the good; [the] good effects … need not be intentional. Nor must one be aware of the effects. Nor does it matter whether the same good would have resulted if one had not existed. What matters is that one is causally responsible for the good.'

33 A. Markus, 'Assessing Views of Life: a Subjective Affair?' *Religious Studies* 39 (2003): 125–43, 133.

34 H. Frankfurt, 'Reply to Susan Wolf', in S. Buss and L. Overton (eds), *The Contours of Agency: Essays on Themes from Harry Frankfurt*, Cambridge, MA: MIT Press (2002), 245–52, 250; H. Frankfurt, 'The importance of what we care about', reprinted in *The Importance of What We Care About*, H. Frankfurt (ed.), New York: Cambridge University Press (1988) [1982], 80–94, and his *The Reasons of Love*, Princeton: Princeton University Press (2004). It is also the view that Taylor is most famous for having endorsed at one stage (e.g. in R. Taylor, *Good and Evil*, New York: Macmillan [1984]) though he later abandoned it, e.g. by the date of his 'Time and Life's Meaning', *The Review of Metaphysics* 40 (1987): 675–86, in which he argued for an objectivist view – meaningfulness in life is creativity.

35 S. Wolf, 'Happiness and Meaning: Two Aspects of the Good Life', *Social Philosophy and Policy* 14 (1997): 207–25, 211.

36 S. Wolf, 'Happiness and Meaning: Two Aspects of the Good Life', *Social Philosophy and Policy* 14 (1997): 207–25, 209.

37 O. Flanagan, *Self-Expressions, Mind, Morals, and the Meaning of Life*, New York: Oxford University Press (1996), viii.

38 Contrast Smuts as referred to in note 32, in this chapter, for whom only the third-personal element is necessary.

39 R. M. Baird, 'Meaning in Life: Discovered or Created?' *Journal of Religion and Health* 24.2 (1985): 117–24, 118–19.

40 T. Metz, *Meaning in Life*, Oxford: Oxford University Press (2013).

41 T. Metz, *Meaning in Life*, Oxford: Oxford University Press (2013), 235.

42 The only notion that might speak against this purely objectivist reading of Metz is expressed by the word 'compelling'. To whom must this person's life story be compelling? The fact is that, with the possible exception of a handful of significant historical figures, nobody's life is compelling to most people. Most people's life stories are not compelling even to themselves. So, if that is the criterion, almost everyone fails it. But, from what he says elsewhere, Metz is clearly of the opinion that a significant majority of people do manage to lead relatively meaningful lives – not just the Winston Churchills of this world. Given that, I think we would do Metz a disservice by placing too much stress on the 'compelling' criterion for a life's being meaningful. (Disservice as it renders his theory incompatible with his commitment to the view that most people do manage to lead relatively meaningful

lives.) Of course one could understand Metz differently here. I tend to think this is the most charitable way to understand him as I think that it is obvious that most people manage to lead meaningful lives (in some senses of meaningful at least and to some extent at least) and I think that it is obvious that it is not true that most people's lives are compelling even to themselves. The sort of people who do find their own life stories compelling are fortunately – fortunately, as they are crushing bores – rare. Their lives certainly seem no more meaningful in virtue of their self-obsession. A few years ago, my wife and I moved from High Wycombe to Oxford. This was significant for my life story – it made my commute a lot easier; it .became practicable to start a family; and various other things that I would bore you with even more than I already have done were I to list them. Though significant for me, I would not describe the story of it as compelling, even to me. I am here then precisely contrary to Wai-hung Wong, who argues in 'Meaningfulness and Identities', *Ethical Theory and Moral Practice* 11 (2008), 123–48, for a view that he says 'can be epitomized in this enticing way: a person's life is meaningful if it contains material for an autobiography that she thinks is worth writing and others think is worth reading' (123).

43 T. Metz, *Meaning in Life*, Oxford: Oxford University Press (2013), 249.

44 Indeed, some contemporary philosophers are still as subjectivist as Frankfurt. See, for another example, Raymond Martin in his 'A Fast Car and a Good Woman', in D. Kolak and R. Martin (eds), *The Experience of Philosophy*, 2nd edn, Belmont, CA: Wadsworth Publishing Co. (1993), 556–62. I do not want to give the impression that this view has vanished from the contemporary scene.

45 See introduction note 14 for how this is only 'in part' true.

46 Typical in this regard is Seachris. Incidentally, Seachris discusses under the name 'the amalgam thesis' a different thesis from that which I endorse under that name later in this book. For Seachris, an amalgam thesis is one that is (a) sceptical of the question, viewing it as 'ill-conceived' or a 'place-holder' and (b) committed to grab-bag polyvalence. (Grab-bag polyvalence will be defined in the next chapter.) It is worth noting now merely as a point of terminological difference that neither of these sub-theses is constitutive of amalgam polyvalence as I am going to define and defend it – (a) is too pejorative and (b) is incompatible with it. I mention Seachris now though as he is typical in showing the '*en passant*' sympathy for pluralism/polyvalence that I talk of in the main text. He says at one stage that there is more than one question of the meaning of life. But, no sooner has he made the point, he suggests we should focus in on one hegemonic interpretation, what it is that makes for meaningfulness in an individual's life. So, for example, in note 35 of his excellent and perceptive paper, 'The Meaning of Life as Narrative' (J. Seachris, 'The Meaning of Life as Narrative: A New Proposal for Interpreting Philosophy's "Primary Question"', *Philo* 12 [2009]: 5–23), he says that one should 'distinguish between two conceptually distinct yet related questions: (i) "What is the meaning of life?" and (ii) "What makes life meaningful?" … I will simply note that there are at least two differences between these questions that are important … First, the question, "What makes a life meaningful?" is more obviously a value-laden question … Conversely, "What is the meaning of life?" seems to be … more about seeking a deep explanation or narrative for why we or anything else for that matter exists. Second, the question, "What makes a life meaningful?" is a question about human life, and not everything that exists in the universe, or the universe itself. However, as a matter of fact, general questions about life's meaning are often motivated out of more global and all-inclusive intuitions. These global intuitions are nicely captured in what I consider to be an equally vague synonym of the question, "What is the meaning of life?" – *What is it all [life, the universe, finite existence] about?* Here, we are not simply asking a question about human life, but about everything in the observable universe. So, the global intuitions out of

which the question, "What is the meaning of life?" are often motivated fit more naturally in the context of the question, "What is the meaning of life?" as opposed to "What makes life meaningful".' All good points, it seems to me, excellent points indeed. But precisely because they are such excellent points, they are ones that cannot just be made and then left to one side as if not needing further reflection. Quinn is another interesting case of the *en passant* sympathy for Pluralism of which I speak in the main text, though, unlike Seachris, he only ever considers meaningfulness as a property that may be had by individuals' lives. But in that (already, to my mind, too-narrow-a) context he distinguishes two senses in which an individual human life may be meaningful, which he calls 'axiological' and 'teleological', before saying 'Though I do not know how to prove it, I think the axiological and the teleological are logically independent kinds of meaning, and so I hold that a human life can have more than one sort of meaning,' (P. Quinn, 'The Meaning of Life According to Christianity', E. D. Klemke and S. Cahn (eds), *The Meaning of Life*, Oxford: Oxford University Press (2008), 35–41, 35). But Quinn then goes on to combine the two as individually necessary and only jointly sufficient for what he calls 'complete' meaning, by which it becomes increasingly obvious as his paper goes on he means meaningfulness when properly understood, i.e. what one might initially be led to think Quinn regards as two different kinds of meaning are in fact thought by him to be two aspects of one unitary value – meaningfulness. He's not a pluralist after all. (Note again then that the term 'pluralist' is being used in this note with a different sense from that with which it was used initially. More details follow in the next chapter.)

Chapter 2

1 As mentioned in earlier notes, there are the senses of it that are sometimes disambiguated as political pluralism and value pluralism. In the main text now I concentrate on pluralism as a thesis about meaningfulness in individual human lives. While some certainly claim to be pluralists about that, I'll argue that – with perhaps just one or two exceptions – they are not to be counted as pluralists in my sense. A point that is worth noting but that I shall not return to often in the main text is that even these one or two exceptions, the people who get to count as pluralists about meaning in my sense, are not pluralists in quite such a full-blooded way as I am. They do not accept – or at least explicitly accept and in fact seem implicitly to reject – that there are plural meanings of 'What is the meaning of life?' and that some of these – the cosmic ones – have different answers to the individualistic ones. They seem to think simply that the individualistic interpretations of the question (which are – they implicitly suggest – the only ones that can be given to it) have different answers.

2 T. Metz, *Meaning in Life*, Oxford: Oxford University Press (2013), 34.

3 T. Metz, *Meaning in Life*, Oxford: Oxford University Press (2013), 36. Oddly, on page 35, he seems more diffident even about the connotation issue, saying there 'The family resemblance proposal is attractive, and I do not have definitive grounds to reject it.' That is not a ringing endorsement, then.

4 T. Metz, 'The Meaning of Life', *Oxford Bibliographies*. (http://www.oxfordbibliographies.com/view/document/obo-9780195396577/obo-9780195396577-0070.xml [accessed 1 November 2011]).

5 Metz is here citing Wolf (S. Wolf, 'Happiness and Meaning': Two Aspects of the Good Life', *Social Philosophy and Policy* 14 [1997]: 207–25, 211).

6 Some of the confusion undoubtedly comes here from the fact that on some, monistic by my reckoning, theories of the meaning of life we may nevertheless, despite their monism

Notes

as I reckon it, sensibly talk about different meanings of life. I have in mind here views such as Frankfurt's: the view is that the unitary value that is meaningfulness in life ('life' being taken to be exclusively meaning the lives of each of us taken individually) is finding or creating a purpose for ourselves to which we may commit wholeheartedly. On that theory, and given the variety across human nature, it follows that for some the meaning of life may be philosophical success; for others, golf; for yet others, the raising of a family; and for yet others, being a nun. So, given the plurality of things that can be taken up by people as their meaning-giving purpose in life, we may say that there are many meanings of life, as many as there are purposes that can fulfil this role for people. Fair enough, that does seem to me a legitimate way of talking. However, that is not a pluralist way of talking. There are not as many values of meaningfulness as there are purposes that can fulfil this role for people. There is one value of meaningfulness, which is fulfilling this role for people. It is just that there are many things that can play that role – undergird it, as I put it previously. So, this is a legitimate way of talking, but it threatens to obscure the value facts behind it. It would be rather as if one insisted on talking of a classical hedonistic Utilitarianism as maintaining a pluralistic view of the good simply because it recognized that plural things could cause pleasure. Classical hedonistic Utilitarianism surely is not a value-pluralistic normative theory!

7 Kekes is worth lingering over, for he uses the term 'pluralistic' of his own approach (J. Kekes, 'The Meaning of Life', in *Midwest Studies in Philosophy* 24 [2000]: 17–34), yet I do not count him as a fellow-traveller either. He says, on page 32, 'According to the pluralistic approach, then, lives have meaning if they meet the following conditions ...': and he then lists seven. As, according to him, there is one thing 'meaning' that is constituted by seven aspects that are, page 33, 'individually necessary and jointly sufficient to make lives meaningful', so, according to him, there are not different sorts of meaning, just one sort composed of several elements. This makes him a monist. He looks for a moment like a pluralist, but his so-called Pluralism collapses back into Monism as all the things that might otherwise have been labelled different sorts of meaning amalgamate in the end – according to Kekes – into one thing, true meaning. I shall talk about the notion of amalgamation in a moment in the main text.

8 I would in fact count as a pluralist someone who did not endorse the plural connotation element, just the plural denotation one. But in fact there are no such people and it is hard to know how one could argue for such a view because, as I shall discuss in the main text, Pluralism at the level of the connotation of the question is the best (even if not the only) evidence one could have for Pluralism at the level of the denotation of the answer. I therefore ignore this possibility in the main text.

9 I actually think that it refers to at least one non-value thing too – the property that a life may have of standing for a particular idea, in the manner that Lenin's stood for the communist revolution; the Dalai Lama's stands for the cultural and religious values of Tibet; and so on. I shall come to this more fully later.

10 'The Evening Star' and 'The Morning Star' famously have different connotations but the same denotation. Someone who was a pluralist about it/them in Metz's sense could believe that. Someone who was a pluralist about it/them in my sense would have to believe that they had different denotations.

11 T. Metz, *Meaning in Life*, Oxford: Oxford University Press (2013), 36.

12 This may be a bit 'rough and ready' and, if it is true, it may be a contingent truth, as to be a pluralist in Metz's sense requires, it seems to me, one to believe in the plural connotation element and/or (it is unclear) to believe that plural things can undergird the one unitary value of meaningfulness. See also previous note about how in principle (though not in practice) one might believe in plural denotation without believing in plural connotation.

13 Julian Baggini is the only one I am sure does, but David Schmidtz can be read this way too (J. Baggini, *What's it All About?*, London: Granta [2004]; and D. Schmidtz, 'The Meanings of Life', in L. Rouner (ed.), *Boston University Studies in Philosophy and Religion* 22, Notre Dame, University of Notre Dame Press [2001]: 170–88).

14 For example, Baggini in the end presents a hotchpotch of meanings of life – a grab bag, indeed (he never takes in the cosmic interpretations). Towards the end of his book he tells us that a meaningful life is one 'with a balance of authenticity, happiness and concern for others; one where time is not wasted; one which engages in the ongoing work of becoming who we want to be and being successful in those terms' (J. Baggini, *What's it All About?* London: Granta [2004], 186).

15 It is also unique in that it locates the polyvalence within the individualistically interpreted question (What is meaningfulness as it occurs in human lives?) within a broader polyvalence, one that takes in the cosmically interpreted question (What is the meaning of life in the sense of humanity's life, or in the sense of biological life, or what is the meaning of it all?).

16 T. Metz, 'The Meaning of Life', *Stanford Encyclopedia of Philosophy* (first published online Tuesday 15 May 2007; substantive revision Monday 3 June 2013).

17 This becomes particularly obvious when one switches back to considering the cosmic interpretations of the question, the ones the answers to which are the right metaphysical and metaethical theories. But it is also true, I shall suggest, of the individualistic meanings of life. Some of them (a life's standing for an idea for example) are not valuable in themselves (though sometimes they get value from the idea or the consequences that flow from the life's standing for that idea).

18 R. Hepburn, 'Questions about the Meaning of Life', *Religious Studies* 1 (1965): 125–40, 126.

19 Seachris says in 'Meaning of Life: Contemporary Analytic Perspectives', *Internet Encyclopedia of Philosophy*, in a passage that I've already referred to: 'Following precedent in the literature … this approach for addressing vagueness in the question of life's meaning may be called the amalgam thesis … Roughly, the amalgam thesis entails that the original question … is a largely ill-conceived place-holder for a cluster of related requests, and thus, not really a single question at all. One way of understanding the amalgam thesis is to view it as making the question of life's meaning little more than a disjunctive question: what is the purpose of life, or what makes life valuable, or what makes life worthwhile?' It should become clear if it is not already that I am using 'the amalgam thesis' to mean something different from this.

20 This is why Kekes ultimately fails to be correctly labelled as a pluralist in my sense. See note 7 to this chapter.

21 This is why I count Quinn as a monist too; see note 46 in Chapter 1.

22 And again, it does so even bracketing-off the cosmic interpretations of the question.

23 There is a third group, who favour saying that water is still essentially H_2O and it is just that there is a lot of 'Fools' Water' around that we did not expect, *viz.* stuff that is superficially a lot like water but is not really water. They are quickly identified as people who happen to be holding their conference on the work of Saul Kripke at the same Conference Centre as the Chemists and have simply wandered into the wrong seminar. They are sent on their way.

24 This is perhaps most quickly and easily seen by bringing back into consideration the distinction between cosmic and individualistic interpretations of the question, the first being plausibly answered by the right metaphysical/metaethical worldview, the second being plausibly answered by the right account of a value (or – as I would maintain – more than one value and some non-value properties) that some individuals' lives may instantiate.

Chapter 3

1 Sometimes I shall call it the 'waiting on metaphysics/metaethics' point, as its resolution depends in part on the metaphysics of morals, or actually value more generally, and I shall wish to acknowledge this.

2 P. Edwards (in P. Edwards (ed.), 'Why', in *The Encyclopedia of Philosophy*, 7–8, New York: Macmillan [1972], 296–302, 298ff.) addresses this issue, though is ultimately sceptical that this, which he calls the 'super-ultimate why-question' makes sense. M. K. Munitz (in his *The Mystery of Existence, An Essay in Philosophical Cosmology*, New York: Appleton-Century-Crofts [1965]) is interesting in that he maintains that the highest-level cosmic interpretation of the question is meaningful, but that the question under that interpretation is unanswerable. See also J. Seachris, in his 'The Meaning of Life as Narrative: A New Proposal for Interpreting Philosophy's "Primary" Question', *Philo* 12 (2009): 5–23.

3 So, for example, Karl Britton, who says that the question, 'What is the meaning of life?', 'is put in many different ways. What is the meaning of it all? What is the meaning of everything? … Why is there anything at all and why just what there is and not something quite different?' in his *Philosophy and the Meaning of Life*, Cambridge: Cambridge University Press (1969), 1–2.

4 The issue of the differing centrality to one's concerns of life in its various senses is an important one when it comes to the issue of ranking as I shall discuss it later. If what I hazard later in this chapter is right – that it is life as individual life that is our main, but not sole, concern when asking 'What is the meaning of life?' – then that will make it the case that interpretations of the question that use that notion of life to refer to individual lives – individualistic ones, as I have been putting it – will seize on issues more central to our concerns and thus these meanings of life are, as I shall later put it, to be ranked intrinsically higher on the chart/list of the meanings of life that we may imagine as constituting our best answer to the question. It is because they are to be ranked intrinsically higher that less harm has been done than one might have expected by the fact that most philosophers have bracketed off the cosmic interpretations. These cosmic interpretations are generally to be ranked intrinsically lower – they are less important. We will come back to this later, but my point now is that life in these broader senses is a part – even if a less important part – of what we are asking for the meaning of when we ask 'What is the meaning of life?'

5 L. Feuerbach, *Thoughts on Death and Immortality*, J. Massey (ed. and trans.), Berkeley: University of California Press (1980), 236–7.

6 R. Taylor, 'The Meaning of Life', *Good and Evil*, New York, Macmillan (1984), 261.

7 J.-P. Sartre, *Nausea*, L. Alexander (trans.), New York: New Directions Publishing (1964), 112.

8 R. Taylor, 'The Meaning of Life', *Good and Evil*, New York: Macmillan (1984), 262.

9 B. Russell, 'A Free Man's Worship', in his *Mysticism and Logic*, London: Penguin (1953), 51.

10 We have come across it already and mentioned Russell in that context (as well as Flew and Klemke). By way of another example, Baier also notes that when we ask the question, we may be asking about whether humanity in general – the species – has a meaning – or whether one's own individual life has a meaning. And he answers the first question negatively and the second positively, or at least potentially positively. (According to Baier it depends what that individual chooses to do with his or her life: K. Baier, *Problems of Life and Death*, Amherst: Prometheus Books [1997].)

11 Indeed, as already mentioned, so much does it preoccupy our interest that it enables those who bracket off the more cosmic interpretations of the question to 'get away with it'. 'I

assume that the person who asks "What is the meaning of life?" is concerned about the meaning of *his or her own life*. Questions about the meaning of life in a broader sense (e.g. "What, if anything, is the meaning of the human race or the universe as a whole?"), if they are of interest to anyone, are not the subject matter of the question that interests me in this book' (S. Goetz, *The Purpose of Life: A Theistic Perspective*, London: Continuum [2012], 2).

12 T. Metz, 'Baier and Cottingham on the Meaningful Life', *Disputatio* I. 19 (2005): 251–64, 253.

13 L. Tolstoy, *A Confession*, a selection from Chapter IV to Chapter V.

14 However, even though it is by the by to our main purpose at the moment, it is perhaps worth noting that if there are different sorts of meaningfulness (as I am arguing that there are), it seems quite possible that 'meaningfulness/meaninglessness' in some senses of 'meaningfulness/meaninglessness' will allow top-down or bottom-up inferences while 'meaningfulness/meaninglessness' in other senses will not. We'll come to this later.

15 Some contend that only lives as a whole may be considered meaningful (P. Tabensky, 'Parallels Between Living and Painting', *Journal of Value Inquiry* 37 [2003]: 59–68 and and J. Levinson, 'Intrinsic Value and the Notion of a Life', *Journal of Aesthetics and Art Criticism* 62 [2004]: 319–29), so no aspects or periods can be meaningful in themselves. On this view, if we are to live forever, we cannot say that anyone's *ante-mortem* life is meaningful. That we can say that some people's *ante-mortem* lives are meaningful means – on this view – that we can say that we are not immortal. But the implication that we can work out that we are not immortal in this fashion is most implausible. So we have reason to reject the view. (We also have reason to reject it from considering the specifics of their arguments for it, which rely on somewhat strained parallels between works of art and lives at crucial points.) It is more plausible to think that both parts of a life and a life as a whole can be bearers of meaning but one has reason to prefer the meaning of a life as a whole over the meaning of its parts – the whole taking in as it would certain holistic and narrative sorts of meaning (we will come to this later). A common assumption, and again one that seems plausible to me, is that an individual life which is meaningless (or at least less meaningful) at one time may become meaningful (or at least more meaningful) later and that the reverse may happen too. We do not wish to commit the fallacy of composition (every grain of sand in the sandbag is light; the bag itself is light; so, the sandbag must be light). But, as discussed in the main text, we seem also to be able to reason that for some senses of meaningfulness, were every period within a given life to be meaningful in that sense, then the whole of it must be meaningful in that sense too. For others, that is less clear. For most senses, it seems that a whole life might be meaningful in that sense yet at least some aspects or periods of it be meaningless in that same sense. The whole of life being meaningless in a given sense (being unworthy of choice) may be precisely what makes it meaningful in another sense (significant) by making it a good example – a cautionary tale.

16 N. Levy, 'Downshifting and Meaning of Life', *Ratio* 18.2 (2005): 176–89, 177.

17 There are similarities here with Nozick's 'meaning as external causal relationship'; see R. Nozick, *Philosophical Explanations*, Oxford: Oxford University Press (1981), 574.

18 I do not put much weight on this particular example in making my case for amalgam polyvalence, as the claim that meaning in life can be a matter of 'mere causal consequence' is more controversial than the claims I need for the other examples I use later.

19 A. Camus, *The Myth of Sisyphus*, O'Brien J. (trans.), London: Penguin, (2005 [1942]), Chapter 4.

20 I say significant here and hereafter, though plausibly all that's needed for this sort of meaning is for the consequence to have non-negligible (and positive) value and there's a gap between non-negligible (positive) value and significant positive value.

Notes

21 As I said in a previous note, while I believe this, I recognize that it is more controversial and thus do not put any weight on it in my developing argument for an amalgam thesis.

22 According to Consequentialism, the moral value of an individual action is determined by the amount of good it produces; that of a life as a whole then by the aggregate (net) of the values of the actions performed during it. Mother Teresa's was a very good life as she helped a lot more people than she harmed and she helped them in significant ways; whatever harms she inflicted were minor. Either of my grandfathers – I have every reason to believe – led on balance good lives. But it seems very unlikely to me that either's was as good as Mother Teresa's in a consequentialist sense. They just did not affect as many people as Mother Teresa did and the effects they produced were of more mixed quality even if, I reasonably hope, on balance they tended to be good. And then – he's such an easy example, why not use him again? – Hitler's was a very bad life. He harmed at lot more people than he ever helped, and harmed them in significant ways; whomever he helped (perhaps he once helped a little old lady across the street in Munich, who knows?) he did not help in any significant way. There's at least an analogy to be drawn with some senses of meaningfulness. So, if we consider the meaningfulness of an individual's life as a matter of its causal significance and are consequentialists about assessing that, we might say that the meaningfulness in one sense of an individual action is determined by the amount of evaluable consequence that it brings, that of a life as a whole then by the aggregate of evaluable consequences that it brings. On that score, Mother Teresa's life would then come out as much more meaningful than those of either of my grandfathers. But then so would Hitler's. If it is just amount of evaluable stuff that he produced that counts, Hitler's life might even come out as more meaningful than Mother Teresa's. And thus there is at least some pressure only to count good consequences as contributing positively towards meaningfulness, at least of this sort. But that cannot be quite all that there is to it. We think that the charity worker who knowingly brings minimal, but non-negligible, good into the world before dying and being forgotten about leads a more meaningful life than the infamous killing-spree mass-murderer whose crimes are made subject of much popular culture and give impetus to new legislation on gun-control thereafter, even though the second may end up having had more meaning as positive causal consequence. (The serial killer's meaning would of course only ever be a meaning in this sense *simpliciter*, not a meaning in this sense for him; the charity worker's meaning by contrast would be as well as a [smaller] meaning *simpliciter*, also a meaning for her.) And one has to 'count on' quite a bit of course to get to the positive in the case of the serial killer. His short-term consequences were negative. However, in the medium-to-long term, if we allow ourselves to stipulate as huge the number of lives saved by the gun-control measures that he inadvertently inspires, he gets to bring about significant positively evaluable consequence. Whether that, which may well happen long after his death, gets to add meaning to his life is something over which intuitions will differ. I personally think it does, but nothing in my main line of argument requires this. And nor does anything turn on any particular answer as to the question of which sort of evaluable consequences count. Is it evaluable consequences or evaluable consequences but with a lesser weighting (possibly a zero or negative weighting) being given to bad ones? And should the consequences we count be only intended consequences? The lives of the progenitors of significant people are in that way significant. Does that get to add to their meaningfulness? Does the grandmother of Mother Teresa get to have had a more meaningful life than the grandmother of my grandfather because of what her granddaughter would one day do relative to what my grandfather did? And Hitler's forebears? My intuitions supply only inconclusive answers, though again a lot of work can be done by drawing on the distinction between meaning *simpliciter* and meaning for the individual concerned and of course bearing in mind polyvalence.

23 This is a bit brisk. One might maintain that the value that one is worried about is the same, before or after – significant positively evaluable casual elements (either before as causes or after as effects). But – as we shall see in the main text – that way out will not work. It is really that the antecedent be purposive (and significantly positively evaluable), not just that it be causal (and significantly positively evaluable), which, we suppose, is needed for this sort of meaning.

24 J. Cottingham, *On the Meaning of Life*, London: Routledge (2003), 47. His surrounding discussion of how this feeling – however real – cannot be used to settle the issue of whether or not the species really is accidental in the worrying sense is good.

25 I think that Brooke Alan Trisel would disagree (from what he says in his 'Intended and Unintended Life', *The Philosophical Forum* 43.4. [2012]: 395–403) but that David Velleman would concur (from what he says in his 'Family History', *Philosophical Papers* 34.3 (2005): 357–78).

26 J. Seachris, 'The Sub Specie Aeternitatis Perspective and Normative Evaluations of Life's Meaningfulness: A Closer Look', *Ethical Theory and Moral Practice* 16.3 (2013): 605–20.

27 'Antecedents' needs to be taken quite broadly, for example to include in principle God's purpose in creating life even if God is outside time and thus not strictly-speaking 'antecedent' to His act of creation.

28 As mentioned in note 46 in Chapter 1, Quinn in 'How Christianity Secures Life's Meanings', claims that 'meaning' in 'What is the meaning of life?' has two meanings – one axiological – to do with its worth – and one teleological to do with its purpose. This is not quite the same distinction as I have drawn then, but it crosses the same conceptual space orthogonally. Or consider R. A. Sharpe who (in his 'In Praise of the Meaningless Life', *Philosophy Now* 24 [1999]: 1) says the following: '"meaning" is ambiguous. It can be equivalent to "significance" or it can connote "purpose" … To say that life is meaningless may be to say that it is purposeless or may be to say that it is of no significance or value'. This is an interesting contribution in that it asserts ambiguity in a crucial term – meaning – in the question. Note that while appreciating bivalence in the concept of meaning, Sharpe does not attribute a richer polyvalence than that, even at the level of connotation; and he does not argue for polyvalence apropos of 'life'.

29 I say this with some confidence, as I know I speak now to people who have got to this stage in reading the book, i.e. people who have already shown themselves to be forgiving.

Chapter 4

1 As we have seen already, Metz calls the questions of 'whether the universe has a meaning or of whether the human species does', 'holistic' or 'cosmic' questions and eschews engaging with them so as to focus on the issue of whether individual humans' lives have meaning. '[I] set aside such holistic understandings of the question of life's meaning, so as to make progress on the individualist construal' (T. Metz, *Meaning in Life*, Oxford: Oxford University Press [2013], 3). The holistic sorts of meaning that an individual life may have (of which more in a moment) he does engage with.

2 'A plausible reading of ["What is the meaning of life?"] … is "What is the purpose of life?". I believe it is plausible to understand the question "What is the meaning of life?"… as the question "What is the ultimate (final or all-encompassing) purpose for which I exist?"' (S. Goetz, *The Purpose of Life: A Theistic Perspective*, London: Continuum [2012], 3, 15). Or 'When we wonder about life's meaning, the question sometimes is less about what makes

life good and more about what makes life significant – what purpose is served by living it' (D. Schmidtz, 'The Meanings of Life', in L. Rouner (ed.) *Boston University Studies in Philosophy and Religion, Volume 22; If I Should Die: Life, Death, and Immortality*, Notre Dame: University of Notre Dame Press [2001], 170–88, 171.)

3 'We can understand the question of something's meaning, roughly, as the question of how it connects up to what is outside it.' (R. Nozick, *Philosophical Explanations*, Oxford: Oxford University Press [1981], 601); Nozick argues that the 'unlimited' can be its own meaning and that connecting up to it can give us meaning (R. Nozick, *Philosophical Explanations*, Oxford: Oxford University Press [1981], 600ff.).

4 'What are we really asking when we ask about the meaning of life? Partly, it seems, we are asking about our relationship with the rest of the universe – who we are and how we came to be here. One aspect of this is a scientific question about our origins.' (J. Cottingham, *On the Meaning of Life*, London: Routledge [2003], 2).

5 Dahl says 'to ask whether life is meaningful is at least to ask whether there is a way of living one's life that will make it overall good' (N. Dahl, 'Morality and the Meaning of Life: Some First Thoughts', *Canadian Journal of Philosophy* 17.1 [1987]: 1–22, 4). Nielsen, by way of another example, says this: 'When we ask: "What is the meaning of life?" or "What is the purpose of human existence?" we are normally asking … questions of the following types: "What should we seek?" "What ends – if any are worthy of attainment?" … [The question of the meaning of life] is in reality a question concerning human conduct.' (K. Nielsen, 'Linguistic Philosophy and "the Meaning of Life"', in E. D. Klemke and S. M. Cahn (eds), *The Meaning of Life*, Oxford: Oxford University Press [2008], 186–93, originally in *Cross Currents*, Summer 1964). Interestingly, this first equates meaning with purpose and then goes on to equate that with worthy purpose (ignoring the possibility that we might have some purpose – being the foodstuffs for returning aliens – that were not worthy of attainment). Again, I disagree then only in thinking of these as all synonymous with one another and with meaning in life; they are all in order, it seems to me, as what I call 'partial unpackings'.

6 According to Britton, for example, if we say of our individual lives that they are meaningful, 'we are saying that we find some things worthwhile on their own account and that we can make these things our aim' (K. Britton, *Philosophy and the Meaning of Life*, Cambridge: Cambridge University Press [1969], 12).

7 Metz says of the project of seeking a more precise articulation of what it is one is asking when asking 'What is the meaning of life?' that 'it of course will not do merely to say that a meaningful life is a life that is "important" or "significant" or that it is an existence that "matters" or "has a point." These terms are synonyms for "meaningful"' (T. Metz, 'The Concept of a Meaningful Life', *American Philosophical Quarterly* 38 [2001]: 137–53, 138). I only disagree with him here in thinking of these things as synonyms, rather than partial unpackings of the meaning of 'meaningful'. As Wong points out, 'a life that is significant in some way may still not be meaningful, such as the life of a comatose person whose unusual DNA is the key to the cure of a serious disease' (Wong, 'Meaningfulness and Identities' *Ethical Theory and Moral Practice* 11 [2008]: 123–48, 145). Of course, I would say of such a life that it has significance-meaning so is meaningful, *pace* Wong, but of course only in that particular sense. It is not meaningful in other senses, e.g. affording the person living it the peculiar feeling of existential repletion that I have interpreted Ayer and Wohlgennant as talking about.

8 On finding meaning in what life is subjectively like now – giving oneself the right feeling towards it – Taylor says this: 'If the builders of a great and flourishing ancient civilization could somehow return now to see archaeologists unearthing the trivial remnants of pots

and vases, a few broken statues, and such tokens of another age and greatness – they could indeed ask themselves what the point of it all was, if this is all it finally came to. Yet it did not seem so to them then, for it was just the building, and not what was finally built, that gave their life meaning. ... The things to which they bent their backs day after day, realizing one by one their ephemeral plans, were precisely the things in which their interests lay, and there was no need then to ask questions. There is no more need of them now – the day was sufficient to itself, and so was the life' (R. Taylor, 'The Meaning of Life', *Good and Evil*, New York, Macmillan [1984]: 266–7). Nozick helpfully distinguishes several senses of meaning, of which the last, V, is: 'Meaning as personal significance, importance, value, mattering: "You mean a lot to me" ... Under this rubric is a completely subjective notion, covering what a person thinks is important to him, and one somewhat less so, covering what affects something subjectively important to him, even if he does not realize it' (R. Nozick, *Philosophical Explanations*, Oxford: Oxford University Press [1981], 574). This seems to me to capture the same notion of meaning in life that I am talking about here.

9 I say 'more centrally', as I do not find the subjectivism of Ayer, Wohlgennant and Frankfurt (or indeed Taylor in the passage quoted in the previous note) plausible and I think most people do not.

10 This may be rather opaque. It is admittedly hard to characterize this sort of holistic property. But it is not hard to spot it and its absence. Sometimes it may be called organic unity – a part of a life that might have been meaningful had the rest of it taken a different shape becomes meaningless with later decisions, e.g. spending years doing a vocational qualification and then not pursuing that vocation. Some people's lives have more of the relevant sorts of internal connections than others; they 'hang together' better (for good or ill). I say for good or ill as these properties of 'internal support', 'organic unity' or what have you do not of themselves make one's life good. Léon Degrelle's earlier career in politics hangs together with his later service in the Waffen SS, which in turn hangs together with his post-war career in Franco's Spain. But his life was much less good than that of almost everyone who fought on the side of the Allies and for whom the war was a severe disruption, i.e. for whom their war service did not 'hang together' with the rest of their lives at all. Pedro Tabensky (in his 'Parallels Between Living and Painting', *Journal of Value Inquiry* 37 [2003]: 59–68) argues that the value of a given part of a life (or painting) is given by its relation to other parts. This is the sort of holistic meaning I have in mind, but I think it is not the exclusive meaning of 'meaning' – or even particularly valuable. Some paintings 'hang together' better than others, but are nevertheless considerably less successful than others as works of art.

11 See Antti Kauppinen, 'Meaningfulness and Time', in *Philosophy and Phenomenological Research* 82 [2012]: 345–77, according to whom life is meaningful in virtue of the pattern it displays over time: 'life is ideally meaningful when challenging efforts lead to lasting successes' (Antti Kauppinen, 'Meaningfulness and Time', in *Philosophy and Phenomenological Research* 82 [2012], 345–77, 346). Perhaps it is simply better if it ends well (F. M. Kamm, 'Rescuing Ivan Ilych: How We Live and How We Die', *Ethics* 113 [2003]: 202–33, 221–33) or simply if the bad parts lead to good parts later (e.g. David Velleman, 'Well-Being and Time', *Pacific Philosophical Quarterly* 72 [1991]: 48–77, who suggests that the narrative order in which value occurs determines the meaningfulness of the life in which it occurs). A good example Velleman gives to illustrate the point is that a failed marriage may teach one something that makes a second marriage successful. It is 'not just offset but redeemed, by being given a meaningful place in one's progress through life' (D. Velleman, 'Well-Being and Time', *Pacific Philosophical Quarterly* 72 [1991], 48–77, 65). An even more extreme example: a rape that in and of itself one would have described as meaningless, indeed meaning-negating for all concerned, leads to a pregnancy and in turn a child. The child is then loved and cared for by the mother. One can drag meaningfulness in this way out of awful

happenings. See also Dale Dorsey, 'The Significance of a Life's Shape', *Ethics* 125.2 (2015): 303–30.

12 J. Seachris, 'The Meaning of Life as Narrative; A New Proposal for Interpreting Philosophy's 'Primary' Question', *Philo* 12 (2009): 5–23, says 'the question, 'What is the meaning of life?' should be understood as the request for a narrative that narrates across those elements and accompanying questions of life of greatest existential import to human beings'. And Garrett Thomson says 'to know the meaning of life is to know a true metaphysical narrative about the human life in general that somehow makes sense of our lives' (G. Thomson, *On the Meaning of Life*, London, Wadworth [2003], 132–3).

13 T. Metz, *Meaning in Life*, Oxford: Oxford University Press (2013), 9. He suggests similar (though subtly different questions) in his 'New Developments in the Meaning of Life', *Philosophy Compass* 2 (2007): 196–217, 211: 'What ought one most strive for besides achieving happiness and satisfying moral requirements? How can one do something worth [*sic*] of great esteem or admiration? What is particularly worthy of love and devotion?' Also, Metz (in 'Could God's Purpose be the Source of Life's Meaning?' *Religious Studies* (2000): 36, 293–313, 293) says 'I take the question of what can make life meaningful to be the question of what about our lives (besides bare survival) could be worthy of great esteem.'

14 My apologies are due to any reading who are Moral Philosophers and could reasonably complain of what follows not only that they would have preferred more detail, but that it conflates in misleading ways certain concepts it would be important to keep separate if one were to gain true traction on the issues.

15 I have tried to frame this so that it does not already direct us towards a particular normative theory. What is it that makes something the best thing to do? What is it that makes something the morally right thing to do? What is it that makes something one's duty to do? What is it that makes something virtuous to do? What is it the doing of which would show one to be virtuous? And so on. All seemed less good than my framing, inadequate as it may be.

16 The case is perhaps not entirely parallel for a number of reasons, one being that there does not (to me anyway) seem to be as much polyvalence at the level of connotation (only denotation) when it comes to moral value. It might seem that were there no polyvalence at all at the level of connotation, the parallel conclusion could only be supported using arguments of the third sort I have sketched, which sort, as I say, are somewhat 'second best', though of course if they are the best available, then 'second best' is not really the right characterization of them. But I would suggest that not only can significant arguments be made in this area, e.g. to the effect that each of the various normative theories fails to square with deep and stable intuitions that we have when we try to understand well-being, say, and whether or not we should maximize the total, the average, some weighted total or average (and whether maximization is a plausible notion to deploy in all such contexts in any case) but also that recent work in experimental philosophy can be argued to support the thesis that the phenomenology of our experience of first-order moral experience is as if of plural moral values (M. Gill and S. Nichols, 'Sentimentalist Pluralism: Moral Psychology and Philosophical Ethics', *Philosophical Issues* 18 [2008]: 143–63). And again I refer the interested reader to the wider topic of value pluralism and the arguments surrounding it.

17 I do not count it as a further line of argument for polyvalence as it seems to me best thought of as an expression of the third.

18 I say 'largely' as of course it is possible for philosophers to disagree about issues internal to a particular sort of meaning of life and other things.

19 T. J. Mawson, 'Recent Work on the Meaning of Life and the Philosophy of Religion', *Philosophy Compass* (2013): 1138–46.

Chapter 5

1 L. Wittgenstein, *The Blue Book*, Oxford: Blackwell (1958), 3.

2 It is perhaps worth stressing the point that there is this consensus because a common view outside the discipline of Philosophy is that the term 'God' is a very vague one or that it means a variety of things to a variety of people. This is probably true of the term 'God' as it finds itself used in the wider population. (That's why opinion pieces in newspapers, people talking about it on the radio, and so forth offer so little connection with the substance of the debate.) But it is definitely not true of the term as it finds itself used within the discipline of the Philosophy of Religion, as it is understood by philosophers who debate whether or not there's a God. Indeed, I would hazard that the term 'God' has a more agreed-upon definition than 'knowledge', 'consciousness', 'physicality', 'science', or indeed almost any of the other things that philosophers inquire about and debate.

3 Maybe this is not such a spoiler; you would probably have already realised that this was likely to be my view.

4 R. Nozick, *Philosophical Explanations,* Oxford: Oxford University Press (1981), 571.

Chapter 6

1 J. Baggini, *What's it All About? Philosophy and the Meaning of Life,* London: Granta (2004), 3.

2 D. Schmidtz, *The Meanings of Life,* in L. Rouner (ed.), *Boston University Studies in Philosophy and Religion, Volume 22,* Notre Dame, IL.: University of Notre Dame Press (2001), 170–88, 177–8. He goes on 'The first feature I will mention, though, does seem just about essential, namely that meaningful lives, in one way or another, have an impact.' His position is also, I think, that it is sufficient that one be doing something with one's life that gives one a feeling of satisfaction. And, as many things can do this – being a mail man, for example, happens to have done it for Schmidtz for a goodly period of his life – so, unless we think that impact could be pretty local (that the mail be delivered on one's route), it seems to me (even though we have to gloss over 'essential' somewhat) that we should interpret him as being a pluralist – a grab-bag polyvalence theorist, in my preferred terms – about meaning in individual humans' lives. According to Schmidtz so interpreted, meaningfulness in human living is two different values (though both may be present at once, indeed one seems likely to be causally related [at least in general] to the other): either impactful living or living in a way that is satisfying to the person. Further, I hazard, Schmidtz holds that one will not be satisfied unless one has an impact – hence his use of 'essential' (he means causally necessary). Now this is reading a lot into him of course, but my inclination to read this into him is why, if I had to put my money somewhere on this issue, I'd put my money on Schmidtz being a grab-bag polyvalence theorist.

3 I call them two features, but, as will become clear, they may perhaps better be thought of as two aspects of one feature of the chart – it being a ranked chart.

4 The same sort of meaning – meaning as standing for something – can be attributed, it seems to me, to parts of individuals' lives. Schmidtz tells us 'A few years ago, I joined thousands of others in trying to save a small community in Kansas from rising floodwaters, as we surrounded it with dikes made of sandbags. We failed … But … the effort meant something – it made a statement' (D. Schmidtz, *The Meanings of Life,* in L. Rouner [ed.], *Boston University Studies in Philosophy and Religion, Volume 22,* Notre Dame, IL.: University of Notre Dame Press [2001], 80). Schmidtz does not have an overarching life-goal of contributing to flood defence, but these efforts had a significance, a meaning, in virtue of

signifying this commitment to flood defence. I have chosen this example precisely because he failed. So the meaning of his efforts does not come from significance in the sense of significant positively evaluable consequence. His actions did not have meaning in that sense. So this is a sort of meaning parts of lives can have as well as lives as a whole.

This is a sort of meaning that is different from others in that if a life has meaning in this sense, there must be something that it means. In this respect, it is close to linguistic meaning. I am here somewhat contrary to a point made by Audi, where he says, 'unlike a linguistic expression, a life can be meaningful even though there is nothing it means' (R. Audi, 'Intrinsic Value and Meaningful Life', *Philosophical Papers* (2006): 34, 331–55, 333). I do not think that is true of this type of meaning (though it is of course true of other types). And of course I'm contrary to those who would equate significance with meaning in life simpliciter, e.g. Metz, who says that 'a meaningful life is one that is "important" or "significant" or that it is an existence that "matters" or "has a point". These terms are synonyms of "meaningful"' (T. Metz, *Meaning in Life*, Oxford: Oxford University Press [2013], 18). And, T. Metz, *Meaning in Life*, Oxford: Oxford University Press (2013), 21, 'synonyms of "meaningful life" include phrases such as "significant existence" and "way of being that matters"'. Not so, according to me: a life may have meaning in the sense of standing for an idea – it signifies and in that sense is significant – but not in the sense of producing significant positively valuable consequences; in that sense it is insignificant. I take it that the period of Schmidtz's life he devoted to defending that Kansas village against flooding would be an example of a period significant in one sense and not in another. Or, consider the actions of Perkins as ordered by his commanding officer in the famous 'Beyond the Fringe' sketch with the words, 'We need a futile gesture at this stage. It'll raise the whole tone of the war.'

5 He refers to A. Gewirth, *Self-Fulfillment*, Princeton: Princeton University Press (1998), 184–5.

6 T. Metz, 'Recent Work on the Meaning of Life', *Ethics* 112 (2002): 801.

7 I prefer 'partial unpackings'.

8 E. M. Adams says 'We have to distinguish between the meaning of life and the meaning of a life. The meaning of a life may be a matter of great concern to a biographer or historian, or to anyone if it concerns one's own life. It is the general question about the meaning of life that is of theoretical interest' (E. M. Adams, 'The Meaning of Life', *International Journal for Philosophy of Religion*, 51 [2002], 71–81, 78). One way to take these comments is to interpret Adams's 'meaning of a life' as what it is that that the life stood for, what a particular – ideologically focused – type of biographer would draw out for attention in rendering the lives of Lenin, Hitler, Gandhi, the Dalai Lama, and so on.

9 J. J. C. Smart and B. Williams, *Utilitarianism For and Against*, Cambridge: Cambridge University Press (1973), 108ff.

10 L. J. Russell, 'The Meaning of Life', *Philosophy* 28.104 (1953): 30–40, 32. Kauppinen considers a similar case – calling it 'Single Purpose' – and says of it that it 'would not be the most meaningful shape of a whole life'. It seems to me it would not be the most overall meaningful shape a whole life might take, or the life of the deepest meaning. But it would be the most meaningful shape a life might take in the sense in question – of necessity.

11 Berit Brogaard and Barry Smith, 'On Luck, Responsibility, and the Meaning of Life', *Philosophical Papers* 34.3 (2005): 443–58, 444.

12 R. Audi, 'Intrinsic Value and Meaningful Life', *Philosophical Papers* 34 (2005): 331–55, 335. He later discusses 'the theistic assumption that pleasing God is sufficient for meaningfulness' ('Intrinsic Value and Meaningful Life', *Philosophical Papers* 34 [2005]: 331–55, 337). As will be expected, I do not think this is an assumption theists need or would be well advised to

make. One may indeed, it seems to me, please God by deliberately eschewing at least some forms of meaningfulness – significance say, or one's life standing for an idea – by knowingly turning from them in order to do one's duty in some more humble, but less meaningful, way. Kekes points out 'Morally good projects may be tedious or painful; they may involve doing our duty at the cost of self-sacrifice, self-denial, the frustration of our desires, and our going against our strong feelings' (J. Kekes, 'The Meaning of Life', *Midwest Studies in Philosophy* 24 [2000]: 17–34, 30).

13 T. Metz, *Meaning in Life*, Oxford: Oxford University Press (2013), 4. He considers Hitler (T. Metz, *Meaning in Life*, Oxford: Oxford University Press [2013], 5, and bites the bullet rather – saying that Hitler's life 'could have been meaningful and even in virtue of having achieved his end of wiping out Europe's Jewish population' (also, T. Metz, *Meaning in Life*, Oxford: Oxford University Press [2013], 5), but goes on to say that of course that is quite compatible with saying that it would then have been 'valuable merely in a certain respect, which would leave open the judgements that what he did was seriously immoral and that he had the most reason not to do it'. In the end, Metz's own account of meaning in life rules Hitler out, so there is no ultimate worry for him.

14 J. Cottingham, 'Meaningful Life', in P. K. Moser and M. T. McFall (eds), *The Wisdom of the Christian Faith*, Cambridge: Cambridge University Press (2013), 175–96.

15 In fact, I would maintain a more controversial thesis – though its truth is not necessary for the argument in the main text. More controversially then, I think further reflection will take us to see that Hitler's life would have been less meaningful *overall* had he stayed as a failed artist in Linz and that Hitler probably did end up leading the most meaningful life that he could have led. Hitler's life was more meaningful overall than it would have been had he done anything morally acceptable with it, e.g. stayed as a failed artist in Linz. (I say this as I presume that it was psychologically impossible for him to have led a life that was committed to a morally acceptable idea or realized any other significant goods.) But Hitler's adding meaningfulness to his life by getting his life to stand for the idea that he did get it to stand for was in and of itself his making his life worse for himself. In, and of itself, even before we consider the effects that his doing this had on other people and values. It was his making his life more meaningful than it could have been made by any other choices that it is plausible he would have been able to make, given the psychological problems that I am assuming he had. But it was making it a lot worse. Possible alternative lives for Hitler – e.g. that of a failed artist in Linz – would have been better, but less overall meaningful ones. So, leading the most overall meaningful life that one can may not be leading the best life that one can. Even if one resists this more controversial point, the point argued for in the main text remains untouched. Leading the most meaningful life *in this sense* may not be leading the best life that one can. Kauppinen perhaps speaks for more (than I have just spoken for) in saying 'Hitler's life was, in fact, meaningless' (A. Kauppinen, 'Meaningfulness and Time', *Philosophy and Phenomenological Research* 82 [2012]: 345–77, 361), though the reasons given for this – 'his projects gave him no reason to live, nor anything to be proud about and celebrate' are to my mind not conclusive. That that is true means that his life failed to be meaningful in some legitimate senses, but not that it failed to be meaningful in all legitimate senses. In particular, these considerations do not mean it failed to be meaningful in the sense of standing for an idea. Nor even do they mean that it failed to be overall as meaningful as it could be. Given the paucity of options open to a person of his psychology, getting his life to stand for an idea of the purest evil was in fact quite possibly – I have hazarded actually – the overall most meaningful thing he could do with his life. He could not access any of the positive sorts of meaning, just this particular negative sort. But of course Kauppinen is a monist, so the fact that these considerations rule out meaningfulness in the sense defended is taken by Kauppinen to be their ruling out meaningfulness altogether. Harry Frankfurt, with his

subjectivism, unsurprisingly thinks that devoting oneself 'to what one loves suffices to make one's life meaningful' and thus concludes that Hitler led a meaningful life despite the fact that the cause to which 'Hitler devoted his life was a dreadful evil' (H. Frankfurt, 'Reply to Susan Wolf', in S. Buss and L. Overton (eds), *The Contours of Agency: Essays on Themes from Harry Frankfurt*, Cambridge, MA: MIT Press [2002], 245–52, 248–9).

16 In fact, if you are typical in having the higher-order desire I spoke of earlier you will, on reflection, give the same ranking as me here, assuming that is that you think I've got my ranking right.

17 A. Smuts, 'The Good Cause Account of the Meaning of Life' *Southern Journal of Philosophy* 51.4 (2013): 536–62, 552.

18 I am somewhat contrary to Kauppinen then who says that 'Feelings of fulfillment would hardly be appropriate if my heart was not in what I was doing – in a sense, it wouldn't really be *my* action to take pride in' (A. Kauppinen, 'Meaningfulness and Time', *Philosophy and Phenomenological Research* 82 [2012], 345–77, 356). Feelings of fulfilment might be appropriate, just hard to generate, in such a case. One's heart is not in the activity; one persists in it nevertheless recognizing that it is the sort of thing that should fulfil one even though it will not, and thus recognizing that feelings of fulfilment would be appropriate, just hardly likely. The activity is meaningful for one in this sense. I am also somewhat contrary to Kekes, when he says that 'Mill reasonably judged his life meaningless [at the stage he suffered the 'crisis' in his mental history], yet it had worth, for it was dedicated to a good cause; it aimed at the important goal of bettering the condition of humanity' (J. Kekes, 'The Meaning of Life', *Midwest Studies in Philosophy* 24 [2000], 17–34, 20). I would say that Mill's life did have some meaning – even for him – at this stage, even though he felt no satisfaction in that meaning. Thus, Mill would have been wrong to have judged his life meaningless in every sense at this stage. A careful reading of the relevant passage from his autobiography would suggest that he did not in fact judge his life meaningless in every sense of the term.

19 On this issue there is room for dispute also, of course.

20 Given that – as already indicated in a few notes – I am not an intersubjectivist about the relevant values, one may press me on how the intersubjectivity that I do endorse here fits with that. The answer is that it is our intersubjective concerns that demarcate which cluster of values and non-values we are asking about and then the ranking of these concerns is an objective matter. It is also intersubjectively something we care about given that we – most of us – have the higher-order desire to have our lower-order desires proportioned to the objective desirability of the things on the list.

Chapter 7

1 One would be forgiven for thinking that discoveries of undermining or exclusion between different meanings of life cannot form a part of the case for amalgam polyvalence over grab-bag, as grab-bag polyvalence asserts the conceptual and metaphysical separateness of all the different meanings of life. However, as I am understanding it, grab-bag polyvalence goes beyond merely asserting separateness. It denies that the reasons for separateness are logical or metaphysical. And thus discoveries of this sort – logical or metaphysical reasons for separateness – would be reasons for rejecting it. In other words, and to repeat, I am understanding grab-bag polyvalence as the view that each item in the grab bag is logically and metaphysically unrelated to any other. For example, the logical relation of mutual exclusion – if a life is meaningful in sense x, then it cannot, of logical necessity, be

meaningful in sense y – is forbidden under grab-bag understandings. Thus any 'mutual exclusion' – findings are a reason to reject grab-bag polyvalence in addition to any mutual 'inclusion' – findings. As I indicated earlier, another way of thinking of this whole issue is to consider what an omnipotent being might be able to do with the various meanings of life – omnipotence securing for him the ability to put in place causal connections wherever they are logically and metaphysically allowed. Were a grab-bag polyvalence true, then an omnipotent being could causally separate out all of them from one another, so that, as one might put it, were one to pull any one out of the bag, none of the rest would come with it. (There's no logical or metaphysical support or inclusion relationship between any of them.) In addition, were a grab-bag polyvalence true, an omnipotent being could instead causally link all the meanings of life together, so that, as one might put it, were one to pull out any one, all the rest would come too. (There's no logical or metaphysical undermining or exclusion relationship between any of them.) So it is that the discoveries of logical and metaphysical support and inclusion between different meanings of life are reasons to reject grab-bag (and direct reasons to endorse amalgam) polyvalence. The discoveries of logical and metaphysical undermining and exclusion between some sorts of meaningfulness are reasons to reject grab-bag (and indirect reasons to endorse amalgam; indirect in that they are compatible with amalgam polyvalence but also with the view that there is no amalgamation at all). They are also reasons of course to endorse polyvalence generally. I have not brought out for discussion this 'third way' within polyvalence, the view that there are many meanings of life but that none of them amalgamate to any extent whatsoever and some of them undermine or exclude one another for non-causal reasons. That is because it seems to me obvious that there is what I call amalgamation. In any case, discovering mutual underminings and exclusions is another way of discovering that grab-bag polyvalence is false, even though it remains true that if that had been the only way of discovering that grab-bag polyvalence was false, it would not have been enough to get one directly to amalgam polyvalence. One needs discoveries of mutual support or inclusion to get one there. But discoveries of this second sort are pretty easily available – I'll give some in this chapter – and thus we have sufficient reason to endorse the amalgam view.

2 R. Taylor, 'The Meaning of Life', *Good and Evil,* London: Macmillan (1984), 258.

3 I. Dilman, 'Life and Meaning', *Philosophy* 40.154 (1965): 320–33, 321.

4 Several unless they all amalgamate into one; I believe they do not (and will later argue for that), but it is not essential, so I leave this claim to there being several undefended in the main text at the moment.

5 It is arguable that there is another sort of meaning that a life might have in virtue of simply having a purpose in an appropriate larger scheme of things. But some think that one's life having a purpose in an appropriate larger scheme of things does not add to the meaning of one's life unless one is to some extent at least fulfilling that purpose, even if unconsciously and/or trying to do so. So, suppose that God's purpose for me is that I give up my work in Philosophy and become instead a missionary to street children in Brazil. If so, then, on this view, that fact does not make my life in any way meaningful (given that I am not to any extent fulfilling His purpose or indeed trying to do so [not least because I assign the hypothesis that that is God's purpose for me a very low probability]). I actually disagree with this view, but – because it is widespread – I pass it by at this stage.

6 This is because it is very implausible to imagine that there is a God or some such who has an appropriate larger scheme of things in mind for you in which obsessively collecting miniature teapots figures.

7 Although of course we have not been considering cosmic meanings of life, which seem unlikely to amalgamate.

Notes

Chapter 8

1 J. Cottingham, *The Spiritual Dimension*, Cambridge: Cambridge University Press (2005), 53, talks about 'minimal' meaning and contrasts it with 'deep' meaning.

2 See e.g. G. Kahane, 'Should We Want God to Exist?', *Philosophy and Phenomenological Research* 82 (2011): 674–96.

3 J.-P. Sartre, *Existentialism is a Humanism*, P. Mairet (trans), London: Methuen & Co. (1980), 26–7.

4 Most charitably for, as the discussion of Baier has already shown, dignity is not plausibly the thing that God threatens/would threaten.

5 J. Cottingham, 'Meaningful Life', in P. K. Moser and M. T. McFall (eds), *The Wisdom of the Christian Faith*, Cambridge: Cambridge University Press (2013), 175–96.

6 Of course even this would not in itself preclude self-creation (as Brian Leftow has pointed out to me), but it would preclude *permissible* self-creation.

7 Of course, your reasoning, if it is as sketched here, is in principle defeasible in its own terms. If the fact is that your friend conceives of himself as needing to be the provider for his family only because he does not feel able – much though he wishes he were able – to go against the gender-stereotyping in his society, then the wider context in which he *qua* worker finds himself would not be any more of an expression of his self-creative autonomy than the narrower context. But let's sweep that possibility to one side for a moment to see how we might understand what is going on more fundamentally when one switches perspectives from one context to another.

8 Brian Leftow points out that one explanation at variance with the one I favour in the main text is that you are perhaps simply reflecting back to him his own dissatisfaction – given that he has placed a value on this, so you are going along with that.

9 The objection is discussed and well critiqued by Metz in T. Metz, *Meaning in Life*, Oxford: Oxford University Press (2013), 102–4. I believe my points complement his.

10 K. Baier, 'The Meaning of Life' in E. D. Klemke and S. M. Cahn (eds), *The Meaning of Life*, Oxford: Oxford University Press (2013), 83–113, 104.

11 Not the peculiar deistic God I mentioned.

12 J. Cottingham, 'Meaningful Life', in P. K. Moser and M. T. McFall (eds), *The Wisdom of the Christian Faith*, Cambridge University Press (2013), 175–96. He makes mention of Nietzsche in this context in a note and the reference to him and Cottingham's criticisms are worth following up: 'Friedrich Nietzsche seems to have imagined that humans [of an exalted type] could somehow create meaning and value for themselves by some exalted act of will or choice; *Beyond Good and Evil* [*Jenseits von Gut und Böse*, 1886], trans. W. Kaufmann, New York: Random House (1966), §203. I have argued elsewhere that this is a thoroughly confused notion; see J. Cottingham, 'The Good Life and the "Radical Contingency of the Ethical"', in D. Callcut (ed.), *Reading Bernard Williams*, London: Routledge (2008), Chapter 2, 25–43.

13 Of course the historical Sartre did not believe in Platonism, but we need not follow him here.

14 One might raise at this point, if not before, the following question: what about 'restrictions' imposed by human nature per se – ones that remain constant in logical space (regardless of whether or not there is a God) and prevent this? Fair enough. If there are such, then we can divide through by them, as it were. They cancel out when considering comparisons between Godly worlds and Godless worlds. I am talking about the difference God makes/would make in particular through being an authority who has purposes for us.

15 In metaphysics, or in human nature (if that's not already included in metaphysics); see previous note.

16 I talk about Sartre's position here not aiming to refer to the position occupied by the actual Sartre, but rather aiming to refer to the view worked out on his behalf as, it has been argued, more plausible than the one that the historical Sartre would himself have endorsed.

17 Or as fully as human nature allows; see previous notes.

18 On Trinitarian Christianity, one perhaps does best to understand this claim as being made only about the Trinity as a whole. For if God is three persons in one substance, the second person of which became incarnate in order to atone for the sins of mankind, then this second person of the Trinity would lead a very meaningful life in the sense of having a purpose in an appropriate larger scheme of things even whilst leading a less meaningful life in Sartre's sense (through having this part of His essence precede at least his human existence). There are deep theological issues that affect these ones. In any case, it seems at least worthy of further investigation whether God as Trinity might lead a life that is fully meaningful in every desirable sense of meaningful through localizing different and incompatible sorts of meaningfulness in His different persons. Perfect Being Theology might suggest we should think that God would lead a fully meaningful life in every desirable sense of meaningful, which then might provide a reason for Trinitarianism.

Nozick, in the final essay of his *Socratic Puzzles*, Cambridge, MA: Harvard University Press (1997), wonders whether God's life gets meaning in virtue of His creating (for no purpose?) the larger plan that gives meaning to our lives.

19 It thus can be a source of rational regret, in the sense that Williams has argued – to my mind persuasively – that we are able rationally to regret what I would call 'aspects' of what remained overall the right moral choice for us to have made after having made it. The best explanation of rational regret in such cases is that the path not taken had genuinely valuable aspects that the path taken did not have (or did not have to the same degree), even though the path taken was overall the best path to take. This is the best explanation as it is hard – though attempts have certainly been made to do it – to explain the regret as rational if the options should have been compared in terms of a single value, moral rightness. How then could we rationally regret having chosen the path that *ex hypothesi* had more of this than the one not taken? (B. Williams, 'Ethical Consistency', in his *Problems of the Self*, Cambridge: Cambridge University Press [1973], 166–86, and B. Williams, *Moral Luck*, Cambridge: Cambridge University Press [1981]). See also, M. Stocker, *Plural and Conflicting Values*, Oxford: Clarendon Press (1990).

20 Even if they had, there would still have been the cosmic meanings of life to consider of course.

21 I shall come back to this point in a later chapter.

22 See also J. Kekes, 'The Informed Will and the Meaning of Life', *Philosophy and Phenomenological Research* 47.1 (1986): 75–90, especially his discussion of what is wrong with what he calls 'manipulated wants'.

23 As Camus puts it: 'from the point of view of Sirius, Goethe's works in ten thousand years will be dust and his name forgotten' (A. Camus, 'The Myth of Sisyphus', in J. P Brien (trans.), *The Myth of Sisyphus and Other Essays*, New York: Knopf [2005], 78). In the main text, I speak of the time to be considered as a hundred years. If you think the claims I make to be empirically false (claims to the effect that pretty much everyone's life is such that in a hundred years' time the universe will be for evaluative purposes as if they had never existed), then substitute a longer time to make them come out true – perhaps the time suggested by Camus, ten thousand years.

Notes

24 T. Nagel, 'The Absurd' in O. Hanfling (ed.) *Life and Meaning a Reader,* Oxford: Blackwell (1987), 49–59, 49. Originally in *Journal of Philosophy* 68 (1971): 716–27.

25 T. Metz, 'What is this thing called the meaning of life?' in D. Pritchard (ed.), *What is this thing called Philosophy?*, London: Routledge (2015), 319–58.

26 Audi (R. Audi, 'Intrinsic Value and Meaningful Live', *Philosophical Papers* 34 (2005): 331–55, 354–355) is one of many who challenges whether having an infinite effect is necessary for meaning. And we have already come across the option of denying that a lack of meaning in a wider context overwhelms or outweighs meaning in a narrower context.

27 The relation between this sort of meaning – mattering to someone – and the 'other' under discussion here – fulfilling a purpose in an appropriate larger scheme of things – depends on whether all elements that fulfil a purpose in an appropriate larger schemes of things matter to someone. If so, and if everything that matters to someone matters to them at least in part because it fulfils a purpose in an appropriate larger scheme of things, then they are at least coextensive, though in that the facts that would need to be in place to guarantee this sort of coextension are going to depend on metaphysics, they would not be coextensive of conceptual necessity – they would remain logically discrete sorts of meaning conjoined by metaphysical necessity. This then is a case of a connection that draws them into a cluster IFF ('if and only if') metaphysics is a certain way. There's amalgamation here, but only if a certain type of religious hypothesis is true. Here is the sort of religious hypothesis that I have in mind (in essence it is an expanded version of the theistic hypothesis): We are creatures who matter to God. Thus if something matters to us, it matters to Him. And we are creatures for whom things mattering is a part of His intention in creating us (thus fulfilling a part in an appropriate larger scheme of things). To elucidate the model by way of a parallel case: my daughter often finds that things matter to her that it astonishes me can matter to anyone. For example, she wants her dolls lined up in a particular way, rather than some other; they all have to be sitting in the right place and in the right way. I see that objectively it does not matter which way they are lined up. But I also see that – subjectively – it matters a lot to her. That I see that second thing, combined with the fact that she matters to me, makes her whimsical desire that the dolls be lined up one way rather than another consequently matter to me too. So, if there's a God, everything that matters to us – however whimsical it may be – matters to God. Naturally things that matter to us because they objectively matter – that gratuitous suffering be reduced, say – matter to God anyway. But things that do not objectively matter – the equivalent of dolls being lined up one way rather than another – but matter to us in our lives (and even as adults we have many such things, e.g. that the front room be painted one colour rather than another, that we have this for lunch rather than that) matter to God. That people have such whimsical desires fulfils a purpose in God's appropriate larger scheme of things; we are this way because God's purposes in creation were that we be so. And thus there is coextension: everything that matters to anyone matters to God.

    So, we have by these reflections possibly another example supporting the case of amalgamation (if we do think that the right religious hypothesis is true) and certainly a case supporting the thesis that we are likely – collectively – to be dissatisfied with answers to the question of the meaning of life pending a decisive resolution to issues in metaphysics, which is a source of dissatisfaction that I also diagnose in this book and call 'waiting on metaphysics'. I have already discussed it.

28 The thesis that sometimes goes by the name Value Pluralism.

29 God can throw Himself here on some words of mercy from Nagel: 'Provided one has taken the process of practical justification as far as it will go in the course of arriving at the conflict, one may be able to proceed without further justification, but without irrationality either.

What makes this possible is judgment—essentially the faculty Aristotle described as practical wisdom, which reveals itself over time in individual decisions rather than in the enunciation of general principles' (T. Nagel, 'The Fragmentation of Value' in his *Mortal Questions*, Cambridge: Cambridge University Press [1979], 135). Similarly, He can appeal to Sartre's famous example of the person trying to decide whether to stay at home with his ailing mother or go and fight in the war; either is a permissible choice, but that does not mean that whichever the person decides to do he cannot rationally regret it in some respects.

30 I also think the same may be true of aspects, but ignore this in the main text.

31 It is not really another sort, but a reapplication of the Sartrean sort, to the issue of where the balance should be struck between self-chosen meaning and God-chosen meaning; do we get to make that choice or does God?

32 'Meaning luck', I might have called it were it not for the fact that we have already used that term to refer to another phenomenon.

33 Obviously there's a – very weak – sense in which, even were God deistic, we'd still end up serving His purposes by whatever we did, that is the purpose God had for us that we do whatever it was we wanted to do. I am obviously assuming a stronger – content-laden – purpose as being necessary for us to be fulfilling a purpose in an appropriate larger scheme of things generated by His intentions for us. God has a permissive will and a perfect will. His perfect will for me is – say – that I write on just this topic of Philosophy; his permissive will for me is – say – that I be allowed not to write on anything in Philosophy at all. It is only when I act in conformity to His perfect will that I get to count as fulfilling His purpose for me.

34 I draw here on the brilliant work of Brian Dalton, in this case in his sketch 'Mr Deity and the Meaning Game': https://www.youtube.com/watch?v=1Y85yfT0Oug (accessed 11 June 2014).

35 The example of Jonah shows that there are exceptions, at least temporary exceptions. As I say, I like to think that in the end he felt this.

Chapter 9

1 I assume that we do take ourselves to be such.

2 T. J. Mawson, 'On Determining How Important it is Whether or Not there is a God', *European Journal for Philosophy of Religion* 4 (2012): 95–105. This was a development of an argument I presented first in a paper called 'Is Whether or Not There is a God Worth Thinking About?' which appeared in D. Bradshaw (ed.), *Ethics and the Challenge of Secularism*, Council for Research in Values and Philosophy (2013), 5–19. And T. J. Mawson 'An Agreeable Answer to a Pro-Theism/Anti-Theism Question', forthcoming.

3 This is an example, of course, only on the assumption that time travel is metaphysically impossible but not logically impossible. If you do not happen to so grade it, you could consider arriving at a hotel late at night and being told that all the rooms are occupied, the last one being taken only ten minutes before you arrived. Counterfactual question: would it have been better for you had you arrived fifteen minutes earlier? Counterpossible question: would it have been better for you had this been Hilbert's Hotel? If you think actual infinities are metaphysically possible, then I give up.

4 The method then, it will be noticed, cannot be used to evaluate logically impossible worlds – that seems fine to me; there are no such.

5 So, if the truth on which they agree is Optimism, that will be a truth expressed by the theist

Notes

as its being the case that given that God does exist, the world is in fact more meaningful than it would have been if He had not existed. For the atheist, it will be expressed as its being the case that were God to have existed, the world would have been more meaningful than in fact it is. And for the agnostic it'll be expressed as a disjunction of these two claims and a knowledge-denial claim, i.e. as its being the case that one of those things the theist or atheist says in expressing Optimism is true, but we cannot know which.

6 It is even perhaps paradoxical-sounding – cosmic meanings of life are not intrinsically deep? How could that be? We should remind ourselves then that all that is being said with such a claim is that, absent these connections with our more individualistic concerns, God's answering the cosmic concerns by tying together the fabric of reality at its most fundamental level, isn't actually His contributing that much to answering the question 'What is the meaning of life?' because the cosmic concerns in themselves are not central to that topic. There are obviously other senses of deep in which He is contributing at a deep level. In being that in terms of which the fact that there are laws of nature at all is explained, He is contributing at a level that is metaphysically deeper than the laws of nature themselves, for example.

7 This is assuming that He is a net contributor at all at the cosmic level.

8 Milder variants of Optimism could also be defended (e.g. God adds more to the meaning of most of our lives than He takes away). The same goes *mutatis mutandis* for Neutralism and Pessimism. In fact, I think the stronger form of Optimism may be defended so that's what I've confined myself to considering here.

9 Again there are relevant complications to this suggestion, ones that are addressed in the two papers I mention.

10 Not that many theists do think this; it is a tenet of all the monotheistic religions that there's an afterlife awaiting at least some of us.

11 I take it that this is a commitment of the justification-by-faith approach which is common within Protestant Christianity: one is saved by having faith in Christ, its being a necessary (though not sufficient [even the demons believe, and tremble]) condition of one's having saving faith that one believes a certain thing about Christ *ante-mortem*; that's why, on the view, Jehovah's Witnesses, say, or Mormons, will not be saved – they allegedly do not satisfy the accuracy-of-*ante-mortem*-belief condition that's allegedly necessary.

12 I give the argument for Theism implying Universalism in T. J. Mawson, *Belief in God*, Oxford: Oxford University Press (2005), 99ff. It is simple: God wants want what's best for us; it will be best for us to have an everlasting afterlife in perfect communion with Him and with one another (Heaven); so God will give us that.

13 See e.g. F. Tipler and J. Barrow, *The Anthropic Cosmological Principle*, Oxford: Oxford University Press (1986); F. Tipler, *The Physics of Immortality: Modern Cosmology, God and the Resurrection of the Dead,* New York: Doubleday (1994); and F. Tipler, *The Physics of Christianity,* New York: Doubleday (2007).

14 I talk this way as technically it is a potential infinite, in contrast to an actual infinite; we will never in fact achieve it. I actually think this makes quite a difference, undercutting many of the traditional arguments against the desirability of immortality per se – ones that are based on the faulty application of the principle that after an infinite time everything that can happen will have happened (infinitely, many times indeed). It is faulty to apply this as we'll never actually have lived anything but a finite amount of time. This faulty reasoning can be found in many places in the literature. By way of one example, 'If our powers are limited, the number of significant projects that we are capable of completing is finite, but the time span of an immortal life is infinite.' So an 'immortal life would be either frustrating or boring,

and long. Very long.' (A. Smuts, 'Immortality and Significance', *Philosophy and Literature* 35 [2011]: 134–49, 148). Not so, or at least not so as a matter of logic. Even with a potential infinite ahead of us, we will only ever have a finite past behind us and thus even if we retain finite powers, we will never – of logical necessity – need to have completed all of the finite significant projects that we are capable of completing. We will always be able to think of new aesthetically valuable ways to worship God and please ourselves and our fellow men.

15 Or at least the form of Atheism I am engaging with.

16 Nor is it that we would be demotivated. Some say that knowing that we have an infinite Heaven ahead of us would demotivate us – we've come across this point before. As already mentioned, intrinsically valuable things are worth doing and thus worth doing now, not postponing. The fact that I could worship God tomorrow (and will) is no reason not to worship God today. And the fact that one has a potential infinity ahead of one does not stop that. Consider this choice. God tells you that you can have one of two Heavens, each qualitatively the same except that in one you have twice as much hedonic pleasure per day as you do in the other. You would be rational in choosing the twice-as-much-per-day Heaven even though each offers you a potential infinity of pleasure. Even though each offers you a potential infinity, you'll never get an actual infinity, and in the twice-as-much-per-day Heaven you'll always be doing twice as well on the hedonic scale as you would have been doing in the other.

17 For example, C. Belshaw, *10 Good Questions about Life and Death*, Malden, MA: Blackwell (2005), 82–91; and Joseph Ellin, in *Morality and The Meaning of Life*, Fort Worth TX: Harcourt Brace College Publishers (1995) argue that immortality would have to become boring.

18 In my *Belief in God*, Oxford: Oxford University Press (2005), I say, 'The news delivered by John Newton in the famous words, "When we've been there ten thousand years, bright shining as the Sun, there's no less days to sing God's praise, than when we've first begun," I admit, is not entirely welcome to me with the level of enthusiasm I can currently muster for hymn singing, even John-Newton-hymn singing. But this failure is a failure of character and imagination (and very probably musical ability) on my part, not an incoherence or implausibility in the doctrine; indeed, the failure on my part and resultant difficulty is precisely what one would expect on Theism. This moves me on to the second point. Second, it is not obviously true that thinking away the reaction of boredom to a situation in someone is always to posit an impoverishment in his or her consciousness of it. As anyone who has taught Philosophy will know, students can get bored even when the subject matter does not by any means warrant it. This is a deficiency in them (and perhaps reveals that one has not done all that one might *qua* educator). To remove someone's capacity for inappropriate boredom is not to suppose an impoverishment in his or her consciousness of the object, which he or she might otherwise find boring; rather it is to suppose an improvement. I do not have educated musical tastes and as such I would find an opera by Gilbert and Sullivan much less boring than one by Wagner. However, I am quite prepared to assent to Mark Twain's claim that Wagner's music is a lot better than it sounds. If, as Twain's way of putting it well captures, I can't now really imagine how that could be, I'm prepared to think that that's precisely because I am not musically educated; not being musically educated I would not expect to be able to envisage what it would be like to be transformed into the sort of person who could listen to Wagner without getting relatively bored except by rather artificially "thinking away" the boredom. But – however artificial – I can think this reaction away and I realize when I do so that – assuming the truth behind Mark Twain's aphorism – were such a change to be effected in me, I would have been quite the opposite from being impoverished in my appreciation of what it was I was hearing' (247). Bortolotti and

Nagasawa, in 'Immortality Without Boredom', *Ratio* 22 (2009): 261–77, and Quigley and Harris in 'Immortal Happiness', in *Philosophy and Happiness*, L. Bortolotti (ed.), New York: Palgrave Macmillan (2009), 68–81, esp. 76–8, also challenge the idea that immortality would have to get boring.

19 T. Metz, 'The Meaning of Life', *Stanford Encyclopedia of Philosophy* (first published online Tuesday 15 May 2007; substantive revision Monday 3 June 2013).

20 D. Brukner, 'Against the Tedium of Immortality', *International Journal of Philosophical Studies* 20 (2012), 623–44.

21 See also T. Chappell, 'Infinity Goes Up on Trial: Must Immortality be Meaningless?' *European Journal of Philosophy* 17 (2009): 30–44 and, the most influential defence of immortality not needing to be boring, John Martin Fischer, 'Why Immortality is Not So Bad', *International Journal of Philosophical Studies* 2 (1994): 257–70.

22 T. Metz, 'What is this thing called The Meaning of Life' in D. Pritchard (ed.), *What Is This thing called Philosophy?*, London: Routledge (2015), 341.

23 R. Taylor, 'The Meaning of Life', in *Good and Evil*, London: Macmillan (1984), 26.

24 This name has become quite standard. See, e.g. T. Metz, *Meaning in Life*, Oxford: Oxford University Press (2013), Chapter 5 and following. Although the idea is as old as the hills, I believe Metz was in fact the first to so name it, in his 'Could God's purPose be the Source of Life's Meaning?' *Religious Studies* 36 (2000): 293–313, where he defines it thus: 'Purpose theory is the view that a life is meaningful insofar as one fulfils a purpose that God has assigned' (295). Of course, given polyvalence, I am operating with a more relaxed understanding of purpose theory whereby it asserts merely that fulfilling a purpose that God has assigned (or even, I would maintain, simply having been assigned a purpose by God [whether one fulfils it or not]) is one of the meanings of life. There may well be others and thus a life may be meaningful in many senses even if one does not fulfil a purpose that God has assigned. Affolter – responding directly to Metz's piece – sums it up nicely by way of contrasting it with a popular misunderstanding (or rather – I would say – partial understanding), when he says 'The idea is not that God decides on some goal that He wants to fulfil and then chooses or even designs a person to fulfil that goal. The idea is that God designs a person in such a way that the need to fulfil some purpose is built into the person's very nature, such that his life makes no sense apart from that goal' (J. Affolter, 'Human Nature as God's Purpose', *Religious Studies* 43 (2007): 443–55, 453). This, it seems to me, well characterizes God's generic purposes for us as humans. Sometimes though, *pace* Affolter, God will have particular goals that He will choose some people to fulfil. The most obvious case: they will be given a vocation revealed to them in a religious experience. And of course, given my polyvalence, I do not wish to say as Affolter does that life could make *no* sense apart from the goals that God has assigned them (either generic or particular). There are lots of meanings of life that a person might have quite apart from God's goals for him/her. Most notable are self-assigned purposes that he/she finds satisfying, possibly more satisfying (in the short-term anyway) than he/she would find fulfilling his/her God-assigned objective purposes.

25 Some of the generic purposes God has for us are ones that we cannot wholly fail to fulfil anyway; and the same probably goes for some of the peculiar purposes He has for us as individuals. And it may well be that God has for some people peculiar purposes that it is essential for the Divine Economy they fulfil – perhaps Jonah's preaching to Nineveh is one such. If so, then, one way or another, Jonah was going to have to fulfil this purpose God had for him.

26 That the larger scheme of things is appropriate is rather under-determined by the

details in the main text, but these can be added in – it is the factory that is producing mini-ambulances, let's say.

27 Affolter, in J. Affolter, 'Human Nature as God's Purpose', *Religious Studies* 43 (2007): 443–55, discusses some of the issues here. Though he in the end endorses the view that God as creator is uniquely qualified to give our lives a certain type of purpose, he says at one stage the following: 'It is not immediately clear why we should privilege the designer [and, one might add, creator] of an object over anyone else who finds a better use for it. It may be the case that a person makes something as an engine that turns out to be much more effective as a heater … the fact that a person designs or makes some object with a certain purpose in mind does not entail that the designer's purpose is the object's unique purpose' (J. Affolter, 'Human Nature as God's Purpose', *Religious Studies* 43 [2007]: 443–55, 445–6). It seems to me that the creator and designer has a unique authority in determining the ultimate purpose of an object. It seems to me – though not perhaps to Affolter – that this is so even when that creator and designer is working far from *ex nihilo*, but in any case it is all the more clearly so if He is. So, for example, it may well be that the creator of a piece of machinery creates it with the intention that it be an engine, but in fact it is used solely as a heater. That, it seems to me, is a case of an engine being used as a heater. Its later use does not stop its being an engine. It is of course an engine being used with the purpose of heating, so it is, as Affolter says, not the case that it has a unique purpose – being an engine. It now has the purpose of heating. But its now having the purpose of heating does not stop its being the case that its ultimate purpose – even though now that purpose is failing to be fulfilled – is to be an engine.

28 At one stage, Waghorn says that 'If purpose theory is true, we seem to have to face the uncomfortable idea that, if God were to make our purpose a lowly one, say to act as food for intergalactic travellers, then fulfilling this purpose would make our lives meaningful. This is counterintuitive' (N. Waghorn, *Nothingness and the Meaning of Life: Philosophical Approaches to Ultimate Meaning Through Nothing and Self-reflexivity*, London: Bloomsbury [2014], 198). But he himself warms to the idea, pointing out that 'it is a purpose, in the sense that an even more depressing scenario (analogous to there being no divine plan at all) in which we were slaughtered arbitrarily or by accident by intergalactic travellers who happened to be passing through our solar system would not provide us with a purpose' (N. Waghorn, *Nothingness and the Meaning of Life: Philosophical Approaches to Ultimate Meaning Through Nothing and Self-reflexivity*, London: Bloomsbury [2014], 199). I agree, and would only add the obvious points made earlier, including the most important one that we are here discussing, a counterpossible: God of metaphysical necessity could not assign us a purpose that would be lowly in any problematic way.

29 T. Metz, 'Recent Work on the Meaning of Life', *Ethics* 112 (2002): 781–814, 810.

30 A common point made against the suggestion that immortality is key to our lives' meaningfulness is to argue that if our *ante-mortem* lives were not meaningful, then there's no way that merely extending them into a *post-mortem* realm would make them meaningful. It would just prolong them in all their meaninglessness, making things, if anything, worse. My counter of course may be anticipated: on my polyvalence, our *ante-mortem* lives have – and would have, even if they were not to be prolonged into a *post-mortem* realm – meaning of many sorts. It is not that I am saying that without immortality, our mortal lives would not be meaningful at all. Indeed quite the contrary: it is precisely because our *ante-mortem* lives do have meaning that in extending them *post-mortem*, God gives our lives (understood as *ante-mortem* and *post-mortem* wholes) more meaning.

31 See also J. Wisnewski, 'Is the Immortal Life Worth Living?' *International Journal for Philosophy of Religion* 58 (2005), 27–36, and T. Chappell, 'Infinity Goes Up on Trial: Must

Immortality Be Meaningless?' in *European Journal of Philosophy* 17 (2009): 30–44. Morris suggests (in T. Morris, *Making Sense of it All: Pascal and the Meaning of Life*, Grand Rapids, MI: William B. Eerdmans Publishing Company [1992]) that meaning in life comes from loving what is most worth loving, which is permanent persons – God (and the rest of us, *contra* the appearance of mortality). Augustine had in effect pre-figured this debate and its conclusion by conceding that the love of any finite good would become unsatisfactory, but not of an infinite good.

32 N. Levy, 'Downshifting and Meaning in Life', *Ratio* 18 (2005): 176–89. As he says, 'I suspect that the theological solution to the problem of the meaning of life might be taken as satisfying these conditions' (184).

33 I have again rather chopped up Tolstoy's text. The full version may be found in several translations free of charge online, by looking up 'L. Tolstoy, *A Confession*'.

34 A. Flew, *The Presumption of Atheism and Other Essays*, London: Elek Books (1976), 160–1.

35 As Iddo Landau argues at length, we may 'examine our lives *sub specie aeternitatis*, and we may adopt godlike standards of affecting the whole universe [to judge of their meaning]; but we need not adopt the latter *because* of the former' (I. Landau, 'The Meaning of Life *Sub Specie Aeternitatis*', *Australasian Journal of Philosophy* 89.4 [2001]: 727–34, 731).

36 W. Craig, 'The Absurdity of Life Without God', *Reasonable Faith: Christian Truth and Apologetics*, Wheaton, IL: Crossway Books, 3rd edn (2008), 73.

37 I. Dilman, 'Life and Meaning', *Philosophy* 40.154 (1965): 320–33, 328.

38 S. Goetz, *The Purpose of Life: A Theistic Perspective*, London: Continuum, 2012, 2.

39 A. Flew, *The Presumption of Atheism and Other Essays*, London: Elek Books (1976), 158.

40 B. Trisel, 'Human Extinction and the Value of Our Efforts', *The Philosophical Forum* 35.3 (2004): 371–91, 391.

41 It does not matter that other things could give the world and our lives the 'religious character' needed for ultimate significance-meaning. The point relevant to the case for Optimism is that God could do this.

42 Waghorn defines what he calls 'ultimate' meaning this way – 'an existence the meaningfulness of which cannot be improved upon' (N. Waghorn, *Nothingness and the Meaning of Life*, London: Bloomsbury [2014], 3). This is not the same as ultimate significance-meaning. It is not clear that Heaven will have ultimate meaning in Waghorn's sense, for by being – by definition – a maximally desirable *post-mortem* state of existence for us and meaningfulness (even overall meaningfulness) being just one value, it may be that our heavenly afterlives will be ones the meaningfulness of which could be improved upon but only by making them, all things considered, worse.

43 D. Schmidtz, 'The Meanings of Life', in L. Rouner (ed.), *Boston University Studies in Philosophy and Religion*, Vol. 22, (Notre Dame, University of Notre Dame Press (2001), 170–88, 178.

44 R. Taylor, 'The Meaning of Life', in his *Good and Evil*, London: Macmillan (1984), 263.

45 The way I put things in the main text is somewhat misleading perhaps in that theists and atheists are unlikely to be polyvalence theorists and thus unlikely to think of the issue in terms of the chart/list that I have been encouraging us to think of it in terms of. The phenomenon I track here then is that theists tend to enthuse about it (e.g. Tolstoy) and atheists tend to dismiss it (e.g. Flew). At least those atheists who think it undesirable seem to me to be provably mistaken. It is in fact somewhat desirable that some of what we do has ultimate significance-meaning, but how much is this 'somewhat'? That, I concede to the other atheists, seems to me far less certain.

46 Craig sometimes tends to see the danger of Atheism being that it would lead to top-down spread; if nothing has ultimate significance-meaning, then nothing can have non-ultimate significance-meaning either. But as already indicated, I don't think that is right and nor do I think it essential to Craig's overall picture. Indeed in a later note, we will see that it is essential to his view that this not happen.

47 See for example B. Trisel, 'Human Extinction and The Value of Our Efforts', *The Philosophical Forum* 35.3 (2004): 371–91, though his argument in this respect is somewhat suspect. It starts from the assumption that immortality is impossible; adds that to desire the impossible is irrational; and concludes that immortality is undesirable.

48 This is another place at which it may seem I endorse intersubjectivism – in this case, I endorse it, it should be noted, merely as a thesis about how our intersubjective reactions are the best evidence we could ever get about the objective ranking.

49 Though, through 'clustering' with ultimate significance-meaning *for us*, it is pulled higher up, as I shall show in a moment.

50 C. Hartshorne, *The Logic of Perfection,* Lasalle, Illinois: Open Court (1973), 259. See also Hartshorne 'God and the Meaning of Life', in L. S. Rouner (ed.), *Boston University Studies in Philosophy and Religion*, Vol. 6, Notre Dame: University of Notre Dame Press (1984), 154–68.

51 Thus ultimate significance-meaning *simpliciter* is pulled up the chart by its being a necessary condition of something that is high up – ultimate significance-meaning *for us*. That explains why theists rank it higher than atheists, and if their metaphysics is right, rightly so. Is it right? Another 'waiting on metaphysics' issue.

52 C. Hartshorne, 'God and the Meaning of Life', in L. S. Rouner (ed.), *Boston University Studies in Philosophy and Religion*, Vol. 6, Notre Dame: University of Notre Dame Press (1984), 154–68, 160.

53 A. Smuts, 'Immortality and Significance', *Philosophy and Literature* 35 (2011): 134–49, 136.

54 J. Cottingham, 'Meaningfulness, Eternity and Theism', in B. Himmelmann (ed.) *Meaning in Life,* Berlin and Boston: De Gruyter (2014), 99–112.

55 Of course, if my brand of Theism is right, when Sartre gets to Heaven he will find his temperament changed to be like mine in this respect, but that – I concede – is not going to be of comfort to him *ante-mortem*.

56 In short, it makes the problem of preserving personal identity easier – most clearly seen by the thought that God needs somewhere to send Hitler in between his death and his being suitable for Heaven to have him prepared so that he will not mess it up for the rest of us (and himself).

57 T. J. Mawson, *Belief in God*, Oxford: Oxford University Press (2005), 84ff.

58 By mess up, I mean render less than ideal.

59 I say objectively, as we may have subjective preferences of our own creation – *'Shall I play the harp today or play the trumpet? Since I've got here, I've developed a preference for the harp.' 'Oh really, in my case it's the trumpet.' 'But you know what, today, somewhat whimsically, I'm going to choose the harp myself.' 'How delightful.' 'Yes it is, isn't it? But then again everything everyone's ever done here in Heaven has been delightful.' 'Hasn't it just?'* These sorts of differences and choices can be preserved (on the presumption that harp playing and trumpet playing are each objectively as good as the other).

Notes

Chapter 10

1 Unless perhaps there is more than one person in the Godhead, as discussed in page 207, note 18 in chapter 8 on Trinitarianism.

2 Bernard Williams is one of many who points out that pluralism about values does not imply that comparisons are always impossible. He says 'There is one motive for reductivism that does not operate simply on the ethical, or on the non-ethical, but tends to reduce every consideration to one basic kind. This rests on an assumption about rationality, to the effect that two considerations cannot be rationally weighed against each other unless there is a common consideration in terms of which they can be compared. This assumption is at once very powerful and utterly baseless. Quite apart from the ethical, aesthetic considerations can be weighed against economic ones (for instance) without being an application of them, and without their both being an example of a third kind of consideration' (B. Williams, *Ethics and the Limits of Philosophy,* Cambridge, MA: Harvard University Press [1985], 17).

3 Of course, if there is a God, then in the chart as seen by us *post-mortem*, these boxes will be filled in by special divine revelation. I am here in the main text simply commenting on the *ante-mortem* chart as it could be discovered after an idealized (but still *ante-mortem* and absent special divine revelation) investigation. Of course this is to simplify rather too. As Laurence James points out (in L. James, 'Achievement and the Meaningfulness of Life', *Philosophical Papers* 34.2 [2005], 429–42, 43) 'Projects that are clearly beyond one's abilities will be avoided because one knows it is futile to attempt those projects.' But quite what projects are beyond one's abilities depends on whether or not there is a God around to augment one's abilities – if prayer is efficacious; if there's an afterlife; and so on. All these have an effect on what projects are futile and what not; what then it will add to the meaningfulness of our *ante-mortem* lives to commit ourselves to and what it will not.

4 See earlier discussion of how best to think of metaphysical and logical modal space.

5 Craig thinks this way, it seems to me, which is why he places such great emphasis on ultimate significance-meaning being the deepest sort.

6 Occasionally, one gets an echo of this point in the monist literature, when it has been admitted that the allegedly single value of meaningfulness nevertheless has different components and one might not find them lining up perfectly. Thus Kauppinen says 'Difficulties begin when one life rates higher than another on, say, value of the goal, but lower in terms of capacity exercise [these both being components of meaningfulness as Kauppinen understands it]. Which is more meaningful? Here we must say ... assigning lexical ordering or weighting to meaning-conferring properties of lives would distort the facts' (A. Kauppinen, 'Meaningfulness and Time', *Philosophy and Phenomenological Research* 82 [2012], 345–77, 365).

7 The important point to bear in mind in what follows is that overall meaningfulness is not what Griffin calls a 'super-value'. That is, it's not what is genuinely one value in terms of which all sub-values are ranked. But of course, as Griffin also is one who points out, 'there being no super-value [does not imply] that there is no super-scale. To think so would be to misunderstand how the notion of 'quantity' of well-being enters. It enters through ranking; quantitative differences are defined on qualitative ones. ... All that we need for the all-encompassing-scale is the possibility of ranking items on the basis of their nature. And we can, in fact, rank them in that way. We can work out trade-offs between different dimensions of pleasure or happiness. [Griffin is talking about well-being, not meaning.] And when we do, we rank in a strong sense: not just choose one rather than the other, but regard

it as worth more. That is the ultimate scale here: worth to one's life.' (J. Griffin, *Well-Being: Its Meaning, Measurement and Moral Importance*, Oxford: Clarendon [1986], 90)

8 Elizabeth Anderson gives a good example to show that it is a mistake to understand all moral goods on 'the maximizing model'. As the father of two daughters, I should not, she plausibly argues, see my love for my children as something I direct towards a child-aggregate the well-being or what have you of which I should be maximizing. Anderson herself would take this observation in a slightly different direction from the one that I would take it in, stressing that we can make rational choices between conflicting values without ranking values: '... choices concerning those goods or their continued existence do not generally require that we rank their values on a common scale and choose the more valuable good; they require that we give each good its due' (E. Anderson, "Practical Reason and Incommensurable Goods", in R. Chang (ed.), *Incommensurability, Incomparability and Practical Reason*, Cambridge, MA: Harvard University Press [1997], 104). I myself am more sanguine about thinking of a 'super-scale' as I would stress [see the quotation from Griffin on page 216, note 7] that thinking in terms of a super-scale does not commit one to thinking of there being a super value that the scale articulates. And thus, I believe that thinking of ranking is sometimes – though not always – the appropriate way to configure the issues that face one. So, consider this: a terrorist tells me that if I do not select one of my daughters for him to execute, he will execute them both. There is no way to knock his gun from his hand deftly, using the Ninja-like martial arts skills for which I am justly famous. And so on. Either I choose one or he kills both. Let us suppose my elder daughter is an adult, my younger, not; the elder suffers from a terminal illness that will kill her in weeks if the terrorist does not; my younger, not; the elder volunteers to be the one executed in the light of this, indeed she begs that I choose her so that her death can mean something (the life of her sister) that if I do not choose her, it cannot. I think that in those circumstances, I could and should rank the options and choose the highest-ranked one, the death of my eldest daughter although of course this is not to take back any of what I have said about there being cause for rational regret in the choice I should make or to suggest that the moral reality underlying the morally rational – indeed I would push the boat out and say obligatory – choice to select my elder daughter is best described as there being a child-aggregate the well-being of which I should be aiming to maximize.

9 P. Singer, *How are we to live?* Oxford: Opus (2007), 251.

10 Waghorn's notion of 'ultimate meaning' is a tricky one; he would not regard our heavenly afterlives as ultimately meaningful in that they could be improved upon by reference to at least some of the values of meaningfulness; but if we allow ourselves some leeway in understanding 'ultimate meaning' in what follows, we can agree with him when he says 'only if one had already achieved ultimate meaning could one have phrased perfectly the question to which such an achievement is the answer' (N. Waghorn, *Nothingness and the Meaning of Life*, London: Bloomsbury [2014], 190).

11 S. Wolf, 'Happiness and Meaning: Two Aspects of the Good Life', *Social Philosophy and Policy* 14 (1997): 207–25, 224.

12 If one thinks that even Wooster had some meaning-generating engagement with people, then imagine that at this extreme the Wooster-like life is lived in a virtual reality, so that his carefree japes don't affect anyone else.

13 R. Hepburn, 'Questions about the Meaning of Life', *Religious Studies* 1 (1965): 125–40,128.

14 Monty Python, *The Meaning of Life* (Celandine Films, 1983).

15 T. Metz, in 'The Concept of a Meaningful Life', *American Philosophical Quarterly* 38.2 (2001): 137–53, 137, says of the lack of interest in the topic of the meaning of life among analytic

philosophers that it is unfortunate, for 'a theory of life's meaning would help to answer the following important questions, among others: Why might a good marriage be considered more desirable than a great one-night stand? In what sense do strong candidates for euthanasia have 'nothing left to live for'? What disadvantages are there to living in a highly industrialized, consumer society? What makes certain kinds of knowledge worth pursuing? Which attitudes should one have toward the prospect of one's death? Why might people need God in their lives? Is there any independent reason for being moral? What should the goal of psychotherapy be? How do the arts figure in the best life?' But, though we perhaps naturally presume it, I think on reflection we can see that knowing the meaning of life would not help us in all these respects.

BIBLIOGRAPHY

Adams, E. M. 'The Meaning of Life'. *International Journal for Philosophy of Religion* 52 (2002): 71–81.

Affolter, J. 'Human Nature as God's Purpose'. *Religious Studies* 43 (2007): 443–55.

Anderson, E. 'Practical Reason and Incommensurable Goods'. In *Incommensurability, Incomparability and Practical Reason*, R. Chang (ed.), 90–109. Cambridge, MA: Harvard University Press, 1997.

Audi, R. 'Intrinsic Value and Meaningful Life'. *Philosophical Papers* 34 (2005): 331–55.

Ayer, A. J. 'The Meaning of Life'. In *The Meaning of Life and Other Essays*, 178–97. London: Weidenfeld & Nicolson, 1990.

Ayer, A. J. 'The Claims of Philosophy'. Repr. in *The Meaning of Life*. 2nd edn. E. D. Klemke (ed.), 219–32. New York: Oxford University Press, 2000 [1947].

Baggini, J. *What's It All About? Philosophy & the Meaning of Life*. Oxford: Oxford University Press, 2004.

Baier, K. 'The Meaning of Life'. Repr. in *The Meaning of Life*. 2nd edn. E. D. Klemke (ed.), 101–32. New York: Oxford University Press, 2000 [1957].

Baier, K. *Problems of Life and Death: A Humanist Perspective*. Amherst: Prometheus Books, 1997.

Baird, R. 'Meaning in Life: Discovered or Created?' *Journal of Religion and Health* 24.2 (1985): 117–24.

Belshaw, C. *10 Good Questions about Life and Death*. Malden, MA: Blackwell, 2005.

Bortolotti, L. 'Agency, Life Extension, and the Meaning of Life'. *The Monist* 93:1 (2010): 38–56.

Bortolotti, L. and Y. Nagasawa. 'Immortality Without Boredom'. *Ratio* 22 (2009): 261–77.

Britton, K. *Philosophy and the Meaning of Life*. Cambridge: Cambridge University Press, 1969.

Brogaard, B., and B. Smith. 'On Luck, Responsibility and the Meaning of Life'. *Philosophical Papers* 34 (2005): 443–58.

Brukner, D. 'Against the Tedium of Immortality'. *International Journal of Philosophical Studies* 20 (2012): 623–44.

Camus, A. *The Myth of Sisyphus*. J. O'Brien (trans.). London: Penguin, 2005 [1942].

Chappell, T. 'Infinity Goes Up On Trial: Must Immortality Be Meaningless?'. *European Journal of Philosophy* 17 (2009): 30–44.

Clack B., and B. Clack. *The Philosophy of Religion*. Cambridge: Polity, 2008.

Cottingham, J. 'Meaningful Life'. In *The Wisdom of the Christian Faith*, P. K. Moser and M. T. McFall (eds). 175–96. Cambridge: Cambridge University Press, 2012.

Cottingham, J. 'Meaningfulness, Eternity and Theism'. In *Meaning in Life*, B. Himmelmann (ed.), 99–112. Berlin and Boston: De Gruyter, 2014.

Cottingham, J. *On the Meaning of Life*. London: Routledge, 2003.

Cottingham, J. 'The Good Life and the "Radical Contingency of the Ethical"'. In *Reading Bernard Williams*, D. Callcut (ed.), Ch. 2, 25–43. London: Routledge, 2008.

Cottingham, J. *The Spiritual Dimension: Religion, Philosophy and Human Value*. Cambridge: Cambridge University Press, 2005.

Craig, W. 'The Absurdity of Life Without God'. In *Reasonable Faith: Christian Truth and Apologetics*. 3rd edn., 65–90. Wheaton, IL: Crossway Books, 2008.

Dahl, N. 'Morality and the Meaning of Life'. *Canadian Journal of Philosophy* 17 (1987): 1–22.

Bibliography

Darwall, S. *Impartial Reason.* Ithaca: Cornell University Press, 1983.

Davis, W. 'The Creation of Meaning'. *Philosophy Today* 30 (1986): 151–67.

Davis, W. 'The Meaning of Life'. *Metaphilosophy* 18 (1987): 288–305.

Dilman, I. 'Life and Meaning'. *Philosophy* 40. 154 (1965): 320–33.

Dorsey, D. 'The Significance of a Life's Shape'. *Ethics* 125.2 (2015), 303–30.

Ellin, J. *Morality and the Meaning of Life.* Fort Worth, TX: Harcourt Brace, 1995.

Feuerbach, F. *Thoughts on Death and Immortality.* J. Massey (ed. and trans.). Berkeley: University of California Press, 1980.

Fischer, J. 'Why Immortality is Not So Bad'. *International Journal of Philosophical Studies* 2 (1994): 257–70.

Flanagan, O. *Self-Expressions: Mind, Morals, and the Meaning of Life.* New York: Oxford University Press, 1996.

Flew, A. 'What Does it Mean to Ask: "What is the Meaning of Life?"'. In *The Presumption of Atheism and Other Essays.* London: Elek Books, 1976.

Frankfurt, H. 'The Importance of What We Care About'. *Synthese* 53 (1982): 257–72.

Frankfurt, H. 'Reply to Susan Wolf'. In *The Contours of Agency: Essays on Themes from Harry Frankfurt*, S. Buss and L. Overton (eds), 245–52. Cambridge, MA: MIT Press, 2002.

Frankfurt, H. *The Reasons of Love.* Princeton: Princeton University Press, 2004.

Gewirth, A. *Self-Fulfillment.* Princeton: Princeton University Press, 1998.

Gill, M. and S. Nichols. 'Sentimentalist Pluralism: Moral Psychology and Philosophical Ethics'. *Philosophical Issues* 18 (2008): 143–63.

Goetz, S. 'The Meaning of Life'. In *The Routledge Companion to Theism.* C. Taliaferro, V. Harrison and S. Goetz (eds), 698–709. New York: Routledge, 2012.

Goetz, S. *The Purpose of Life: A Theistic Perspective.* London: Continuum, 2012.

Griffin, J. *Well-Being: Its Meaning, Measurement and Moral Importance.* Oxford: Clarendon, 1986.

Hanfling, O., ed. *Life and Meaning: A Reader.* Oxford: Blackwell, 1987.

Hare, R. M. 'Nothing Matters'. Originally published as '"Rien n'a d'importance": l'anéantissement des valeurs est-il pensable?' In *La Philosophie Analytique,* L. Beck (ed.). Paris: Editions de Minuit (1959/60); reprinted in English as '"Nothing Matters": Is "the Annihilation of Values" Something That Could Happen?'. In *Applications of Moral Philosophy*, 32–47. London: Macmillan, 1972.

Hartshorne, C. 'God and the Meaning of Life'. In *Boston University Studies in Philosophy and Religion, Volume 6: On Nature,* L. Rouner (ed.), 154–68. Notre Dame: University of Notre Dame Press, 1984.

Hartshorne, C., *The Logic of Perfection.* Lasalle, Illinois: Open Court, 1973.

Hartshorne, C. 'The Meaning of Life'. *Process Studies* 25 (1996): 10–18.

Hepburn, R. 'Questions About the Meaning of Life'. *Religious Studies* 1 (1965), 125–40. Repr. in *The Meaning of Life,* 2nd edn., E. D. Klemke (ed.), 261–76. New York: Oxford University Press, 2000.

James, L. 'Achievement and the Meaningfulness of Life'. *Philosophical Papers* 34.2 (2005): 429–42.

James, W. 'Is Life Worth Living?' In *The Will to Believe and Other Essays.* London: Longmans, 1897, 57, originally published in *International Journal of Ethics* 6.1 (1897): 1–24.

James, W. 'What Makes a Life Significant?'. In *Talks to Teachers on Psychology, and to Students on Some of Life's Ideals.* New York: Henry Holt, 1899.

Kahane, G. 'Should We Want God to Exist?' *Philosophy and Phenomenological Research* 82.3 (2011): 674–96.

Kamm, F. 'Rescuing Ivan Ilych: How We Live and How We Die'. *Ethics* 113 (2003): 202–33.

Kass, L. 'L'Chaim and Its Limits: Why Not Immortality?'. *First Things* 113 (2001): 17–24.

Kauppinen, A. 'Meaningfulness and Time'. *Philosophy and Phenomenological Research* 82 (2012): 345–77.

Kekes, J. 'The Informed Will and the Meaning of Life'. *Philosophy and Phenomenological Research* 47 (1986): 75–90.

Kekes, J. 'The Meaning of Life'. *Midwest Studies in Philosophy* 24 (2000): 17–34.

Klemke, E. D. 'Living Without Appeal: An Affirmative Philosophy of Life'. In *The Meaning of Life*, E. D. Klemke (ed.), 184–95. New York: Oxford University Press, 1981 and 1999.

Klemke, E. D. and S. M. Cahn (eds). *The Meaning of Life: A Reader*. 3rd edn. New York: Oxford University Press, 2007 [1st edn., E. D. Klemke (ed.), 1981].

Landau, I. 'The Meaning of Life *Sub Specie Aeternitatis*'. *Australasian Journal of Philosophy* 89 (2011): 727–34.

Landau, I. 'Why has the question of the meaning of life arisen in the last two and a half centuries?'. *Philosophy Today* (1997), 263–9.

Law, S. 'The Meaning of Life'. *Think* 11 (2012): 25–38.

Levinson, J., 'Intrinsic Value and the Notion of a Life'. *Journal of Aesthetics and Art Criticism* 62 (2004): 319–29.

Levy, N. 'Downshifting and Meaning in Life'. *Ratio* 18 (2005): 176–89.

MacIntyre, A. 'Comments on Frankfurt'. *Synthese* 53 (1982): 291–4.

Markus, A. 'Assessing Views of Life: A Subjective Affair?'. *Religious Studies* 39 (2003): 125–43.

Martin, R. 'Fast Car and a Good Woman'. In *The Experience of Philosophy*. 2nd edn. D. Kolak and R. Martin (eds), 556–62. Belmont, CA: Wadsworth Publishing Company, 1993.

Mawson, T. J. 'An Agreeable Answer to a Pro-Theism/Anti-Theism Question', forthcoming.

Mawson, T. J. *Belief in God*. Oxford: Oxford University Press, 2005.

Mawson, T. J. 'Is Whether or Not There is a God Worth Thinking About?'. In *Ethics and the Challenge of Secularism*, D. Bradshaw (ed.), 5–19. Council for Research in Values and Philosophy, 2013.

Mawson, T. J. 'On Determining How Important it is Whether or Not there is a God'. *European Journal for Philosophy of Religion* 4 (2012): 95–105.

Mawson, T. J. 'Recent Work on the Meaning of Life and the Philosophy of Religion'. *Philosophy Compass* (2013): 1138–46.

Metz, T. 'Could God's Purpose be the Source of Life's Meaning?'. *Religious Studies* 36 (2000): 293–313.

Metz, T. 'The Concept of a Meaningful Life'. *American Philosophical Quarterly* 38 (2001): 137–53.

Metz, T. 'Recent Work on the Meaning of Life'. *Ethics* 112 (2002): 781–814.

Metz, T. 'Critical Notice: Baier and Cottingham on the Meaning of Life'. *Disputatio* 19 (2005): 251–64.

Metz, T. 'New Developments in the Meaning of Life'. *Philosophy Compass* 2.2 (2007): 196–217.

Metz, T. 'God, Morality and the Meaning of Life'. In S. Vice and N. Athanassoulis (eds), *The Moral Life*, 201–27. London: Palgrave Macmillan, 2008.

Metz, T. 'The Meaning of Life'. *Oxford Bibliographies*. (http://www.oxfordbibliographies.com/view/document/obo-9780195396577/obo-9780195396577-0070.xml [accessed 1 November 2011]).

Metz, T. *Meaning in Life*, Oxford: Oxford University Press, 2013.

Metz, T. 'The Meaning of Life', *Stanford Encyclopedia of Philosophy* (first published online Tuesday 15 May 2007; substantive revision Monday 3 June 2013).

Metz, T. 'What is this thing called The Meaning of Life?' In *What Is This Thing Called Philosophy?*, D. Pritchard (ed.), 319–58. London: Routledge, 2015.

Morris, T. *Making Sense of It All: Pascal and the Meaning of Life*. Grand Rapids, MI: William B. Eerdmans Publishing Company, 1992.

Munitz, M. *The Mystery of Existence, An Essay in Philosophical Cosmology*. New York: Appleton-Century-Crofts, 1965.

Bibliography

Nagel, T. *Mortal Questions.* Cambridge: Cambridge University Press, 1979.

Nagel, T. *Secular Philosophy and the Religious Temperament: Essays 2002–2008.* Oxford: Oxford University Press, 2010.

Nagel, T. 'The Absurd'. *Journal of Philosophy* 68.20 (1971): 716–27.

Nagel, T. *The Last Word*, Oxford: Oxford University Press, 1997.

Nielsen, K. 'Linguistic Philosophy and "The Meaning of Life"'. Rev. edn. In *The Meaning of Life.* E. D. Klemke (ed.), 177–204. New York: Oxford University Press, 1981.

Nozick, R. *Philosophical Explanations*, Cambridge, MA: Harvard University Press, 1981.

Nozick, R. *Socratic Puzzles.* Cambridge MA: Harvard University Press, 1997.

Nussbaum, M. 'Mortal Immortals: Lucretius on Death and the Voice of Nature'. *Philosophy and Phenomenological Research* 50 (1989): 303–51.

Perry, J., M. Bratman and J. Fischer (eds). *Introduction to Philosophy, Classical and Contemporary Readings.* Oxford: Oxford University Press, 2012.

Pojman, L. 'Religion Gives Meaning to Life'. In *The Meaning of Life*, E. D. Klemke (ed.), 27–30. New York: Oxford University Press, 1999.

Pritchard, D. 'Absurdity, Angst, and the Meaning of Life'. *The Monist* 93.1 (2010): 3–16.

Quigley, M. and J. Harris. 'Immortal Happiness'. In *Philosophy and Happiness*, L. Bortolotti (ed.), 68–81. New York: Palgrave Macmillan, 2009.

Quinn, P. 'How Christianity Secures Life's Meanings'. In *The Meaning of Life in the World Religions,* J. Runzo, and N. Martin (eds), 53–68. Oxford: Oneworld, 2000.

Quinn, P. 'The Meaning of Life According to Christianity'. In *The Meaning of Life*, E. D. Klemke and S. M. Cahn (eds), New York: Oxford University Press (1981), 35–41.

Russell, B. 'A Free Man's Worship'. In *Mysticism and Logic*, 9–37. Bungay: Penguin, 1953.

Russell, L. J. 'The Meaning of Life'. *Philosophy* 28.104 (1953): 30–40.

Schlick, M. 'On the Meaning of Life'. *Philosophical Papers II.* Dordrecht: D. Reidel Publishing Co., 1979.

Schmidtz, D. 'The Meanings of Life'. In *Boston University Studies in Philosophy and Religion, Volume 22; If I Should Die: Life, Death, and Immortality,* L. Rouner (ed.), 170–88. Notre Dame: University of Notre Dame Press, 2001.

Seachris, J. 'The Meaning of Life as Narrative: A New Proposal for Interpreting Philosophy's 'Primary' Question'. *Philo* 12 (2009): 5–23.

Seachris, J. 'The Sub Specie Aeternitatis Perspective and Normative Evaluations of Life's Meaningfulness: A Closer Look'. *Ethical Theory and Moral Practice* 16.3 (2013): 605–20.

Sharpe, R. 'In Praise of the Meaningless Life'. *Philosophy Now* 24 (1999).

Singer, P. *How are We to Live? Ethics in an Age of Self-Interest.* Amherst, MA: Prometheus Books, 1995.

Singer, P. *Practical Ethics.* 2nd edn. New York: Cambridge University Press, 1993.

Smart, J. J. C., and B. Williams. *Utilitarianism For and Against.* Cambridge: Cambridge University Press, 1973.

Smith, Q. 'Moral Realism and Infinite Spacetime Imply Moral Nihilism'. In *Time and Ethics: Essays at the Intersection,* H. Dyke (ed.), 43–54. Dordrecht: Kluwer Academic Publishers, 2003.

Smith, Q., ed., 'Special Issue: The Meaning of Life'. *The Monist*, 93 (2010): 3–165.

Smuts, A. 'Immortality and Significance'. *Philosophy and Literature* 35 (2011): 134–49.

Smuts, A. 'The Good Cause Account of the Meaning of Life'. *Southern Journal of Philosophy* 51.4 (2013): 536–62.

Stocker, M. *Plural and Conflicting Values.* Oxford: Clarendon Press, 1990.

Tabensky, P. 'Parallels Between Living and Painting'. *Journal of Value Inquiry*, 37 (2003): 59–68.

Taylor, R. *Good and Evil.* New York: Macmillan, 1984.

Taylor, R. 'Time and Life's Meaning'. *The Review of Metaphysics* 40 (1987): 675–86.

Thomas, L. 'Morality and a Meaningful Life'. *Philosophical Papers* 34 (2005): 405–27.

Thomson, G. *On the Meaning of Life*. London: Wadsworth, 2003.

Tipler, F. *The Physics of Christianity*. New York: Doubleday, 2007.

Tipler, F. *The Physics of Immortality: Modern Cosmology, God and the Resurrection of the Dead*. New York: Doubleday, 1994.

Tipler F., and J. Barrow, *The Anthropic Cosmological Principle*. Oxford: Oxford University Press, 1986.

Tolstoy, L. *A Confession*. [1884].

Trisel, B. 'Human Extinction and the Value of Our Efforts'. *The Philosophical Forum* 35.3 (2004): 371–91.

Trisel, B. 'Intended and Unintended Life'. *The Philosophical Forum* 43 (2012): 395–403.

Uygur, N. 'What is a Philosophical Question?'. *Mind* 73.289 (1964), 64–83.

Velleman, J. D. 'Well-Being and Time'. *Pacific Philosophical Quarterly* 72 (1991): 48–77.

Velleman, J. D. 'Family History'. *Philosophical Papers* 34 (2005): 357–78.

Waghorn, N. *Nothingness and the Meaning of Life: Philosophical Approaches to Ultimate Meaning Through Nothing and Self-reflexivity*. London: Bloomsbury, 2014.

Wielenberg, E. *Value and Virtue in a Godless Universe*. Cambridge: Cambridge University Press, 2005.

Williams, B. 'The Makropulos Case: Reflections on the Tedium of Immortality'. In *Problems of the Self*, 82–100. Cambridge: Cambridge University Press, 1973.

Williams, B. 'Ethical Consistency'. In *Problems of the Self*, 166–86. Cambridge: Cambridge University Press, 1973.

Williams, B. 'Persons, Character and Morality'. In *The Identities of Persons*. A. O. Rorty (ed.), 197–216. Berkeley: University of California Press, 1976.

Williams, B. *Moral Luck*. Cambridge: Cambridge University Press, 1981.

Williams, B. *Ethics and the Limits of Philosophy*, Cambridge, MA: Harvard University Press (1985), 17

Wittgenstein, L. *Tractatus Logico-Philosophicus*. C. Ogden (trans.). London: Routledge & Kegan Paul, 1988.

Wittgenstein, L. *The Blue Book*. Oxford: Blackwell, 1958.

Wisdom, J. 'What is There in Horse Racing?'. *The Listener*, 10 June 1954.

Wisnewski, J. J. 'Is the Immortal Life Worth Living?'. *International Journal for Philosophy of Religion* 58 (2005): 27–36.

Wohlgennant, R. 'Has the Question About the Meaning of Life Any Meaning?'. Reproduced in *Life and Meaning: A Philosophical Reader*. O. Hanfling (ed.), 34–38. Cambridge: Basil Blackwell Inc., 1987 [1981]; originally Chapter 4 of Wohlgennant, R., *Philosophie als Wissenschaft*. Chicago: Open Court, 1911.

Wolf, S. 'Happiness and Meaning: Two Aspects of the Good Life'. *Social Philosophy and Policy* 14 (1997): 207–25.

Wolf, S. 'The Meanings of Lives'. In *Introduction to Philosophy, Classical and Contemporary Readings*, J. Perry, M. Bratman and J. Fischer (eds), 62–73. Oxford: Oxford University Press, 2012; and in S. Wolf, *The Variety of Values, Essays on Morality, Meaning, and Love*, 90–104. Oxford: Oxford University Press, 2015.

Wong, W. 'Meaningfulness and Identities'. *Ethical Theory and Moral Practice* 11 (2008): 123–48.

FURTHER READING

Antony, L. M., ed. *Philosophers Without Gods: Meditations on Atheism and the Secular Life.* Oxford: Oxford University Press, 2007.

Benatar, D., ed. *Life, Death & Meaning.* Lanham, MD: Rowman & Littlefield Publishers, Inc., 2004.

Blumenfeld, D. 'Living Life Over Again'. *Philosophy and Phenomenological Research* 79 (2009): 357–86.

Brännmark, J. 'Leading Lives'. *Philosophical Papers* 32 (2003): 321–43.

Brown, D. 'Process Philosophy and the Question of Life's Meaning'. *Religious Studies* 7 (1971): 13–29.

Cooper, D., 'Life and Meaning'. *Ratio* 18 (2005): 125–37.

Dworkin, R. *Sovereign Virtue.* Cambridge, MA: Harvard University Press, 2000.

Edwards, P. 'Why'. In *The Encyclopedia of Philosophy.* Volumes 7–8. P. Edwards (ed.), 296–302. New York: Macmillan, 1972.

Edwards, P. and A. Pap, eds. *A Modern Introduction to Philosophy.* 2nd edn. New York: The Free Press, 1965.

Feinberg, J. 'Absurd Self-Fulfillment'. In *Freedom and Fulfillment: Philosophical Essays,* 297–330. Princeton: Princeton University Press, 1992.

Ferry, L. *Man Made God: The Meaning of Life.* Chicago: University of Chicago Press, 2002.

Fischer, J. 'Free Will, Death, and Immortality: The Role of Narrative'. *Philosophical Papers* 34 (2005): 379–403.

Fischer, J. *Our Stories: Essays on Life, Death, and Free Will.* New York: Oxford University Press, 2009.

Flanagan, O. *The Really Hard Problem: Meaning in a Material World.* Cambridge, MA: The MIT Press, 2007.

Gordon, J. 'Is the Existence of God Relevant to the Meaning of Life?'. *The Modern Schoolman* 60 (1983): 227–46.

Griffin, J. 'On Life's Being Valuable'. *Dialectics and Humanism* 8 (1981): 51–62.

Haber, J. 'Contingency and the Meaning of Life'. *Philosophical Writings* 5 (1997): 32–44.

Hanfling, O. *The Quest for Meaning.* Oxford: Blackwell, 1987.

Haught, J. *Is Nature Enough? Meaning and Truth in the Age of Science.* Cambridge: Cambridge University Press, 2006.

Heinegg, P., ed. *Mortalism: Readings on the Meaning of Life.* Amherst, N.Y.: Prometheus Books, 2003.

Hooker, B. 'The Meaning of Life: Subjectivism, Objectivism, and Divine Support'. In *The Moral Life: Essays in Honour of John Cottingham,* N. Athanassoulis and S. Vice (eds), 184–200. New York: Palgrave Macmillan, 2008.

Jacquette, D. *Six Philosophical Appetizers.* Boston: McGrew-Hill, 2001.

James, L. 'Shape and the Meaningfulness of Life'. In *Philosophy and Happiness.* L. Bortolotti (ed.), 54–67. New York: Palgrave Macmillan, 2009.

Kekes, J. *The Human Condition.* New York: Oxford University Press, 2010.

Kurtz, P. *Embracing the Power of Humanism.* Lanham, MD: Rowman & Littlefield, 2000.

Landau, I. 'Immortality and the Meaning of Life'. *Journal of Value Inquiry* 45 (2011): 309–17.

Levine, M. 'What Does Death Have to Do with the Meaning of Life?' *Religious Studies* 23 (1987): 457–65.

Margolis, J. 'Moral Realism and the Meaning of Life'. *The Philosophical Forum* 22 (1990): 19–48.

Martin, M. *Atheism, Morality, and Meaning*. Amherst, N.Y.: Prometheus Books, 2002.

Mawson, T. J. 'Morality and Religion'. *Philosophy Compass* 6 (2009): 1033–43.

Mawson, T. J. 'Sources of Dissatisfaction with Answers to the Question of the Meaning of Life'. *European Journal for Philosophy of Religion* 2 (2010): 19–41.

Metz, T. 'The Immortality Requirement for Life's Meaning'. *Ratio* 16 (2003): 161–77.

Metz, T., ed. 'Special Issue: Meaning in Life'. *Philosophical Papers* 34 (2005): 330–463.

Metz, T. 'God's Purpose as Irrelevant to Life's Meaning: Reply to Affolter'. *Religious Studies* 43 (2007): 457–64.

Metz, T. 'Imperfection as Sufficient for a Meaningful Life: How Much is Enough?'. In *New Waves in Philosophy of Religion*, Y. Nagasawa and E. Wielenberg, 192–214. London: Palgrave Macmillan, 2009.

Metz, T. 'The Good, the True, and the Beautiful: Toward a Unified Account of Great Meaning in Life'. *Religious Studies* 47 (2011): 389–409.

Metz, T. 'The Meaningful and the Worthwhile: Clarifying the Relationships'. *The Philosophical Forum* 43 (2012): 435–48.

Mintoff, J. 'Transcending Absurdity'. *Ratio* 21 (2008): 64–84.

Moser, P. 'Divine Hiddenness, Death, and Meaning'. In *Philosophy of Religion: Classic and Contemporary Issues,* P. Copan and C. Meister (eds), 215–27. Malden, MA: Blackwell Publishers, 2008.

Munitz, M. *Cosmic Understanding*. Princeton: Princeton University Press, 1986.

Murphy, J. *Evolution, Morality, and the Meaning of Life*. Totowa: Rowman and Littlefield, 1982.

Nagel, T. *The View from Nowhere*. New York: Oxford University Press, 1986.

Nozick, R. *Anarchy, State and Utopia*. New York: Basic Books, 1974.

Nozick, R. *The Examined Life*. New York: Simon & Schuster, 1989.

Oakley, T. 'The Issue is Meaninglessness'. *The Monist* 93 (2010): 106–22.

Perrett, R. 'Regarding Immortality'. *Religious Studies* 22 (1986): 219–33.

Rescher, N. *Human Interests*. Stanford: Stanford University Press, 1990.

Rosenburg, A. *The Atheist's Guide to Reality: Enjoying Life Without Illusions*. New York: Norton, 2011.

Sartre, J.-P. *Existentialism is a Humanism*. P. Mairet (trans.). London: Methuen & Co, 1980 [1946].

Sartre, J.-P. *Nausea*. L. Alexander (trans.). New York: New Directions Publishing, 1964.

Seachris, J. 'Death, Futility, and the Proleptic Power of Narrative Ending'. *Religious Studies* 47 (2011): 141–63.

Starkey, C. 'Meaning and Affect'. *The Pluralist* 1 (2006): 88–103.

Swinburne, R. *Faith and Reason*. Oxford: Oxford University Press, 2005.

Taliaferro, C. 'Jesus Christ and the Meaning of Life'. In *Jesus and Philosophy: New Essays,* P. Moser (ed.), 215–29. Cambridge: Cambridge University Press, 2009.

Taliaferro, C. *The Golden Cord. A Short Book on the Secular and the Sacred*. Notre Dame: University of Notre Dame Press, 2012.

Trisel, B. 'Futility and the Meaning of Life Debate'. *Sorites* 14 (2002): 70–84.

Vernon, M. *After Atheism: Science, Religion, and the Meaning of Life*. New York: Palgrave Macmillan, 2008.

Walker, L. 'Religion and the Meaning of Life and Death'. In *Philosophy: The Quest for Truth*, L. Pojman (ed.), 167–71. Belmont, CA: Wadsworth Publishing Co., 1989.

Wolf, S. 'Meaningful Lives in a Meaningless World'. *Quaestiones Infinitae, Volume 19*. Utrecht: Utrecht University (1997): 1–22.

Further Reading

Wolf, S. 'The True, the Good, and the Lovable: Frankfurt's Avoidance of Objectivity'. In *The Contours of Agency: Essays on Themes from Harry Frankfurt,* S. Buss and L. Overton (eds), 227–44. Cambridge, MA: The MIT Press, 2002.

Wolf, S. *Meaning in Life and Why It Matters.* Princeton: Princeton University Press, 2010.

Young, J. *The Death of God and the Meaning of Life.* London: Routledge, 2004.

INDEX

Index

holistic questions 187, 188, 197

I-desires 11
ideological fracture 88, 91, 165
immortality 10, 12–13, 141–2, 146, 154–7, 181,
182, 210, 211, 212, 213, 215
incommensurability 3, 17, 129, 130, 160, 165, 169,
176–7, 217
individualistic interpretations of the question/
individualistic meanings of life 39, 40, 41,
48, 51, 69, 87, 108, 123, 134, 135, 137, 138,
139, 159, 162, 164, 168, 173, 188, 191, 193,
194, 210
integrity 89, 92, 165, 168

Jacquette, D. 224
James, L. 216, 220, 224
James, W. 11, 14, 25, 26, 27, 30, 181, 183, 184, 185,
220

Kahane, G. 3, 176, 206, 220
Kamm, F. 199, 220
Kant, I. 10, 24, 117, 121
Kass, L. 182, 220
Kauppinen, A. 183, 199, 202, 203, 204, 216, 221
Kekes, J. 34, 45, 180, 181, 187, 192, 193, 203, 204,
207, 221, 224
Klemke, E. D. 2, 5, 6, 176, 177, 178, 180, 181, 185,
187, 191, 194, 198, 206, 219, 220, 221, 222

Landau, I. 184, 214, 221, 224
Levinson, J. 195, 221
Levy, N. 61, 145, 179, 180, 195, 214, 221
life
    ante-mortem 11, 12, 13, 17, 22, 101, 124, 139, 140,
    141, 143, 144, 152, 153, 155, 156, 158, 159,
    166, 167, 170, 174, 181, 182, 195, 213, 216
    aspects of a 7, 16, 60–1, 67, 98, 106, 111, 113,
    116, 119, 127, 130, 131, 132, 153, 154, 155,
    172, 195, 209
    exclusion/undermining between different
    meanings of life 98, 204–5
    inclusion/support between different meanings
    of life 63, 98, 99, 102, 104–7, 173, 199, 205
    logical and metaphysical
    periods of a 16, 31, 60–3, 67, 98, 106–7, 113,
    117, 145, 153, 164, 172, 181, 182, 195
    post-mortem 12, 13, 22, 140–5, 154–9, 166, 167,
    174, 213, 214

MacIntyre, A. 184, 221
meaning
    in the for-the-individual-concerned mode 1,
    7–9, 89–93, 99, 100–8, 117, 124–6, 143,
    146, 165–7, 175, 196, 204, 215

    in the simpliciter mode 79, 90, 91–3, 100–5,
    143, 146, 152, 196, 215
    maximization 164–5, 168, 173
    overall 12, 13, 16–17, 64, 121, 122, 131, 134,
    140, 141, 155, 158, 159, 161, 164–71, 173,
    202, 203, 214, 216
meaning-luck 6, 9, 11
Markus, A. 189, 221
Martin, R. 190, 221
Mawson, T. J. 46, 200, 209, 210, 215, 221, 225
meticulous God 8, 111, 119, 123, 127, 128, 131,
135, 157, 164, 174, 178
Metz, T. 14, 39–46, 59, 67, 68, 69, 73, 85, 88, 90, 91,
127, 141, 142, 143, 168, 177, 178, 179, 183,
184, 187, 188, 189, 190, 191, 192, 193, 195,
197, 198, 200, 202, 203, 206, 208, 212, 213,
217, 221, 225
monism 16, 44, 45, 48, 88, 108, 110, 112, 123, 164,
176, 180, 181, 191, 192, 193, 203, 216
Morris, T. 213, 221
Munitz, M. 194, 221, 225

Nagasawa, Y. 211, 219, 225
Nagel, T. 1, 2, 5, 6, 14, 16, 65, 127, 152, 175, 176,
178, 187, 208, 209, 222, 225
neutralism 110, 136, 138, 139, 210
Nichols, S. 200, 220
Nielsen, K. 198, 222
Nozick, R. 7, 80, 81, 182, 195, 198, 199, 201, 207,
22, 225
Nussbaum, M. 181, 222

optimism 4–17, 110, 134–59, 174, 177, 209, 210,
214

pluralism 3, 15, 16, 43–5, 85, 110, 128, 129, 145,
176, 177, 181, 183, 190, 191, 192, 193, 200,
201, 208, 216, 220 see also polyvalence
Pojman, L. 181, 222, 225
polyvalence 15–16, 45–51, 58, 59, 63–78, 81, 85–6,
95, 97, 98, 102–4, 108, 110, 114, 122, 141,
171, 172, 173, 176, 183, 190, 193, 195, 196,
197, 200, 201, 204, 205, 212, 213, 214 see
also pluralism
Pritchard, D. 176, 208, 212, 221, 222
providence 8, 111, 112, 127, 128, 131, 178
purgatory 166
purpose 1, 5–10, 22, 29, 39, 54, 56, 57, 65, 67, 79,
80, 83, 87, 89, 93, 99, 104, 105, 106, 108,
111, 112, 115–20, 122–32, 140, 142–6, 159,
163, 167, 173, 175, 178, 179, 180, 188, 192,
197, 198, 205, 206, 207, 208, 209, 212, 213

qualitative point, the 139, 145, 154, 155, 158
quantitative point, the 12, 139, 141, 145

228